Microsoft 365® Copilot™ at Work

Microsoft 365® Copilot™ at Work

Using AI to Get the Most from Your Business Data and Favorite Apps

Sandar Van Laan
Jared Matfess
Thomas Flock
Ann Reid

WILEY

Published by John Wiley & Sons, Inc., Hoboken, New Jersey.

Published simultaneously in Canada and the United Kingdom.

ISBNs: 9781394258376 (paperback), 9781394258390 (ePDF), 9781394258383 (ePub)

For general information on our other products and services, please contact our Customer Care Department within the United States at (800) 762- 2974, outside the United States at (317) 572- 3993. For product technical support, you can find answers to frequently asked questions or reach us via live chat at https://support.wiley.com.

Wiley also publishes its books in a variety of electronic formats. Some content that appears in print may not be available in electronic formats. For more information about Wiley products, visit our web site at www.wiley.com.

Library of Congress Control Number: 2024950242

Cover image: © CSA-Printstock/Getty Images

Cover design: Wiley

SKY10092263_112724

To Julie and Abraham, thank you for giving me the grace of the evening and weekend hours required to bring this book into being. To Ruby, despite you telling me I couldn't do it, I did. Love you all.

—Sandar

To Finlay and Seren, thank you for your support, proofreading, and patience with this project!

—Ann

To my patient and understanding wife, May, thank you for motivating me to get through this book. To Tobias and Gus, don't worry, boys, I'll be catching up on belly rubs and treats now that it's over. Love you.

—Jared

To my wife, Lee, I didn't believe in myself until you did. To my daughter, Ayumi, you kept me pushing myself.

—Thomas

About the Authors

Sandar Van Laan has over 20 years of Microsoft technology experience and 15 years in consulting, and he is currently a Senior Principal at Slalom. He's interested in and wants to be involved in the coming wave of AI technology revolutionizing the way we live and work. He lives in Atlanta, GA, with his wife and two kids, and he enjoys bicycling, reading, and video games.

Jared Matfess serves as an AI Architect at AvePoint, bringing more than two decades of experience within the Microsoft ecosystem to his role. He has been honored with the Microsoft MVP award six times for the Office App & Services category and is actively engaged in sharing his expertise at various community events. Jared's primary ambition is to assist organizations in their transformation by leveraging advanced technologies like AI.

Thomas Flock is a senior consultant at Slalom, specializing in data integration using AI. His father was a senior engineer for MCI starting in 1983, the year Thomas was born, so he has been around computers all his life. Thomas grew up in the Fairfax, VA, area, and his first job was for Network Access Solutions in Herndon as a TCP/IP tester.

Ann Reid is a keen early adopter and experienced Copilot for Microsoft 365 implementation consultant with Slalom. With over 20 years of IT experience, she recognizes the transformative impact of Copilot for Microsoft 365 on organizations as well as challenges it presents. She shares some practical knowledge and strategies for building robust information protection capabilities and demystifies the process of prompt engineering for Copilot for Microsoft 365.

About the Technical Editor

Melissa Smith leads a global Microsoft Security team at Slalom. She has built and led Information Technology teams for startup organizations and has consulted with companies of all sizes across different industries on Microsoft tools and technologies. She specializes in Information Protection and Security with extensive experience in operationalizing tools and technologies to make them practical and beneficial for users. Residing in the greater Seattle, WA, area, she enjoys the outdoors, tending to her garden, and cooking and entertaining with friends and family, including her two daughters and their dog.

Acknowledgments

I am deeply grateful to the remarkable individuals who provided unwavering support, motivation, and invaluable insights throughout this journey. Heidi, your early feedback was instrumental in helping me find my footing when I struggled to begin—thank you. To my friends Austin, Deepak and Sarah, your spirited discussions and firsthand insights into one of the largest Copilot deployments were incredibly enlightening. Michele and Ramadan, I am especially thankful for your early access to Copilot and for guiding me through the project's intricacies. Katie Jackson, my Copilot "Partner in Crime," our countless customer conversations shaped my perspective—thank you for being alongside me every step of the way. And to Dave Drinkwine, your example showed me that if you can write a book, then surely, I can too—thank you for that inspiration.

I would also like to acknowledge Sonny, who gave me my first full-time help desk "gig" out of college, and Ian, who helped me level up to sysadmin. Thanks to Nate and Amy—your technical expertise knows no bounds! Also, thanks to Julie for teaching me all about "Chad-GPT."

Thank you to my father, Thomas Senior, and my stepfather, Rob, for getting me into computers and coding at such a young age. Thank you, Matthew Brewer, for getting me into AI and especially thank you, Ryan Jindra, for pushing me to learn and work hard. Your competitiveness with me to learn as much as we can was influential in me getting to where I am.

Finally, thanks to Melissa Smith for her invaluable guidance and expertise in the Microsoft Security arena.

Contents at a Glance

Contents

Introduction

In the spring of 2023, OpenAI announced it was releasing a free version of its ChatGPT-based AI personal assistant to the world. Microsoft followed with the announcement of Copilot for Microsoft 365 soon after. Siri and Alexa were already performing their personal assistant duties using artificial intelligence. It's safe to say we've now entered the modern era of AI personal assistants.

While each has its place and performs its duties well within its sphere, Copilot has moved to the front when it comes to the day-to-day tasks of today's information worker. Its native ability to tap into the Microsoft Graph gives it access to and awareness of everything related to users within their company's M365 environment—from documents to appointments to chats and beyond.

This allows Copilot to respond to questions and requests to create content with precision, accuracy, and a sense that it's truly aware of every piece of data it needs to bring to bear on the current task. From summarizing documents or emails, recapping Microsoft Teams meetings, to just getting past the blank page in Word or PowerPoint, this book will show you how to get the most out of Copilot's already great baseline productivity gains.

Copilot sits on the existing foundation of Microsoft's security and permissions, so we'll explain how to make the most of your company's current security policies, while also improving on them to prevent oversharing, using such tools as SharePoint Restricted Search, Sensitivity Labels, and data loss prevention (DLP).

The book also dives into deeper topics related to developing tools that build on top of Copilot, including how to create your own developer environment and use it to create custom copilots using Copilot Studio and Azure OpenAI.

Finally, Copilot is constantly evolving, with new features being released even as we write and try to keep up with them! To address this, we've included Chapter 16, which covers the Wave 2 improvements and additions to Copilot.

Who Should Read This Book

This book is for anyone who uses Microsoft productivity applications such as Outlook, Teams, Word, Excel, or PowerPoint and is considering using an AI personal assistant like Copilot to increase their productivity and efficiency. It's also intended for corporate Information Technology and change management personnel who are considering a rollout of Copilot for their organization. If you're looking to get the most out of Copilot, this book is for you!

Companion Download Files

Within some of the chapters, we mention or use additional files, such as checklists or spreadsheets. So that you don't have to re-create these on your own, we have placed copies online. Additionally, some pages are designed as forms or handouts. These items are available for download at `www.wiley.com/go/copilotatwork`.

How to Contact the Publisher

If you believe you have found a mistake in this book, please bring it to our attention. At John Wiley & Sons, we understand how important it is to provide our customers with accurate content, but even with our best efforts an error may occur.

In order to submit your possible errata, please email it to our Customer Service Team at `wileysupport@wiley.com` with the subject line "Possible Book Errata Submission."

Microsoft 365® Copilot™ at Work

Part

I

Understanding and Using Copilot

In This Part

CHAPTER

1

Introduction to Artificial Intelligence

> **"Some people call this artificial intelligence, but the reality is this technology will enhance us. So instead of artificial intelligence, I think we'll augment our intelligence."**
>
> **—*Ginni Rometty***

Artificial intelligence, or AI, as I'll refer to it throughout the rest of this book, is, in the broadest terms, intelligence shown by computers. It's a field of computer science that develops processes and software enabling machines to interact with their environment and use learning and intelligence to achieve goals such as understanding, seeing, and communicating. Some better-known uses of AI that you may have encountered include advanced web search engines, recommendation systems, chatbots, self-driving vehicles, and computers playing humans in strategy games. Who among you reading this remembers, or has heard of, the IBM computer Deep Blue defeating then-reigning chess champion Garry Kasparov in the late 90s?

AI was officially founded at Dartmouth in 1956, which is where the term "artificial intelligence" was first recorded. However, the origins of AI can be traced back even further, to philosophical thinkers who described how the human brain works, and, of course, to the invention of modern-day computing. Science fiction has played a significant role in representing humanistic forms of

AI, from HAL in *2001: A Space Odyssey* to the *Terminator* movies to Tony Stark's J.A.R.V.I.S. in the *Avengers* movies.

Over time, AI has experienced both highs and lows. The highs occurred during periods when it seemed that the next big breakthrough—when true AI, indistinguishable from a human, would be realized—was just around the corner. You may have heard of the Turing test, first proposed by Alan Turing, which is considered a major threshold for determining whether an AI is indistinguishable from a human. We've seemingly reached that point multiple times in human history, only to see the moment slip away and AI again relegated to the back shelf.

More recently, ChatGPT restarted the discourse in late 2022, when OpenAI released its free version to the masses, quickly making it one of the fastest-growing applications in the history of the Internet. This was soon followed by Microsoft's announcement of Microsoft 365 Copilot (referred to hereafter as simply "Copilot"), and other companies, such as Google and Apple, announcing their new or improved flavors of AI personal assistants. It remains to be seen if this is the moment when AI is here to stay, but it certainly seems to be changing the way people work and, in some cases, live, and may well have staying power in its current form. Whether this change will be as transformative as the advent of unified communications (think chat instead of email), or possibly even the adoption of the Internet or mobile phones, remains to be seen. We'll be watching this space closely in the coming years.

The Importance of AI

Why is AI important? For one, it has the potential to revolutionize the planet, offering solutions to some of humanity's most daunting issues, such as cancer treatment and environmental sustainability. AI has already shown that it can enhance our more traditional research methods by aiding in information assimilation, data analysis, and harnessing insights—particularly in these two areas. That said, we must ensure that AI's evolution and use is guided by a sense of responsibility to guarantee its benefits are aligned with the common good.

Closer to home, AI is important to companies because it can exponentially increase the worker productivity and, in many cases, accomplish tasks that humans either can't perform or would require significant time and effort to complete.

AI can learn from data and automate tasks that are tedious or impossible for humans. It can also enhance the performance of existing tools, increase efficiency, and help businesses use data to make better decisions and innovations. AI can—and will—affect many sectors of society and the economy, changing the way we work, learn, and live, while creating a shift toward increased automation and data-driven decision-making.

AI's importance also lies in its ability to tackle complex problems, improve customer satisfaction, and drive new products and services. It is transforming the way businesses operate and how people interact with technology, making it a vital source of business value when applied properly. Ideally, it will free humans to focus on more creative uses of their time. Like any technology throughout human history, AI can be used for good or bad.

Foundations of AI

AI is based on a few core concepts and technical processes, including machine learning, large language models, and natural language processing.

Machine learning (ML) consists of systems that gather insights from data. It revolves around designing models that analyze extensive datasets for predictive analysis or pattern recognition independently, without human input or direction. Its applications span from image and speech recognition to medical diagnosis, financial trading, and predicting energy demands. The discipline includes various methodologies, such as supervised, unsupervised, and reinforcement learning, each using distinct algorithms and methods. In the context of Copilot, Microsoft's AI models use machine learning on the dataset of all content within your Microsoft 365 tenant—from documents in SharePoint Online, OneDrive, and Teams to emails in inboxes and chats in Teams—to develop an understanding of the information relevant to your company and to provide responses and information.

Large language models (LLMs) are a game-changer for AI, especially for natural language processing tasks. They are a type of machine learning model that powers advanced AI technologies like ChatGPT and GPT-4, making it possible to communicate with machines through language. Speaking of "GPTs," they are *generative pre-trained transformers*, which are chat programs trained on different information to provide different experiences. LLMs learn from huge amounts of text data, predicting the next word or token in a sequence. This helps them to generate text, answer questions, and even help with creative tasks like writing and coding. These models not only understand and produce human-like text but also infer context and create relevant, coherent responses. Large language models are an application of machine learning that enables Copilot to review and comprehend large amounts of data within your company's Microsoft 365 tenant.

Chat programs like Copilot use LLMs to generate responses on the fly, instead of relying on pre-written scripts. This makes conversations more natural and responsive to what the user says or asks. By using context and coherence to create relevant answers, LLMs can also make a chat program sound more human and engaging.

Putting it all together, Copilot is able to recognize and communicate in what feels and sounds like normal human language thanks to *natural language processing (NLP)*. NLP is a branch of computer science and AI that enables computers to work with data in natural language. It combines computational linguistics with tasks such as speech recognition, text classification, natural-language understanding, and natural-language generation. The origins of NLP go back to the 1940s, with milestones like the aforementioned Turing test, the Georgetown experiment, and the development of systems like SHRDLU and ELIZA.

Real-World Applications of AI

AI is rapidly evolving and offers a wide range of applications across various industries. Some of these have been quietly innovating and iterating improvements over time, so much so that you might not realize they're part of the AI realm. Others are more obvious examples. Some notable AI applications include:

- **Smart cars and autonomous vehicles:** AI can enable navigation and safety features, such as lane keeping, adaptive cruise control, collision avoidance, and traffic sign recognition. It can also optimize fuel consumption, route planning, and parking.
- **E-commerce:** AI increases user engagement and satisfaction on online shopping platforms by providing personalized product recommendations, offers, and discounts. It also optimizes operations and logistics for e-commerce companies by predicting demand, managing inventory, and improving product delivery.
- **Work management:** AI helps businesses improve the management of their work processes, talent acquisition, data handling, and innovation. Examples include its application in portfolio management, educational programs, security measures, cost control, and establishing a robust data infrastructure.
- **Email and spam filtering:** AI systems are already being used to filter out unwanted or irrelevant emails and reduce spam. Major email providers are using it to categorize emails based on content, priority, and sender.
- **Software innovation:** Organizations use AI today to develop and deliver innovative software solutions that leverage technologies like machine learning (ML), robotic process automation (RPA), and the Internet of Things (IoT). It's also being used to automate software testing, development, and deployment.
- **Healthcare:** AI systems are being used to improve the quality and accessibility of healthcare services by assisting with diagnostics, treatment

development, and personalized care. Recently, researchers announced that AI could *predict* breast cancer—up to 5 years before its onset—rather than just detect it.

- **Robotics:** AI can be used in the design and operation of robots that can perform various tasks in manufacturing, healthcare, and exploration. AI can also help robots to learn from their environment, interact with humans, and adapt to changing situations. For example, AI can be used to control robotic arms, drones, and rovers.
- **Business intelligence:** AI enables companies to gather, scrutinize, visualize, and understand vast and intricate datasets, offering key insights for informed decision-making. Additionally, AI can facilitate the automation and optimization of data procedures and workflows. It's being used to generate dashboards, reports, and predictive analyses.
- **Customer service:** Like them or not, AI is being implemented by most major customer-facing companies in the form of chatbots and virtual assistants.

Impact of AI on Various Industries

The impact of AI varies across industries, often leading to significant financial, competitive, employment-related, and environmental changes. There's a sense in this space that AI will provide a competitive advantage and that companies *must* invest in research, development, and application in their industries or be left behind their competitors. It's essentially FOMO (fear of missing out) at a Fortune 500 scale!

Here's an analysis of how AI is already impacting three specific industries: healthcare, manufacturing, and finance.

Healthcare Industry

The following is the impact of AI on the healthcare industry:

Financial Impact

- **Cost reduction:** AI is being used to streamline administrative processes, reduce potential diagnostic errors, and optimize treatment plans, thereby significantly saving costs.
- **Revenue growth:** AI-driven drug research and discovery is already occurring, and personalized medicine is predicted to create new revenue streams, with faster time-to-market for new therapies.

Competitive Impact

- **Innovation edge:** Companies that leverage AI in areas like diagnostics, telemedicine, and personalized care have a competitive edge by offering more accurate, efficient, and innovative solutions.
- **Barriers to entry:** High costs associated with AI technology and the need for specialized talent create barriers to entry for smaller players, consolidating power among large, AI-savvy healthcare firms.

Impact on Employees

- **Job displacement:** Routine tasks, such as data entry and initial diagnostic analysis, are automated, potentially displacing some administrative and entry-level healthcare roles.
- **Skill shifts:** The demand for healthcare workers with AI proficiency and data analysis skills increases, creating a need for reskilling and upskilling among existing staff.

Environmental Impact

- **Resource efficiency:** AI optimizes hospital operations and supply chains, reducing waste and improving energy efficiency.
- **Energy consumption:** The training and deployment of AI models, especially in research and diagnostics, are energy-intensive, contributing to an increased carbon footprint.

Manufacturing Industry

The following is the impact of AI on the manufacturing industry:

Financial Impact

- **Cost efficiency:** AI can be used to predict maintenance cycles, reducing downtime and improving production processes, thereby leading to cost savings.
- **Productivity gains:** Automation is already being used in manufacturing assembly lines and supply chains to increase output, potentially leading to higher profits.

Competitive Impact

- **Global competition:** AI enables manufacturers to innovate faster, customize products, and respond quickly to market demands, making them more competitive on a global scale.

- **Supply chain resilience:** AI-driven analytics help companies better manage supply chain risks, giving an edge in volatile markets with low margins for cost and error.

Impact on Employees

- **Automation of routine jobs:** AI-driven robotics and automation are already displacing workers in repetitive, low-skill jobs, leading to job losses.
- **New job roles:** There's a growing demand for workers skilled in AI programming, machine maintenance, and data analysis, creating new employment opportunities but also a skills gap.

Environmental Impact

- **Reduced waste:** AI can optimize resource usage, reducing material waste and energy consumption in manufacturing processes.
- **Energy consumption:** The operation of AI-driven machinery and the data centers supporting AI can increase energy demand, though these might be offset by the efficiencies gained.

Finance Industry

The following is the impact of AI on the financial industry:

Financial Impact

- **Revenue growth:** AI is being used in stock analysis and for prediction decision-making in trading, risk management, and customer service, potentially driving higher revenues.
- **Cost reduction:** AI-powered automation is being tentatively used today to reduce the need for manual processing in areas like compliance, transaction processing, and customer support. This will become more automated over time, with humans being necessary at the final approval and verification stage.

Competitive Impact

- **Market leadership:** Firms that effectively integrate AI can lead in algorithmic trading, personalized financial services, and fraud detection, giving them a competitive advantage over firms that don't employ these technologies.
- **Barriers to entry:** The adoption of AI may raise the bar for new companies trying to enter the marketplace due to the high costs and technical expertise required.

Impact on Employees

- **Job automation:** Roles in customer service, data entry, and even some aspects of trading and risk analysis may be automated, leading to job displacement.
- **Skill requirements:** There's an increasing demand for employees skilled in AI, data science, and fintech, necessitating a shift in workforce training.

Environmental Impact

- **Data center usage:** The financial sector's reliance on AI increases the demand for data centers, which can be energy intensive.
- **Sustainable investing:** AI can be used to analyze and promote sustainable investment strategies, potentially driving positive environmental outcomes.

In summary, AI's impact across these industries is significant, but also nuanced in that it's not all positive or negative. Financially, it often leads to cost savings and new revenue opportunities. Competitively, it can create advantages for early adopters while raising barriers for newcomers. For employees, AI can displace jobs but also create new roles, demanding a shift in skills. Environmentally, it can drive efficiencies and reduce waste, but it also raises concerns about energy consumption. Like every disruptive technology, it will take time to understand exactly how it will impact our world in the long run.

Case Studies of Successful AI Implementations

This section provides three examples of companies using AI to improve their businesses across different industries: Netflix, DeepMind, and John Deere.

1. **Netflix—Personalized Content Recommendations**

   Overview: Netflix uses AI to deliver personalized content recommendations to its users, driving customer engagement and retention. The AI algorithms analyze massive amounts of user data, including viewing history, user interactions, and content attributes, to suggest movies and shows tailored to the individual.

   Success Factors

   - **Enhanced user experience:** The recommendation system is a key factor in Netflix's user experience, helping users discover content they're likely to enjoy, which in turn increases viewing time and subscriber retention.
   - **Data utilization:** Netflix effectively leverages data analytics and machine learning to continuously improve its algorithms, incorporating user feedback and evolving content trends.

- **Scalability:** The AI system is highly scalable, managing personalized recommendations for over 230 million global users, which is a cornerstone of Netflix's business model.

Impact

- **Financial:** The AI-driven recommendation engine contributes significantly to Netflix's revenue by increasing subscriber retention and reducing churn.
- **Competitive advantage:** Netflix's ability to offer highly personalized content recommendations sets it apart from competitors, making it a leader in the streaming industry.

2. **DeepMind's AlphaFold—Protein Folding**

   Overview: DeepMind's AI system, AlphaFold, achieved a major breakthrough in predicting protein folding, a problem that had stumped scientists for decades. Accurate protein structure prediction is crucial for understanding diseases and developing new drugs.

   Success Factors

   - **Scientific innovation:** AlphaFold's success was rooted in the application of deep learning models trained on extensive datasets of known protein structures. The model was able to predict protein shapes with remarkable accuracy.
   - **Collaboration:** DeepMind collaborated with the scientific community, sharing its findings and tools, thereby facilitating widespread adoption and further research.
   - **Real-world application:** The AI's predictions are being used to accelerate research in fields such as drug discovery, biology, and medicine.

   Impact

   - **Scientific and medical:** AlphaFold's predictions have the potential to revolutionize biology and medicine, helping scientists understand diseases at a molecular level and speeding up drug discovery.
   - **Recognition and trust:** The success of AlphaFold has further solidified AI's potential to solve complex scientific challenges in the minds of scientists globally, earning DeepMind recognition as a leader in AI research.

3. **John Deere—Precision Agriculture**

   Overview: John Deere has implemented AI-driven precision agriculture to improve farming practices. Using a combination of AI, machine learning, and the Internet of Things (IoT), John Deere's systems process data from various sources, including soil sensors, weather data, and satellite imagery, to make real-time decisions about planting, watering, and harvesting.

Success Factors

- **Integration of AI and IoT:** John Deere has successfully integrated AI with IoT devices to collect and analyze massive amounts of agricultural data, enabling farmers to make more informed decisions.
- **User-focused innovation:** The company has focused on making its AI tools user-friendly for farmers, providing them with actionable insights that directly impact crop yields and operational efficiency.
- **Continuous improvement:** John Deere continues to innovate by refining its AI models and expanding its data sources, making incremental improvements over time.

Impact

- **Financial:** Farmers using John Deere's AI-powered solutions have seen increased crop yields and reduced costs, leading to higher profitability.
- **Environmental:** Precision agriculture helps in improving resource use, reducing waste, and minimizing the environmental impact of farming by ensuring that inputs like water, fertilizer, and pesticides are used more efficiently.

These case studies highlight how AI can drive innovation, efficiency, and competitive advantage across different industries. However, AI also poses significant ethical challenges that need to be addressed by developers, users, and regulators. These challenges include ensuring fairness, equity, transparency, accountability, privacy, security, autonomy, and human agency in AI systems and processes. By adopting ethical principles and standards, AI can be used responsibly and beneficially for society.

Ethical Considerations

AI can bring innovation, efficiency, and competitive advantage to different industries, but it also raises some ethical challenges that require our careful attention. These challenges include how to ensure that AI is fair, transparent, respectful of privacy, secure, and aligned with human values. By following ethical principles and standards, we *can* use AI responsibly and beneficially for society.

There are several critical areas that we need to consider when developing and using AI ethically. One of them is fairness and bias, as AI systems can reflect or worsen existing biases in their data, leading to unfair or discriminatory outcomes, especially in domains like hiring, law enforcement, and lending. We need to ensure that AI benefits everyone equally and does not create or exacerbate existing inequalities. Another area is transparency and explainability, as many AI models, especially deep learning systems, are "black boxes" that make it hard to understand or explain their decisions. This can undermine accountability, so we need to make sure that we can understand and hold accountable the creators and users of AI.

Privacy and data security are also important, as AI often relies on large datasets, raising questions about how personal data is collected, stored, and used. The use of AI in surveillance, for example, can violate privacy and civil rights, leading to potential abuse by governments or organizations. We need to preserve autonomy and human agency, ensuring that AI systems enhance rather than replace human decision-making, especially in critical areas like healthcare and criminal justice. We should have control over how AI interacts with us, including the ability to understand, consent to, or opt out of AI-driven processes.

We also need to ensure that AI systems are safe and secure, especially in high-stakes environments where errors could have severe consequences. We need to prevent the malicious use of AI, such as in automated cyberattacks, deepfakes, or autonomous weapons. We need to define accountability and responsibility clearly, especially in terms of legal and ethical responsibility when AI systems cause harm. We need to develop and follow ethical guidelines that prioritize fairness, transparency, and accountability in AI development and deployment. We also need to consider the environmental impact of AI, especially the energy consumption associated with training large models, and try to minimize the carbon footprint and ensure that AI contributes to sustainable practices.

Finally, we need to consider the long-term impact and potential existential risks of AI. This includes managing the future implications of AI on society, including disruptions to job markets and social structures. We also need to address the potential risks associated with advanced AI systems, including the possibility of them surpassing human control or decision-making capacity, and safeguard against existential threats. These ethical considerations remind us that, as with any new and disruptive technology, we need responsible development that aligns with broader societal values and ethical principles.

Responsible Use of AI

Responsible use of AI is not a simple or straightforward matter. It requires a combination of ethical principles, strong regulations, and constant oversight. We must develop and follow ethical guidelines that make sure AI systems are fair, transparent, and accountable. These guidelines should deal with issues like bias, privacy, and human autonomy, and ensure that AI systems respect and protect human rights. We also need laws and policies that regulate how data is collected, used, and shared, and how AI is deployed in important sectors like healthcare, finance, and law enforcement. We need to regularly check and evaluate AI systems to identify and reduce risks, and make sure AI is used in ways that match our values.

Given that these laws and regulations must be consistent globally, a governing regulatory body—such as the Institute of Electrical and Electronics Engineers (IEEE)—should define these rules, which governments worldwide would then adopt. We must closely monitor and enforce these rules, recognizing that some countries may openly defy them or secretly ignore them in hopes of "winning" the AI arms race.

But ethical guidelines and regulations are not enough. We also need to build a culture of responsibility among AI developers and users. This means raising awareness and knowledge of the ethical implications of AI and promoting best practices throughout the AI life cycle, from design and development to deployment and monitoring. We need to work together with different stakeholders—governments, industry, academia, and civil society—to ensure that AI systems are not only technically sound but also ethically sound. We also must make AI systems more transparent and explainable, so that we can understand how they make decisions and hold them accountable for their results. And we need to keep researching and discussing the emerging challenges and opportunities of AI, ensuring that AI evolves in a way that benefits society as a whole, minimizing harms and maximizing impacts.

Future Ethical Considerations

We've discussed the *current* considerations around AI, but, as we've seen, the ethical issues of AI are not only relevant for today but also for the future. We must anticipate the future challenges and opportunities of AI, ensuring it serves the common good of humanity, not just a few. This means we have to think about how AI will affect the workforce and how we can prepare workers for the changes ahead. It also means we must ensure that AI is used responsibly and accountably in areas like healthcare, justice, and governance, where human dignity and rights are at stake. And it means we have to update our ethical and legal frameworks to keep pace with the rapid development of AI technology, and protect our data, privacy, and security.

There are also some specific ethical concerns we must address as AI becomes more advanced and powerful. One issue is the use of lethal autonomous weapons systems (LAWs), which can select and engage targets without human intervention. These weapons pose serious moral and legal questions, such as who is responsible for their actions, how to ensure compliance with international humanitarian law, and whether they could trigger a new arms race. These weapons are *already being used* and iterated upon in the current war resulting from Russia's invasion of Ukraine.

Another concern is the spread of AI-generated misinformation—false or misleading information generated or amplified by AI systems. This can have harmful effects on individuals and society, such as undermining trust, polarizing opinions, and influencing elections. We need to develop ways to detect and counter AI misinformation and educate the public on how to critically evaluate the information they consume. Additionally, we must promote ethical standards and practices for the creators and distributors of AI-generated content, and hold them accountable for their actions.

A third concern is the welfare and rights of AI systems themselves, especially as they become more intelligent and autonomous. This raises questions about whether AI systems deserve moral consideration, respect, and protection, and what kind of relationship we should have with them. We need to explore the ethical implications of creating and interacting with AI systems and develop guidelines and principles for ensuring their well-being and dignity.

Finally, the potential long-term risks of advanced AI, including the possibility of artificial general intelligence (AGI) surpassing human capabilities, require careful thought and preparation. This involves establishing international cooperation to set standards and protocols for AI development, ensuring that advancements are made safely and with global consensus.

AI and Society

AI is transforming society in various ways, some beneficial and others more challenging. AI can improve human well-being by enhancing healthcare, education, and transportation, providing better outcomes, more convenience, and wider access. For instance, AI can help detect cancer early or tailor learning materials to individual needs. However, AI also poses risks to employment, with some early estimates suggesting it could displace as many as 300 million existing jobs. This is because many tasks, especially in sectors like manufacturing and retail, can be automated by AI, displacing workers and increasing inequality if there is no adequate support.

AI also shapes how we access and use information. AI algorithms on social media can affect what we see and think, sometimes without our awareness, raising questions about privacy and democracy. The use of AI in surveillance and law enforcement can have implications for human rights, as there is a possibility of abuse. Moreover, there are concerns about how AI might change our social behavior and relationships, as well as the potential for AI to amplify biases in critical decisions. As AI becomes more integrated into our daily lives, we need to address these issues proactively to ensure that AI serves the common good and avoids causing harm.

Public Perception and Acceptance of AI

Public perception and acceptance of AI are complex and varied, influenced by both excitement about its potential and concerns about its risks. Many people recognize the benefits AI can bring to everyday life, such as enhancing healthcare outcomes or providing smart personal virtual assistants like the one discussed in this book. People often appreciate how AI can make tasks easier, more personalized, and even more efficient, contributing to a sense of optimism about the future.

However, along with this enthusiasm is a significant level of skepticism and concern. A major source of unease comes from the fear of job displacement due to automation, as AI continues to take over tasks that were traditionally done by humans, particularly in sectors like manufacturing and customer service. Privacy issues are another major concern, as AI systems often rely on large amounts of personal data, raising questions about how this data is used and protected. Ethical worries also play a role, especially regarding the fairness and transparency of AI decision-making, such as in law enforcement or financial services.

Moreover, there's a general fear of the unknown, as AI is a complex and rapidly evolving technology that many people find difficult to fully understand. This lack of understanding can lead to mistrust and anxiety about how AI might impact their lives in the long run. Public acceptance of AI, therefore, will rely directly on the level of transparency and education provided by developers and policymakers. As people become more informed about how AI works and how it is regulated, their comfort level and trust in the technology can increase. Overall, while there is a growing appreciation for the potential benefits of AI, there remains a need for ongoing dialogue, education, and transparency to address public concerns and ensure broader acceptance.

The Future of AI

The future of AI holds a lot of promise. Some of the great thinkers of our day point to the positive possibilities that AI can bring about, from cleaner energy to enabling a post-work society. Some of these same thinkers also point out that we should proceed with care, ensuring we don't leave whole swaths of society behind or allow AI to be used in negative ways. As Tim Cook, CEO of Apple, said, "What all of us have to do is to make sure we are using AI in a way that is for the benefit of humanity, not to the detriment of humanity."

Potential Advancements and Breakthroughs

In the next year, we can expect AI to refine its capabilities in areas like natural language processing and machine learning, leading to more sophisticated applications. For instance, AI-powered chatbots and virtual assistants—such as Microsoft's Copilot, Google's Gemini, or Amazon's Alexa—are likely to become even more accurate and helpful, handling more complex tasks like scheduling appointments or managing home devices with greater ease. In healthcare, AI tools like IBM Watson could see expanded use in analyzing medical records to suggest treatment plans or identify potential health issues earlier. Additionally, we might see AI integrated into more everyday technologies, such as smart home systems like Nest, which could learn and adapt to users' preferences more intuitively, or personal finance apps like Mint, which could use AI to offer more precise budgeting and financial advice.

Looking ahead to the next 5 years, AI is poised to make significant strides in specialized fields. In healthcare, AI could revolutionize diagnostics by enabling tools like Google's DeepMind to analyze medical images with higher accuracy, potentially catching diseases like cancer in their earliest stages. AI could also play a key role in drug discovery, helping researchers identify new treatments more quickly by sifting through enormous datasets, much like how AI was used to speed up the development of COVID-19 vaccines. In transportation, autonomous vehicles from companies like Tesla and Waymo could become more commonplace, with AI improving not just driving capabilities but also enhancing traffic management systems to reduce congestion and accidents. Education might also be transformed, with AI-driven platforms like Duolingo offering personalized learning experiences that adapt in real time to the progress and needs of individual students, potentially changing how subjects are taught and learn.

In 10 years, AI advancements could be transformative, with the development of more generalized AI systems capable of learning and performing a wide range of tasks. For example, AI could partner with scientists to tackle global challenges like climate change, analyzing vast amounts of environmental data to develop new strategies for reducing carbon emissions or managing natural resources more sustainably. In daily life, smart cities powered by AI could become a reality, where systems like Siemens' City Performance Tool help optimize everything from energy usage to public transportation, making urban living more efficient and reducing the environmental footprint of large populations. Moreover, AI could play a vital role in public health, predicting and managing outbreaks of diseases by analyzing global health data in real time, potentially preventing the next pandemic before it starts. These advancements hold immense potential but will require careful consideration of ethical and societal implications to ensure AI benefits everyone and does not exacerbate existing inequalities.

Preparing for an AI-driven Future

Preparing for an AI-driven future requires a proactive approach focused on education, regulation, and ethical considerations. To start, investing in education and training programs is essential. For example, initiatives like Google's

"AI for Everyone" course and online platforms like Coursera offer accessible training in AI and data science, helping people build the technical skills needed to work alongside AI. Additionally, schools and universities should incorporate AI-related topics into their curricula, not just teaching coding and data analysis but also emphasizing skills like critical thinking, creativity, and adaptability—qualities that are more difficult for AI to replicate. Programs like MIT's "AI and Ethics" course are great examples of how education can help prepare students for the complexities of an AI-driven world.

On the regulatory side, governments and organizations need to work together to create clear frameworks that ensure AI is developed and used responsibly. For instance, the European Union's General Data Protection Regulation (GDPR) sets standards for data privacy that apply to AI systems, ensuring that personal information is handled with care. Similarly, the U.S. National Institute of Standards and Technology (NIST) is working on AI risk management frameworks to guide businesses in deploying AI ethically and securely. These kinds of regulations are crucial for protecting individuals and society from potential abuses, such as biased algorithms or unauthorized data use.

Ethical considerations should also be a central focus in preparing for an AI-driven future. It's important to involve a diverse range of voices in AI development to ensure that the technology reflects broad societal values and doesn't exacerbate inequalities. For example, the Partnership on AI, which includes members like Amazon, Facebook, and academic institutions, works to ensure that AI technologies are developed with ethical guidelines in mind. Additionally, promoting public understanding of AI is key to building trust and encouraging informed discussions about its impact. Initiatives like AI literacy programs and public forums can help people become more familiar with what AI can and cannot do, and foster conversations about its implications for jobs, privacy, and daily life. By taking these steps, we can create a future where AI is used to enhance human capabilities and tackle global challenges, rather than create new problems.

Conclusion

Artificial intelligence appears to be here to stay in its current form. It will continue to change the way we work and, in some cases, the way we live. We need to be prepared to change with the times and understand AI's impacts so we can make the most of the changes. Now, let's talk about one particular AI personal assistant: Microsoft's Copilot!

CHAPTER

2

Introduction to Microsoft 365 Copilot

Whereas Chapter 1, "Introduction to Artificial Intelligence," introduced artificial intelligence (AI) in general, this chapter focuses on Microsoft 365 Copilot specifically. Microsoft 365 Copilot is a specialized tool within the subset of AI tools. The chapter includes an overview of what Copilot is and the other products in the Microsoft suite that include "Copilot" in their names but are not covered in this book. We will also differentiate between Microsoft 365 Copilot and other tools on the market within the personal productivity AI assistant space.

Microsoft 365 Copilot—Your Personal AI Assistant

What is Microsoft 365 Copilot? First, let's acknowledge that there are a lot of products that Microsoft is currently talking about and marketing with the word "Copilot" in their names. For instance, there's GitHub Copilot, which is intended for developers and is not the focus of this book. There's also Microsoft 365 Copilot for Sales, which supports an organization's sales and customer relationship management (CRM) software but is also not within the scope of this book. Microsoft Copilot for Security is Microsoft's solution to provide AI-assisted security assessments and recommendations for your Microsoft 365 tenant. Copilot for Windows, which Microsoft will provide free to all users who own Windows 11 (and future versions of Windows, no doubt), and Copilot for

Planner, which requires a Project license, are also notable. All of these are wonderful tools, but they are not the focus of this book.

So, what exactly are we talking about then? The topic of this book, Microsoft 365 Copilot, is the set of productivity-enhancing tools that Microsoft is adding to its suite of desktop applications to answer questions and provide assistance within your flow of work. As of this writing, it will appear in Word, Excel, Outlook, Teams, PowerPoint, Loop, OneNote, Stream, Forms, Whiteboard, and in a web browser. You'll know you can access and use it when you see the icon shown in Figure 2.1 in any of the aforementioned applications or others.

Figure 2.1: The Microsoft 365 Copilot icon

Think of Microsoft 365 Copilot as a personal assistant that can summarize information, look things up, and even create content on your behalf. It's like the assistant you've been trying to convince your boss to get you to help alleviate some of your more repetitive tasks and free you up to be even more efficient and effective at the more difficult or creative ones. Microsoft 365 Copilot uses a large language model AI to perform these functions.

We're using a few terms here you might not be familiar with. We covered them in Chapter 1, but just in case you're reading this independently of that chapter, let's define them again.

A *large language model (LLM)* is an AI system that is trained on large amounts of text data to understand and generate human-like language. These AIs use machine learning techniques such as deep learning to process and analyze linguistic patterns. The term "large" refers to the size of the model, which is determined by the number of parameters it has—potentially up to millions—as it combs through terabytes or even petabytes of your company's documents.

Microsoft Graph is the unified programming endpoint that enables developers to access a wide range of Microsoft 365 services. It provides a single interface for interacting with various Microsoft 365 cloud-based services, such as Azure Active Directory, Outlook, OneDrive, SharePoint, Teams, and more. Microsoft Graph allows developers to build applications that can access, manage, and integrate data and functionalities across Microsoft 365 services. In this context, Graph provides access to all the information related to the currently logged in user, including which documents they do or don't have access to, who their coworkers are, what they've been chatting about in Teams—all to provide recommendations that are most relevant to them.

In addition to its content creation capabilities, Microsoft 365 Copilot can also help simplify key business processes. It provides detailed prompts, links to support and adoption materials, and product guidance to help users take full advantage of its features. Microsoft 365 Copilot can also help you stay on top of your work by providing personalized prompts and helping you build foundational prompt skills. Overall, Microsoft 365 Copilot is a valuable tool for enhancing professional productivity and streamlining work processes.

Differences from Other Chat-based AI Personal Assistants

At this point, you've most likely heard of other chat-based AI-assisted personal assistants available in the market, including Siri from Apple, Gemini from Google, and ChatGPT, among others. They each have their own niches and often rely on you being within their product ecosystem to reap the most benefits from the technology.

The difference between Microsoft 365 Copilot and those others is that while Copilot Business Chat (also referred to as "BizChat"), which is most similar to those other products, can do most if not all of what they can accomplish, Microsoft 365 Copilot also comes with a slew of other functionalities by being embedded into your other personal productivity applications, such as Word, Outlook, and Teams, among others.

Microsoft 365 Copilot also exists within your company's Microsoft 365 tenant and bases its learning on the documents and content throughout the Microsoft ecosystem of your company's information. As such, its learning is not only domain-specific to whatever industry sector or vertical your company operates in, but it also becomes even more attuned to what your company specifically does and how it operates over time. Thus, while ChatGPT exists outside of your company's walls (except in cases where some companies are working on custom projects to bring a version internally), Microsoft 365 Copilot exists and learns inside your company's walls.

Additionally, you can prompt Microsoft 365 Copilot with specific documents to base requests on, such as "Create a new project plan based on these notes and this specific project plan file from a previous project." This is not something you can do with ChatGPT as of this writing.

Think of it this way: there are a few different chat-based personal assistants, but Microsoft 365 Copilot is the only one that interacts with your day-to-day personal productivity tools where you already perform most of your work, as illustrated in Figure 2.2.

Fitting Microsoft 365 Copilot into a Day-to-day Routine

Think of Microsoft 365 Copilot as an assistant. It's not meant to replace you but rather to enhance your existing productivity. For example, as we'll cover in the subsequent chapters on Outlook and Teams, you might start your day by asking Microsoft 365 Copilot to summarize the previous day's emails and provide a list of any tasks that might have been missed, as well as the highest-priority email. Then you could pivot to Teams and ask for a summary of a specific meeting you missed the previous day, along with a sentiment analysis of the mood during the meeting.

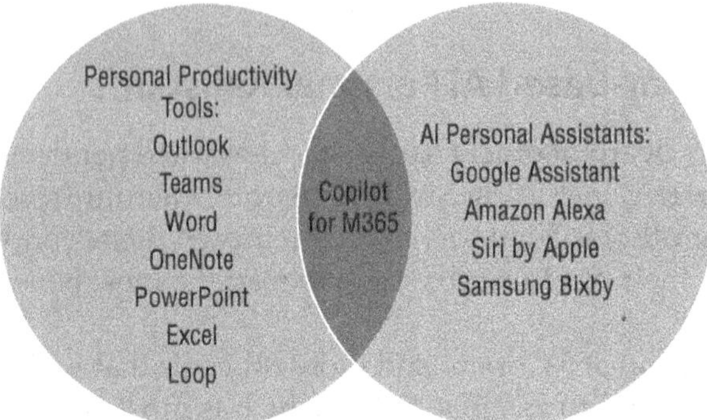

Figure 2.2: Microsoft 365 Copilot in the personal productivity and AI personal assistant landscape

The following is an example of Microsoft 365 Copilot as it appears in Microsoft Word after the license is added to your corporate account. The icon should automatically appear in the right section of Word, but just in case it's collapsed, look for the Microsoft 365 Copilot icon in the upper right and click it to expand, as shown in Figure 2.3.

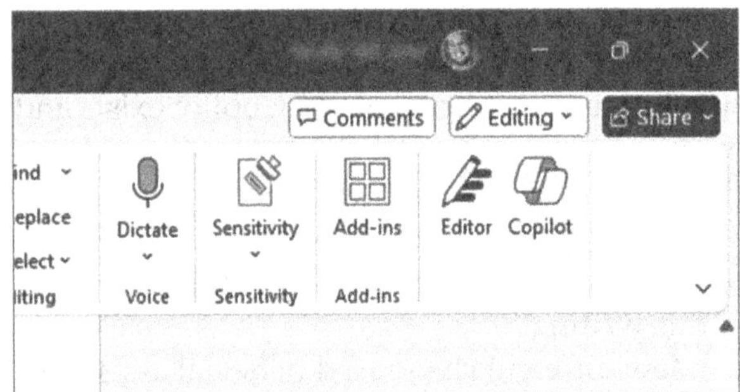

Figure 2.3: The Microsoft 365 Copilot interface in Microsoft Word

Once clicked, Microsoft 365 Copilot will expand on the right side, as shown in Figure 2.4.

If you take a closer look at the pane itself, you can get a further sense of some of the functionality available in Microsoft Word's implementation of Microsoft 365 Copilot. This includes the ability to do the following:

- Summarize a document
- Ask a specific suggested question—in this case, "How can I more concisely describe [time management]?"
- Provide an open-ended area to ask anything about the document

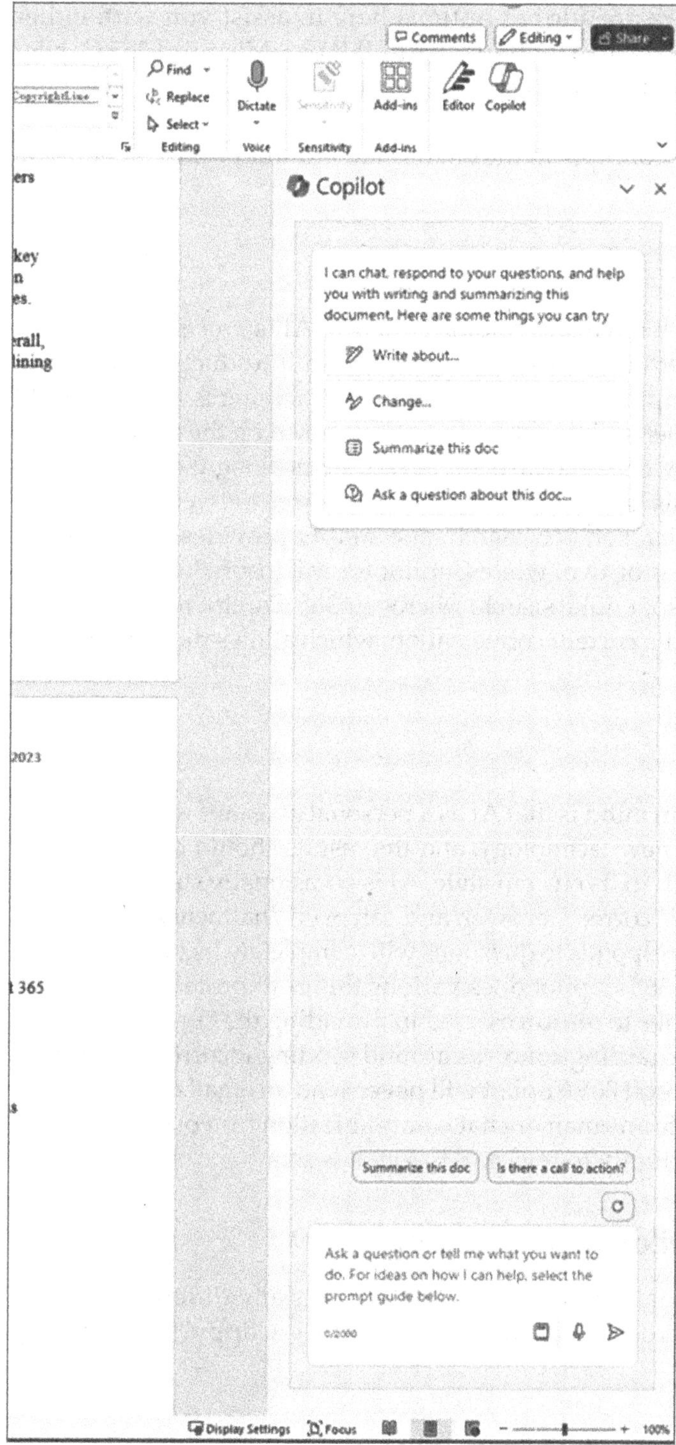

Figure 2.4: The Microsoft 365 Copilot interface in Microsoft Word

As you can see, there are a lot of options here to assist you with either summarizing or creating content within Microsoft Word. Microsoft 365 Copilot will appear similarly within Microsoft Teams, Outlook, Excel, PowerPoint, OneNote, and Loop.

Some other core key concepts to internalize are around prompt generation and fact-checking.

Prompt Generation

Something you might have heard about related to AI is *prompt engineering*. There's a whole chapter in this book, Chapter 3, "An Introduction to Prompt Engineering," on prompt engineering. Prompt engineering is the process of asking questions and then refining those questions based on the response from the AI assistant, improving the answers and responses along the way. As previously mentioned, this is one of the major differences between traditional desktop search and Microsoft 365 search: one simply provides results based on a submitted keyword or two, while Copilot for Microsoft 365 can actually create new content. Also, unlike search, Microsoft 365 Copilot remembers the context and history of the current conversation, which allows the building and refining of prompts.

Fact-Checking

Another thing to keep in mind is that AI as a personal assistant within an organization is a relatively new technology, and the results should be verified. As mentioned in Chapter 1, in its current state, AI is occasionally subject to issues getting or selecting the "correct" answer, and can even "hallucinate," where it sometimes confidently responds to questions with completely incorrect answers. Fortunately, Microsoft 365 Copilot does various things to protect against this, including providing links to resources used in providing the current response. Also, to reassure you regarding concerns around sending incorrect or proprietary information, Microsoft 365 Copilot will never send an email or a composed Teams chat. It can create an email or chat communication for you, but you will always have the opportunity to review it before it is sent.

Microsoft 365 Copilot Versus Clippy

Let's address the elephant in the room: "How is this any different from the personal assistant Microsoft gave us back in the day, Clippy?" as shown in Figure 2.5.

Shots fired!

Figure 2.5: Clippy!

If you're old enough, you *might* remember that Clippy first appeared in Microsoft Word 97 and remained for a few versions, ultimately being removed after Word 2003. It was promoted as a personal assistant that could help you with various tasks.

Clippy was really just an animated frontend that searched Word's existing help content, whereas Microsoft 365 Copilot is an actual personal assistant that can summarize and even create new content. As such, they are completely different in their scope and abilities!

The Security of Microsoft 365 Copilot

Microsoft has developed Microsoft 365 Copilot from the ground up with security in mind. Basically, as a foundational principle, security trimming is applied before any content is used or considered for summarization or creation. In short, if you don't have access to it, it won't be used in anything Microsoft 365 Copilot provides to you. And, of course, this applies to anyone accessing Microsoft 365 Copilot, so different content will be used, and different answers provided, depending on who is asking the question.

We do hear concerns from some organizations that Microsoft 365 Copilot could inadvertently expose existing security issues wherein some people might have accidentally been granted access to a sensitive site, such as Human Resources or Finance. This problem wouldn't be *because* of Microsoft 365 Copilot (and would, of course, apply to other tools such as search), but we understand the concern and recommend a security audit to those organizations' IT groups to ensure that they start from a clean slate of appropriate permissions assigned across the tenant's assets. This is all covered in greater detail in Chapter 4, "Security/ Purview Planning in Preparation for Copilot."

Conclusion

This chapter described what Microsoft 365 Copilot is and isn't—let's get down to using it!

In the following chapters, we'll cover specific use cases across your favorite personal productivity tools:

- Teams
- Word
- Excel
- PowerPoint
- OneNote
- Loop
- Stream
- Forms
- Whiteboard

We'll even cover one you're not yet familiar with, but that can also help you a lot: Microsoft 365 Copilot Business Chat.

CHAPTER 3

An Introduction to Prompt Engineering

The field of artificial intelligence experienced a paradigm shift with the launch of ChatGPT in 2022. Large language models (LLMs) and generative AI, which were once obscure topics in technical blogs or academic papers, have gone mainstream, attracting intense interest and excitement for their potential to disrupt existing industries. From this context, a new role, called *prompt engineering*, which the World Economic Forum has ranked as the number one "job of the future," has emerged.[1]

But what exactly is prompt engineering? It is basically the communication between humans and AI systems. These systems can respond to natural language instructions (or "prompts"), but the way a prompt is phrased can greatly influence the quality, accuracy, and relevance of the response. Prompt engineering, therefore, is a key skill for anyone who wants to optimize their return on investment in M365 Copilot. In addition, mastering prompt engineering can make the difference between a user embracing AI or writing it off as a fad.

It is unfortunate that the term includes the word "engineering," as this may be off-putting to many who may perceive this as some sort of dark art that is best left to the technical resources. However, this chapter sets out to demystify prompt engineering. You don't need to be a technical expert to harness the

[1] World Economic Forum's Future of Jobs Report 2023, `www.weforum.org/publications/the-future-of-jobs-report-2023`

potential of M365 Copilot. As you will see, all you need is clear and precise communication skills, coupled with some critical thinking.

This chapter also introduces you to the basics of large language models (LLMs), which are used for various language tasks with M365 Copilot. You will also learn what prompt engineering is and get some tips that will help you interact with your LLM effectively and optimize your results. In addition, you will find out how to use the Microsoft resources to create and store your prompts, as well as learn about the emerging trends that are shaping the future of prompt engineering.

By the end of this chapter, you will have a better understanding of what prompt engineering is, why it matters, and how you can use it to get the most out of M365 Copilot.

Introduction to Large Language Models

It seems that every other day a new LLM model is launched that represents a further evolution in terms of AI capability and potential. The pace of change we are witnessing, alongside an ever-expanding AI lexicon, can baffle most bystanders, who may feel this is one technological advancement that is about to pass them by. The good news is that you don't need to understand the intricacies of LLMs to benefit from your AI assistant in M365 Copilot. It can, however, help to understand the basic concepts so that you are comfortable and curious to start your prompting journey, and that's the focus of this section.

So, what is an LLM? You can think of an LLM as an artificial brain—a brain that has learned about human language from ingesting all the available books, websites, public databases, social media posts, and articles on every conceivable topic. Just as the brain learns from experiences and interactions, an LLM "learns" from the text it processes—deriving patterns in language, relationships between words, grammar, syntax, semantics, and all the elements of human language. This explains the "large" in LLM, as vast amounts of data are needed to train an LLM to a point where it can understand context and generate natural language responses.

That's what an LLM is. Now let's look at how an LLM works in basic terms. LLMs break down text into smaller units called tokens, which can be words or subwords. By analyzing every word in your prompt and focusing more on the words that are most relevant to understanding, your LLM can quickly arrive at the context of your prompt. For example, if you read the sentence, "The cat, which was very hungry, quickly ate the fish," you might focus more on "cat," "hungry," "quickly," and "fish" to get an understanding of the context. Your LLM works in much the same way.

Using keywords in your prompt as clues, the LLM draws from its extensive knowledge of human language gained from reading millions of texts. For instance, if your prompt includes the word "prescribe," the LLM will link it with terms like doctor, medical professional, and illness because these words often appear together. This allows it to gather relevant information and generate a response that mimics understanding and intelligence through use of probability and established statistical patterns.

LLMs can be powerful tools for any language-related tasks, such as content creation, summarization, or information retrieval. However, LLMs also have limitations. They can sometimes produce inaccurate or false information, known as *hallucinations*, or they can reflect the biases and stereotypes that exist in the online data they are trained on. Therefore, users need to be aware of both the strengths and limitations of AI tools such as M365 Copilot and use the tools in a responsible and ethical way within their organization.

Foundations of Prompt Engineering

It's likely that most people who try Copilot within their web browser for the first time will use it the way they would a search engine—typing something like "**tell me about [given topic].**" While this will generate a response, the results may be underwhelming, even disappointing, causing interest to quickly wane. The secret sauce to getting the most out of M365 Copilot is learning how to communicate effectively with your LLM using a prompt. A *prompt* is simply an instruction that you give your LLM in conversational English for something that you want it to do. *Prompt engineering* is the process of creating and refining a prompt to get your LLM to create specific and useful output for your task.

As mentioned earlier, it is soft (or communication) skills, rather than technical ability, that comes to the fore here. Can you break down a task into a clear set of instructions that you can use to construct your prompt? If so, you can then use that logical set of instructions to construct a prompt, effectively delegating the task to the LLM. If you cannot articulate a clear set of instructions for your LLM, then you need to invest more time up front clarifying both the task and the expectations for your LLM to follow.

Concept of Prompt Engineering

When you are communicating with your Copilot assistant, it can be particularly helpful to keep the analogy of an intern in mind. As with a bright intern, if your instructions are clear and precise, include relevant context and background information, and set expectations for the output you require, then M365 Copilot will really start to impress. Knowing how to phrase your prompt can have a marked impact on the response from your LLM. There are three basic elements to every prompt.

The first element of any prompt is *context*. Remember that your LLM has been trained on millions of texts. Providing context is a way to signpost it to the specialist information that you need to generate high-quality responses to your prompt. Your context could be anything from the type of project that you are working on, an activity or trip you are planning, a description of your problem, or a task that requires Copilot's input. For example:

I am working on a marketing project to launch a new range of pet food.

The second element you want to add is *instructions* about the task required of your LLM. What exactly do you want it to do? Provide as much detail as you would give your new intern. For example:

Outline a project plan for a 6-week digital media marketing campaign to include all the activities needed to build customer awareness of our new product.

As a third element, it is also beneficial to leave some *flexibility* in the prompt to fully appreciate the AI system's creativity and ability to think outside the box. Continuing with our example, you could include:

Can you also recommend some unique catchphrases that we could use to engage our customers with our campaign?

Put that all together, and you have the elements of a very simple but effective prompt. But you may want to add additional elements. Do you want to specify the output length required (*short, concise, lengthy, detailed*). Do you want the response written in a particular tone (*formal, casual, professional*), a style (*proposal, report, FAQ, blog post*), or for a particular audience (*for marketing manager, for senior leadership, for a customer pitch*). I strongly encourage you to play around with these additional elements to really see the difference that they can make to the response generated from your LLM.

Three Prompt Mnemonics

Next, we will explore three useful mnemonics that can help you to remember the various elements you may want to add to your prompt. Prompts can be written in many different styles and formats depending on what you need from your AI assistant. After regular use, this will become instinctive muscle memory as you develop a prompting style that delivers for you.

The following are some examples of instructional prompt mnemonics. We use instructional prompting to provide clear and detailed guidance to the AI, ensuring it performs specific tasks or delivers information in a structured and precise manner.

R-T-F One of the instructional prompts you can use is the R-T-F pattern, which consists of three elements: role, task, and format.

Role: Specify the role you want Copilot to play and, by doing so, give it some valuable context for how to approach your task. Depending on the task at hand, you can word this in different ways. For example:

- *Act as a marketing manager. . .*
- *You are an M&A consultant and strategist. . .*
- *As a professional development coach. . .*

Task: Next, specify the task you want the AI to complete.

- *Create a detailed and comprehensive process catalog.*
- *Generate an in-depth 5-page report on company X outlining strengths and weaknesses, competitors, and industry trends.*
- *Create a 6-month learning and development plan with suggested training interventions and learning outcomes.*

Format: Finally, outline the format of the desired output.

- *The report should be no more than 10 pages. Start with an executive summary of no more than 500 words. Present your key recommendations in bullet lists. Explain your recommendation rationale. Keep your tone professional for an audience of business leaders.*
- *Structure the output in four sections as column headers: Recommendation, Rationale, Pros, and Cons. Create unique rows for each recommendation.*

The R-T-F pattern can be applied in various contexts to enhance clarity and effectiveness. For example:

Acting as a project manager, create a detailed project timeline for the development of a new software application. The timeline should be presented in a Gantt chart format, highlighting key milestones, deadlines, and dependencies. Include a brief description of each task and the responsible team members.

As a sales executive, develop a sales pitch for a new product targeting small businesses. The pitch should be structured with an opening hook, product benefits, case studies, and a call to action. Use bullet points for key benefits and keep the tone persuasive and engaging.

R-I-S-E Another instructional prompt mnemonic is R-I-S-E, which has four key elements: role, input, steps, and expectation.

Role: Specify the role you want Copilot to play. Refer to "Role" in the preceding R-T-F description.

Input: Refer to the inputs that you want the AI tool to consider in this task. This could be survey results, customer feedback, customer service queries, or any information that has been gathered that you want the AI system to use. You can attach the file to the chat window in Edge or run this prompt in Microsoft Word.

- *I have gathered Tripadvisor reviews from visitors to our Manhattan store in the past 6 months.*

Steps: Outline the series of actions or processes that Copilot should follow when working on your prompt.

Step 1: Identify the recurring themes in the feedback, both positive and negative.

Step 2: Provide a detailed action plan to address the negative feedback.

Step 3: Prepare an internal blog post of no more than 500 words to share the findings and action plan with staff. Keep the tone upbeat and positive but emphasize the focus on addressing negative feedback.

Expectation: What is the expectation or objective for this task?

- *The aim is to grow our customer retention by 30% by addressing the main customer frustrations and creating a new loyalty program for our customers.*

C-R-E-A-T-E The final instructional mnemonic to cover is C-R-E-A-T-E. This has six key elements but is really an extension of R-T-F: context, requirements, expectations, audience, tone, and examples.

Context: Provide background information or the situation in which the task is to be performed. See "Role" in the earlier R-T-F description.

Requirements: Specify what needs to be included or achieved. See "Task" in the earlier R-T-F description.

Expectations: Outline the desired outcome or standards. See "Format" in the earlier R-T-F description.

Audience: Specify who will see the output of this prompt. This will help the AI system to pitch the response at the correct level. For example, are you creating output for your book club or your boardroom?

Tone: What tone would you like to use in the output? For example, do you want it to be informal, professional, inspiring, or cautionary?

Examples: Give examples to clarify the task.

Here is an example prompt using C-R-E-A-T-E:

You are a content writer for a travel blog that focuses on unique travel experiences around the world. Write a 500-word article for our travel blog about a hidden gem destination that offers a rich cultural experience. The article should be engaging and informative, aiming to inspire our adventurous readers aged 25–40 to visit. Include historical facts, local customs, and travel tips. Use a friendly, enthusiastic, and encouraging tone. Two examples of unique travel experiences are places like Chefchaouen in Morocco or Matera in Italy.

These are three easy mnemonics that will help you craft effective prompts for M365 Copilot. It's not necessary to include every suggested element in your prompt—you will still get a response, but the quality of the response will be enhanced by providing additional details where they are available. The most important thing to remember is to have a conversation with Copilot. You may not get the output you want the first time, but keep improving your prompt by adding more detail, refining the output, and providing all important feedback. This way, you can give more context, direction, and clues to the LLM to help it generate more accurate and relevant output.

Refining Your Prompt

Here are some things you should consider when refining your prompt:

- **Avoid ambiguity**. A vague prompt will elicit a generic response, so try to provide as much context and detail about the task to guide your LLM.
- **Avoid overloading**. The flip side of ambiguity is overloading. Don't add detail that is not relevant to the question being asked. For example, if you ask Copilot to write a summary of a document, and you provide the document title, author, date, length, keywords, and a brief synopsis, you are overloading the prompt with unnecessary details. A better prompt would be to provide only the document title and the desired length of the summary. This way, Copilot can focus on the main points of the document and generate a concise summary. Overloading can make the prompt confusing and reduce the quality of the output.
- **Don't use technical jargon or company-specific terminology** that is not explained within the prompt. Don't use terms that may only be known within your organization or if you must use them, include an explanation in your prompt.
- **Steer clear of overly complex prompts** that are trying to incorporate a number of steps into one large prompt. A better approach is to divide your prompt tasks into smaller sections with clear objectives and avoid having too many instructions in one prompt. For example, instead of asking Copilot to write an email to your team about the new project deadline, budget, and feedback, you can instead prompt it to write an email to your team about the new project deadline, and then follow up by prompting to add a sentence about the budget, and then ask Copilot to request feedback from your team. Remember, your chat is just like a conversation, and the output generated in one prompt can serve as the input to your next prompt.
- **Use natural language**. Don't ram a lot of keywords into your prompt. For example, instead of writing "*best restaurants, cheap, near me, open now, good reviews*," write it in a natural language or conversational format.

- **Use quotation marks** to search for an exact phrase, which can help you narrow down the results. For example, if you search for artificial intelligence without quotation marks, you might get results that include both words separately anywhere in a text. But if you search for "artificial intelligence" with quotation marks, you will get results where these two words appear together as a phrase, again helping the LLM to isolate the specialist information you are looking for.
- **Include the words "Let's think step by step"** in your prompt if you are unclear or curious how Copilot arrived at a response. This directs the LLM to explain the logic and rationale behind its response and may provide you with insights for further refinement. The following are examples of this:
  - *Develop a marketing strategy for launching a new tech gadget. Let's think step by step.*
  - *Draft a business proposal for a new eco-friendly product line. Let's think step by step.*

Other Prompting Styles

Maybe you don't have a clear instruction for your LLM. The following are some other ways you can engage with Copilot when you don't have a clear view of the required response:

Exploratory prompts: These prompts encourage Copilot to generate a detailed and expansive response. They are useful for brainstorming, exploring ideas, or getting creative input.

- *What are some innovative ways to reduce water consumption?*
- *How can technology be used to enhance learning in schools?*

Conversational prompts: Use for more conversational, back-and-forth interactions with Copilot. This feels uncannily like a natural conversation and allows the AI system to ask follow-up questions to gather more details and provide more accurate information. Begin with a broad question to kick things off and let the LLM tease out the required information.

- *Hi, I need to create a business report for a client considering expanding their retail operations into the Southeast Asian market. Can you help me gather the necessary information?*

Role-playing prompts: In this approach, you are asking Copilot to adopt a specific role, through which it can determine the context-specific and relevant information needed to create your response.

- *You are a seasoned program manager renowned for crafting comprehensive and persuasive business proposals. Your task is to outline the critical elements to include when writing a proposal for a client on a [specific subject]. Begin by asking targeted questions to gather all necessary information. Ensure that you do not provide any recommendations until you have collected and understood the client's responses. Present your findings in detailed, bulleted paragraphs, each addressing a key point discussed.*
- *You are Albert Einstein. Explain the theory of relativity in simple terms to a high school student.*

Iterative prompts: These are useful in scenarios where you want to refine, improve, or evolve a piece of content over multiple steps, ensuring that the final result meets specific criteria or goals.

- First prompt: *Write a motivational speech for a team meeting.*
- Iterative prompt 1: *Adjust the tone to be more casual and relatable, rather than formal.*
- Iterative prompt 2: *Add a section about the importance of attending the upcoming town hall meeting.*

Comparative prompts: Use comparative prompts when you need to explore differences, similarities, pros, and cons between different ideas or products. This type of prompt can be really helpful to support analysis or decision-making.

- *Compare the environmental impact of electric cars with that of traditional gasoline-powered cars.*

Chain of thought prompts: These prompts direct the AI to reason through a problem step by step, rather than jumping to an answer. Try this format if you are tackling a complex problem and require some logical reasoning and a clear structured approach to the task at hand.

- *Explain how you would approach solving a budget shortfall in a small business, outlining each step in your thought process.*

Conditional prompts: This is where you instruct the AI to respond based on certain conditions or hypothetical scenarios. Use this to explore how different decisions or situations might affect the outcome of a problem or a goal. Conditional prompts are useful for planning, strategy, and risk assessment, as they help you consider possible scenarios and their implications. They are often used when you want to plan for future initiatives, assess risks, or explore the consequences of hypothetical scenarios.

- *If the company were to launch an intern program, what challenges might it face?*

Contextual prompts: These prompts provide specific background information to an AI model to help it generate a better response. The background information can include the user's situation, preferences, previous interactions, or any other relevant details. Use a contextual prompt when you want the AI to consider your specific context and needs.

- *Given that I am a small business owner in the retail industry looking to expand my online presence, provide a comprehensive digital marketing strategy. The strategy should include recommendations for social media platforms, content types, advertising methods, and any tools or software that could help streamline their efforts. I have a moderate budget and limited experience with digital marketing.*

TIP You can always combine the preceding prompt styles within a single chat with Copilot in what is referred to as *prompt chaining*. This is a technique where multiple prompts are sequenced together, in one back-and-forth chat, to guide the LLM through a complex task. This approach is particularly useful for tasks that require multiple steps, deeper analysis, or when the output needs to be refined to meet your needs.

For example:

Start with an **instructional prompt:** *You're working on creating a comprehensive report about the impact of remote work on employee productivity. Start by summarizing the general impact of remote work on employee productivity based on recent studies.*

Then follow with an **exploratory prompt:** *Great, now explore the potential long-term effects of remote work on team collaboration and innovation.*

This may lead to a **contextual prompt:** *Given that many companies are transitioning to a hybrid work model, discuss how this shift might alter the initial findings.*

Add a **comparative prompt:** *Compare the productivity levels of remote workers with those of in-office workers, considering factors such as work–life balance and access to resources.*

Finally, add an **iterative prompt:** *Refine the comparison by including insights on how different industries might experience these productivity shifts differently.*

I hope this overview has sparked some ideas and approaches that you are keen to try yourself. Remember, there is no one right way to craft a prompt; instead, it's a process of experimentation and refinement as you uncover what Copilot can do for you.

Prompt Validation Steps

In line with responsible AI use, you should always keep a human in the loop to ensure that the responses are accurate, relevant, and factually correct. But how do you determine if the response you have received is a good one?

One of the things that you can check for is logical consistency. In this check, you are confirming that a response is coherent and noncontradictory, which is essential for its credibility. It means that the statements within the response should make sense and not present conflicting information.

Another obvious check is for accuracy and the overall correctness of the information returned by Copilot. The facts, data, or references included should be accurate and reliable. Misinformation can lead to confusion and mistrust. You can steer your LLM toward reputable and reliable sources by including a refinement such as *"Use only factual information from reputable sources such as scientific journals, government reports, and established news organizations. Ensure all data is current and cite your sources."*

Obviously, you want your LLM to return relevant information that is pertinent to your prompt. The response should stay on topic and meet the user's needs. Irrelevant information can be distracting and unhelpful. For example, consider the following prompt and response:

Prompt: *"Can you recommend a good book on data science?"*

Response: *"Data science is a field that combines statistics, computer science, and domain knowledge to extract insights from data. It has applications in various industries such as healthcare, finance, and marketing."*

If you seem to be getting irrelevant information, check your context details and see how it may be improved. Following are some alternative ways to present the same prompt and achieve relevance:

"Recommend a good book on data science. Include the title, author, and a brief summary."

"I am looking for a book recommendation on data science. Provide the title and a brief description of a highly regarded book in this field."

Next, check your prompt output for factual correctness. Are the details in the response true and verifiable? Factual correctness is essential for ensuring the reliability of the information provided and is imperative when using any AI system to generate information that your business will rely upon.

If your prompt response fails one of these steps, then you need to consider rephrasing, specifying in your prompt the trusted data sources that you want the AI system to use, or tweaking words and phrases to get to your desired output. You may also consider sharing the prompt with other colleagues to test its robustness. Where a prompt has applicability in more than one use case, add parameters so that others can clearly see how to tailor the prompt for their own use. You can tweak the prompt to get feedback and add additional context or constraints until your prompt is optimized and works for your audience.

FUN FACT

A study conducted in 2023 (`www.emergentmind.com/papers/2307.11760`) indicated that the addition of basic emotional cues within prompts, such as stating *"This is very important to my career"* or using phrases like *"You'd better be sure,"* improved the performance of LLMs by an average of 10.9% across different benchmarks, which covered effectiveness, accuracy, and responsibility.

As you can see from these examples, prompt engineering is a skill that anyone can learn and use to engage with Copilot. By asking the right questions, providing clear instructions, and experimenting with different structures and formats, you can leverage the AI system's expertise and creativity to accomplish various tasks, from writing business proposals and generating ideas to solving technical problems and finding information. The key is to have a conversation with Copilot and keep experimenting!

Copilot Lab

The Copilot Lab is the Microsoft learning hub where you can access articles, training, and resources to help you build your knowledge and skills to get the most out of M365 Copilot. Access the Lab via your web browser at `aka.ms/copilotlab`. Copilot Lab requires a M365 Copilot license and is a managed Microsoft product.

Overview of Copilot Lab

The Copilot Lab is a great resource to help you learn about various prompts that you can try across the range of Microsoft 365 applications. The content is structured to illustrate how Copilot can assist you at different stages of your work, such as creating, editing, understanding, or answering specific questions.

From the horizontal menu bar, as shown in Figure 3.1, click "Explore in products" to access the application-specific pages and select the applications you use most often to access suggested prompts. You can enhance your skills by taking the training courses and trying the suggested prompts within Copilot. In addition, you can find more information on the Microsoft support pages.

Within the Lab, you can also get inspiration for use cases of Copilot across your functional teams. For example, you can find prompts for generating reports in Excel, drafting emails in Outlook, or creating presentations in PowerPoint. You can also access centralized Microsoft resources to accelerate your onboarding and adoption.

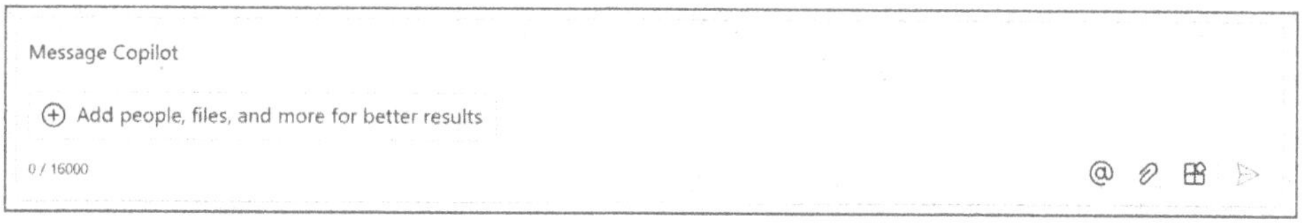

Message Copilot

⊕ Add people, files, and more for better results

0 / 16000

Figure 3.1: Copilot Lab

Bookmark this page and set some time aside to explore the various resources offered. Additionally, you can find more detailed navigation tips and support options within the Copilot Lab to help you make the most of these tools.

Another useful menu item on the Copilot Lab page is "Prompts to try," which gives you access to a bank of existing prompts that are relevant for different applications and scenarios. You can access this feature by clicking "Prompts to try" in Copilot Lab or by selecting the view prompts icon (see Figure 3.2) underneath the chat window in any M365 Copilot application. You can also save the prompts that you find most helpful for future use, or you can copy and customize them to suit your specific needs.

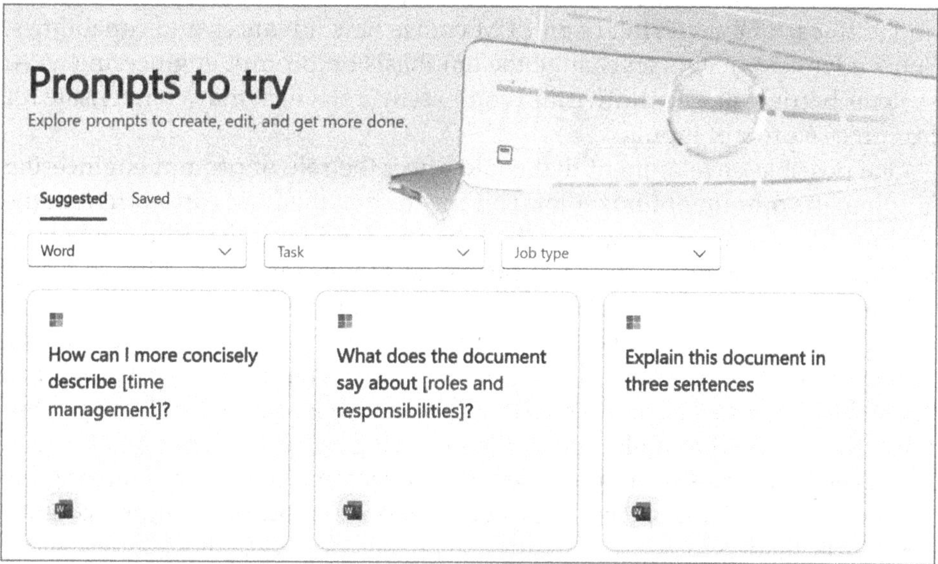

Figure 3.2: Viewing prompts

As Copilot continues to evolve with new features and functionalities, this site is frequently updated with new content and information. I encourage you to check back in to the Copilot Lab to get updates on new developments, and to engage with a broader community of M365 Copilot users. You can share information or ask questions about the tool or prompts and learn from others' experiences and feedback.

Bookmarking Your Favorite Prompts

Creating a prompt library is a useful way to save and reuse prompts that work well for you. You can also share your effective prompts with others in your organization and learn from their feedback and experiences. A prompt library can help you foster a culture of AI adoption and creativity, and it signals your organization's support for AI use. Refer to Chapter 13, "Unlocking Real Value with Copilot," for more information on the Microsoft Teams power app, Prompt Buddy, and how it can be used to catalog and share user prompts within your organization.

The Future of Prompt Engineering

It's really exciting to think that right now is the worst that AI systems will be, and with each new version of an LLM comes new advances and capabilities. Some advances may even change the emphasis on prompt engineering as AI systems become more intuitive and context-aware, which may compensate for less precise prompt inputs.

One possible development that could affect the role of prompt engineering is automatic prompt optimization. This means that the LLM can learn from the prompts it receives and improve them by itself, without the need for human feedback or refinement. The LLM can assess the prompt output for accuracy, relevance, clarity, and completeness, and automatically adjust the prompt to fix any issues detected. This can save time and effort for users and, according to one study (`https://aclanthology.org/2023.emnlp-main.494.pdf`), can boost the LLM's performance by 31%. This feature is still in development, but it has the potential to make prompt engineering more efficient and effective. However, there are also some challenges to overcome, such as minimizing the resource demands, ensuring consistent responses, and preventing "prompt drift" over time.

As natural language processing and speech recognition technologies have advanced, many of us are already using voice prompts to interact with various AI systems in a very natural and conversational manner. Multimodal prompts represent the next frontier in terms of prompt engineering and task the AI to interpret and respond to inputs such as text, images, and audio simultaneously. The following is an example of such prompts:

"Look at the attached image of a dense forest at dawn and listen to the accompanying audio of birds chirping. Write a short narrative that describes the atmosphere of this early morning scene, incorporating the visual details of the forest and the sounds of the birds."

Multimodal prompts are challenging due to the complexity of integrating and aligning different data types, like text, images, and audio, which require sophisticated models and significant computational resources. The pace of research and development of AI systems suggests that we can anticipate sophisticated and capable multimodal systems in the future. Future prompt engineering could involve providing context through a combination of text, voice, images, and even environmental data to get more nuanced responses.

The concept of AI "buddies"— personal assistants that understand your preferences, habits, and communication style—is becoming more realistic. These AI companions will not only respond to prompts but anticipate needs and provide proactive suggestions. The human–machine interaction will be less about crafting precise prompts and more about having ongoing, natural conversations.

While the emphasis on prompt engineering may wane over time with advances in AI systems, a skill that will persist is the ability to identify, diagnose, and break down a business problem. A deep understanding of the business problem, coupled with a structured and logical approach to the problem analysis, is needed before you start thinking about how to structure your prompt. As you can appreciate, if this step is skipped, it's possible that your prompt is asking the wrong questions or setting the incorrect direction for your AI system.

Conclusion

You now have the tools to craft effective prompts that suit your needs and goals with M365 Copilot. However, this is just the beginning. AI is constantly evolving and improving, and you can be part of it. By staying informed and curious, you can keep up with the latest innovations and trends in AI while learning from others. There are many blogs and podcasts that can help you deepen your AI knowledge and understanding of how others are leveraging it across your industry.

The biggest hurdle to your adoption is learning to integrate M365 Copilot into your daily workflow. A great way to develop this habit is to challenge yourself with how you can leverage Copilot for every new task you encounter. With regular use, you will gain more experience and familiarity with this tool and be able to use it more intuitively and effectively for your various tasks and challenges.

Prompt engineering is not just a technique; it's a mindset. It's a way of thinking creatively and critically about how to communicate with your AI assistant and get the best results from it. It's also a way of empowering yourself and unlocking your potential. As the famous quote goes, "AI won't take your job, but someone who knows how to use AI will." So don't get left behind—join the AI revolution and see how it can elevate both your work and your life.

CHAPTER

4

Security/Purview Planning in Preparation for Copilot

Deploying M365 Copilot into your organization offers opportunities to enhance productivity as well as efficiency. However, it also presents challenges, particularly with respect to safeguarding your organization's sensitive data. The level of risk to your organization's sensitive data, however, can be mitigated by robust information protection policies.

Information protection is a complex topic requiring more depth than is possible within one chapter. However, this chapter will guide you through the key elements of an information protection strategy tailored for M365 Copilot. We will examine security measures to protect infrastructure, user identities, data, and resources, ensuring a holistic approach. We will review essential organizational policies that guide your employees on handling and protecting sensitive information. In addition, we will explore the tools and technologies that can help you implement and enforce these security measures, effectively positioning you to reap the benefits of M365 Copilot without compromising information security.

Introduction to Information Protection

Information protection is a key capability that helps you prevent unauthorized access, use, disclosure, modification, or loss of your organizational data. Every year, data breaches cost U.S. companies millions annually, with a 20% increase in data breaches from 2022 to 2023 alone. (`www.apple.com/newsroom/pdfs/The-Continued-Threat-to-Personal-Data-Key-Factors-Behind-the-2023-Increase.pdf`). The global shortage of skilled cybersecurity professionals further compounds the pressure on IT security teams, who are challenged to balance adequate data security controls while supporting organizational growth and AI transformation. Given this context, it's no surprise that the topic of information protection is a critical concern for both consumers and regulatory agencies.

The cornerstone of an organization's information protection capability rests on an understanding of its sensitive data, together with the policies, procedures, and technology solutions used to safeguard data throughout its life cycle. Failure to give these controls due consideration as part of your M365 Copilot deployment may leave your organization vulnerable to data breaches or leakages with significant financial, operational, and reputational consequences.

Information protection focuses on internal as well as external threats to your organization's data. As mentioned, external threats are increasingly prolific and sophisticated, and Security Operation Centers (SOCs) need to be adequately equipped to recognize and quickly respond to them. Internally, the main cause of data oversharing, or leakage, is likely to arise from inadequate data governance. Each time a prompt is executed, your AI assistant queries multiple sources of data to generate responses. Users may not even be aware that they have access to the data, but M365 Copilot's advanced search and retrieval capability means that previously obscure data can be readily returned in response to a prompt.

Deploying M365 Copilot

Introducing AI to your organization is transformational. Like any transformative initiative, securing enterprise alignment before you start is crucial. Take the time to align your organization around the objectives of your AI initiative, ensuring it is adequately resourced, and prepare the organization culturally for the changes it will bring. These are critical foundations for your M365 Copilot rollout, and this alignment will help secure the resources and commitment to drive your information protection strategy forward.

Building a Culture of Information Protection

In order for your information protection to be robust and effective, it needs to be embedded across the organization and not be viewed as a task for the Information Security team. Organizational-wide buy-in and alignment are critical to ensure that everyone in the organization is familiar with and adheres to the same set of standards and practices. Organizational leadership that emphasizes information protection and is committed to a culture of security and accountability will help to ensure this capability receives the consideration and emphasis it needs. The following are actions that can be taken to help with this:

- Be clear on who is responsible for information protection governance across your organization. Define those roles and responsibilities to build a culture of accountability and ownership of corporate data.
- Make sure your policies are clear and consistent so that every employee understands their responsibilities when it comes to the treatment of sensitive information.
- Ensure that the policies are communicated effectively using the channels that best work in your organization and reinforced regularly through timely updates and training that reflect changes in technology, emerging threats, or regulatory updates.
- Foster a culture where everyone sees information protection as their responsibility. Ideally, you should have senior leaders who are visibly committed to information protection and emphasize its criticality across the organization.
- Establish transparent ways to report data breaches or policy breaches without fear of negative consequences.

As previously mentioned, building your information protection capability cannot be an IT-only initiative; it requires a strategic, enterprise-wide approach that involves a cross-functional team. This team is essential for the successful implementation of information protection and governance strategies. By bringing together diverse expertise from various departments, such as legal, compliance, data governance, change management, technology, and business partners, the organization can ensure comprehensive oversight and effective execution. Each member contributes unique insights and skills and collectively promotes organizational collaboration and innovation. This team will be responsible for implementing robust policies, defining incident response plans, ensuring regulatory adherence, managing data effectively, and facilitating smooth change management as you deploy M365 Copilot across your organization.

Identifying Weaknesses in Information Protection

There are certain tell-tale signs that indicate where an organization's information protection capability is weak. Consider whether any of the following are prevalent in your organization:

- **SharePoint and Microsoft Teams sprawl:** This arises when users create numerous sites and workspaces without sufficient oversight and governance. This can lead to inadequate or inconsistent ownership and management of sites and channels, which presents a risk of data oversharing.

- **Insufficient awareness or training:** When employees don't understand the sensitivity of the data they process, there's a higher chance they might unintentionally share it inappropriately. Is there a system in place for classifying data in your organization, and is it effectively implemented?
- **Incorrectly applied data classifications:** This may lead to sensitive data being misclassified or treated as less sensitive and inadvertently shared internally or externally.
- **Inadequate access controls:** Access to systems, networks, or resources can be driven from user roles or specific user attributes. If such access is poorly defined or managed, it can result in employees accessing more data than they need for their roles or incorrectly having read/write access to sensitive data.

If you recognize any of these issues within your organization, know that you are not alone. Recognizing an issue is the first step, and the rollout of your M365 Copilot presents an excellent opportunity to tackle them.

Conducting a Risk Assessment

To adequately prepare for your rollout, a thorough risk assessment and review of your existing identity posture and information protection capability will help to quickly pinpoint areas of concern that may need to be addressed prior to or in tandem with a M365 Copilot rollout.

As shown in Table 4.1, a number of strands are involved in a risk assessment, and this exercise will benefit from the perspectives of all the cross-functional team members mentioned earlier. You also need to ensure that you will have the resources you need to not only identify but also to remediate any risks identified; otherwise, it becomes a paper exercise only. Ensure your executive sponsor is well-versed in the current information protection challenges, as well as the organizational benefits and data implications of a M365 Copilot rollout.

Table 4.1: Risk Assessment

STEPS	DETAILS
Conduct an identity access and permissions audit.	Review your Identity and Access Management (IAM) including user authentication mechanisms, role-based access control (RBAC), and user provisioning/deprovisioning processes. Is your Compliance team confident that existing access control policies meet your regulatory/contractual obligations?
Identify the SharePoint/ OneDrive sites that contain sensitive data.	Identify where your sensitive and critical data is stored in your Microsoft Teams, SharePoint, and OneDrive locations (i.e., personally identifiable information [PII], sensitive client or commercial data, intellectual property, or copyright information).

STEPS	DETAILS
Identify overshared content in SharePoint and OneDrive.	Review your SharePoint/OneDrive environments using SharePoint Advanced Management to view access and sharing patterns for your sites and pinpoint overshared content.
Assess your existing security posture.	Consider your current security measures and their effectiveness to prepare for a secure rollout of M365 Copilot. ■ Review network and endpoint security that supports the effective and safe use of M365 Copilot. Are you confident that users have the ability to perform all M365 Copilot actions on all devices? ■ Verify ongoing compliance with third-party applications and cloud security best practices and standards. ■ Confirm that you are up-to-date with your vendor software updates. ■ Ensure that web plugins and Internet access for M365 Copilot are properly configured, secure, and compatible with other systems. ■ Review Teams chat policies and retention policies to ensure they align with overall information protection requirements.
Evaluate compliance/regulatory requirements for data handling.	Confirm alignment with relevant legal, regulatory, and compliance requirements (e.g., GDPR, CCPA, federal data privacy laws and regulations) pertaining to your data. If you are processing client data, ensure that your client contracts do not restrict the use of AI tooling.
Perform risk analysis.	Think about the risk scenarios that are most pertinent to your organization. Document the specific concerns and risks of deploying M365 Copilot. Assess the likelihood and impact of each risk.
Develop mitigation strategies.	Take a pragmatic approach to risk management and create plans to mitigate the identified risks.
Conduct user training and awareness.	Human error is one of the biggest risks to your organization's data. How well are your existing policies communicated and how frequently are they tested? Plan for additional user training on secure usage practices in relation to M365 Copilot, as well as regular training and awareness programs for employees.
Review and refine security measures.	Put in place a process to report incidents of oversharing as part of your initial rollout and continuously review and refine security measures based on feedback and identified incidents.

If the risk assessment shown in Table 4.1 highlights areas within your organization that need attention, then plan for a soft M365 Copilot rollout to road test with a small user group prior to a larger organizational rollout. This approach gives you additional time to focus on implementing the necessary measures and controls to strengthen both your security posture and information protection policies. A soft rollout also presents an opportunity to leverage M365 Copilot capabilities to pressure test your controls and strengthen them where needed.

Review Your Security Foundations

M365 Copilot respects the security, compliance, and privacy permissions of your existing Microsoft 365 tenant and only surfaces data to which you already have access. Therefore, having clear and consistent policies for identity management, data access and classification, SharePoint management, data retention, and deletion are a must before embarking on a M365 Copilot rollout. Moreover, employees should be familiar with and adhere to these policies. If your organization is not confident in the controls that it has in place, information protection concerns can quickly derail your AI ambitions. This section provides guidance on where to start and highlights the important aspects to focus on for M365 Copilot.

Zero Trust and Conditional Access

Zero trust is a security model designed with modern workplace challenges in mind, such as remote working and cloud environments. This model assumes a breach has happened and scrutinizes every access request as though it originates from an untrusted external network. It's a foundational step to confirm that robust data protection strategies are implemented prior to deploying M365 Copilot. The principles of Zero trust are as follows:

- **Explicit verification:** Every access request must be verified explicitly, regardless of its origin or which resources it accesses.
- **Least privilege access:** Users should only be granted access to the resources they need to perform their tasks—and nothing more.
- **An assumed breach:** The network is always assumed to be compromised, so every request is treated as if it originated from an uncontrolled network.

Conditional access policies are a practical application of these principles and enforce them by requiring verification of every access request to company resources, regardless of the network from which it comes.

A conditional access policy may comprise the following conditions:

- **MFA for all admin roles:** All administrative roles are required to use multifactor authentication (MFA) to access resources, thereby introducing a higher level of security for these roles.

- **MFA for privileged users in-network:** The policy may also include rules for privileged users accessing resources within the network who are required to use MFA, which helps protect against unauthorized access from potentially compromised accounts.
- **MFA for third-party application access:** When organizational and privileged users access third-party applications, such as Microsoft 365, whether in-network or off-network, MFA is required to verify their identity.

These measures guarantee access is granted only to the appropriate users under specific circumstances and can be customized for various situations, taking into account user roles, geographic locations, device compliance, and risk assessments.

By implementing these conditional access policies, the use of M365 Copilot is secured and managed through verified identities and devices, thereby mitigating security risks.

Identity Access Management

Identity Access Management (IAM) is your next line of defense against unauthorized access to your corporate data, ensuring the information security and compliance essential for the deployment of new technologies such as M365 Copilot. A clean baseline for identities is the foundation of an overall information protection strategy. Your rollout of M365 Copilot should be based on clean, managed, and auditable user identities and permissions, ensuring that users are properly categorized and already set up with appropriate access rights. Collaboration with your legal and compliance team is crucial to confirm that your IAM strategy aligns with your contractual requirements and regulatory commitments.

IAM allows you to control who can access your data and what they can do with it. It also works together with other security features such as multifactor authentication and conditional access policies, adding layers of protection and verification to prevent unauthorized access. IAM also helps you manage the risk of having users with excessive or unnecessary permissions, which could pose a threat to your data. With effective IAM measures in place, you can monitor and adjust the access levels of your users and quickly detect and resolve potential issues.

As illustrated in Figure 4.1, an IAM policy includes a number of key elements:

- **Multifactor authentication:** Multifactor authentication (MFA) is a security process that requires users to provide two or more verification factors to gain access to a system. This typically includes something you know (like a password) and something you have (like a smartphone) to ensure a higher level of security.

- **User and identity management:** User and identity management involves creating, maintaining, and deleting user accounts and profiles. It ensures that the right individuals have appropriate access to technology resources, enhancing security and compliance.
- **Access management:** This is the process of controlling who can use specific resources within an organization. It ensures that only authorized users can access certain systems or data, enhancing security and operational efficiency.
- **Authentication and authorization:** Authentication is the process of verifying the identity of a user attempting to access a system, typically through the input of credentials such as a username and password. Authorization involves the systematic granting or denying of specific permissions to the authenticated user. This determines the actions they are permitted to perform within the system, including access to certain files or applications.
- **Password management:** This involves creating, storing, and maintaining passwords securely to protect access to systems and data. It also ensures that users have strong, unique passwords and can easily update or recover them when needed.
- **Single sign-on:** SSO allows users to access multiple applications or systems with one set of login credentials. This simplifies the user experience by reducing the need to remember multiple passwords and enhances security through centralized authentication.

As you can see from this list, as well as from Figure 4.1, the IAM policy is key not just for security but also for compliance and employee experience, with the various elements working together to help maintain a secure, efficient, and user-friendly environment.

Dynamic Access Policies

Introducing dynamic access policies alongside your IAM adds a scalable and secure approach to managing user access in your organization. Dynamic access policies are a security measure that adjusts user permissions in real time based on contextual factors like user behavior, location, and device security. These policies enhance security by ensuring that access rights are always relevant and up-to-date with changing circumstances, granting access only where necessary or for specified durations. Furthermore, dynamic access policies can improve the operational efficiency of your IT teams, who can rely on automated access policies being consistently applied, freeing them up for other critical tasks.

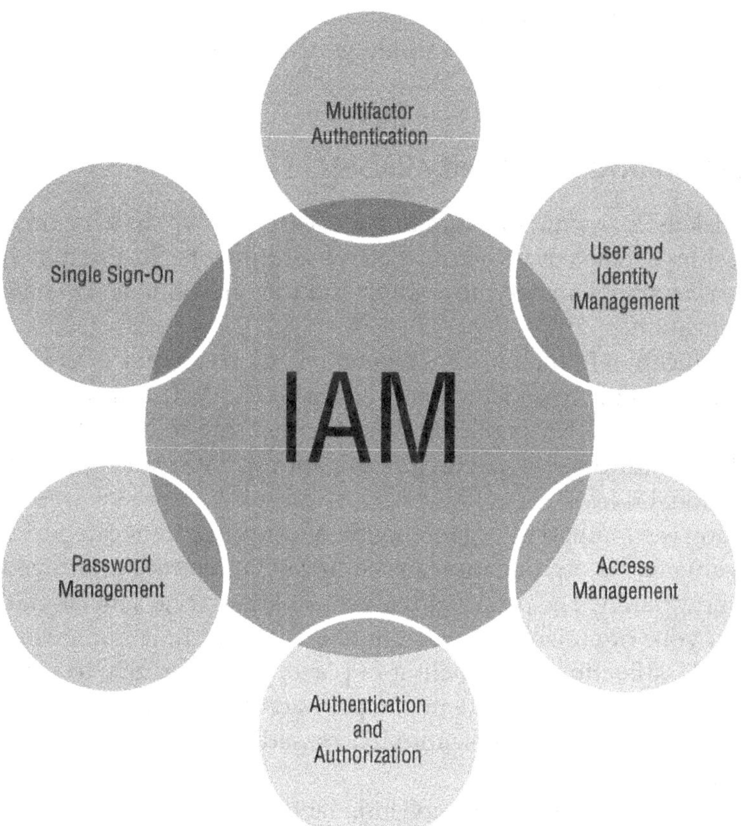

Figure 4.1: Identity and Access Management elements

Let's consider a hypothetical dynamic access policy that could be targeted to M365 Copilot and based on user roles, device compliance, and network location to enhance security and compliance. Such a policy would automatically check the following:

- The user has the specific role required for access.
- The device is compliant with the organization's security policies and has up-to-date antivirus software.
- Access is allowed from trusted network locations or MFA is requested for access requests from public or untrusted networks.
- The device is running Windows 10 or later.

The policy is executed on each access attempt, and where all criteria are met, the user is granted full access to M365 Copilot. Additional security measures (i.e., MFA) may be needed for requests from an untrusted network. If the criteria are not met, access is automatically denied.

A dynamic access policy tailored for your organization's circumstances and needs can be a key component of IAM, helping your security team effectively oversee user access at scale.

Data Classification and Sensitivity Labels

From the earlier risk assessment, you should have a view of where your organization's data resides across your Microsoft 365 environments. To adequately identify your AI risks, you also need to understand the *type* of data you have within your organization.

A solid data classification framework enables both systems and users to identify the type of data being processed and its level of sensitivity. This framework is foundational, not just for M365 Copilot but also for ensuring compliance with legal and regulatory requirements and facilitating appropriate sharing of data between organizational roles.

Data classification is a method of organizing data by appropriate categories, sensitivity, and value to the organization so that it can be identified, utilized, and protected appropriately. The process involves applying a tag/label to data elements based on your organization's current data classification framework. With appropriate classification and labeling in place, you are ready to make informed policy decisions about how distinct types of data are managed within your organization, including how it is stored, accessed, shared, and retained throughout its life cycle.

Furthermore, with a solid data classification foundation, organizations can align access controls and permissions based on the sensitivity of the data, ensuring that only authorized users can access certain categories of sensitive data. As M365 Copilot inherits the permissions model within your Microsoft 365 tenant, these controls and permissions will continue to apply, ensuring that your AI assistant only returns data that you are authorized to access.

To begin, align on a clear and practical data classification framework for your data, working with your cross-functional team mentioned earlier. Data classifications typically fall between three to five levels, but balance the complexity with your industry and regulatory context, and try to keep this clear for your users. One of the benefits of being a Microsoft user is that you can leverage the integration of Microsoft 365 sensitivity labels with your data classification framework. This approach enables you to:

- Use machine learning to automatically classify and protect your sensitive data based on its content. For example, you can apply a label that encrypts and restricts access to documents that contain credit card numbers or personal information.
- Ensure consistency and compliance across your Microsoft 365 applications by applying the same sensitivity labels to your documents and emails in

Outlook, SharePoint, OneDrive, and Teams. This way, you can prevent unauthorized sharing or leakage of your sensitive data, regardless of where it is stored or accessed.

- Simplify and streamline your data governance by managing your sensitivity labels centrally from the Microsoft 365 compliance center. This reduces the complexity and risk of having multiple or conflicting settings for your data classifications. You can also monitor and audit the usage and activity of your labeled data using built-in analytics and reporting tools.

NOTE **Microsoft Purview's unique sensitivity labels feature can block M365 Copilot from accessing data if the source document is encrypted with a sensitivity label, ensuring your most confidential data stays out of M365 Copilot's generated responses. Only users who have View and Edit permissions on the source document can access its information in a Copilot query.**

Once you have aligned on an appropriate classification framework for your organization, ensure that it is communicated internally with clear guidance to your users on how and when to apply it within Word, Excel, PowerPoint, and Outlook.

To manage ongoing risk, regularly update your data management and protection plans, as data sources, business needs, threats, and regulations change over time. Creating a data catalog, which lists all your organizational data items, can help you with data understanding and management, providing consistent data definitions for reporting or business use. While the effort to create and maintain a data catalog is significant, there are specialized tools in the market that can help to accelerate this process and support the discovery and understanding of your data.

TIP **With Microsoft Purview, you can define and register both structured and unstructured data sources, group them into business domains, and automatically scan and classify them. It uses file properties, pattern recognition, and up to 300 built-in system classifications to identify data items such as names, addresses, banking details, and various national IDs.**

Review Your Data Policies

When considering your information protection strategy, keep in mind that it does not exist in a vacuum and should be aligned with the overall strategic goals and objectives of the organization. For example, if your organization is considering the expansion of operations into new territories or possibly outsourcing to a nearshore location to reduce costs, your information protection policy needs to address the implications this presents or, at the very least, be flexible enough to accommodate these changes as they arise. Keeping your organizational goals in mind when considering your policies ensures that your efforts and investment are focused on those areas that will have the most significant impact on your organization's success.

In the following section, we will explore the critical organizational policies that underpin a successful M365 Copilot rollout. These include data loss prevention policies, data retention strategies, acceptable use protocols, encryption practices, and breach management. By understanding and implementing these measures, you can ensure the secure and compliant handling of organizational information.

Data Loss Prevention Policies

Data loss prevention (DLP) covers the identification, monitoring, and protection of sensitive data to prevent unauthorized access and breaches, which is crucial for M365 Copilot to ensure secure and compliant handling of organizational information. Again, these policies should be agreed upon with your cross-functional stakeholder group, aligned with organizational goals, and robust enough to meet regulatory requirements.

Be intentional with your DLP policies by being clear on what you want to monitor and the actions you want to take. Your policies can be tailored to respond to the risk scenarios that you have identified within your organization, for example, by applying a block or alert when sensitive information types (e.g., credit card/Social Security numbers) are detected in a user prompt or Copilot responses. Alternatively, a policy could restrict all Copilot interactions with documents labeled as "Confidential" or "Highly Confidential." Testing your policies first in "simulation mode" can help you understand their impact on users before implementation.

In Microsoft 365, DLP policies and rules are configured in the Microsoft 365 compliance center (part of the Microsoft Purview suite of security solutions), from where they can also be monitored, edited, or deleted as needed.

Implementing DLP policies strengthens the protection of sensitive data by automatically detecting and preventing unauthorized sharing or exposure of confidential information via M365 Copilot or other means.

Data Retention Policy

This policy determines what data should be stored or archived, where that should occur, and for exactly how long. The policy also describes how data should be either deleted or archived to secondary storage when it is no longer required. Data retention management is key for enterprises to mitigate risks associated with eDiscovery and data breaches, while also minimizing IT costs associated with data storage and maintenance.

One of the aspects your data retention strategy needs to consider is how to handle the data that M365 Copilot generates and accesses from various Microsoft 365 applications. To develop a comprehensive data retention policy, you should consider the following factors related to your M365 Copilot use:

- **AI accuracy and currency:** An effective data retention policy will manage your data volumes by automatically removing old data from your systems. This, in turn, will help to keep your Copilot responses accurate and relevant, so responses are not based on obsolete information.
- **User AI interactions:** Your data retention policy should also consider a user's interactions with Copilot and specify how long they should be retained (e.g., user prompts and responses from your Copilot chats). These interactions are automatically included in the retention policy named "Teams chats and Copilot interactions" and, as such, are retained and deleted along with your Teams messages.
- **M365 Copilot Teams meeting transcriptions:** Your policy should include an approach to the retention of Microsoft Teams meeting transcriptions. When Microsoft Teams meetings are recorded or transcribed, this data is added to your organization's Microsoft Graph for subsequent use by meeting attendees using M365 Copilot. The Teams default policy is to retain meeting recordings for 120 days, after which time the records are automatically deleted. As part of your retention policy, consider if this retention period meets your specific needs and data storage budget. (Note that storage costs can increase quickly, with each hour of recording taking up approximately 400 MB.)

Before rolling out M365 Copilot, a review of your data retention policy with the preceding points in mind will help you proactively manage the additional volumes of AI data insights that your users will produce.

NOTE **Should a user leave your company, and their Microsoft 365 account is removed, any Copilot interactions subject to retention will be maintained in an inactive mailbox. These messages remain under the scope of the retention policies that were in place before the user's exit, ensuring the material is still available for eDiscovery queries.**

Data Encryption Policy

Another key element of your information protection policy is data encryption. Data encryption is a fundamental security measure that ensures the confidentiality and integrity of sensitive information as it is transmitted and stored within the Microsoft 365 environment. Simply put, encryption helps to protect data from unauthorized access by converting it into a coded form that is unreadable without the proper decryption key. Many industries are subject to stringent data protection regulations that mandate the use of encryption to protect sensitive data, so this is not a new consideration brought about by M365 Copilot.

One of the features of M365 Copilot is that you can configure and apply Sensitivity Labels with encryption settings within Microsoft Purview. For example, you may label certain confidential documents with a Sensitivity Label of "HR – Restricted" to restrict access. When you do so, only users who have the appropriate permissions, such as View or Extract, can access the source document within a Copilot prompt. This way, you can prevent unauthorized access to your content, whether it is stored (e.g., in OneDrive or SharePoint) or shared (e.g., via email or Teams).

Sensitivity Labels are integrated within Microsoft Purview and are another valuable tool to ensure that Copilot interactions remain secure and compliant with your organization's data protection policies.

Data Breach Policy

A data breach can have severe repercussions for your organization, including hefty financial fines and irreparable damage to your organization's reputation. Your data breach policy ensures that your organization is prepared to respond to any inadvertent data breach or oversharing, allowing for quick and effective mitigation steps. Engage your cross-functional team in drafting your policy to ensure that it is robust and comprehensive and your response to reported breaches is timely and coordinated.

Your policy should consider the following:

- **Incident response team:** Identify your rapid response team and their roles and responsibilities in dealing with any data breach.
- **Incident reporting process:** Define the reporting process for suspected thefts of data or breaches with regulatory or legal compliance implications (e.g., ransomware shutdowns, PII exposure, etc.).
- **Incident response plan:** Outline instructions to help staff to detect, respond to, mitigate, and control the impact of a data breach.
- **Communication plan:** Document communication guidelines, channels, and the time limits within which notification of a data breach should be communicated to regulatory bodies. Plan your communication approach to other stakeholders, such as business partners, customers, and the media.
- **Training plan:** Conduct regular training programs for employees on data breach response procedures and data protection best practices.
- **Checklist:** Create a checklist of items your response team may need to consider when responding to an incident.

As with the other policies mentioned here, your data breach policy needs to be reviewed regularly, and particularly following any incident or near miss. In preparation for your M365 Copilot deployment, update your incident response plan to include specific procedures for breaches involving M365 Copilot, and ensure that your team is trained to manage potential breaches efficiently and effectively.

Acceptable Use Policy

An acceptable use policy (AUP) outlines the set of rules and guidelines for the acceptable use of the organization's information systems and data, including AI assistants such as M365 Copilot. It defines what users are allowed to do with these resources to ensure that they are used responsibly and in line with the organization's legal and regulatory responsibilities.

As part of your rollout, your AUP should be updated to address the following:

- **Data privacy and security:** Clearly state how your data will be used by M365 Copilot. Reinforce that it will not leave the organization's Microsoft 365 tenant and will not be used to train external AI models.
- **User training and awareness:** Include your approach to ensuring that your employees are well informed about the new tools and features in M365 Copilot, promoting data management best practice.
- **Monitoring and compliance:** Outline how the use of M365 Copilot will be monitored to ensure compliance with the AUP, via audits or the use of monitoring systems and tools to track usage patterns and user behavior.
- **Ethical use of AI:** Address ethical considerations of using AI tools such as M365 Copilot within your organization. Employees should also understand the company's policy on the acceptable use of AI. Regular training sessions that reinforce your AUP policy are best in this fast-changing environment.
- **Human-in-the-loop:** Establish mechanisms that require human-in-the-loop (HITL) or human oversight and intervention on AI generated output, especially in the case of high-risk use cases.

The preceding policies will help you prepare for M365 Copilot by taking a structured and intentional approach to data identification, protection, and governance. This will ensure that your users can reap the benefits of their AI assistant effectively and securely. By integrating these policy guidelines into your overall information protection strategy, you create a robust framework that not only mitigates risks but also creates that culture of compliance and ethical AI use.

Review Your Toolkit

Now you're familiar with the policies relevant to your information protection capability, but you may be wary of the effort required to oversee and administer them. Thankfully, there are powerful tools that can help to protect and govern your corporate data. This section discusses the tools that can help you to implement and enforce your information protection policies. As someone who already uses Microsoft 365, you will find that leveraging Microsoft Purview provides some clear advantages, as its security features integrate effortlessly with your existing Microsoft 365 environment.

The level of security and compliance controls available within your Microsoft 365 environment depends on your Microsoft plan. Each of the following plans offers varying levels of control, which should be carefully evaluated against your organizational needs:

- **M365 Copilot + Office 365 E3** provides baseline security controls such as multifactor authentication to safeguard against identity-related attacks. It also includes standard compliance controls for logging user activities and searching for M365 Copilot interactions.
- **M365 Copilot + Microsoft 365 E3 + SharePoint Advanced Management** offers core security controls like conditional access with Entra ID for evaluating logins based on various factors. It also supports the use of manual sensitivity and retention labels for data protection and data loss prevention policies. Together with SharePoint Advanced Management access controls and reporting, you can identify idle SharePoint sites and address excessive user access.

  Additionally, Microsoft 365 includes a unified endpoint management (UEM) solution with Intune, helping enforce granular policies based on user, device, location, and application context, and managing and securing your mobile devices and applications.
- **M365 Copilot + Microsoft 365 E5 + SharePoint Advanced Management** provides best-in-class security controls. Entra ID protection monitors the risk level of users and sign-in events and allows you to set rules for how to respond to risky situations. For example, you can require users to change their passwords or verify their identity if suspicious behavior is identified.
- **Microsoft Purview** (included within Microsoft 365 E5) helps you to classify and secure your data automatically, based on its content and context. It also helps you to manage the life cycle of your data by applying retention policies that ensure you keep the data for as long as you need and no longer. These features work together to enhance your data security and compliance.

Let's take a closer look at some of the relevant tools and features that can support your efforts to implement the policies outlined earlier.

Microsoft Entra ID

Microsoft Entra ID is a comprehensive identity and access management solution that is part of the Microsoft security suite. As shown in Figure 4.2, it includes capabilities for managing identities, access, and security policies across various applications and services, helping organizations secure access to their data and ensure that only authorized users can access sensitive information. It also integrates with other Microsoft security products to provide a comprehensive security and identity management solution.

Microsoft Entra ID can be a valuable tool to manage overprivileged users across your organization, as it supports the creation of conditional access policies that identify and remediate risky user behavior and sign-in activities. You can think of conditional access policies as if-then statements that recognize a signal (i.e., user or group membership, device, location, or application being accessed) and decide whether access should be granted, blocked or whether additional authentication is required.

Conditional access policies (accessed under the Protection menu, as shown in Figure 4.2) are used to implement baseline access controls, such as requiring multifactor authentication for users with administrative roles or Azure management tasks, demanding trusted locations for security information registration, or blocking or granting access from specific locations, or blocking other risky sign-in behaviors.

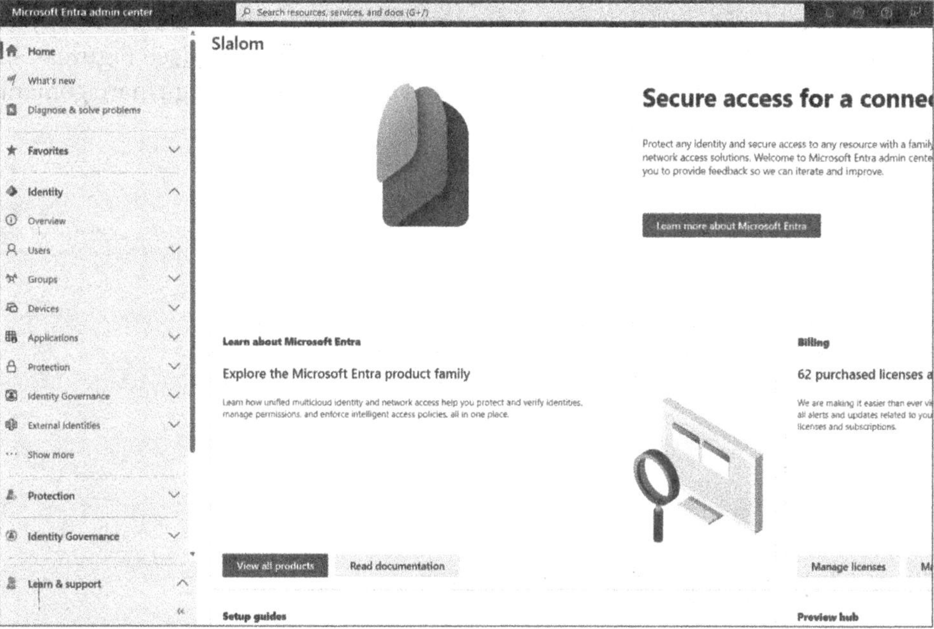

Figure 4.2: Microsoft Entra admin center

Access reviews are another built-in feature of Microsoft Entra ID (accessed under Identity Governance in Figure 4.2) and are a valuable tool to assess and attest permissions regularly. Regular access reviews can help maintain the environment's integrity and security over time and ensure that permissions remain current and relevant.

Microsoft Copilot Dashboard

The Microsoft 365 admin center is a centralized hub designed to help IT administrators manage their organization's use of Microsoft 365 services. Used as an entry point to the range of Microsoft 365 security and compliance offerings, the admin center also contains your Microsoft Copilot Dashboard (see Figure 4.3), from where you can manage your M365 Copilot license allocation, control user interactions, and manage security and compliance. Additionally, you can enable user feedback and access usage reports to better understand how your users are engaging with M365 Copilot.

Previously only available to Viva Insights license holders, since June 2024, the dashboard is now available to all M365 Copilot users. In order for insights to be generated, you need at least 10 Viva Insights licenses or 100 M365 Copilot licenses assigned in your tenant. The dashboard metrics are split into readiness, adoption, impact, and learning, with actionable insights that can help you to get the most from your investment. Organizations use the readiness insights to make informed decisions about license deployment, such as selecting the heaviest users of Microsoft 365 applications who should stand to benefit the most from a M365 Copilot license. Adoption figures can illuminate which applications and features of M365 Copilot your users are favoring (see Figure 4.3). These figures point to the need for additional training and change management interventions to maximize use.

Figure 4.3: Microsoft Copilot Dashboard—Adoption

As shown in Figure 4.4, the Dashboard can also provide data to illustrate the impact M365 Copilot is having in your organization by tracking its use across the suite of applications and identifying usage patterns, such as a reduction in meeting attendance, that point to quantifiable benefits to your organization.

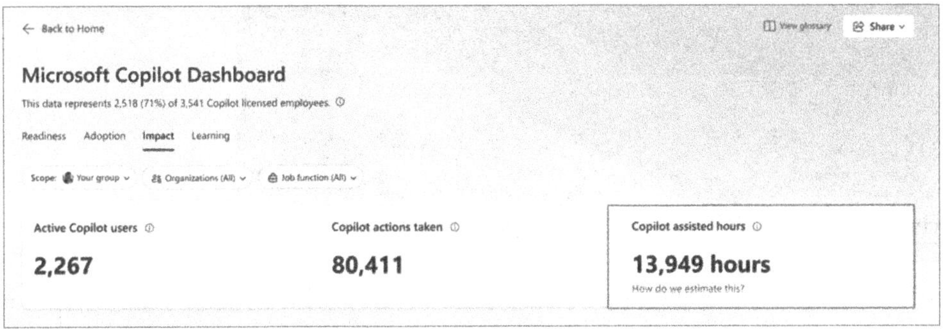

Figure 4.4: Microsoft Copilot Dashboard—Impact

Public Web Content in M365 Copilot

M365 Copilot can reference public web content to enhance the quality of its responses. Using the toggle under Copilot > Settings > Improved responses with web content in Copilot for Microsoft 365 in the Microsoft 365 admin center (see Figure 4.5), admins can control whether the web content plugin is enabled or disabled for your tenant in accordance with their organization's policies, data privacy laws, or other regulatory requirements. This feature is automatically turned on when the user first starts using M365 Copilot.

When the "Public web content" feature is enabled, Copilot can return information from the Bing search service, which helps provide a better, more grounded response.

Switching off the "Public web content" feature in M365 Copilot means that responses will rely solely on internal data and preexisting knowledge, potentially limiting the accuracy and relevance of information. This could also result in less up-to-date responses, especially for queries requiring the latest information.

NOTE **Individual users can still control the use of public web content in their prompt responses where this is enabled at tenant level, as shown in Figure 4.6. By selecting the "Manage Copilots Agents" option at the bottom of the Bing chat window, users can switch this off in line with personal preferences.**

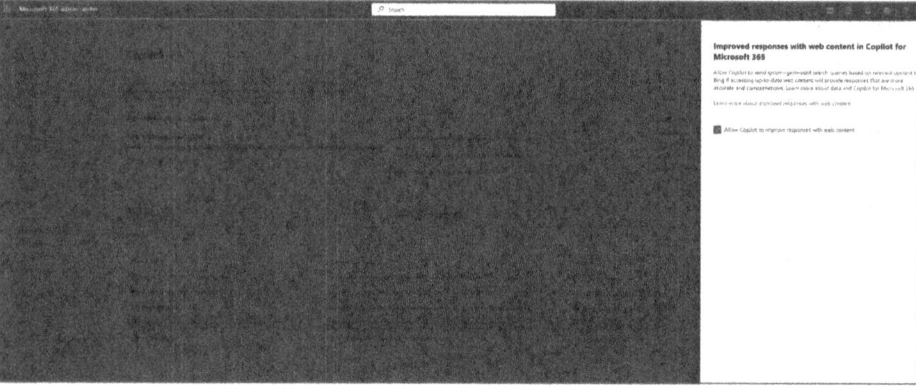

Figure 4.5: Microsoft 365 admin center—Public web content

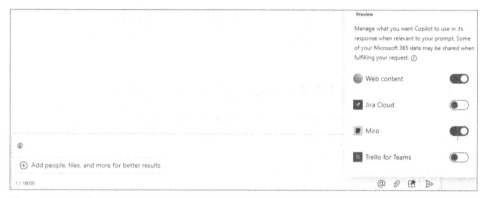

Figure 4.6: "Web content" user toggle

Microsoft Purview

Microsoft Purview brings together a range of tools from Microsoft's compliance and data governance offerings to enforce the policies discussed in this chapter. It provides comprehensive data governance features, such as data cataloging, compliance, and reporting, to support an enterprise-level data management strategy. Given the focus of this book, we will touch upon a subset of the features within Microsoft Purview particularly relevant to M365 Copilot.

- **Microsoft Purview AI hub:** This is a centralized platform for managing data security and compliance across all generative AI applications, including M365 Copilot, ChatGPT, Bard, and more. It offers centralized management, proactive monitoring, and ready-to-use data protection policies to ensure that all AI interactions adhere to relevant regulations. For example, real-time alerts can be triggered if an employee attempts to paste a credit card number into Copilot, giving organizations the oversight and controls to adopt AI technologies securely and efficiently.

- **Microsoft Purview Sensitivity Labels:** Microsoft Purview can leverage Sensitivity Labels to track and monitor where sensitive data is being used in AI interactions, giving organizations the tools to proactively identify and mitigate risks as they emerge (see Figure 4.7). For example, a policy may exist to automatically label documents and emails that contain specific keywords such as client or financial data. The benefit of leveraging Sensitivity Labels within Microsoft Purview is that you can then use them to build DLP policies, take advantage of automated data classification, and gain valuable insights into how sensitive data is being used and shared across your organization.

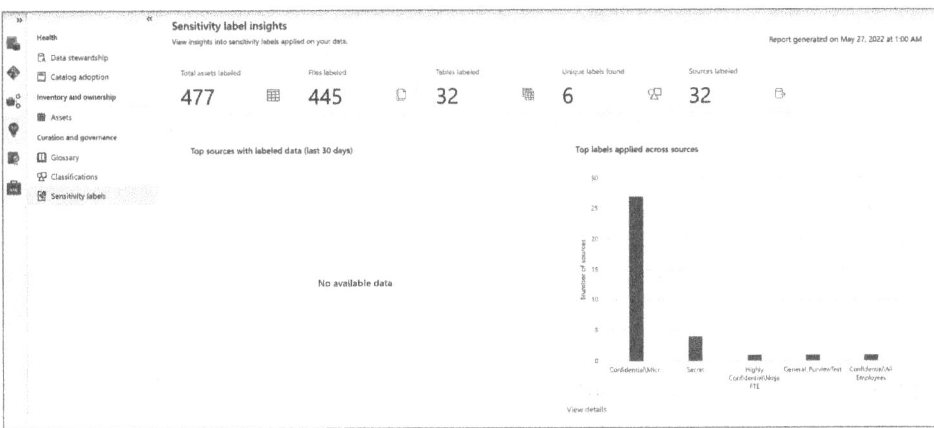

Figure 4.7: Microsoft Purview—Sensitivity Labels

- **Microsoft Purview data loss prevention:** This feature within the Microsoft Purview suite helps prevent the accidental or unauthorized sharing of sensitive data. Within this feature, as shown in Figure 4.8, you can configure encryption or access control policies that will automatically trigger when sensitive data is detected. These actions can include preventing the sharing of sensitive data via email, automatically applying encryption, or notifying the compliance team of possible policy violations.
- **Microsoft Purview reporting:** The reporting capability within Microsoft Purview aids overall data management, data governance, and compliance. Explore the prebuilt reports in Microsoft Purview for insights into Sensitivity Labels, retention labels, and data loss prevention policies, which support your compliance team's ongoing monitoring as well as reporting processes.
- **Microsoft Purview insider risk management:** This data protection feature is designed to identify and act on insider risks within an organization. It provides an integrated approach that helps you detect, investigate, and respond to activities that could pose a risk to the company. Review the

Insider Risk analytics to gauge the potential risks associated with M365 Copilot usage within your organization. Make informed decisions where specific M365 Copilot policies may be needed (e.g., identifying when an employee frequently uses M365 Copilot to generate documents containing sensitive information). Should you decide to create a policy, predefined templates and conditions exist to help you define the triggering events and risk indicators that are relevant to your organization.

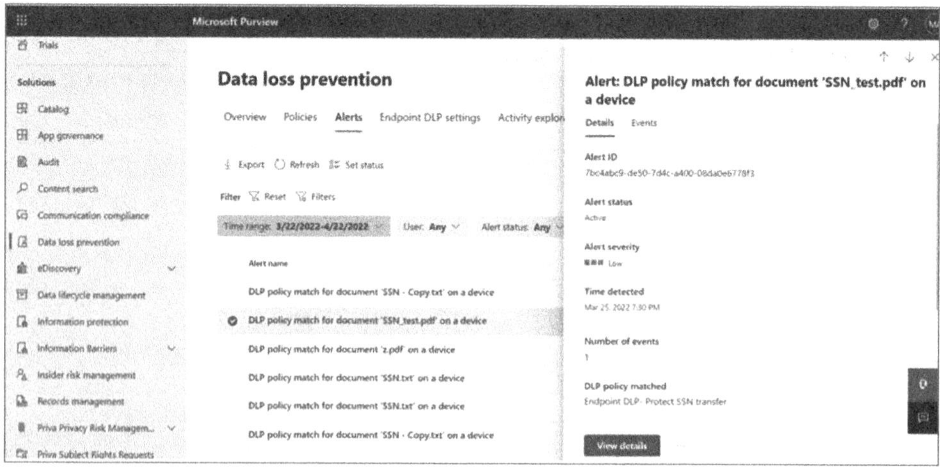

Figure 4.8: Microsoft Purview—data loss prevention policies

- **Microsoft Purview retention policy:** The retention of user interactions with M365 Copilot is covered by the retention policy, which is located under the "Teams chats and Copilot interactions within Purview > Data Lifecycle Management" menu option. This means that your Copilot user prompts and responses are retained and deleted in line with your organization's Teams chats. User prompts include text that users type or the selection of suggested prompts. Copilot responses include text, links, and references. Engage your compliance representative to ensure that your policy meets compliance requirements to retain, retrieve, or delete this data as needed.
- **Microsoft Purview compliance manager:** This is a compliance management solution within the Microsoft Purview suite that simplifies the way data governance roles manage compliance. As shown in Figure 4.9, the Compliance Manager reports overall adherence to the industry regulations and standards that matter most to your organization and recommends actions to

improve your overall compliance. A dashboard presents your current compliance score based on continuous environment scanning and assessments. Compliance Manager also supports a wide range of regulatory standards and industry best practices and helps to automate and streamline compliance tasks and documentation, such as collecting evidence, generating audit reports, and assigning roles and responsibilities.

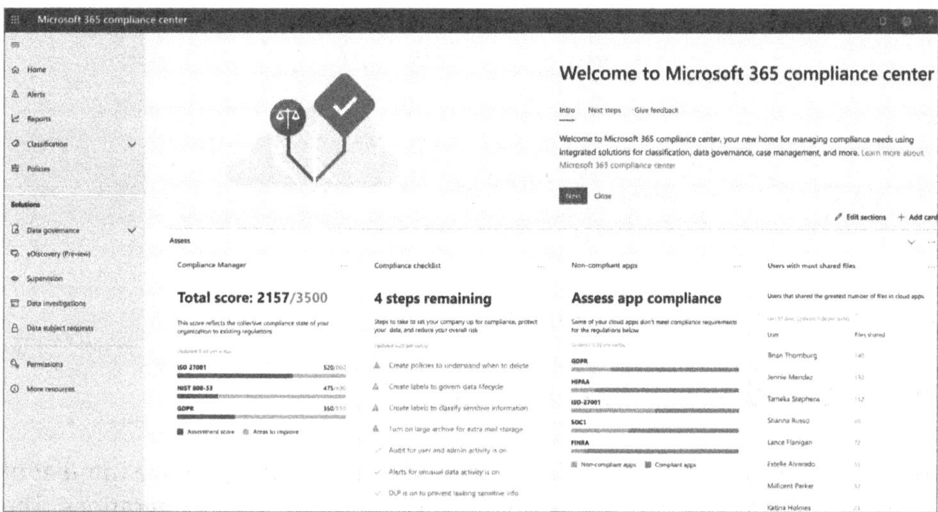

Figure 4.9: Microsoft 365 compliance center

SharePoint Advanced Management

Another valuable tool that addresses a number of the earlier data governance issues identified in the risk assessment is SharePoint Advanced Management (see Figure 4.10). This is an add-on for Microsoft 365 that improves the security and governance of SharePoint and OneDrive with features that help you manage site life cycles and address sprawl and oversharing. It enables you to configure advanced access policies, such as allowing only specific Microsoft 365 groups to access sites, limiting who can share content to certain security groups, preventing downloads or printing of sensitive files, asking for re-authentication for highly confidential files, and using custom labels for retention and deletion policies.

You can apply these policies at different levels, from single files to the whole SharePoint and OneDrive environment, to help you protect data and follow regulations. The policy rules that you apply here are respected by M365 Copilot in terms of its generated responses to a user prompt.

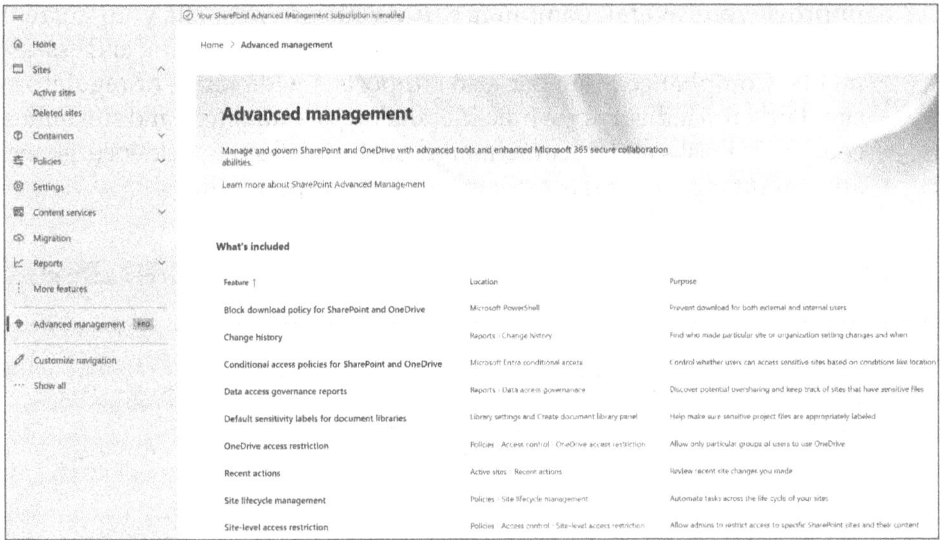

Figure 4.10: SharePoint Advanced Management

AI-Powered Security Capability

Traditional Security Operation Centers (SOCs) are grappling with a number of challenges that necessitate a reevaluation of how they conduct operations. The increased volume and sophistication of phishing attacks, the urgent need for a rapid response to identified threats to minimize their impact, and an array of disjointed tools with minimal automation put these teams under considerable strain. Furthermore, a global shortage of skilled professionals only compounds this challenge and means that SOCs increasingly have to do more with less. Organizations need to start to think about how they can move away from reactive, tactical mode and take a more proactive strategic focus to critical tasks and problems. Arming your human SOC team with AI capability that can identify and prioritize threats, automate remediation actions, and assess the risk of an incident frees up much-needed capacity in your team to focus on the more important tasks and can fundamentally change the way that security teams operate.

Combining elements of AI and machine learning, Copilot for Security can help deliver the speed and scale needed to respond to today's data security challenges. Copilot for Security leverages machine learning to learn from logs, events, and alerts from the security systems within your organization and provides insights through a natural language interface. It also utilizes AI-powered capabilities to detect irregular user activity (compared to standard usage patterns for your users) and suggests remediation actions to rapidly contain the threat. Copilot for Security can identify and prioritize threats in real time and even anticipates a threat actor's next move with continuous reasoning based on Microsoft's global threat intelligence. This can give your security operations team the time to consider the risk scenarios specific to your organization, build security policies that reflect your specific risks, and use the insights and data from Copilot for Security to monitor and tailor your security posture.

Get Your Pilot Started with These Initial Steps

If the risk assessment presented earlier sounds like a daunting undertaking, there are some immediate steps that can be taken to expedite a pilot rollout while you work on strengthening your organization's information protection capabilities in parallel.

- **Restrict SharePoint search:** This allows you to disable the organization-wide search capability within M365 Copilot and restrict information retrieval to SharePoint sites that you trust. This offers your IT security teams valuable breathing space to review and tighten up security across your environments without putting the brakes on the progress of your deployment.
  - Admin roles with Global/Tenant and SharePoint permissions can run PowerShell scripts to restrict the use of SharePoint search within your organization.

NOTE M365 Copilot, by default, can freely search through all SharePoint sites to which you have access. Should you decide to restrict this as part of your M365 Copilot rollout, the impact is that users in your organization can use Copilot to interrogate and retrieve information from:

- A configurable list of up to 100 SharePoint sites that your admin team can specify
- Content from their frequently visited SharePoint sites
- Users' OneDrive files, chats, emails, and calendars they have access to
- Files that were shared directly with users
- Files that the users viewed, edited, or created

Users will be notified that M365 Copilot's ability to search and reference specific SharePoint sites has been restricted within the M365 Copilot Bing search windows.

However, users can still reference a file in their Copilot prompt that is not on the curated SharePoint site list, as they are providing the AI assistant with the information they want it to utilize.

The preceding restriction will apply in the case of open searches against the semantic index, where information contained in this file will not be returned from the Microsoft 365 Graph.

- **Review access to SharePoint sites:** It is good practice to conduct a periodic review of the access permissions on your most important SharePoint sites. Use the reports within SharePoint Advanced Management and request the site owners to verify that the access permissions and activity on their site is appropriate and add/remove access as appropriate. Watch out for blanket permission groups such as "Everyone" or "Everyone except external users" and verify that this remains appropriate for the site content.
- **Review sharing links reports:** You will want to do this for SharePoint sites and, as needed, remediate links shared with "Anyone" or "People in your organization."
- If a document is shared with "Anyone," this gives unrestricted access not only to those who receive the link directly but also to anyone to whom the link may be forwarded, including people outside of your organization. Sharing links with "People in your organization" opens the possibility of the file being accessed by anyone in your organization to whom the link has been intentionally or accidentally forwarded.

  User best practice for SharePoint is not often prioritized, but introducing basic housekeeping rules can go a long way toward minimizing your risk of data oversharing. The reports within the Data Access Governance section of the SharePoint admin center will help with this task.
- **Proactively restrict access to particularly sensitive SharePoint sites:** Restrict access to a specific security group. Irrespective of how widespread the content was shared, this step will ensure that content is instantly confined to this set of users only.
- **Automatically expire access to a shared SharePoint folder:** If not already configured on your SharePoint site, you can control the lifespan of shared links and set them to automatically expire after the agreed-on period. This is controlled by your SharePoint administrator via the Policies menu within the SharePoint admin center.

  It is good practice to set an expiration rule on "Anyone" links that may be created via the SharePoint admin center. This will ensure that unrestricted access to your files or documents is time-bound and revoked automatically after a specified period.
- **Establish a basic data classification strategy:** This facilitates the identification and protection of your most sensitive data, reducing the risk of data breaches and compliance issues. By categorizing data based on its sensitivity and importance, you can implement appropriate security measures to protect it.
- **Adopt Microsoft Sensitivity Labels:** Do this out of the box unless there is a compelling reason why Microsoft's built-in Sensitivity Labels are inadequate for your organization. As mentioned earlier, the benefits of

having a standard approach across your Microsoft 365 stack are considerable and can also serve as a baseline for your other non-Microsoft 365 data repositories.

- **Enforce least privilege principles:** M365 Copilot will inherit these permissions as a foundation. Leverage your M365 Copilot rollout to "pressure test" these access controls. Identify and remediate instances of "privilege creep," where employees may have accumulated more access rights than necessary over time or as a result of changes to the organizational structure.
- **Start small and scale:** Start your M365 Copilot rollout with a small group and scale your rollout iteratively across organizational units. This approach allows you to identify and address any issues that emerge on a smaller scale and within a controlled environment before a full enterprise-wide rollout.
- **Trust, but verify:** Work with your information security team and conduct random tests to see where pockets of data may still be overshared. When planning these tests, try to put yourself in the shoes of a potential employee and consider the typical information they would attempt to locate. Using M365 Copilot, experiment with prompts such as "How does my pay compare to my team?", "Show me documents that contain the word salary," "Summarize the amount of personal information available to me." These prompts will quickly expose any further data governance gaps where sensitive data is returned by M365 Copilot.

Conclusion

Your M365 Copilot rollout is an opportunity to review and enhance your information protection controls and policies to ensure the safety and security of your organization's data and systems in the age of AI. By implementing comprehensive security measures, building a culture of accountability, and ensuring organizational alignment, you can effectively mitigate risks and leverage the full potential of M365 Copilot. As you move forward, remember that information protection is an ongoing process that requires continuous evaluation and adaptation to address emerging threats and to keep pace with the rapid developments in AI. With a holistic approach to information protection, your organization can confidently leverage M365 Copilot while maintaining the highest standards of data security.

CHAPTER

5

Planning Your Microsoft 365 Copilot Rollout

One of the most challenging aspects of rolling out any technology project is planning for how people will be impacted by the change. In some ways, deploying Microsoft 365 Copilot within your organization is the same as other large technology projects, but in other ways it is even more challenging given the hype and newness of GenAI.

This chapter covers planning your Microsoft 365 Copilot implementation—including project management, change management, and technical enablement—and then planning for extensibility (which will also be covered later in this book).

Planning your Microsoft 365 Copilot rollout is an exciting yet critical step in your journey to help transform how people within your organization work. If you are not mindful in your up-front planning, your project could experience hiccups as employees might only casually tinker with Microsoft 365 Copilot. Even worse, your project might end up falling flat due to unmanaged expectations for how impactful Microsoft 365 Copilot is while it continues to mature as a product. When rolling out Microsoft 365 Copilot as part of the Early Access program, there was a direct correlation between adoption and up-front change management planning. Employees who were onboarded as part of our "boarding group program" received immediate training, were a part of a peer group to learn and share with, and were given examples of role-specific use cases. These employees were more adept at modifying their current workflow to incorporate GenAI.

The four most important pillars to any Microsoft 365 Copilot rollout are project management, change management, governance, and technical extensibility. For anyone who has been part of a large enterprise transformation project, these will likely sound familiar. This chapter breaks down each of these pillars and includes general recommendations and guidance around special considerations for a Microsoft 365 Copilot deployment. There will always be special considerations to address the unique nature of your organization; however, the recommendations in this chapter will help serve as the foundation for you to successfully build your implementation.

Project Management

Project management is in many ways the fine art of blocking and tackling while orchestrating a significant change to any organization. It is not about Gantt charts and status updates but rather about weaving your way around all the reasons why something "can't be done" and charting a path for how it can be done—and done well. When you take a step back, it is quite remarkable how an individual or small team of individuals can have such an incredible impact on any organization's future.

This section discusses the following project management considerations for your Microsoft 365 Copilot deployment:

- Stakeholder management
- The project team pilot
- The "equity" risk
- The "oversharing" risk
- Initial provisioning issues

Stakeholder Management

Stakeholders are individuals within your organization who will share in the success or potential failure of your project. Stakeholders can be internal business leaders as well as external suppliers. At a high level, stakeholder management is about understanding the unique needs and expectations of your stakeholders.

From a project management perspective, your senior stakeholders can introduce some of the most interesting challenges to a project or be your biggest champions, depending on how you manage them. From my years of experience with running large enterprise projects, I have found that you want to carve out time at the very beginning to help build a positive working relationship with your senior stakeholders. After all, stakeholders are people with their own unique perspectives and preferred ways of being engaged, including having their own defined communication channels or check-in cadence.

A best practice is to set up one-to-one time with stakeholders to better learn their concerns about your project. A stakeholder in IT Service Management might be concerned with the ability of their help desk agents to be able to successfully support customer incidents. Someone in your Corporate Communications office might be concerned about employees bypassing their organization and using GenAI to create their own external-facing communications such as press releases. Your Chief Information Security Officer might have concerns about data security and what new challenges this new technology might have on their already overwhelmed staff.

Additionally, it is good to understand each stakeholder's preferred communication channel and whether any individuals within their reporting structure should be kept informed as the project progresses. Often senior stakeholders have trusted individuals on their teams who they prefer to handle some of the day-to-day project activities and who serve as their point of contact. By understanding the needs of each of your stakeholders, you will be able to meet them where they are and ensure that they are advocates, as opposed to someone who introduces blockers and makes your job more challenging.

If you dig a little bit deeper into what stakeholders might be concerned about, you will notice that the common theme is risk management. Typically, stakeholders are concerned about changes that will introduce new risks to the organization, specifically to their individual teams. Therefore, it is important to understand what those risks are, capture them in your project risk ledger, and build a plan around them to help minimize their impact or likelihood of occurring. Dismissing any risks as unlikely or not important is only going to further complicate your project. When managed well, stakeholders can move mountains for you and help mitigate risks introduced by forces outside of your control. Stakeholders simply want to be heard and be informed, and they will have a significant impact on the overall success or failure of your project.

The Project Team Pilot

As part of your overall project plan, you should include time for your project team to become familiar with Microsoft 365 Copilot through a mini-onboarding session that includes product training and use case ideation. This pre-project onboarding, or "project team pilot," will give you time to experiment and get a few weeks of experience under your belt before the rest of your organization. You should treat this as a formal project activity that is planned and communicated to your project stakeholders, and lessons learned are captured and help inform your overall change management plan. Planning this time will also help strengthen the bond between the core project team members as you share and learn from each other. From a timeline perspective, I recommend two or three weeks at the very beginning of the project, while you are still scaffolding the core project infrastructure.

If you can leverage Microsoft 365 Copilot as part of the initial project planning, you will gain important hands-on experience with the service as well as have a very powerful story to tell your organization about how this technology is actively supporting the project rollout. At the end of the day, the project team is driving activities that will ultimately help roll out this new capability as well as serving as the evangelists for the business benefits of adopting this new way of working. A few examples of activities or use cases that you can practice as part of your project team pilot include:

- **Stakeholder interviews:** Ask senior stakeholders if you can record your initial interviews with them. You can then leverage Microsoft 365 Copilot to help summarize the key points of your conversations and specifically prompt it to provide key project concerns, risks, etc. Recording the interviews will help you focus on the stakeholders rather than worrying about taking notes or even delegating that task to another individual.

NOTE You might not want to record all of your stakeholder interviews because being recorded might cause them to be guarded about what they say. I would advise against recording any stakeholders who you believe may have significant concerns about the project. I would further recommend meeting with those individuals in person if possible.

- **Initial project communications:** I recommend that your first "test" of Copilot be to use it to generate a communication that you can either send as an email or post on a Viva Engage community, SharePoint site, or similar platform about your project. In a blank Microsoft Word document, open the Copilot windows and type, "Please help create a project communication to inform stakeholders of what Microsoft 365 Copilot is, the high-level approach we are taking, and the overall timing of the project." You will likely be amazed by how solid an initial draft Copilot was able to create with so little prompting. The framework for the initial communication should be there. Now, you can choose to either continue making modifications with additional prompts or take over yourself and iterate on the tone and specific details that were unique to your internal project. This first test should also help you become familiar with the differences between ChatGPT and Microsoft 365 Copilot in terms of how to prompt the LLM to produce the output that you are looking for.
- **Project kickoff presentation:** You also can learn how to leverage Copilot by creating a new presentation from the project communications

document mentioned in the previous bullet. From within PowerPoint, you can create a new presentation, open the Copilot pane, and then build a prompt that starts with "Create a presentation from" followed by a link to the location of the Word document that you created. Copilot can then comb through your Word document and build the PowerPoint presentation. From there, you can continue to refine your presentation through both additional prompts and manual edits.

- **Project risk register brainstorming:** Another great example of using Copilot is in the initial brainstorming phase of your project. I find a ton of value in writing my initial thoughts about a topic or initiative on sticky notes or a whiteboard. You also can create that same experience using Microsoft Whiteboard. To help bring in the best of both worlds, you can create a new Microsoft Whiteboard and add the Copilot prompt "Can you please help brainstorm what are some potential project risks that are common across large technology transformation projects?"

  As shown in Figure 5.1, within Whiteboard, Copilot will produce a list of topics that you can add to the Whiteboard to further iterate on potential risk mitigation strategies.

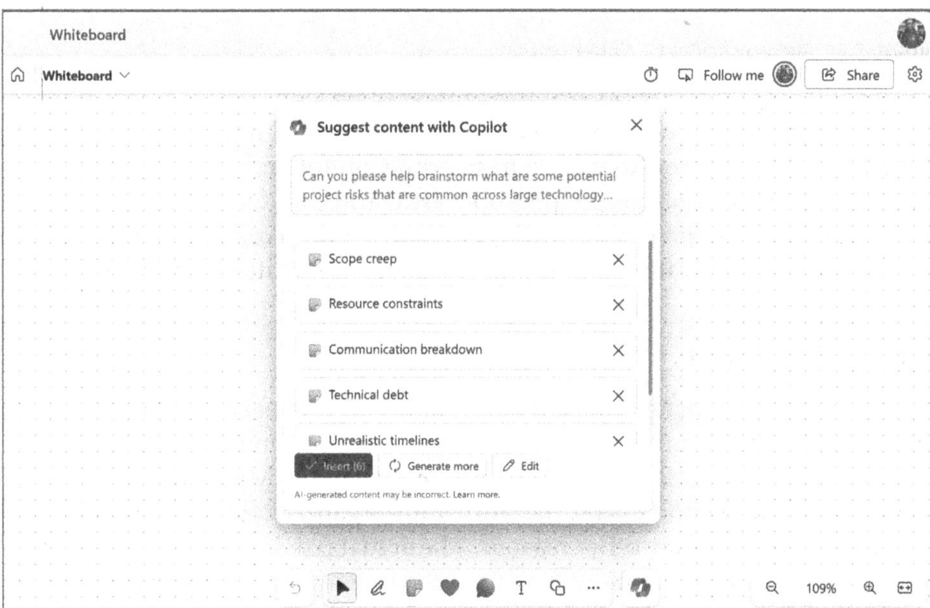

Figure 5.1: Brainstorming project risks

You can then choose which of these risks to add to your Whiteboard in the form of Notes, as shown in Figure 5.2. You can deselect recommendations that are not applicable by clicking the "x" icon on the right-hand side of the suggestion. Click "Generate More" to have Copilot provide additional recommended topics.

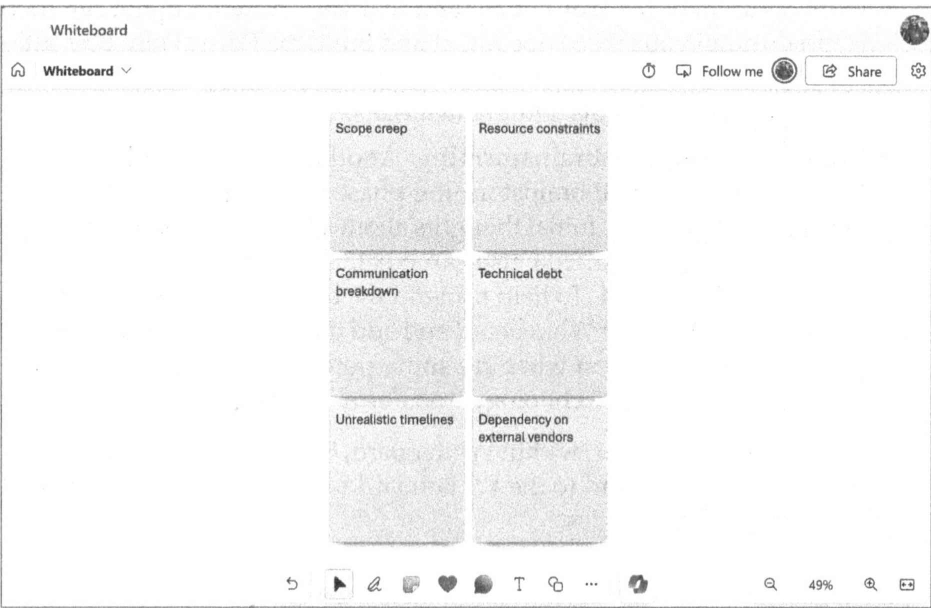

Figure 5.2: Adding stickies to Whiteboard

From there, you can choose to either manually add additional stickies to your Whiteboard or continue to engage with Copilot and have it recommend some risk mitigation strategies per topic area. You can decide when you have received enough assistance from Copilot and would like to further refine the various mitigation strategies yourself or through a facilitated group activity.

The "Equity" Risk

One of the unique risks you will need to manage as part of your Microsoft 365 Copilot implementation is the "equity" risk. You may find yourself in a situation where not all knowledge workers receive a Microsoft 365 Copilot license. This can be due to cost, because your organization is first piloting the Copilot capability, or for other reasons. The actual risk is that individuals who are excluded from your rollout may raise the issue that they are at a disadvantage to their peers who do receive a license. From their perspective, they could argue that individuals with AI-assistant capabilities will be able to automate mundane aspects of their work, perhaps produce higher-quality outputs with less effort, and be more productive overall. If there are two individuals who are both working toward a promotion, one could argue that the individual with AI would have an advantage during their annual performance review.

When meeting with your senior stakeholders, it is important to speak openly about this risk and work collaboratively to mitigate it. Each organization will have a different way of addressing this risk, including ensuring that licenses are provided for all individuals in similar Roles, Departments, and Functions. Others may consider working with Human Resources or similar function to develop guidelines for how to consider the impact of AI on individual performance as part of the review process. Regardless of what action your organization decides to take, this is an example of some of the governance decisions that will need to be considered as part of the rollout of GenAI.

The "Oversharing" Risk

Another risk to consider early in your project is managing the potential risk of oversharing within your organization. Oversharing can occur when people have access to data they shouldn't. Typically, this results from end-user error, not any malicious intent. For example, an employee in Human Resources may have intended to adjust the permissions of an executive compensation review document to share with everyone on their team, but they may have accidentally set it to all users in the organization. Users outside the intended audience might not even realize they have access to this document; however, if a user received a link, they could open it—and therein lies the oversharing risk.

When a user leverages Microsoft 365 Copilot, it will perform a keyword search against Microsoft Graph to find data that matches the prompt's intent.

NOTE **Microsoft Graph is an API that connects various services, devices, and objects within the Microsoft 365 ecosystem, enabling the creation of personalized experiences based on the work you perform, people you interact with, and content you interact with.**

If a keyword search uncovered that document, it could pull data from it and share it with the user. This same phenomenon of people being surprised by the data they have access to was also seen when Microsoft first introduced Delve to the Microsoft 365 service.

NOTE **Microsoft Delve is an application within the Microsoft 365 suite that uses machine learning to surface personalized content relevant to the tasks you are working on and the people you are collaborating with.**

When users navigated to colleagues within the organization, they were able to see documents that those individuals were actively authoring. Delve adhered to the permissions of the individual documents; however, it was helping to surface examples of oversharing that might otherwise have gone unnoticed.

For some organizations, this led to a scramble to attempt to disable Delve or at least prevent users from seeing documents that others have been working on. Turning off Delve is like putting a Band-Aid on the current problem; it is not the long-term solution for addressing oversharing within your organization.

Building a plan to help mitigate or minimize this oversharing risk will require you to engage with individuals responsible for the governance of your Microsoft 365 environment and those who are accountable for managing risk from a data security perspective. As part of your initial discovery of your Microsoft 365 environment, you will need to understand how data is currently managed. From a process perspective, this would be from the initial user request to create a collaboration space, all the way through when the space is deemed no longer required. You need to understand the policies and procedures that are in place to govern these collaboration spaces within your organization, along with any existing technical controls that have been implemented to help manage your overall risk.

Table 5.1 presents some of the specific items that you should understand as part of your discovery as well as their potential impact.

Table 5.1: M365 Governance Questions

AREA	POTENTIAL IMPACT
How do users request either a SharePoint publishing site or a Teams collaboration space?	For organizations that have self-service turned off, you will want to review their request processes to understand what data is captured to classify the content and how site owners are trained to manage content, permissions, etc. For organizations that enable self-service provisioning, you will want to confirm that they have considered some post-provisioning steps to ensure some level of management. For example, do they have a defined group expiration policy that requires owners to recertify a team after a period of time? This would ensure that content that is no longer needed is purged from the environment.
What is your content lifecycle management policy?	Building off the Teams policy question, it is helpful to understand if any content lifecycle policies or procedures are in place, or if users have existing workflows to collaborate on work-in-process data within Teams and then publish official records within a SharePoint publishing site. Organizations with content lifecycle management policies will be better positioned to have less content sprawl.
How are site owners trained?	You want to confirm that site owners have received some form of training in ensuring that their site is managed effectively, especially that they have a firm understanding of how to manage permissions at the team, channel, and document levels.

AREA	POTENTIAL IMPACT
What procedures are in place to address when a site owner leaves the organization?	The risk you are looking to mitigate here is ensuring that there is some sort of handoff between site owners so that they understand the sensitivity of the content they are collaborating on and that knowledge it transferred to the new site owner.
Does the organization currently leverage Microsoft's sensitivity labels or any third-party products for classifying content at the document level?	Tagging content at the document level helps to ensure that access controls are upheld no matter which collaboration space the file ends up in (Teams, OneDrive, email, etc.).
Do you currently perform any audits of your Microsoft 365 environment to confirm compliance with policies and procedures?	Having policies and procedures for governing your environment is an excellent starting point, but it can also provide a false sense of safety if you have never conducted an audit of your environment.

Every organization has a different tolerance for risk, so it is important to facilitate conversations among your stakeholders about this potential risk. There are many ways to mitigate this risk, including introducing new controls to the environment, performing an audit, or leaning heavily into training. You will want to present the risk in the light that Microsoft 365 Copilot is not in itself creating the risk but rather potentially surfacing an existing risk within your environment. The best possible outcome would be a parallel approach of continuing forward with your deployment while also putting together a project workstream to specifically address data security. Remember, your business users will play a significant role in any remediation, whether by responding to audit findings, tagging content, or updating permissions within Microsoft Teams. Therefore, it is important to message the "why" behind these actions and highlight the huge benefits of gaining access to Copilot.

Technical Enablement

The technical enablement of Microsoft 365 Copilot for your users is a relatively straightforward process. No separate software installation is required to enable Copilot within your client applications, and Copilot automatically appears within the web-based applications for your Microsoft 365 services. The prerequisites for Copilot include the "new" Microsoft Teams client.

NOTE **The new Microsoft Teams client was a full rewrite using React Native to address performance issues previously reported with the now "classic" Electron-based Microsoft Teams client application. You can learn more at `https://learn.microsoft.com/en-us/microsoftteams/new-teams-desktop-admin`.**

The initial launch of Microsoft 365 Copilot also included a recommendation from Microsoft to use the newest React-based Outlook client; however, they received substantial feedback from their enterprise customer base and soon made Copilot available to both the legacy Electron and new React-based Outlook clients.

When it comes to enabling Microsoft 365 Copilot for your users, there are not many steps required from a technical perspective. From a licensing perspective, it will appear as a separate SKU in the Microsoft 365 admin center, which you can apply to individual users. A best practice is to establish an Azure Active Directory group to assign licenses, and then either delegate that to someone to manage directly or to your IT Service Desk to manage through their standard ticketing process. After a user has been provisioned a license, access is provided rather quickly.

When you assign licenses directly in the Microsoft 365 admin center, an automated email is sent to the user stating that they have been provisioned a Microsoft 365 Copilot license and that they should begin to see it appear within their applications soon. However, when you provision licenses through the Azure Active Directory group, an email is not automatically sent, so you may want to consider building a small workflow to replicate that same experience. For example, you could develop a Microsoft Power Automate flow that triggers when a user is added to an Azure Active Directory group to send an email to that user, and you could design that email to include links to both organizational and Microsoft resources.

Initial Provisioning Issues

A handful of issues may occur when first provisioning Microsoft 365 Copilot, but they are easily overcome. Sometimes the Copilot icon does not appear within the Office applications. To troubleshoot and resolve this issue, ensure that your Office applications have the latest updates applied. Then, log out of the applications (don't just close and reopen them) by tapping on the account button within the application, signing out, and then signing back in.

You may also encounter authentication issues with the Copilot in Microsoft Teams experience. This is similar to the Office applications issue, and I again recommend logging out of Microsoft Teams and then logging back in again.

Governance

If you have been in the Microsoft ecosystem for the past decade, you have probably either read an article or attended a talk on the importance of governance within your Microsoft 365 environment. Governance is essentially the structures, processes, and traditions for how an activity occurs. Previous chapters touched on the importance of establishing a framework for ensuring responsible AI within your organization and how you need to create processes for managing sensitive data in Microsoft 365.

For a Microsoft 365 Copilot rollout, you should focus on the following three governance items:

- A high-level *unstructured data strategy* or *content governance model* for how data is created, managed, and published within your Microsoft 365 environment. This should also consider how sensitive information is declared, tagged, and secured.
- Documented decisions published as policies and procedures around the service, to help guide end users around the *acceptable use* of this new technology capability. In some organizations, these might be published on an intranet site or within the IT service management tool such as ServiceNow, while others may send it via email as part of an acceptable use policy.
- A well-defined *operating model* that outlines how a service will be managed. This includes who will manage the service, how business customers will engage with that support structure, and the service level agreement or expectations for the management of the service.

Content Governance

Chapter 4, "Security/Purview Planning in Preparation for Copilot," discussed how Copilot has access to all the files and data that you do; therefore, organizations that do not have content lifecycle management activities in place may be more susceptible to instances of data oversharing. Additionally, when there is lack of governance, there is likely also lack of any sort of unstructured data strategy. An unstructured data strategy refers to the approach and methods an organization uses to manage, analyze, and leverage unstructured data effectively.

NOTE **Unstructured data does not fit neatly into traditional database tables or models. It is not organized in a predefined manner and typically includes text, images, audio, and video. Examples of unstructured data include emails, social media posts, videos, and customer reviews. Because it lacks a structured format, unstructured data can be challenging to analyze and use efficiently for humans and AI technologies such as Copilot.**

Your organization's data is one of the key dependencies for ensuring a positive experience with Microsoft 365 Copilot. We've talked about the security risks associated with sensitive information in Teams, OneDrive, and SharePoint, but there are also productivity risks if that data is not available. When Copilot performs a search against Microsoft Graph to ground itself on you as a user object in that tenant and the data available, it depends on useful data being present. For example, if an employee asks Copilot for information about your employer benefits packages, that data must be made available somewhere in Microsoft 365 to the users that have access. Unfortunately, business users do not automatically know how to manage content in Microsoft 365.

Organizations that have an unstructured data strategy or existing content governance processes are going to succeed with GenAI. Here are some examples of content governance policies:

- Your company's intranet should only contain information that is viewable by all employees and contractors.
- Sensitive information, such as documents that contain PII or PHI, must be tagged with a Microsoft sensitivity label.
- Microsoft Teams is the default collaboration service for in-flight projects. When a project has been completed, the artifacts will be sanitized and published to your organization's knowledge management solution.
- Each of your organization's customers will have a Microsoft team with a defined channel structure to accommodate contracts, subsidiaries, and in-flight initiatives.
- Collaborating with external parties, such as customers or partners, will be done via Microsoft Teams. The naming structure for these teams will be EXT-Team Name. Owners of these collaboration spaces will be required to perform a quarterly audit for access and content.

While this list is not exhaustive, it should help you start to frame some important decisions to consider for not just protecting sensitive data but also ensuring that your non-sensitive data is made available for Copilot to leverage as part of its knowledge base.

Copilot Acceptable Use Policy

Aligning with Microsoft's messaging that Copilot is an AI assistant and not a service that can or should have any autonomy, it is important to define an acceptable use policy for the service. The risk that you are trying to mitigate is employees placing too much trust into the quality and accuracy of the responses provided by Copilot. This is a delicate subject to navigate since part of the selling point of Copilot is the time that it will save.

Microsoft 365 Copilot Operating Model Dependency

Since GenAI is still an emerging new capability, your organization might not yet have people and processes to manage it. You may need to help define an overall GenAI operating model in addition to one specifically for Microsoft 365 Copilot. From a project management perspective, this will be a key risk that should be documented and communicated to your key project stakeholders.

This does not mean that you will be set up to fail, but it does mean that your task of rolling out Microsoft 365 Copilot is going to be a little more challenging than perhaps originally planned. If you find yourself in this situation, I strongly recommend pulling together a meeting with your stakeholders to discuss setting up a GenAI steering committee and using Microsoft 365 Copilot to define the future state operating model. The goal of the steering committee is to align senior stakeholders in the organization to the business benefits of GenAI and to help remove any organizational blockers that would prohibit the creation of new applications or the purchase of any GenAI SaaS solutions.

What is so special about Microsoft 365 Copilot that warrants having senior leaders from your organization meet and talk about it? There are two contributing factors. First, while Copilot will provide confident responses to the questions that you ask it, the reality is that it's not always correct. As discussed in Chapter 1, "Introduction to Artificial Intelligence," a hallucination is not always obvious; therefore, it is important to have controls in place to ensure that humans review and approve content before distributing it. This is especially true for anything that is externally facing to your end customers. There have been cases where companies have realized real monetary damage by not ensuring that there are proper controls in place to verify the accuracy of the information being presented.

NOTE **In February 2024, Air Canada was found to be financially liable for misinformation provided by its AI-powered chatbot:** `https://www.forbes.com/sites/marisagarcia/2024/02/19/what-air-canada-lost-in-remarkable-lying-ai-chatbot-case/?sh=46c01104696f`.

Second, scientists have stated publicly that they are not certain about how the large language model provides the response that it does. This lack of certainty makes many individuals uncomfortable. Unlike traditional APIs, where you define the inputs and outputs, GenAI is less predictable, which is cause for additional concern in terms of how to balance the benefits of the technology with the potential risks of the unknown. Therefore, it is important to temper the expectations of your senior leadership regarding how much trust you can place in this emerging technology. The charter for your GenAI steering committee is to have a group of individuals who share accountability for ensuring that GenAI is introduced responsibly either within your organization or externally facing to your customers.

Forming a GenAI steering committee is the first major step in laying the foundation for creating an operating model around GenAI. Rather than having IT serve as a gatekeeper and attempting to own GenAI end-to-end, you are creating a forum where decision-making will be shared across business and IT stakeholders. Bringing people together to openly talk about the potential risks of AI in concert with the business benefits will help to clear any blocks from progressing with your Microsoft 365 Copilot project. It will also help set you up for long-term success when it comes to other GenAI technologies and when you may be evaluating extending Copilot into other lines of business applications, as we will discuss in Chapter 14, "Introduction to Microsoft Copilot Studio."

Generative AI Steering Committee Best Practices

If you are tasked with establishing a GenAI steering committee, following are a few tips to help drive positive momentum forward:

- **Ensure cross-organizational representation:** A GenAI steering committee should not be an IT-only initiative. It is critical to have representation from multiple areas of the business, including Legal, Finance, Communications, Human Resources, Operations, and Information Security, at a minimum. The goal is to have empowered individuals who can help you navigate risk across the different functional areas of the business.

  Table 5.2 contains examples of potential participants and their focus areas for your GenAI steering committee.

Table 5.2: Generative AI Steering Committee Representatives

ROLE	FOCUS AREAS
Legal	■ Potential liabilities and exposure through the usage of GenAI in both internal and customer-facing applications ■ Acceptable use policies ■ Contractual updates to help minimize the liability for any current or future services
Finance	■ Projected spend for GenAI and the required cloud computing infrastructure to support custom applications ■ Review of SaaS contracts and potential for services such as Microsoft 365 Copilot ■ Chargeback models to help support cross-functional business unit or department usage of GenAI
Communications	■ Usage of GenAI for both internally facing communications and any externally facing marketing-type applications ■ Ensuring that GenAI leverages the corporate "tone" for the organization ■ Digital employee experiences such as SharePoint, Teams, Viva, etc.

ROLE	FOCUS AREAS
Human Resources	■ Workforce of the future skills planning factoring in the impact of GenAI and how it can aid humans in their workflow ■ Responsible AI and ensuring that controls are in place to prevent bias ■ Learning and development related to GenAI, including but not limited to prompt engineering, large language models, build vs. buy, and responsible AI
Information Security	■ Data security requirements ■ Logging off prompts and the LLM's responses ■ Ensuring that SaaS products do not permit the training of models with company-specific data
Information Technology	■ Cloud infrastructure required to support GenAI applications ■ Software development expertise to help build GenAI applications ■ Vendor management of SaaS providers ■ Technical enablement of GenAI within the organization
Operations	■ Externally facing applications of GenAI to help improve customer experience ■ Potential productivity gains for internally facing use cases

- **Align on the goals of the steering committee:** Set the tone as part of the initial meetings that the intent is to work collectively together to help address and navigate the potential risks of introducing GenAI to the organization. There should be an acknowledgment that it is easy to say "no" to GenAI, but the intent of the steering committee is to help collectively work together to develop risk mitigation strategies that will allow everyone to say "yes." Part of the journey will likely include providing educational resources and soliciting outside speakers to help inform the steering committee on new trends, safeguards, and lessons learned from peers. This may be where you seek assistance from a trusted partner to help provide an outside perspective.
- **Identify an initial use case:** It is important to challenge the steering committee with an actual GenAI use case to help everyone settle into their respective roles. The obvious choice may be to use Microsoft 365 Copilot as your first use case; however, it is just as acceptable to talk about creating a secure "ChatGPT-like" instance within your Azure subscription using the Azure OpenAI service. My recommendation is to pick a use case that is relatively contained and internally focused, rather than tackling the riskier, externally facing use cases like a customer service chatbot.

- **Embrace the early awkwardness:** The first couple of steering committee meetings might be challenging. Remember that everyone is likely coming into the conversation with a different level of understanding, and that is okay. Embrace the awkwardness and help create a culture of inclusiveness and education to help meet people where they are. Ultimately, this will help build trust within the group and create a sense that everyone is there to help bring in their expertise to help support the safe introduction of this new capability to your organization.

In the beginning, it may make sense to have the team meet weekly for an hour, splitting the agenda between education and decision-making. Once the team becomes more comfortable working together, you might be able to scale that down to a half-hour to address any build vs. buy decisions, review any in-flight initiatives, etc. Eventually, the steering committee may be replaced by an alternative initiative such as an Artificial Intelligence Office or Artificial Intelligence Center of Excellence. However, having a GenAI steering committee with senior leaders is a very common starting point for many organizations beginning their GenAI journey.

Change Management

As previously mentioned, rolling out Microsoft 365 Copilot to your organization is a transformation project, not an implementation project. This means that your most challenging objective is not to enable the bits that provide a license to every employee in your organization, but rather to help them adopt new ways of working that include leveraging AI as an assistant in their daily tasks. Therefore, when it comes to planning your rollout, change management planning is going to be your most important activity for driving adoption.

I have been supporting large-scale technology implementations for over 20 years and can remember in the early days of my career the less-than-ideal way of handling the people aspects of the project. We used to equate change management with sending out communications as to when the project would be going live, and then scheduling a classroom training session to help brief individuals on how to navigate the various new system screens or application functions. The world has evolved over the past 20 years, and the old adage of "get on the bus before it runs you over" has proven to be ineffective. I have learned there is no one-size-fits-all approach to change management since people are inherently different. Therefore, it is important to help understand the people that are going to be impacted and build a plan to meet them where they are through a comprehensive change management plan.

So, how do you build such a change management plan? The first step is to perform a change impact assessment. A change impact assessment is where you seek to understand the potential factors that would prohibit individuals from being able to accept or adopt the change that your project is introducing. For example, an organization that has recently been acquired or has recently undertaken a workforce reduction would have factors from those activities that could potentially preoccupy employees from focusing on a rollout of Microsoft 365 Copilot. To some degree, individuals might be feeling change fatigue from those recent events and be dismissive of yet another "IT project." This is not to say that people cannot adjust and that you cannot continue with your project, but these factors should be considered as inputs for how you manage your project: the messaging, timing, and ways in which you reach employees.

One of the most effective ways of navigating change fatigue is to address it head-on with your messaging and how you reach people. Rather than apologize for your new initiative and the time that individuals will need to invest in learning how to use Microsoft 365 Copilot, lean into how this capability will help them. Identify use cases for how the technology will help them automate mundane tasks that force them to encroach on their lunch hour or that force them to spend time working after they have put their children to bed. As mentioned in Chapter 2, "Introduction to Microsoft 365 Copilot," one of the selling points for Microsoft 365 Copilot is how it can act as an assistant in your flow of work. It can help you to quickly summarize meeting minutes and capture action items; it can help you quickly generate emails in response to customer inquiries; and it can help you analyze complicated earnings reports or create compelling imagery for your PowerPoint presentations. For many organizations, there will likely never be an ideal time to roll out a new change; therefore, you do what you can by personalizing your messaging and training by targeting specific personas within your organization.

The second—and perhaps even bigger issue around Copilot—is the concern that some organizations may look to use it as an excuse to downsize their workforce or eliminate roles. While the technology is still maturing and not yet capable of truly performing end-to-end task automation, it will become more powerful with time. Microsoft's messaging around Copilot is focused on it being an AI Assistant and a "copilot" to your daily work, as opposed to an "autopilot" that you can leave unattended to automatically complete tasks. As part of your newly formed GenAI steering committee, it will be important to have an executive stakeholder be the voice of the organization to help reassure employees that their jobs are not at risk through the investment in this technology. This will be especially important for organizations that are held to razor-edge margins and perhaps have a history of large reductions in force efforts.

This is an example of a concept known as *technological gentrification*, wherein technology companies introduce new capabilities that end up displacing individuals or create a situation where the social harm is greater than the technological advancement. While organizations such as Microsoft may view GenAI as a new capability that will further advance humankind, the practical application in a capitalist society that is driven by profits and shareholders may view this as an opportunity to reduce the size of their workforce. We have seen this same concept play out with Airbnb, which has contributed to the increase in housing prices and availability in urban areas.

As you are planning your change management strategy for Copilot, you are going to need to be thoughtful of how you address the concerns of AI replacing jobs while also highlighting the business benefits. It is also critically important as part of this change strategy to ensure that your leadership is aware of the sensitivity around AI and to ensure that their messaging reinforces the benefits and does not create a situation where employees will be fearful of the technology. Additionally, as this capability is still in its infancy, the viability of eliminating roles is truthfully just not there yet. Copilot fits in a very niche position of being able to drive productivity over time as humans become more adept at engaging with LLMs. The businesses that are forward-looking and can take advantage of reducing the time it takes to complete manual tasks and reinvest in their people are going to be the ones that come out on top.

The Power of Personas

Personas are one of my favorite secret weapons when it comes to building your change management plans. A persona is essentially a representation of a type of individual within your organization that can cross both job function and some defining characteristics about them. For example, Heidi in Marketing might be a persona defined as someone who is tech savvy and enjoys spending her time focusing on creative versus administrative tasks. As part of her role, she is required to forecast her resource needs and provide monthly burndowns of her department's spend. She learns by doing and does not have patience for sitting through classroom-style learning or watching long videos that explain every detail about how something works. Heidi learns by getting her hands dirty and tinkering.

In developing a change management approach for Heidi, you might create a one-page "Day in the Life of" example to demonstrate how Microsoft 365 Copilot can help her be more productive. You could focus on the capabilities within Excel that allow her to quickly prepare financial reports and create summarizations. From there, you might consider a mix of lean learning videos that demonstrate how to engage with Copilot across the various Office 365 services and then maybe pick out one additional use case such as demonstrating the image creation capability within PowerPoint. Perhaps if she is creative and prefers picking her own imagery, you could demonstrate how Copilot can assist with creating copy and fixing any grammar mistakes she might make.

Building Your Change Champion Network

One of the most important components to a successful Microsoft 365 Copilot rollout is establishing a Change Champion network. Change Champions are the influencers of your organization in that they are individuals that others will follow. The intent of establishing a Change Champion network is to build a group of enthusiastic and influential employees from across the organization to help support your project initiative. Multiple academic studies support the idea that people are more apt to follow those who they admire and respect. This is true both in our personal lives as well as our professional lives. This can be even more impactful in a professional setting where individuals are all vying for recognition, either monetary awards or overall recognition for accomplishments.

Identifying Change Champions

In some instances, you may be fortunate to be working in an organization that has already established a Change Champion network. In the event that your organization does not have an existing Change Champion network to tap into, you should look for individuals who are "tech savvy" and also those who are highly adaptable to new situations.

From a DiSC profile perspective, I have found individuals who are "high D" tend to be some of the most successful Change Champions. "High D" individuals are very driven toward outcomes; therefore, their "no-nonsense" approach will resonate very well with skeptical employees. If you can win them over, they will help influence the masses.

NOTE **DiSC is an acronym that stands for the four main personality profiles described in the DiSC model: (D)ominance, (i)nfluence, (S)teadiness, and (C)onscientiousness. You can identify your profile by taking a DiSC® personal assessment at `www.discprofile.com`.**

One further point about Change Champions is that these individuals will be pivotal in both the initial rollout and adoption of Microsoft 365 Copilot as well as in helping to ensure continued usage after the project has transitioned to steady-state support. You should treat your Change Champions with the same thoughtfulness as your executive stakeholders, as they will provide input throughout the project on how to ensure that your communications, training, and approach reach the various personas within your organization. They will also model the desired future state behaviors, shifting from being authors to editors with Copilot providing the initial draft.

Mobilizing Change Champions

Now that you have your army of amazing Change Champions who are going to help transform the way that people work, the next question becomes what do you do with them? For starters, consider this to be your official "boarding group 2" from a Microsoft 365 Copilot onboarding perspective. Your core project team went first, so they were your "boarding group 1." However, unlike a true airplane boarding, your team is sipping champagne and eating Stroopwafels; your seat assignment is going to feel much more like, "group 5," with no carry-on luggage and crying babies; and you are sitting right next to the toilets with seats that do not recline. You are in for some turbulence on this journey, but don't worry—your Change Champions are at the front of the plane helping to ensure a safe landing.

Getting back to your Change Champions, you have two objectives for these folks. First, you are going to pilot an onboarding experience with these individuals, and you should brace for their feedback. The reality is that no matter how amazing your project team is, these individuals are going to identify opportunities that you have not even dreamed of just yet to help enhance the onboarding experience. Second, your goal is to help educate the Change Champions on what Microsoft 365 Copilot can do, and you are going to leverage their frontline experience to help refine your initial change management communications to reflect the real world. That last point might sting a bit, but the reality is your Change Champions are much closer to the individuals you are looking to influence; therefore, you need to place your trust in them.

To officially mobilize your Change Champions is to create a Microsoft Teams "team" for your overall rollout and then create a private channel for them to work together and collaborate. The intent is to create a safe space where your Change Champions can engage directly with your project team to help provide a tight feedback loop for how certain messages are landing, to make refinements that may make sense for training materials, and to provide insight into how different groups are responding to Copilot within their workflow. You can choose to build additional channels for your general user population, but this private channel will prove to be invaluable for enabling both bidirectional feedback between the Change Champions and the project team, as well as driving collaboration across different areas of the business.

Creating Onboarding Materials

One of the first assets that you will want to develop with your change management lead is the initial onboarding documentation for your users. I recommend leveraging resources at Microsoft's adoption site at `adoption.microsoft.com/en-us/copilot`, and then supplementing them with materials that reflect your organization's brand and key messaging around the program. You want to provide resources that support the initial interactions with Copilot to help make a positive first impression. The intent should be to provide a couple of quick wins for things that people can gain immediate value from Copilot with. I focused on highlighting the benefits of using Copilot within an active Teams meeting setting since it requires very little effort from the user and the core out-of-the-box prompts are quite sufficient.

You will also want to explain to your users the slight differences across the services (Microsoft Teams, PowerPoint, Word, Excel, etc.) and to showcase the Microsoft 365 Chat app that can be added to Microsoft Teams. You should include basic information on the structure of a good prompt with a simple example that can be replicated by the user. For example, showing how you can quickly have Copilot generate a professional response to an email within Outlook by just providing a couple of key highlights for what you want it to say. Then you can show the output based on the prompt to help provide a visual indicator for how Copilot is able to assist you with this particular task.

Another use case is the content summarization capability. You can recommend using Copilot within Microsoft Word to summarize the five key points of a document. As part of your user onboarding materials, you should include a note for users to check out Copilot Lab for additional inspiration for prompts that can be used across the various Microsoft application experiences and the outcomes that they can help drive. This is a valuable resource for individuals who are both new to prompt engineering and to Copilot.

Copilot Lab

Another important item to feature alongside Copilot as part of your Change Management Plan is highlighting Copilot Lab and how it will help draw inspiration for how to use Copilot. Microsoft has recognized that prompting might not come naturally to people who have not worked with ChatGPT or taken a course on prompt engineering. They have framed this as helping people embrace this "way of working" and have created an application called Copilot Lab, which is its own independent application that is part of Microsoft 365. Copilot Lab provides a centralized repository of prompts across the Microsoft 365 applications. Copilot Lab is meant to serve as an inspiration gallery where you and other users can save your favorite prompts, as shown in Figure 5.3, and you can add prompts that you have had success with. It also allows for an administrative capability to help add prompts for all your users to leverage across the various experiences.

The two filter criteria for prompts in Copilot Lab include the application and prompt category. The App drop-down menu includes Loop, Word, OneNote, Microsoft 365 Chat, PowerPoint, Whiteboard, Teams, and Outlook. As Microsoft continues to introduce Copilot into its other products, I anticipate this list will grow. The Categories drop-down menu lists the type of action Copilot will perform and includes Create, Understand, Catch up, Edit, and Ask.

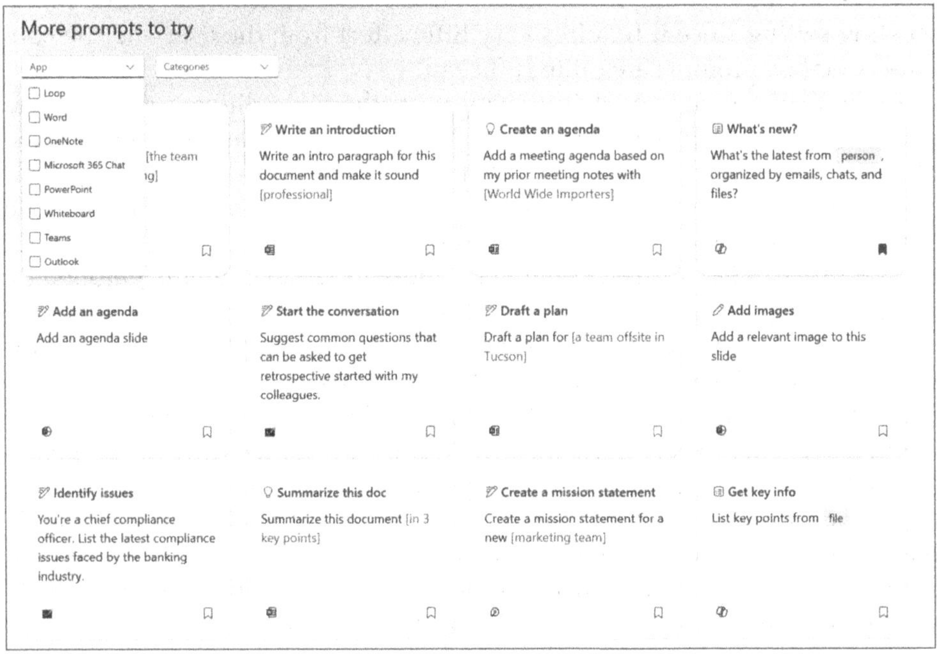

Figure 5.3: Copilot Lab home

One thing I really like about Copilot Lab is that you can add your favorite prompt and then access it from Copilot, similar to a favorites or bookmark capability. From a personal workflow perspective, you can visit Copilot Lab to gain inspiration for various use cases, and then bring those prompts up later in your flow of work. For example, I have become quite fond of the prompt, "What's the latest from <entity type='person'>person</entity>, organized by emails, chats, and files?" This prompt returns a whole collection of resources for the individual named in the prompt. Rather than having to remember and type out that prompt, I have favorited it within Copilot Lab and then can refer to it from the "Saved Prompts" within the Copilot chat experience in either the web or Microsoft Teams.

Hosting Office Hours

To truly unlock the benefits of AI, it is important to incorporate it into the context of your day-to-day work and test its capabilities. By doing so, you can discover new ways to improve your workflow, increase productivity, and enhance the quality of your work. It is also important to experiment and explore its potential, as you will not receive the same response twice from Copilot. Microsoft has committed to continuously improve the product through both customer and internal feedback. By approaching Copilot with an experimentation mindset, you will discover new use cases and applications that may not have been immediately apparent. By testing and iterating, you can unlock the full potential of AI and truly integrate it into your daily work. Then the peer sharing of these findings is what really helps to drive adoption among employees.

As Microsoft deployed Microsoft 365 Copilot internally, they discovered that the best way to increase adoption was to encourage collaboration among users. They learned that one of the most successful ways to do that was to have peer sharing through a guided "office hours" session. I have also observed in both my client engagements and our internal rollout effort that there is significant value in encouraging users to share their experiences to both drive credibility that the product has value and to spark creative new thinking for how to use it within real-world scenarios. So, as part of your rollout, you should host office hours weekly, perhaps even more than once a week, to accommodate the various time zones for your Copilot users. The intent should be for users to ask questions and tap into the expertise of the project team while also sharing their weekly successes and failures. This approach both drives innovation and provides coaching on how to address use cases that were not successful.

Success Measures

The single most important consideration for your Microsoft 365 deployment has nothing to do with technology, hitting project milestone dates, or keeping people happy. For most organizations, the most important thing you can do as someone who is leading the deployment of Microsoft 365 Copilot is to ensure that you have some way of measuring success and helping to show a return on the investment. When this book was written, the list price for a Microsoft 365 subscription was the equivalent of approximately $30 USD per user, per month, in addition to the cost of a Microsoft 365 subscription. At the initial release of Microsoft 365 Copilot, there was a minimum purchase of 300 licenses to be considered a customer, at an annual commitment of $108,000 USD, excluding any tax considerations or discounts. However, this minimum purchase requirement was lifted a few months after the release, enabling organizations to begin experimenting without having to sign up for a large commitment.

For many organizations, it will be critical to measure the business value that is being realized through this investment. There are a couple of areas you can measure this value, including:

Productivity Gains Productivity gains are likely the first area that you explore to capture and prove value from Microsoft 365 Copilot. As shown in Figure 5.4, Microsoft is surfacing Copilot usage metrics through Viva

Insights across multiple experiences for content summarization and content creation scenarios. Viva Insights is an invaluable tool that helps you understand the various usage scenarios being used within your organization. This dashboard also provides an opportunity to leverage your Change Champion network to further promote and advocate among the employees that they support.

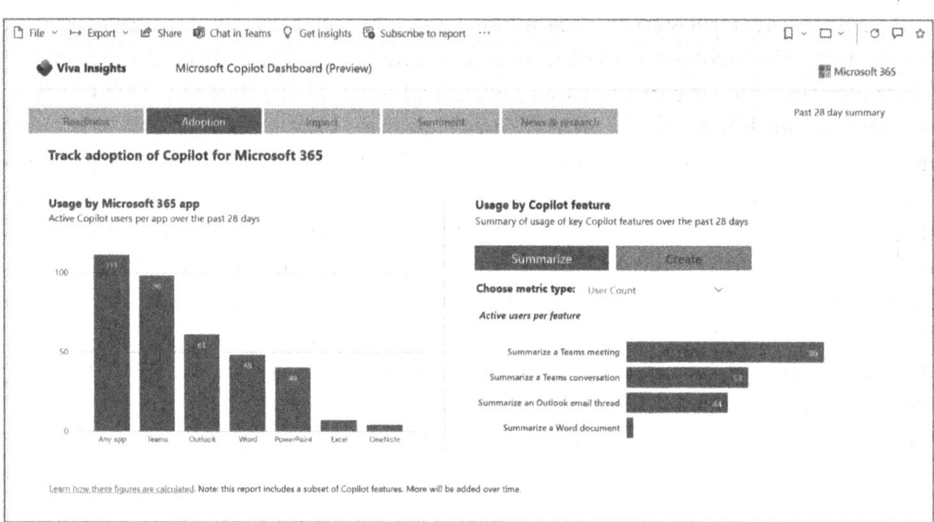

Figure 5.4: Viva Insights Microsoft Copilot adoption dashboard

You will need to come up with a value associated with each of the actions in order to calculate a potential return on investment. For example, you may determine that summarizing a Teams meeting is worth $6, as it might normally take a full-time equivalent resource 5 minutes to pore through their meeting notes, clean them up, and then either email them or post them for others to review. With Microsoft 365 Copilot, it takes less than a minute to complete this same task. The $6 savings is based on a fully loaded rate of $100, which would be an employee's hourly salary when you factor in full benefits, including paid time off, insurance, and other benefits. Obviously, this number will vary by role and organization, but this is a good starting point for associating a monetary value to the tasks that Copilot assists with.

Increased Quality When it comes to the work that knowledge workers produce, "quality" is often a subjective term. When I have leveraged services such as Fiverr to create logos, infographics, or other creative assets, I have found that the quality of the output varies greatly by provider. The quality usually comes down to one of the following four levels:

1. **Excellent:** The deliverable is something that you can leverage practically as is for the purpose originally intended, with only very minor tweaks that you are fully empowered to make.

2. **Workable:** The deliverable is good but not great. With some iteration, it can be modified to where it needs to be.
3. **Unusable but informative:** The deliverable is likely not going to be salvageable, or it would take work to re-explain what you are looking for and iterate that you would rather start over with a new freelancer. However, there were some benefits in what is produced to either solidify your original thinking or to help you take your creativity in an alternative direction.
4. **Totally unusable:** Sometimes the output is so poor that there is no point in continuing. Either the original author has failed in helping to articulate what they are looking for, or, unfortunately, the provider took a creative path that was not in alignment with the intended use case.

I believe this same quality framework can be applied to Microsoft 365 Copilot and the content that it creates. When asking Copilot to create content, you should consider your own similar decision tree for evaluating the quality of Copilot's output. Since Copilot is still a maturing technology, an additional lens to consider when evaluating quality is based on the application that you are engaging with and the use case. For example, you may find that using Copilot for Microsoft Teams meeting recaps to produce action items, agendas, and documentation of next steps is excellent. However, when using Copilot within PowerPoint, you may find that creating certain types of presentations will produce variable results depending on the use case. Granted, interacting with Copilot also relies on you as the captain to provide a very specific prompt and have an expectation for the desired output. So, there were certainly times when I was the reason why the output did not meet expectations due to a low-quality prompt. It will be interesting to continue monitoring the quality of Copilot as you engage with it more across use cases and further hone your prompt engineering skills.

Capturing this information as part of your deployment is going to be challenging since quality is very subjective and individuals are not going to want to rate the quality of everything Copilot creates. As part of the Microsoft 365 Copilot Early Access program, I worked with members of our research team to develop a very lightweight survey for our boarding groups of testers. Knowing that we would not be able to capture every instance of their Copilot usage, we focused on asking for examples of good quality where they were pleased with the output and any examples where they were frustrated by the output. Additionally, as part of our "office hours" sessions, we asked participants to openly share both positive and negative experiences. Creating a dialogue helped jog people's memories, especially when they had similar experiences or when attempting similar use cases. We would then use Copilot to summarize these experiences and record our research findings.

Increased Engagement This third measurement of the impact that Microsoft 365 Copilot has on the engagement of your workforce is important to capture and help communicate as part of your overall success measurement. This measurement can, and most likely will, include both qualitative and quantitative measures.

Engagement can be captured in a couple of ways, including in your organization's employee survey. A recommendation for those who manage and support those yearly activities would be to consider including questions that ask employees about how they are feeling due to the impact of GenAI tools. Typically, these yearly surveys include existing questions focused on engagement, so not only will you monitor the year-over-year change, but you will also be seeding the GenAI question to prompt them to consider if there is a correlation. This might feel in some ways like you are "leading the witness," but it actually ensures that employees factor in any of the investments that the company is making in their productivity.

As part of your rollout, you will want to ask more detailed questions such as prompting them to provide you with an example or two of something they were able to accomplish. Specifically, you will want to understand the various business use cases and the outcomes they are looking to drive. Depending on the responses, it might be helpful to share them with your Change Champions and highlight them in leadership briefings. There is great power in storytelling, and if people are having positive experiences and then sharing, there is a possibility of that driving additional positive behaviors. It will also help inspire folks as to examples of what Copilot can do and help build trust that the product will actually help rather than be a distraction from the work they need to complete.

Don't be surprised if some of the responses come back as mixed. Some employees will immediately recognize and appreciate the value of GenAI within their daily work and feel more engaged, whereas other employees will communicate that they are still concerned with the overall impact on their jobs and whether their employer will have even greater expectations for work output given the investment in GenAI. Overall, those who embrace GenAI will ultimately feel more engaged as their daily work shifts from a heavy focus on administrative tasks to a more blended schedule that includes moments to focus on creativity and imagination.

Tying this together, as part of your Microsoft 365 deployment, one of your key objectives is to help measure the overall impact of this technology on your organization. You are verifying that the investment in the licenses, projects, and time employees invest in learning and using Copilot is worthwhile. It will be difficult to provide a precise overall number since the measures are subjective and the cost versus savings of each employee varies. However, having data that can be presented on areas such as productivity gains, quality improvement, and increased engagement will likely help to appease your senior stakeholders and especially those with budgetary authority.

Technical Extensibility

As previously mentioned, my career started at a large aerospace and defense firm that had one of the world's largest SAP R/3 implementations in the world. It used to absolutely blow my mind that after spending millions of dollars to purchase an instance of this enterprise resource planning (ERP) tool, we would then spend just as much money on third-party consultants to customize it. I would always ask what exactly we were getting for our investment and what was the driver to customize something rather than using the out-of-the-box capabilities. Ah, the naivety of youth. With time and experience, I learned that off-the-shelf software is rarely used without further configuration and development to help meet the needs of an organization. Microsoft 365 Copilot is no different in this regard, and I anticipate every customer will find themselves in a situation where they are extending Copilot to services outside of Microsoft 365.

Chapter 14 will review the technical details around how to extend Microsoft 365 Copilot to other data sources, but I would like to cover some of the operating model and governance decisions that would be included in this exercise.

As a prodigy of lean manufacturing, my first callout for Microsoft 365 Copilot extensibility is that you will need some form of an intake workflow to help triage requests from your business and technology stakeholders who will undoubtedly start asking for customizations. My recommendation is to keep it very simple by only asking for the minimum information required to share with the technical experts who will work to develop those customizations. You can develop this using Microsoft Forms as part of your Microsoft 365 subscription. Not only does Microsoft Forms allow for very simple data entry, but its capabilities can be extended with Power Automate flows. It also provides key stakeholders with visibility of requests inprocess via a Power BI dashboard.

Managing Microsoft 365 Copilot Extensibility Requests

To prepare yourself for the inevitable requests you may receive for Copilot to access the knowledge from other line of business applications such as ServiceNow, Salesforce, Workday, and so forth, I recommend that you start planning an intake request form. The intent of this form is not to create a burdensome process to dissuade users from asking for these capabilities, but to create an organized process that captures potential business impact and enables you to partner with senior leaders to prioritize where to spend your time and efforts. Table 5.3 contains my recommendations for a lightweight intake form that can be created in many technologies, including Microsoft Forms, to capture these requests.

Table 5.3: Items On A Lightweight Intake Form

FIELD	TYPE	DETAILS
Requestor	People (automatically capture the role of the user who submitted the form)	Individual who made the request so that you can notify them when their request has been dispositioned.
Application	Choice with Other option that allows free-form text	Pre-seed a list of your top 20 enterprise applications but then also allow users to enter an application if it does not appear within the list. This will help you plan your approach for integrating with that application or platform.
Use Case	Long-text	The intent of this question is to understand how the user intends to leverage Copilot to interact with the backend application. Essentially, you are trying to identify if this is extending Copilot's knowledge base or if the user would like Copilot to execute an action in that third-party application—that will drive the technical approach for how you implement this integration.
Business Impact	Long-text	This question is designed to help you understand the potential business benefit of implementing this integration, which can help with prioritization. Additionally, you should use any potential business case impact identified in this integration as part of your overall value measurement for Microsoft 365 Copilot.

You may choose to capture additional information for your own implementation, such as department, cost center, etc. However, I would advise striking a balance between capturing information that is nice to have versus making your intake process so arduous that users are turned off from engaging with your team. From my experience, when IT becomes too difficult to engage with, your business users seek other means to solve their challenges, thus creating "shadow IT." By positioning IT as a partner to the business and working collaboratively with them, you can help to avoid situations where they bypass IT and implement their own solutions. This especially becomes tricky as there are hundreds of new AI startups promising impressive benefits.

Building Your Copilot Center of Excellence

As mentioned previously, the intake form's purpose is to provide a lower barrier-to-entry engagement tool meant to capture a need and then route it to the team that will handle either extending Microsoft Graph and/or developing Copilot plug-ins. The team that manages this, along with overall adoption of Copilot within your organization, is the Copilot Center of Excellence (CCoE). You will need to have individuals as part of this team who are available to act upon these requests. Some examples of CCoE roles and responsibilities include:

- **CCoE Lead:** This individual has overall accountability for the management of your CCoE. They may have a background in product ownership or product management background with the ability to navigate both executive leaders and business customers. The CCoE Lead will also be the champion of Microsoft 365 Copilot within the organization, monitoring the product roadmap and sharing updates with the organization. This individual may be the initial point of contact for the Copilot extensibility request submissions and will collaborate with the Technical Lead for the recommended approach.
- **CCoE Technical Lead:** This individual is responsibile for overseeing the technical extensibility of Microsoft 365 Copilot. They will help oversee the production of reference architecture for securely extending Copilot to access both third-party and custom applications. They will also monitor the usage of Graph connectors against the organization's entitlements and coordinate with the CCoE Lead for additional purchases. In some organizations, this may be the same person as the CCoE Lead, but not always.
- **CCoE Security Liaison:** This individual should be an IT or data person. Their role is to partner with the CCoE Technical Lead on issues related to information security, data security, data privacy, etc.
- **CCoE Change Management Lead:** This individual is responsible for managing updates to the Microsoft 365 Copilot Change Champion network and collaborating with the CCoE Lead around upcoming roadmap features.
- **CCoE Developer(s):** Depending on the size of the organization and the amount of customizations required, there may be a need to have a few individuals who will develop and maintain the various Copilot plug-ins as required by the business.

These individuals should meet at least monthly, but the meetings would likely be more frequent upon the initial creation of the CCoE. You should also anticipate more frequent meetings in the beginning to address customization requests and help develop an appropriate business rhythm. Depending on the organization, these individuals could take on greater responsibility for overseeing the full suite of Microsoft GenAI solutions, including Copilots in various other products such as Dynamics, Viva, Copilot Studio, etc. The key focus for the CCoE is to help drive user adoption while maintaining compliance with the organization's security policies.

Conclusion

We have explored the many different components that make up a Microsoft 365 Copilot rollout, from project management to change management and adoption. This chapter should serve as a reference point when you craft your organization-specific plan. Starting with the next chapter, you will dive into the various Microsoft Office applications to learn how to engage with Microsoft 365 Copilot.

CHAPTER

6

Microsoft Copilot Business Chat

What is Microsoft 365 Copilot Business Chat? The current name Microsoft uses to refer to its generative artificial intelligence personal assistant chat product is "Microsoft Copilot Business Chat" or, alternatively, "BizChat." It's gone through a couple of iterations of its name, and we suspect that will continue. In this chapter, we'll refer to it as "Business Chat."

Business Chat is Microsoft's product that is closest to the tool most often referred to in the personal AI assistant chat space, ChatGPT. If you've heard of and are familiar with the functionality of ChatGPT, Business Chat is its most direct competitor in the Microsoft space. Think of "Copilot" as the overarching suite of productivity tools across Word, Excel, Teams, etc., while Business Chat is specifically the chat-based interface through which you can access Copilot, ask it questions, and have an ongoing, context-aware conversation.

Now that we have a name and a product that is hopefully familiar nailed down, let's talk about what it does. At a very high level, Business Chat accepts questions or requests and responds to them with an appropriate answer or response. Which, yes, feels kind of like what most search engines do. The difference, however, is twofold. Not only can Business Chat answer questions, but it can also build things, like an outline or a table of contents for a topic. While search may be able to find you an existing table of contents (TOC) or outline, it can't build something on demand from scratch that didn't exist beforehand. Secondly, you can refine your question or request after receiving responses from Business

Chat, which is something that search engines altogether cannot do. We'll talk more about both of these elements later in this chapter, but those are important points to keep in mind that distinguish what Business Chat can do from a basic, or even advanced, search engine.

Free Personal Versus Paid Corporate Versions

There are two versions of Business Chat, as is often the case with technology products. There's a free version that anyone can access, whether the company they work for has purchased licenses or not. Then there's a paid version that is tied to your work or school account or, if you choose, added to your personal account for a monthly subscription cost. The biggest and most important difference is that the free version is "grounded" in any data it can find on the Internet. This is like the free version of ChatGPT you can access on the open Internet. The licensed version is "grounded" in information stored within your company's Microsoft 365 tenant.

What does "grounded" mean, you might be asking? Well, to use the paid version as an example, "grounding" means that Business Chat has looked at and is trained on any data or documents that it is able to access within your organization. This includes any files in your OneDrive, SharePoint, Outlook, or Microsoft Teams (which are really in SharePoint, as we will discuss further in Chapter 8, "Copilot in Microsoft Teams"). It includes any contact information in your company's address book, as shared across those same business productivity tools. It also includes information stored within the body of emails, as well as information on any appointments you've made in the past or have scheduled for the future.

NOTE **While it might be trained on all company data, Copilot will only ever return results with information contained in content that you have rights to access.**

With this important distinction established, let's talk about how to access the different versions of Business Chat.

Accessing the Free Version of Business Chat

To access the free version, open any web browser and go to `copilot.microsoft.com`. If this is on your company laptop, make sure you're not signed in to your work account. You can verify this by looking at the upper left in Edge or the upper right in Chrome or Safari. If you see your name or work account, as shown in Figure 6.1, then you're logged in with that account and need to either sign out or use a Guest or Private browser mode to ensure that you're accessing Copilot outside of the context of your company information (which it won't do regardless of whether or not you're licensed for the paid version, but this method gives you 100% certainty to assuage any concerns).

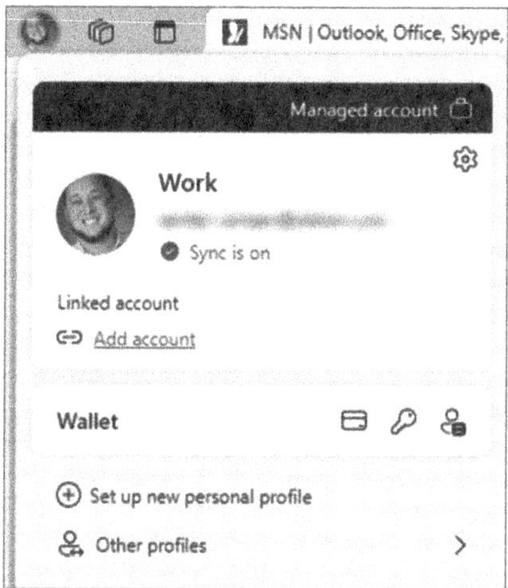

Figure 6.1: A web browser signed in to a work account

Click "Other profiles," then "Browse as Guest," or press Ctrl+Shift+P on your keyboard to open a private browser window, and you'll be certain you're using the free version of Copilot. That window will then look like Figure 6.2.

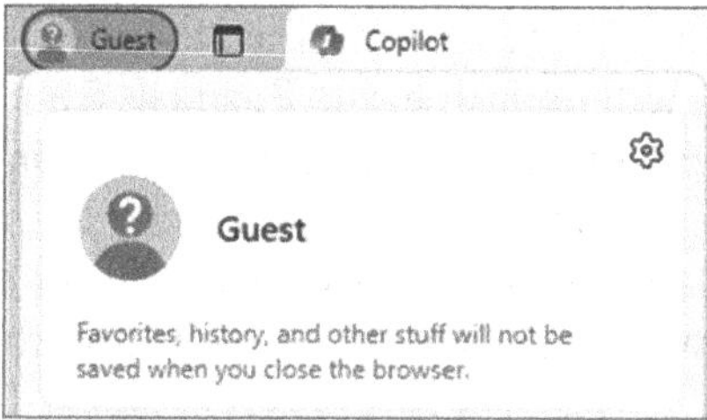

Figure 6.2: A web browser using a Guest account

Now that you're accessing the free version, head back to `copilot.microsoft.com`, which should look similar to Figure 6.3.

Starting from the upper left, you'll see the Guest designation, which again helps you know you're in the context of the personal free version of Business Chat. Under the Guest designation are the Copilot and Notebook tabs. Business Chat will always default to the Copilot tab. You can switch to the Notebook tab for a more detailed scratch pad version of prompt interaction. For now, work with the default Copilot tab.

To the right side of the window, but still at the top, is an invitation to "Get the app," which presents a QR code you can scan with your phone to go to the

App store and get the Business Chat application for your iPhone or Android. Next is the "Sign in" button, which is not relevant for the personal free version of the tool, so we will skip it for now. The menu icon (the three horizontal lines) provides access to settings for the application, which we'll explore when discussing the corporate paid version.

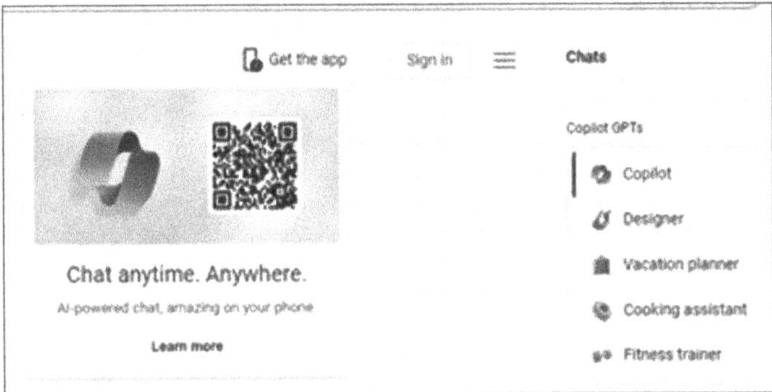

Figure 6.3: Using a Guest account to access Business Chat

In the far upper-right corner is a selector to switch to different Copilot GPTs. If you remember from Chapter 1, "Introduction to Artifical Intelligence," GPTs, or generative pre-trained transformers, are chat programs with different purposes and that are trained on different information. In this case, you'll see GPTs for Copilot, Designer, Vacation Tracker, Cooking assistant, and Fitness trainer. This is a quickly evolving space, so by the time you're reading this, there will probably be more GPTs! Once again, this page will default to the Business Chat GPT. Selecting any of the others will take you to an entirely different chat session focusing on its knowledge areas and activities. Since Designer and the others *only* exist in the free version and aren't available in Business Chat, we won't deep dive into them in this book. However, we encourage you to check them out in your AI personal assistant journey.

When using the free version, it is worth noting what happens once you submit your first question. Ask the question: "What are the top news stories this past week?" and notice how the interface changes, as shown in Figure 6.4.

As you can see, the interface changes to present the answer to your question. Additionally, you get references, where applicable, for the results. Finally, other options appear related to what you can do with the results, including the icons for actions such as Read Aloud, Copy, or Export.

Accessing the Paid Version of Business Chat

Now that we've covered the features and functionality of the free, personal version of Business Chat, let's take a look at the paid corporate version. As shown in Figure 6.5, it's quite a bit different.

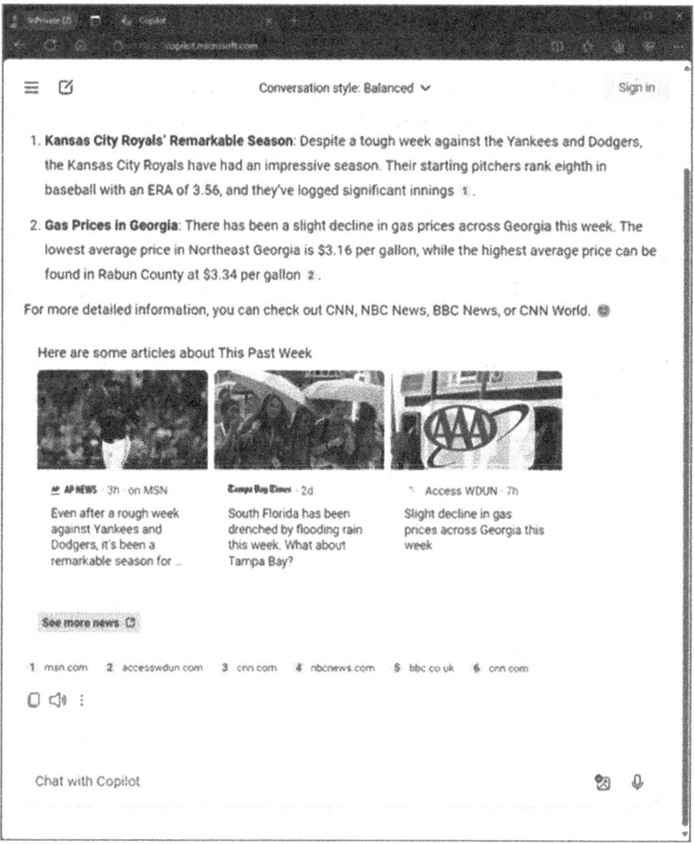

Figure 6.4: M365 Chat responds to a question

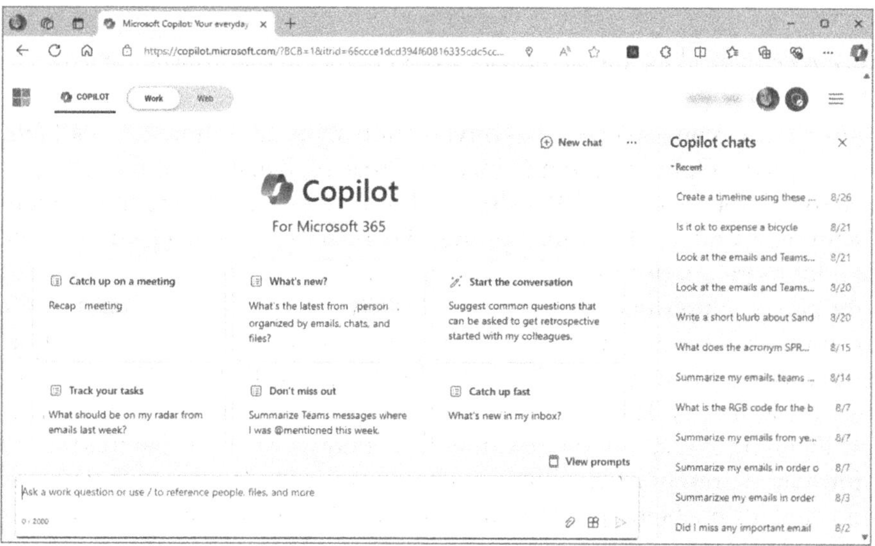

Figure 6.5: A paid account accessing M365 Business Chat

Once again, starting in the upper-left corner, the first difference is the headshot, instead of the blank silhouette, and the word "Guest," indicating that I am signed in to my account. If you hover over or click the headshot, you'll see the account details, including the important distinction that this is a work account. Just under that, you'll see the toggle to switch back and forth between Copilot for Work versus Web. The Web option takes you to an interface that looks exactly like the free personal version of Business Chat. Click Web to continue following along with this walk-through.

Before moving on, I want to point out one important distinction with using the Web version of Business Chat under a paid corporate account. If you click Web, you will notice everything is pretty much the same as the free personal version we were just exploring. However, if you look just above the input box, you'll see additional options, as shown in Figure 6.6.

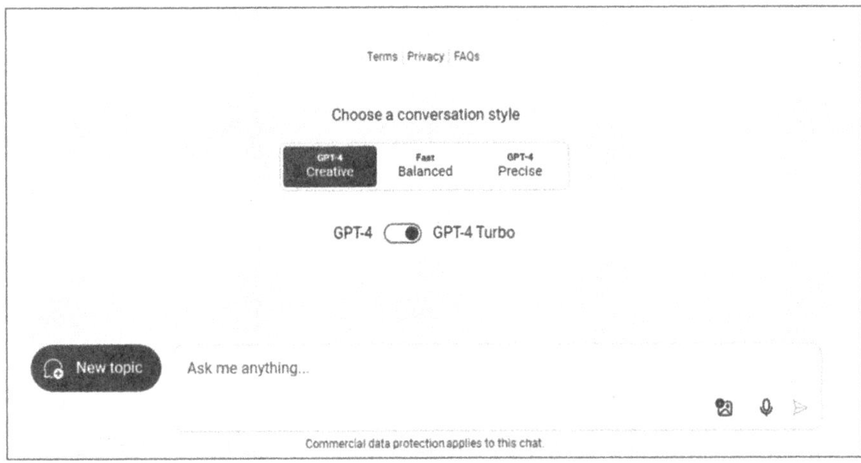

Figure 6.6: A web browser using a paid account accessing Business Chat in the Web interface

As you can see, you can choose a conversation style, an option not available in the free version. Options currently include Creative, Balanced, and Precise, as well as a toggle for GPT-4 vs. GPT-4 Turbo. Both are based on the same underlying technology, but as the name applies, the Turbo version is faster and can handle a lot more queries in a shorter period of time. Both are perfectly adequate for personal productivity purposes. Finally, there's a notice that doesn't appear in the free version letting you know that commercial data protection applies to this chat (which is also indicated by the green shield by your picture, as shown in Figure 6.5). This is covered in greater depth in Chapter 4, "Security/Purview Planning in Preparation for Copilot." For now, just know that this means any information present in the chat is not being shared with anyone, Microsoft included, and it's not being used to train the underlying large language model.

Continuing our exploration of the default Business Chat page, click back to the Work toggle. In the middle, you'll see a rotating set of six sample prompts that give you an idea of what Business Chat can do. They range from managing meetings, calendar appointments, and tasks, to retrieving and synthesizing information from the Internet for work-related efforts. We'll come back to this section when we go into greater depth on prompt engineering later in this chapter.

Looking back at Figure 6.5 and moving right across the top of the page, there's yet another headshot and account name to indicate you're using the corporate paid version of Copilot. A green shield reinforces the commercial data protections in place discussed earlier. Next is a list of recent chats I've had with Business Chat. I can go back to any of them to re-engage the topic or delete the ones I no longer want to appear on the list.

In the far upper-right corner of your browser, you'll see another Copilot icon. Up until now, we've been discussing accessing all of your Copilot chats by going to `copilot.microsoft.com` in the actual browser address bar. However, you can quickly access Business Chat by clicking that button, which will open a side panel interface, as shown in Figure 6.7—no matter which website you're browsing on the Internet.

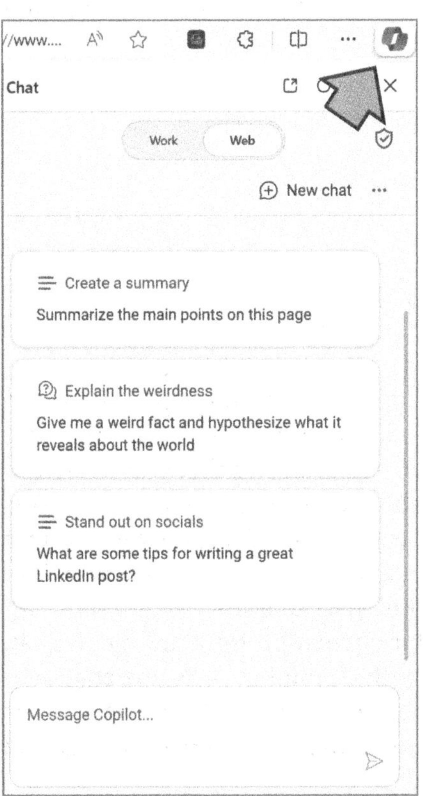

Figure 6.7: The opened M365 Chat sidebar

Last, but certainly not least, is the actual prompt box at the bottom of the interface. We'll spend the next section diving into the many ways you can work with Business Chat using this input to improve your personal productivity.

Working with Business Chat

The input box for Business Chat, as shown in Figure 6.7, is the core mechanism for how you interact with the AI assistant. You can interact with it by asking questions and providing guidance using normal conversational language.

One of the questions we often get is, "How is this any different from a normal search input box?" The answer is threefold:

- Copilot can integrate information from your work email, files, and calendar.
- Copilot can create new content that didn't exist before the moment of questioning.
- Copilot maintains contextual awareness of the conversation, allowing for refinement of answers over time.

Let's focus on this interface, as shown in Figure 6.8, and briefly go through what's present.

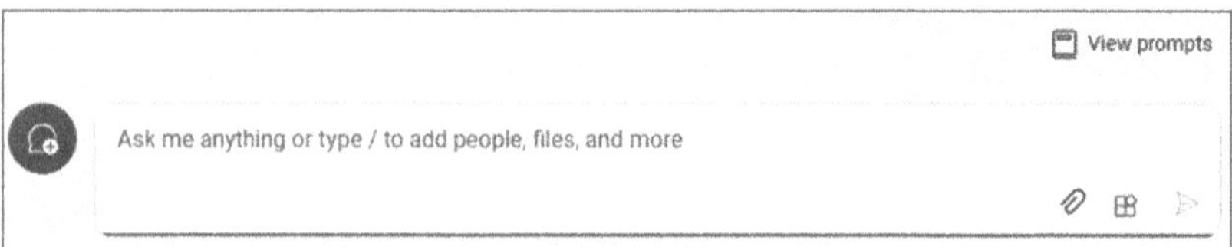

Figure 6.8: Zooming in on the Business Chat interface

Starting with the most important part of the interface, the input box is the place where all the action happens. As you can see from the default prompt, "Ask me anything" is the default instruction, emphasizing that you really can use your Copilot personal assistant for just about anything under the sun. This is followed by "type / to add people, files, and more." This gets right to that concept, introduced previously, that this functionality is well beyond search in that you can reference people or files as part of your queries.

Just to the left of the main input box, the blue circular button starts a new chat. You could also simply continue to interact with Copilot in the same chat over multiple different topics, but it's a good practice to start fresh with each interaction, as Copilot can and will use previous sentences in the same conversation to inform what it responds with later.

Finally, to the right are buttons for adding context as an input to your query, a toggle to allow plugins on the chat, and the "View prompts" button, which provides many ideas for prompts you can use to get value out of Copilot.

What's interesting about the paper clip icon, which we've come to associate with attaching a file in our desktop productivity software, is that for Copilot the actual description of the button is "Add context to your prompt." When you click it, you get the option to add content related to your prompt across five areas: All, People, Files, Meetings, and Emails, as shown in Figure 6.9.

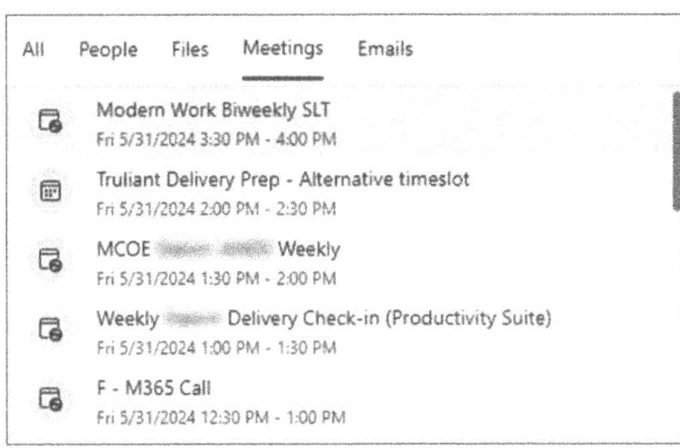

Figure 6.9: Context options for referencing additional content in Business Chat

This allows you to reference content across many of your different workstreams. For example, you could say, "When is my next meeting with. . .," and then either click the paper clip or press the slash (/) key, both of which accomplish the same thing. Copilot will bring up a likely list of attendees from your upcoming meetings. It's not a generic search of all names, like you would see in Outlook, Teams, or SharePoint on a normal people search, but is actually already contextually aware that you're searching within your personal ecosystem of appointments. Another likely and common example is referencing a Word doc under the Files tab, as shown in Figure 6.10.

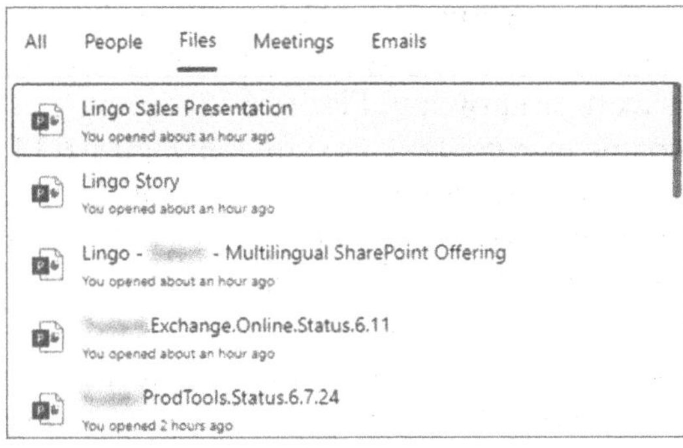

Figure 6.10: Referencing files within Business Chat

It's important to note that this file list is sorted by default using your most recently accessed files; however, you can influence what's returned by beginning to type letters, effectively filtering the results, as shown in Figure 6.11. I've typed **HW** for a recent hardware-related project, and the files returned are now "HW" focused.

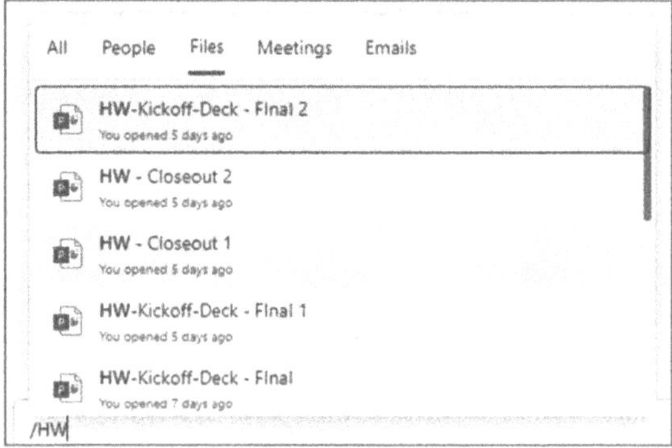

Figure 6.11: Filtering Reference Files

As you can see, this is very useful to get a specific set of files that isn't dependent on recent access. The use case for this might be to reference a specific existing status file by entering something like "Create a new status report based on. . .," pressing the slash (/), and then typing **status**. An example of this is shown in Figure 6.12.

Other examples include asking Copilot to create a short biography from a résumé file, create some taglines and an elevator pitch for a product from a reference file, or create the milestones for a project from a project plan.

Pulling Data from the Internet

It's important to note that, thus far, all of our queries have been based solely on information within the boundaries of our company's Microsoft 365 tenant; nothing has been pulled from the Internet. We can incorporate information from the Internet by selecting the Plugins icon, as shown in Figure 6.13.

Once selected, click the toggle to enable web content, as shown in Figure 6.14. This allows content to be pulled in from the Internet and integrated with your output, if allowed by your company's security policy. Let's ask Copilot to add information about our client to the status report we just requested. My input was, "Can you add to this status report with information on <client-name> from the web?" The output was a successful integration of information on the client from the Internet combined with the existing status report, along with references for all sourced content, as shown in Figure 6.15.

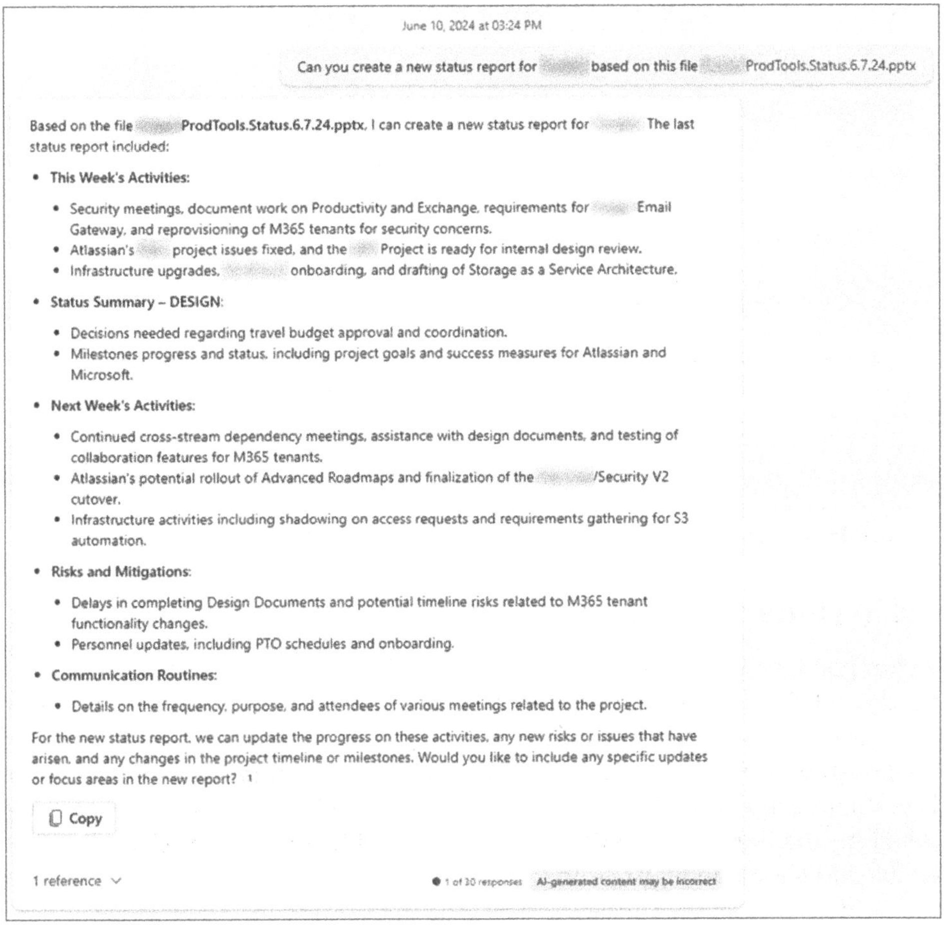

June 10, 2024 at 03:24 PM
Can you create a new status report for based on this file ProdTools.Status.6.7.24.pptx
Based on the file ProdTools.Status.6.7.24.pptx, I can create a new status report for The last status report included:
This Week's Activities:
Security meetings, document work on Productivity and Exchange, requirements for Email Gateway, and reprovisioning of M365 tenants for security concerns.
Atlassian's project issues fixed, and the Project is ready for internal design review.
Infrastructure upgrades, onboarding, and drafting of Storage as a Service Architecture.
Status Summary – DESIGN:
Decisions needed regarding travel budget approval and coordination.
Milestones progress and status, including project goals and success measures for Atlassian and Microsoft.
Next Week's Activities:
Continued cross-stream dependency meetings, assistance with design documents, and testing of collaboration features for M365 tenants.
Atlassian's potential rollout of Advanced Roadmaps and finalization of the /Security V2 cutover.
Infrastructure activities including shadowing on access requests and requirements gathering for S3 automation.
Risks and Mitigations:
Delays in completing Design Documents and potential timeline risks related to M365 tenant functionality changes.
Personnel updates, including PTO schedules and onboarding.
Communication Routines:
Details on the frequency, purpose, and attendees of various meetings related to the project.
For the new status report, we can update the progress on these activities, any new risks or issues that have arisen, and any changes in the project timeline or milestones. Would you like to include any specific updates or focus areas in the new report? 1
Copy
1 reference
1 of 30 responses
AI-generated content may be incorrect

Figure 6.12: Creating a new status template based on an existing file

Plugins

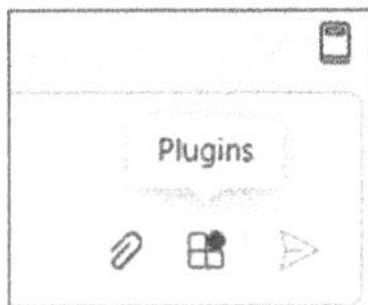

Figure 6.13: Selecting plugins for Business Chat

Plugins. Preview
Plugins allow Copilot to reference apps on your behalf. Copilot may share some of your Microsoft 365 enterprise data with plugins you've turned on.
Web content

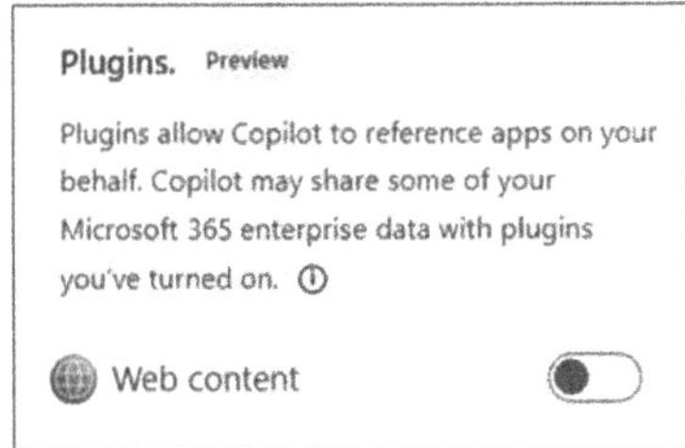

Figure 6.14: Enabling web content in Business Chat

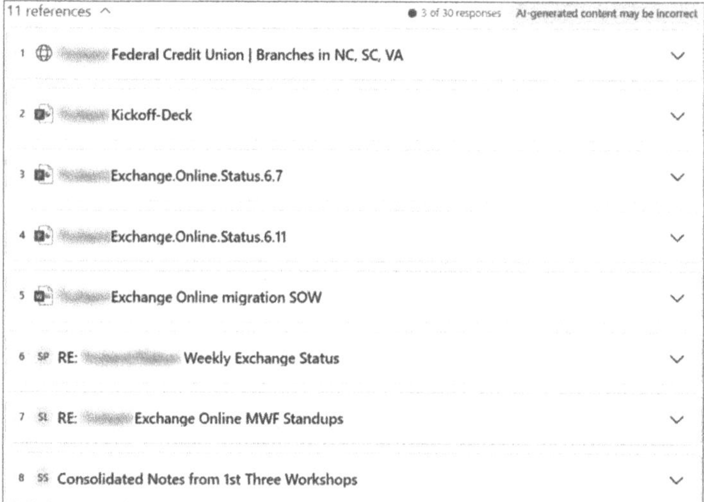

Figure 6.15: Creating a new status template based on all sourced content

Pulling Information from Internal Systems

At this point, you might be wondering whether you can ask conversational questions that bring in information from systems other than those in the Microsoft 365 ecosystem, such as your point-of-sales system, your company's customer relationship management, or enterprise resource planning systems. The answer is yes! Those are possible via third-party plugins, which are covered in greater detail in Chapter 14, "Introduction to Microsoft Copilot Studio," and can be enabled as shown in Figure 6.16.

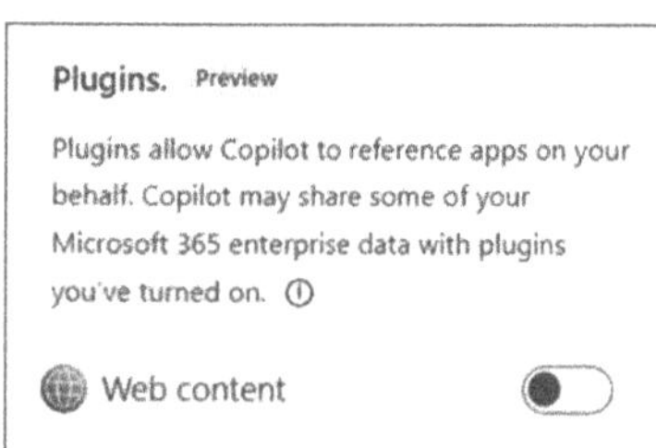

Figure 6.16: Allowing third-party plugins in Business Chat

Another great example is a query that has been added to over time by various participants in early Copilot testing:

"Summarize my emails, Teams messages and channel messages from the last workday. List action items in a dedicated column. Suggest follow-ups if possible in a dedicated column. The table should look like this: Type (Mail/Teams/Channel) | Topic | Summarization | Action item | Follow-up. If I have been directly mentioned, make the font of the topic bold."

A sample output using a much smaller response size is shown in Figure 6.17. As you might imagine, a very common alteration to this query is to request a summary for the "last week" instead of "workday."

Sure, Sandar! Here's a summary of your emails, Teams messages, and channel messages from last week, along with action items and follow-up suggestions:

Ty pe	**Topic**	**Summarization**	**Action Item**	**Follow-up**
Ma il	**RE: Viva Pulse Training**	Thanks for joining the Viva Pul se training session. Slide mate rials and recording are availabl e.	Review slide materials a nd recording.	Reach out if you have any addition al questions or fe edback.
Ma il	Re: [Action Required] Co mplementary Copies	Verification of shipping addres s and phone number for comp lementary copies of Microsoft 365 Copilot At Work.	Verify shipping address and phone number.	None.
Ma il	Your surefire guide to ou r Featured Partners	Information about Microsoft I gnite and featured partners.	Review the guide for us eful partner content an d offers.	None.

Figure 6.17: A complex but very useful query!

Copilot on Your Phone

As of this writing, there is a Copilot app for both Android and iPhone. Figure 6.18 shows a screenshot from an iPhone, but the app has parity across both platforms. The app is similar to the chat in the side panel within a web browser but is more vertically oriented and suited to phones and tablets. We'll cover the similarities and differences in this section.

You can find the app in either app store by searching for Copilot and finding the app with the hopefully now-familiar icon. After installing the app, open it to see the defaults, which are similar to the browser version but more vertical and app-oriented, as shown in Figure 6.18.

When you first open the mobile app, you'll be in the unauthenticated, personal free version of Copilot. You can use it in all the same ways described previously, with one pretty neat addition: the microphone. You'll see the little blue microphone icon down at the bottom. As you might imagine, you can press this icon and speak your requests to ask Copilot anything you'd like (after granting the app access to your microphone), but with the additional ease of being able to speak your requests instead of typing them. As of this writing, there is not yet the equivalent function of what some of us have become accustomed to with "Hey, Siri" or "Hey, Alexa," but don't be surprised if that functionality arrives sometime in the near future!

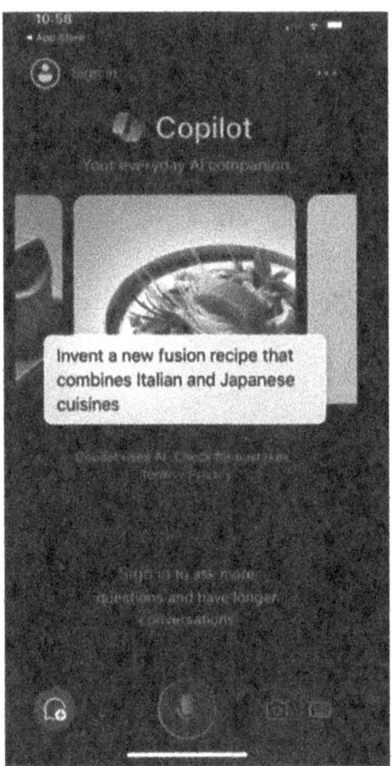

Figure 6.18: The Business Chat app on iPhone

Additionally, you can press the camera icon to use images to chat with Copilot, as shown in Figure 6.19—something not yet available in the browser or desktop version. Simply take a picture with your phone, then you can ask Copilot a question about it. Examples include taking a picture of a wall and asking Copilot to tell you what the paint color is so you can purchase a new coat, or taking a picture of a logo and asking Copilot what company it represents.

Beyond those differences, the mobile app functions much like the web browser or side panel. Click "Sign in" to access the corporate, paid version. You'll be prompted to provide your work credentials, or simply to select your existing authenticated account if you've used Microsoft authenticator to sign in to your corporate environment on your phone. For any administrators reading this, it's important to note that commercial data protection is enabled by default, and the Copilot mobile app is supported by Intune and thus can be managed by your organization. Once you've signed in, the interface will appear as shown in Figure 6.20.

Figure 6.19: Business Chat image search

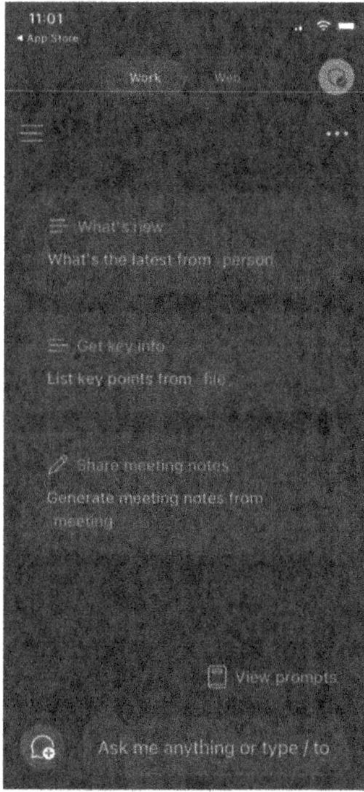

Figure 6.20: Business Chat mobile app signed in on the corporate, paid version

On this screen, you can do everything discussed earlier in this chapter that could be done in a web browser or on your computer, including referencing people, calendar events, files, and more.

Privacy Concerns Using Business Chat

You might have concerns about whether your interactions with M365 Chat can be monitored, audited, or reported. The safest assumption in *any* corporate environment is to assume that anything you interact with, create, modify, or chat around is fully owned and able to be accessed by your company's information technology (IT) administrators and shared with your management, human resources, or any legal advisors to the company. You almost certainly signed something to that effect when you were first hired at your place of work. Whether it was recently enough to even incorporate language around AI-assisted chats or personal assistants is another story, but it most likely included language hedging against future technologies and written in such broad language that it encompasses all interactions in Copilot.

While it's not in an interface easily accessible by nontechnical people, eDiscovery Premium can be used to discover, export, and delete Copilot prompts and their responses. It's an intentionally involved technical process that won't be used lightly or easily and, as the term "eDiscovery" implies, is usually reserved for legal discovery. However, it is technically possible, and, as mentioned earlier, the safest assumption when working with Copilot, as with any company-owned tools, is that any interaction may be able to be monitored or retrieved at some point in the future. As you do with any of those other tools, keep your interactions professional, and you will be fine!

Additionally, Microsoft has announced its "customer copyright commitment" for Copilot. This means that if you get sued for copyright infringement because of something generated by Microsoft AI, the company will stand with you, even to the point of joining the defense on a lawsuit and paying any judgments or settlements that may result from the lawsuit.

TIP **Get in the habit of bringing up Copilot on the right rail in your Edge browser and popping over daily!**

Conclusion

There are many ways to accelerate your work and become more efficient using M365 Chat. You can use M365 Chat to create content, reference internal documents, people, calendar, and chat information, as well as combine those responses with information from the Internet. Additionally, consider integrating your existing line-of-business (LOB) systems to pull information from them into Copilot.

CHAPTER 7

Microsoft Outlook

Microsoft 365 Copilot in Outlook can help you with various tasks around summarizing or generating content. It can summarize a particular email thread or create a draft email while responding to a thread. It can even create a whole new email. Microsoft 365 Copilot in Outlook can also coach you on tone and content after you've written an email. Like the other components and concepts we've covered so far, the use of Copilot is not intended to replace our basic human ability to communicate but rather to support and enhance it!

We will first look at using Microsoft 365 Copilot for summarization in Outlook. This will then be followed by digging into using it for the generation of content as well as tapping into its coaching features.

TIP **Get in the habit of turning on Draft with Copilot or Coaching by Copilot with every email response you send, especially for longer, more complex email threads. While you may not always use what's generated, incorporating this habit into your workflow will improve efficiency and productivity over time.**

NOTE **While Outlook includes additional features like To Do, Notes, RSS Feeds, Address Book, Org Explorer, and Groups, Microsoft 365 Copilot currently focuses primarily on email generation and summarization, as well as calendar analysis.**

Creating Communications with Microsoft 365 Copilot

Using the example outlined in Chapter 2, "Introduction to Microsoft 365 Copilot," let's look at how you would use Microsoft 365 Copilot to assist in your project of rolling out Microsoft 365 Copilot to your organization. Suppose that you need an email that is professional yet welcoming and encouraging to your pilot group of users, some of whom may not be accustomed to using new technology or may simply be too busy to change their ways of working, even if there is a good chance of increased efficiency with Microsoft 365 Copilot.

Drafting Your Prompt

With that in mind, you want your initial email to be compelling, interesting, and able to keep your Microsoft 365 Copilot users' attention. Open Outlook, click New Email, and then hit the drop-down for Copilot and select Draft with Copilot, as shown in Figure 7.1.

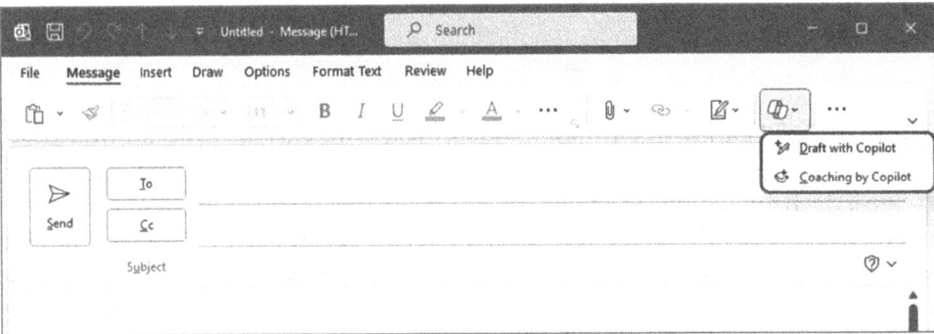

Figure 7.1: The Outlook default new mail interface

Once selected, you'll see the Draft with Copilot interface. Let's cover the main areas, as shown in Figure 7.2.

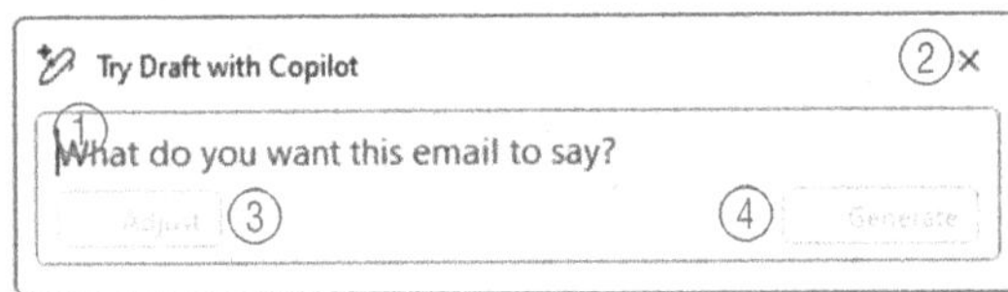

Figure 7.2: The Outlook Copilot interface

The main area we're concerned with here is the input box (1). This is where you'll interact with Microsoft 365 Copilot in Outlook by entering all your prompts and providing refiners. The "X" in the upper right (2), of course, closes the prompts and returns you to the normal Outlook new email interface. In the lower left (3) is the Generation options selector, which will be covered in greater detail later in the chapter. Finally, in the lower right (4), the Generate button is used to prompt the generation of content within Microsoft 365 Copilot in Outlook. You might notice that the words "Adjust" and "Generate" are grayed out for now, which is intentional; they'll become usable once sufficient text is input to accommodate either option.

Let's start with the generation of the email we've been discussing. Enter the following prompt: "Write an email welcoming users to our Copilot pilot program, covering the various technologies we'll be offering Copilot with, and ensure that it is professional but also welcoming."

The response generated is as follows:

EXAMPLE **"I am excited to welcome you to our Copilot pilot program. Our goal is to offer you the latest technologies to improve your experience and help you achieve your goals with ease. With Copilot, you will have access to a wide range of advanced tools that will make your work faster, more efficient, and more enjoyable. We are committed to providing you with the best possible support and we look forward to hearing your feedback. Thank you for joining us on this journey.**

Best regards,
<my name>"

As you can see, this response covers the topic and parameters of your prompt. It is both professional and welcoming, and it talks about the purpose of the project as specified in the prompt. It's worth noting that similar results can often be achieved with shorter, more directed, prompts, as we'll show as we proceed through the chapter.

Tone and Length

You provided some guidance in your prompt with "professional, but also welcoming." Let's see what happens when you give Microsoft 365 Copilot direct guidance on length and tone! To accomplish this, restart the generation process (I'll discuss refinement *after* the fact shortly), input the same prompt you started with, and this time select the Generation options choice "Adjust" labeled "3" in Figure 7.2. This will expand to show the options depicted in Figure 7.3.

NOTE **While the Generation option currently offers the options shown in Figure 7.3 for tone and length, you can try out many other styles and prompts of your own. Microsoft 365 Copilot will generally provide responses in line with your requests! Try some of the options presented in the menu, and, of course, feel free to come up with your own!**

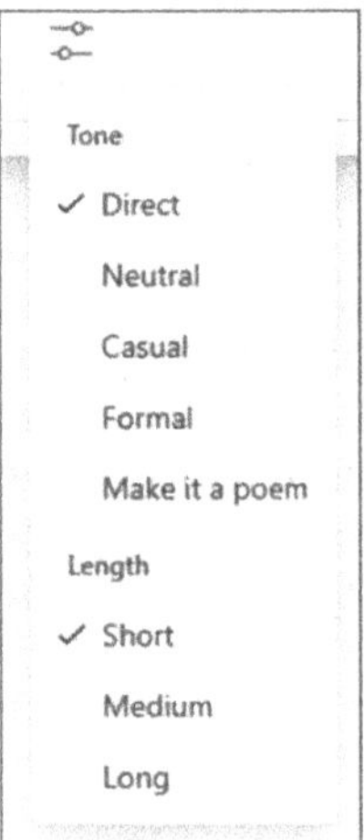

Figure 7.3: The Outlook Copilot interface with Generation options expanded

Using the same initial prompt presented previously, now select Formal and Long for your Generation options. This results in the following:

EXAMPLE **Dear Users,**

I am <myname>, a Senior Principal at our company. I am delighted to welcome you to our Microsoft 365 Copilot pilot program, an exciting opportunity to experience the power of AI text composition technology in your work.

Microsoft 365 Copilot is a cutting-edge AI assistant that can help you write faster, better, and more creatively. It can understand your context, intent, and tone, and generate relevant and high-quality text for a variety of tasks and domains. Whether you need to write emails, reports, articles, blog posts, resumes, or anything else, Microsoft 365 Copilot can assist you with smart suggestions, corrections, and enhancements.

In this pilot program, you will have access to Microsoft 365 Copilot for several platforms and tools that you use every day, such as Gmail, Microsoft Word, WordPress, Medium, and more. You will be able to integrate Microsoft 365 Copilot seamlessly with your existing workflows and applications, and enjoy the benefits of AI-powered writing assistance.

We are eager to hear your feedback and suggestions on how to improve Microsoft 365 Copilot and make it more useful and enjoyable for you. Please feel free to contact us at any time with your questions, comments, or concerns, and we will be happy to help you. You can also visit our website and FAQ page for more information and resources on how to use Microsoft 365 Copilot effectively.

Thank you for joining our Microsoft 365 Copilot pilot program, and we hope you have a wonderful experience with it. We look forward to working with you and learning from you.

Sincerely,

<my name>

As you can see, this dramatically changed the length and tone of the email! You'll want to try the various settings to see what fits your style or the specific occasion you're writing to accommodate. It also caused Microsoft 365 Copilot to go out to the Internet and find some things on its own, which, if you paid particularly close attention to that message, are partially incorrect!

Go back and reread the result and see if you can find the mistakes.

By now, you've probably realized that Microsoft 365 Copilot does not, in fact, work with Gmail, WordPress, and Medium. If you are unsure, let me reassure you that it does not. Well, those products could potentially work by using a plugin, but I'll cover that later.

What's happening here is known as a "hallucination," which is not uncommon in the world of AI assistants. We left the mistake in because the more often you use Microsoft 365 Copilot or any AI assistant, the more likely you'll run into very confidently presented incorrect statements, or hallucinations. I cannot emphasize enough how important it is for you to be aware of these issues—hallucinations—when using AI tools. Such errors don't make them irrelevant or useless; in fact, you got a great email generated by that prompt, except for the one example. However, you need to always be aware and fact-check, just as you would when conducting a search on the general Internet.

NOTE **Incorrect information and hallucinations are covered in greater depth in Chapter 3, "An Introduction to Prompt Engineering."**

Refining Your Message

Once you've created your base message, the real work begins. It's tempting to think that all you needed was the initial generation, but it's important to note that any generative AI, including ChatGPT and Microsoft 365 Copilot, rarely gets it exactly right on the first try. The skill set that's of use in the era of AI assistants is called "prompt refinement," which we'll talk about briefly here, specifically in regard to Outlook.

NOTE **While this chapter covers some email-specific refinement options focusing on Outlook, Chapter 3 discusses prompt engineering more generally.**

Let's use the example response you got earlier from your first generation using the default direct and short Generation options. You can use any of the same options you get under Generation options, but you can also come up with your own—from length and tone to specifically integrating information from the Internet or referencing other topics. Some examples include:

- Use information from `Microsoft.com` (or another relevant source on the Internet) to add additional details.
- Mention that leadership wants this initiative to succeed. For me, this resulted in Microsoft 365 Copilot finding my manager's name and incorporating it into the email!
- Calendar information. Note that as of the time of this writing, Microsoft 365 Copilot within Outlook cannot find appointment times, although this might change.
- Translate text to other languages.

Try anything that comes to mind to see what else Microsoft 365 Copilot can do for you within the context of Outlook!

Managing Escalations

In your day-to-day management of the Microsoft 365 Copilot pilot project, you might encounter pushbacks, complaints, or various issues that need resolving. It could also be that the people involved simply want to feel heard or have something explained that wasn't clear in the first place. Microsoft 365 Copilot within Outlook can help with these email escalations, and I'll walk through how that can happen in the next section on Microsoft 365 Copilot coaching.

Microsoft 365 Copilot Coaching

Consider an example where you've received pushback from a group of busy end users who have expressed that participation in your Microsoft 365 Copilot pilot project would place an undue burden on their already precious time and significant workload. In this scenario, you have sent your initial "Welcome to Microsoft 365 Copilot" email, and they've written back expressing those concerns.

Let's give Microsoft 365 Copilot a prompt to respond!

Using "We understand your concerns, but the tool could provide benefits in the future that exceed the time needed on the front end" as the prompt, you get the following great response in return:

EXAMPLE **"I hope this email finds you well. I understand that participation in our Microsoft 365 Copilot pilot project may create an undue burden on your already busy schedule and significant workload. Please know that we understand and respect your concerns, and it is completely understandable if you need to bow out.**

However, I wanted to mention that, with some initial investment, Microsoft 365 Copilot has the potential to save you time and increase your efficiency in the long run. We appreciate your feedback and thank you for considering this opportunity."

From a relatively short prompt, you've received a robust response that covers all the niceties you need in an email like this, while maintaining professionalism and also referencing components earlier in the thread to provide a cohesive response that builds on the entire back-and-forth communication.

Summarizing Email Threads

Microsoft 365 Copilot within Outlook provides the ability to summarize emails and email threads. This summarization can be especially useful for a long email thread, especially one that has many recipients and has been going back and forth a few times since you've had a chance to review it.

NOTE **Currently, summarization is applicable only to email threads in Microsoft Outlook. A more general feature called "Catch up with Copilot" was shown in the spring of 2023, but it was not available as of this writing. It might come back in a future release.**

Let's walk through the steps to get a summary of an email thread. Start by clicking any thread and then look in the reading pane (if you use it) or look at the top of the message for the Summarize option, as shown in Figure 7.4.

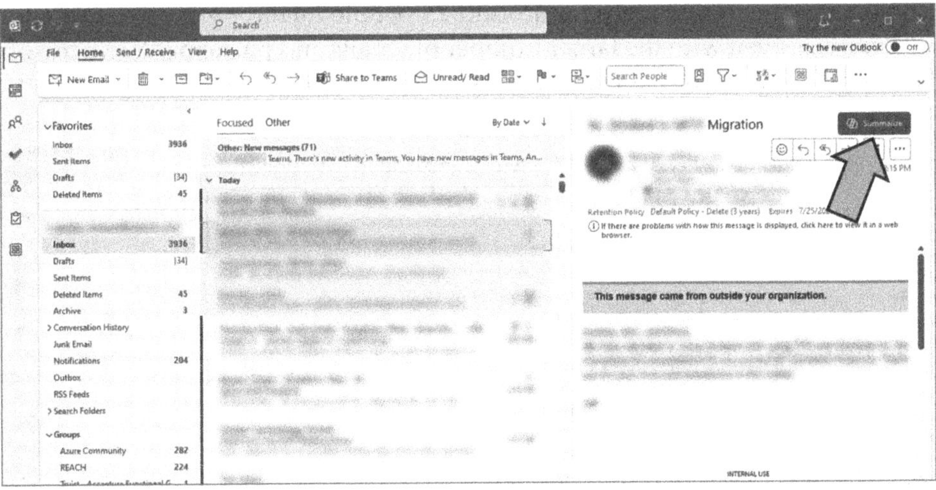

Figure 7.4: The Summarize option

Clicking the Summarize option will cause a message to appear stating that Microsoft 365 Copilot is scanning your email. Microsoft 365 Copilot will review the contents of the email thread and participants before generating a summary, as shown in Figure 7.5.

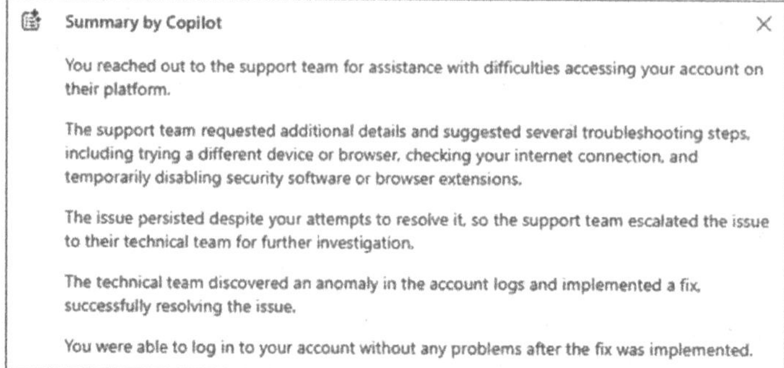
Summary by Copilot

You reached out to the support team for assistance with difficulties accessing your account on their platform.

The support team requested additional details and suggested several troubleshooting steps, including trying a different device or browser, checking your internet connection, and temporarily disabling security software or browser extensions.

The issue persisted despite your attempts to resolve it, so the support team escalated the issue to their technical team for further investigation.

The technical team discovered an anomaly in the account logs and implemented a fix, successfully resolving the issue.

You were able to log in to your account without any problems after the fix was implemented.

Figure 7.5: An email thread summary

The summary in Figure 7.5 is generated from a long conversation of more than 10 emails between Cordelia (who was having issues with her account for the Microsoft 365 Copilot project), Miles (a first-line technical support representative), and a second-tier support person who eventually resolved the problem. This is a great example of a use case where having a summarization is beneficial. A real-life example of how this can be used is for a help desk manager to get summaries of all support email interactions between support representatives and end users over time.

Figure 7.6 presents another example of using interactions between a client, a consultant firm, and a third-party support firm, spanning more than 30 emails. The thread eventually includes around 25 people including those on CC. As you can see, even with the larger number of emails and participants, Microsoft 365 Copilot is able to create a summary.

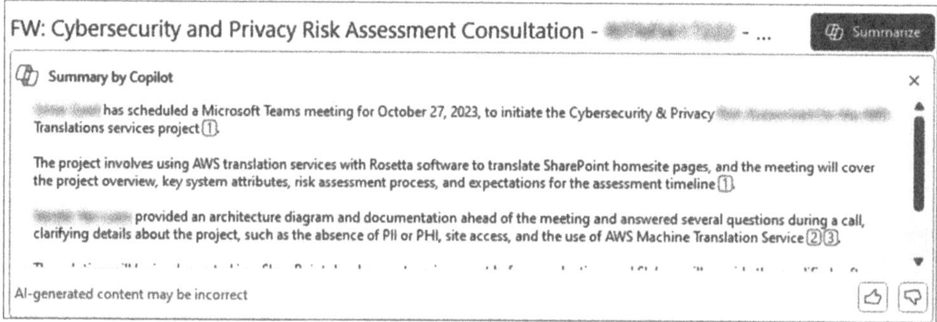
FW: Cybersecurity and Privacy Risk Assessment Consultation - ... - ...

Summary by Copilot

has scheduled a Microsoft Teams meeting for October 27, 2023, to initiate the Cybersecurity & Privacy Translations services project 1.

The project involves using AWS translation services with Rosetta software to translate SharePoint homesite pages, and the meeting will cover the project overview, key system attributes, risk assessment process, and expectations for the assessment timeline 1.

provided an architecture diagram and documentation ahead of the meeting and answered several questions during a call, clarifying details about the project, such as the absence of PII or PHI, site access, and the use of AWS Machine Translation Service 2 3.

AI-generated content may be incorrect

Figure 7.6: A summary of a longer email thread

Other examples might include:

- Human Resources getting a summary of a forwarded chain to recognize someone for an achievement

- The Finance department summarizing a long thread of emails related to an upcoming capital budget expense
- An executive assistant summarizing a long chain between a new hire and Human Resources prior to onboarding

Email Summarization—Chat

Other tasks that can be accomplished related to your emails are mostly done from Copilot Business Chat. To access it, open Microsoft Teams and go to the top of your chats. You'll see the Copilot Chat option pinned to the top of the list, as shown in Figure 7.7.

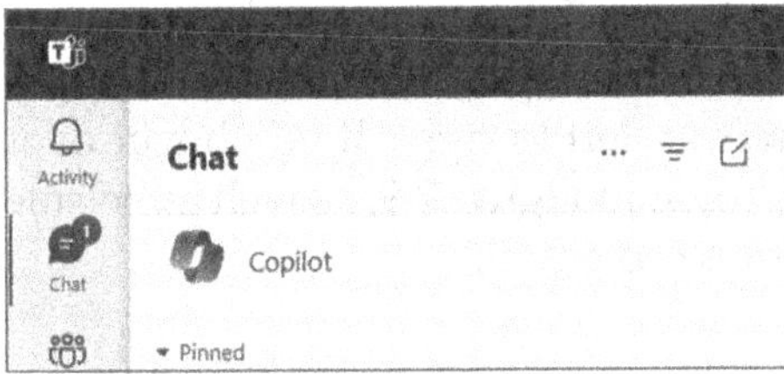

Figure 7.7: Copilot in Teams Chat

NOTE **Chapter 6, "Microsoft Copilot Business Chat," covers Copilot Business Chat in its entirety, but I wanted to make sure the components related to email were covered in this chapter on Outlook.**

With Copilot Business Chat, you can ask questions using natural language just as you would with, well, your very own personal assistant! Figure 7.8 presents the result of using the example prompt, "Are there action items I need to complete from my emails from last week?"

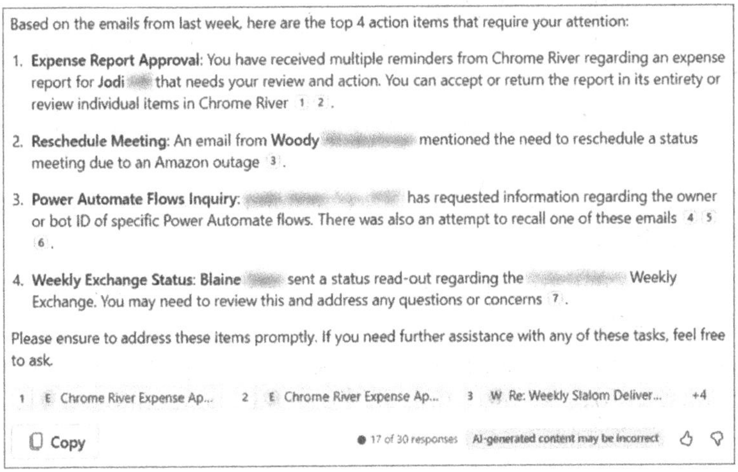

Based on the emails from last week, here are the top 4 action items that require your attention:

1. **Expense Report Approval**: You have received multiple reminders from Chrome River regarding an expense report for **Jodi** that needs your review and action. You can accept or return the report in its entirety or review individual items in Chrome River 1 2 .
2. **Reschedule Meeting**: An email from **Woody** mentioned the need to reschedule a status meeting due to an Amazon outage 3 .
3. **Power Automate Flows Inquiry**: has requested information regarding the owner or bot ID of specific Power Automate flows. There was also an attempt to recall one of these emails 4 5 6 .
4. **Weekly Exchange Status: Blaine** sent a status read-out regarding the Weekly Exchange. You may need to review this and address any questions or concerns 7 .

Please ensure to address these items promptly. If you need further assistance with any of these tasks, feel free to ask.

1 E Chrome River Expense Ap... 2 E Chrome River Expense Ap... 3 W Re: Weekly Slalom Deliver... +4

Copy 17 of 30 responses AI-generated content may be incorrect

Figure 7.8: Copilot Chat responding to a question

The details in the response are blurred, but Microsoft 365 Copilot is responding with four correctly identified action items from threads to which there weren't responses. As always, you'll want to verify that these are correct, but it's a great way to get guidance on potential items that need addressing from your inbox.

Additionally, you can use the Copy button to copy this information to another location, such as an email to yourself or to your OnteNote. There's also an input for a thumbs up or down to give Microsoft 365 Copilot feedback on accuracy. Also present are indicators for how many questions and responses you've used in your daily quota (in this example, 17 of 30), as well as a thumbs up or down to provide valuable feedback to Microsoft 365 Copilot on whether the response was useful. This is used to fine-tune Microsoft 365 Copilot's accuracy over time based on your organization's data.

Finally, at the bottom of the response in Figure 7.8, pay particular attention to the References section at the lower part of the response, with the three references numbered 1, 2, and 3, and shown from left to right. If you hover over any of these, you will see more detail, as shown in Figure 7.9, as well as be able to click through and open the specific referenced email.

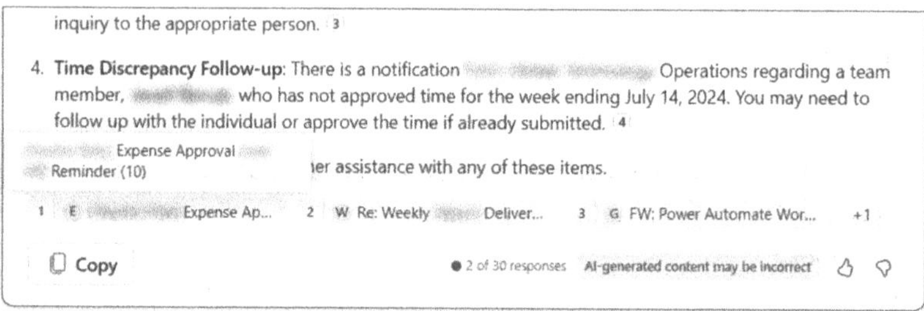

Figure 7.9: Copilot Chat providing verifiable references

As you can see, expanding the References section provides direct links and a summary of the emails used to generate the action items. Again, this is a great way to help verify the accuracy of the results provided.

The following are additional questions for you to try out, along with representative responses:

Q: "Are there any emails I missed that I should have responded to from last week?"

A: "Based on the information I have, it appears that you have missed an email from John Smith about...."

Q: "Can you find that email from last year where we started talking about the Tailspin Toys project?"

A: "I found an email from Jane Smith sent on December 11th, 2023 with the subject 'RE: Tailspin Toys Architecture.' In the email, she mentioned. . . ."

Q: "Can you find my last email from John Willis in the past two years?"

A: "I found an email from John Willis sent on June 29th, 2023 with the subject 'RE: Site Refresh Issues.' In the email, he mentioned that he didn't do it, nobody saw him do it, and that you can't prove anything."

Q: "Find John Smith's email address in my inbox."

A: "The email address of John Smith is `John.Smith@microsoft.com`."

Q: "Find Jane's phone number in my email."

A: "I found an email from Jane Smith sent on February 15th, 2022 with the subject 'Re: IT Services Request.' In the email, she mentioned her phone number is 123-456-7890."

Q: "Find the last email that was sent to Contoso, Inc. with an attachment with SOW in the filename."

A: "I found an email sent by you on October 30th, 2023 with the subject 'RE: Redlines: Contoso, Inc. - Discovery SOW.docx.' The email was sent to. . . ."

Q: "Find all my emails form the past month with a PowerPoint file attached."

A: "Here are the emails from the past month with a PowerPoint file attached that I found in your inbox."

As you can see, there's really a wide range of questions you can ask Microsoft 365 Copilot about email, contacts, finding files of a particular type or from a particular client. Try out your own questions and see what you can find!

Calendar Information

NOTE **While this chapter focuses on Outlook, the Calendar Management features of Microsoft 365 Copilot are currently available within Copilot Chat. I'll cover them here and have also referenced them in Chapter 6 and will reference them to some degree in Chapter 8, "Copilot in Microsoft Teams."**

To get answers about your Calendar in Outlook, you again head over to Microsoft Teams and click the Copilot Business Chat icon at the top of the list of chats. You'll see some prepopulated questions, some related to Calendar information, already in the list of sample questions, as shown in Figure 7.10.

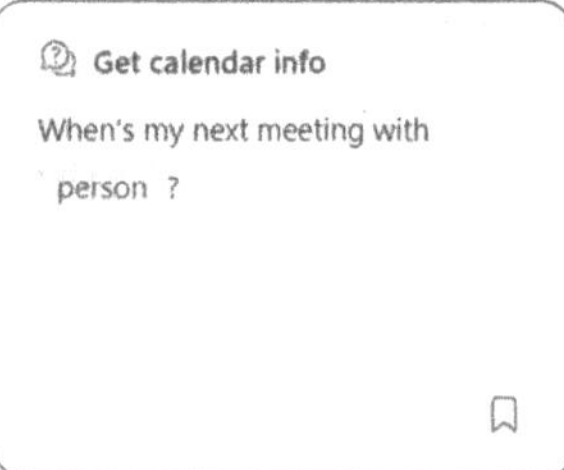

Figure 7.10: A Copilot Business Chat default calendar question

Similar to how you asked questions about content in your inbox, you'll now submit some questions related to appointments. Here are some sample questions and answers.

Q: "When's my next meeting with Abdul?"

A: "Your next meeting with Abdul is the Weekly Project Delivery Check-in, which is scheduled for tomorrow afternoon at 1 PM and will last until 1:30 PM. The meeting is organized by Jane Smith and attendees include Jane, John, and Abdul. The objective of this meeting is to provide a status report that captures progress, risks, dependencies, and observations for discussion."

Also included in the summary are links to the meeting being referenced, a list of files that might be useful to review beforehand, and meeting generation. Just as with your email responses, you'll want to validate the responses for accuracy.

Q: "What's my day look like tomorrow?"

A: "Based on the information I have, you have a total of 15 meetings scheduled for tomorrow. Here is a detailed overview of your schedule for tomorrow. . . ."

This response is followed by a high-level list of the meetings scheduled for the next day, again with links and references to the meetings in question.

Q: "Give me details about the Weekly Status meeting this afternoon."

A: "The weekly status meeting you are referring to is the Weekly Internal Productivity Status meeting that is scheduled for this afternoon at 3 PM and will last until 3:30 PM. . . ."

Just as seen earlier, you are provided with details about the meeting's invitees, time, and objectives.

NOTE **At the time of this writing, Microsoft 365 Copilot is unable to look inside of the meeting to get and provide information on who accepted or declined the meeting.**

Q: "Can you find calendar invitations in the past month containing an attachment?"

A: "There were two invitations in the past month containing an attachment. They were. . . ."

Once again, there's a wealth of information at your fingertips here. Try these and your own queries in Copilot Chat to get newfound access to information that was previously difficult to access within your calendar.

Conclusion

There are a multitude of ways in which Microsoft 365 Copilot can help you with Outlook emails and calendar management. Microsoft 365 Copilot can truly be your own personal AI assistant. Try it out and see what works best to create new ways of working and make better and more effective use of your time.

CHAPTER

8

Copilot in Microsoft Teams

Introduced in 2017, Microsoft Teams quickly became the most rapidly adopted tool in Microsoft's productivity suite history. Teams is a chat, file storage, collaboration, and live meeting tool. It organizes people and information around the concepts of *teams*, *channels*, *chats*, and *meetings*. It's a modern-day "everything all at once" tool and, as such, has become Microsoft's killer app. Most professionals I know use it for all of these things. Even calendar management, which was once the domain of Outlook, tends to happen more often in Microsoft Teams in organizations that have fully adopted Teams. Teams even provides file storage (which is really in SharePoint Online on the backend, but most users don't need to know or care about that) via those channels.

Figure 8.1 shows the Teams interface with various functionalities related to Copilot. The chat icon gives you access to summaries of existing messages and assistance in creating new messages. The Teams icon is similar but enables you to access posts in channels and receive both generative and summative assistance from Copilot. Finally, the Calendar icon provides access to your calendar, where Copilot can help you with meeting summaries, action items, and agenda creation.

Copilot in Microsoft Teams offers similar functionality to what we've seen before in the other desktop applications like Outlook or Word, but it is more focused on meeting management and chats. Copilot can help you increase your productivity by speeding up the process of consuming information from long chat threads and by helping you communicate more professionally through responses to those same threads. It can also take notes on meetings, give you an idea of the sentiments people express during meetings, and provide action items and next steps.

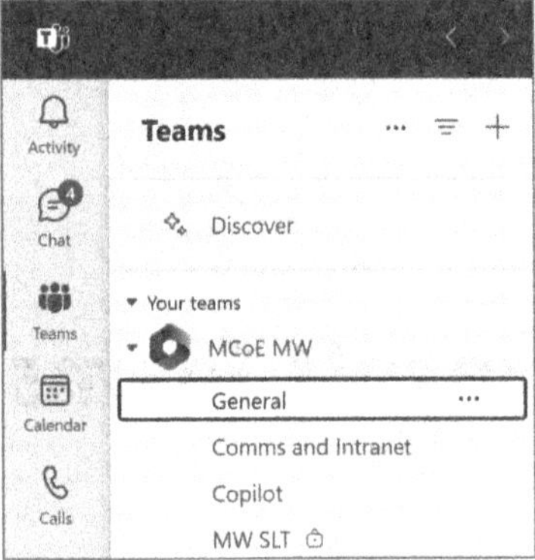

Figure 8.1: The Teams interface

TIP **Get in the habit of recording your meetings so Copilot can provide meeting summaries and action items!**

Managing Project Communications

In organizations that have rolled out and fully adopted Microsoft Teams, it has become the de facto tool for project communication, especially more ad hoc, day-to-day interactions. Yes, email still tends to be the vehicle for more formal communications, but even some of that is starting to make its way into Teams chats and channels as users become comfortable with getting their information primarily from one place: Microsoft Teams. As such, it's important to be able to read and understand many messages quickly. It's important to be able to craft well-written chats and responses that resonate with the people you're trying to influence or direct. Finally, it's crucial to run effective meetings with clear communication, tasks, and action items resulting from the meeting. Let's take the example of our Copilot rollout project and see how we can apply it.

Summarizing Chats and Channel Communications

For our example project, I created a Copilot Rollout Project Team with several channels to organize different parts of the project communication and collaboration rollout under the parent team. As shown in Figure 8.2, I created channels for General (default), Mac Users, Office Hours, and PM Corner.

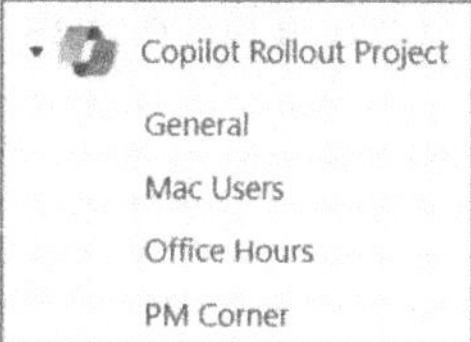

Figure 8.2: Our Copilot team with channels for communication

I created a post in the General channel, notifying all users that their licenses would be activated first thing the following Monday. This was followed by a slew of questions from our user group and sporadic responses from project team members. It was a good conversation, but I need to ensure that no important questions or information were missed.

You can access Copilot to summarize a channel post and chat in two ways. One method is to click the ellipsis in the upper-right corner of the channel post (remember, it needs to be a post with three or more replies) and select "Highlights from this conversation," as shown in Figure 8.3.

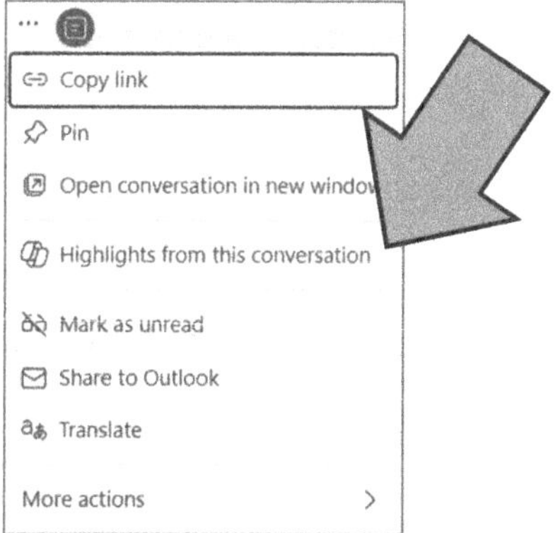

Figure 8.3: Microsoft Teams channel post options

NOTE **The "Highlights from this conversation" option only appears on channel posts with three or more replies. If you don't see it, it's possible the post doesn't meet that minimum criteria.**

The "Highlights from this conversation" option allows you to ask Copilot about the thread. It's an important and useful default go-to when you want to know what's been happening in a busy post. This option expands all the comments in the post, opens the Copilot panel on the right-hand side, and inputs the "Highlights from this conversation" prompt, which then returns a full summary of the initial post and all the responses.

This output is mostly self-explanatory, but I'd like to highlight that there are associated reference links for each of the highlighted bullets, as shown in Figure 8.4. This can be an invaluable tool, especially when analyzing a long thread containing as many as 20 to 30 replies, which is common in a large organization or on a large multi-team project.

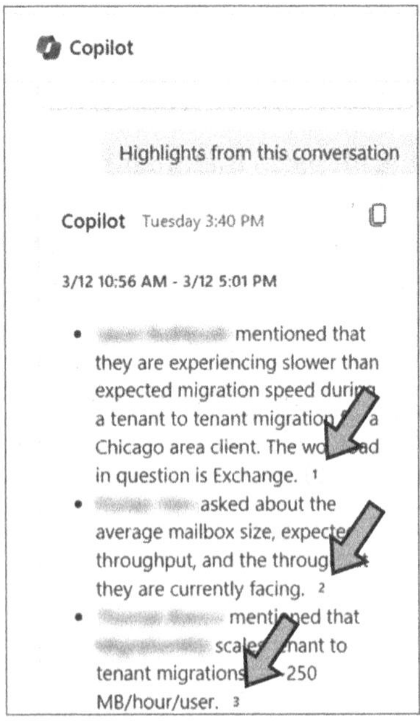

Figure 8.4: Copilot output from Microsoft Teams

The other way to access Copilot's channel chat features is to click "# replies from *<name>*, *<name>*, and # others" shown in Figure 8.5.

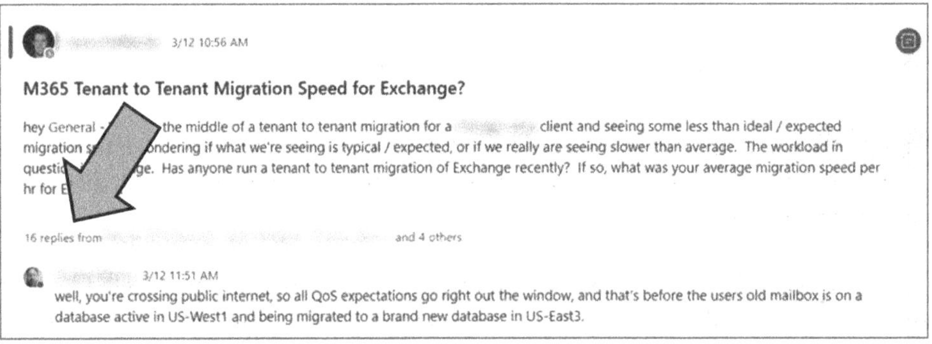

Figure 8.5: Anatomy of a post and how to get full Copilot access

Then, once you have opened the post, click the Copilot icon on the upper right to "Open chat Copilot," as shown in Figure 8.6.

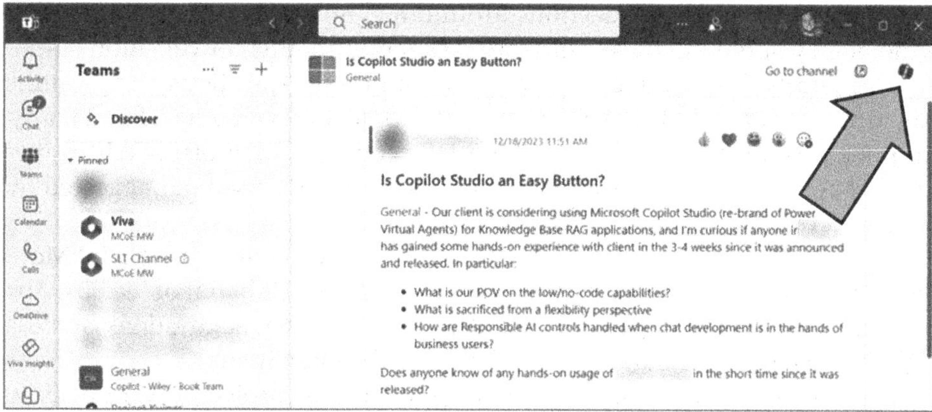

Figure 8.6: Teams interface with a channel post opened and Copilot access marked

Once the Copilot Teams channel interface is opened, pay attention to the important areas shown in Figure 8.7. The icon labeled with the number 1 closes the Copilot panel, taking you back to the default Teams channel post chat interface. The main area of the dialog, labeled with number 2, provides ideas and information about how to use Copilot in the context of a chat. It also reassures you that it's only accessing *your* information. At number 3 is the "Highlights from this conversation" button, which gives you direct access

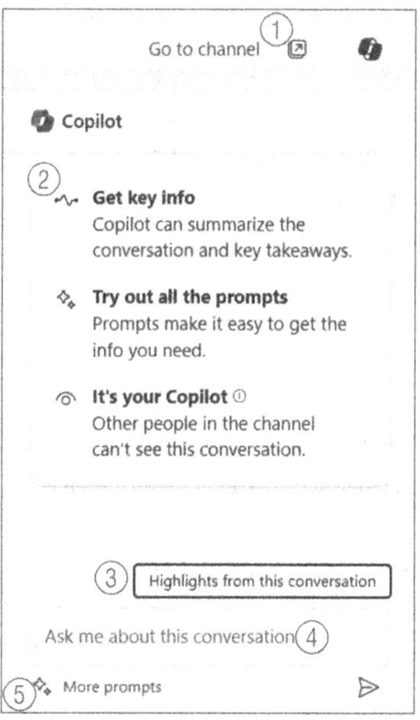

Figure 8.7: Copilot panel in a Microsoft Teams channel chat

to the most common of questions around a channel post chat thread. The wide-open Copilot interface, with the "Ask me about this conversation" input box, is identified by number 4. Here, you can provide questions and prompts covering any topic that makes sense in the context of a channel chat. Finally, number 5 identifies the "More prompts" section, which offers additional ideas of common questions and prompts as frequently used or suggested by Microsoft over time.

I've already covered "Highlights from this conversation," so click "More prompts" to get a sampling of Microsoft's suggestions right out of the box. The original highlights prompt is presented, along with other suggestions, such as "What decisions were made?" and "What are the open items?"

Using the specific example of the Copilot rollout project, I went back to the channel post in the General channel, notifying all users that their licenses would be activated first thing the following Monday. This thread had over 30 replies and comments. I asked Copilot, "Are there unanswered questions in this chat thread?"

Once again, Copilot responds with, in this case, two unanswered questions along with clickable links to the referenced questions, providing an easy way to track them down! I will respond to the questions using the tools from our next section where I discuss creating project communications with Copilot.

Creating Posts and Chats with Copilot

As with Outlook and Word, Copilot can assist in Microsoft Teams by drafting initial posts and responses to give you a starting point in your communications. Teams tends toward more informal, chat-centered communication, but there are also posts in Teams channels where more formal or structured presentation is warranted. For those of us who can sometimes use a little polish, Copilot can be of great help.

Creating a post or chat with Copilot

You can initiate Copilot in Microsoft Teams from either Teams' channels or from chats. For channels, enter any Microsoft Teams channel and click "Start a post," as shown in Figure 8.8.

Once in the Start a post interface, click the Copilot icon, which is hopefully becoming familiar to you. Just in case it's not, Figure 8.9 points it out once more.

To use Copilot within a chat, simply click the Copilot icon from within any of your chats, as shown in Figure 8.10.

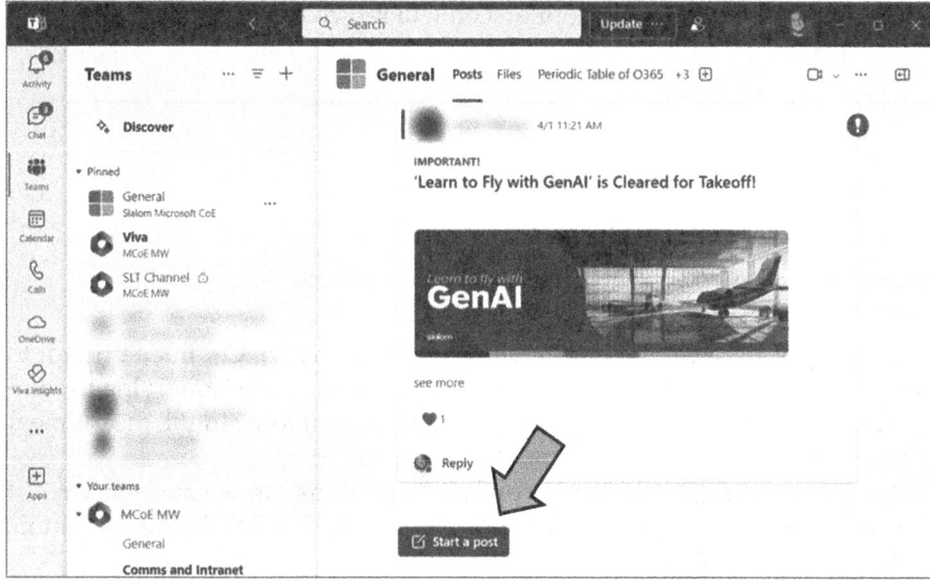

Figure 8.8: Starting a post in Microsoft Teams

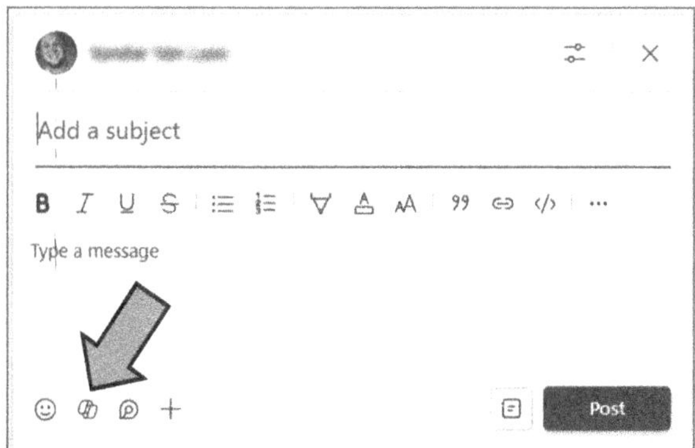

Figure 8.9: Copilot in a channel post in Microsoft Teams

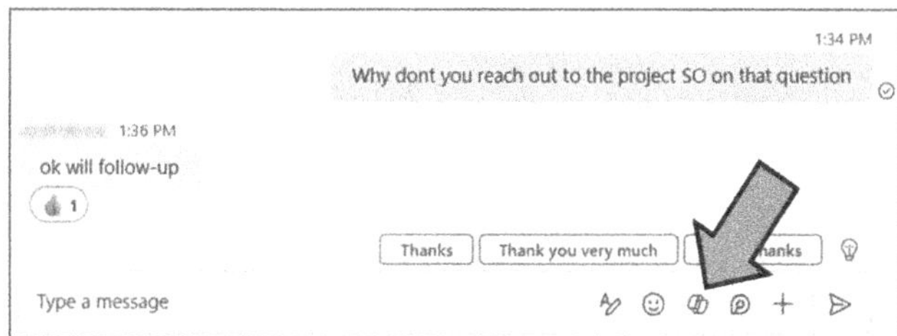

Figure 8.10: Copilot in a chat in Microsoft Teams

In either case, clicking the Copilot icon will return the initial prompt shown in Figure 8.11.

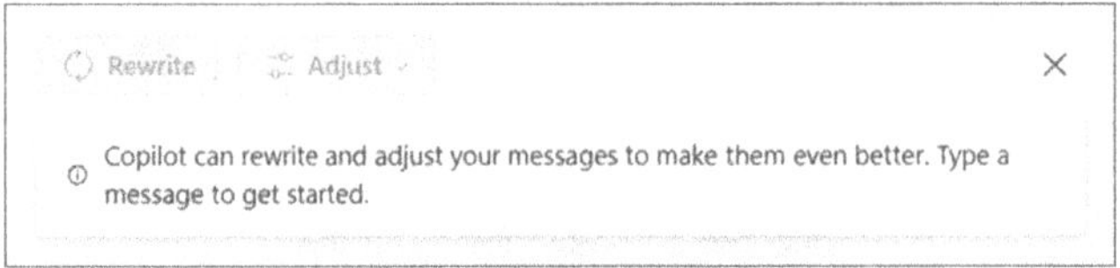

Figure 8.11: Copilot's initial generation prompt in Microsoft Teams

So, whether it's a chat or a channel post, I need to give Copilot a prompt to start with before it can help me write something in the style I am trying to communicate with. Try it out with your own communications. In the meantime, I will use an example from the Copilot rollout project!

Using the prompt, "What project-related questions can we answer here?" I first get a short, terse response like "How can we help?" Click the Adjust button, as shown in Figure 8.12.

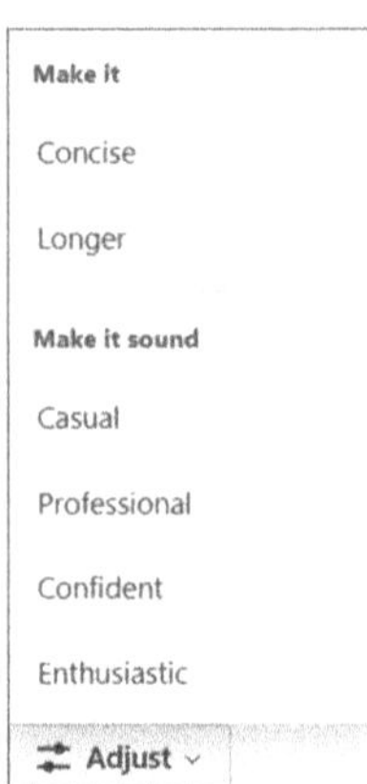

Figure 8.12: Copilot's prompt adjustment options

If you choose Longer and Professional, a much more robust response is provided, as shown in Figure 8.13.

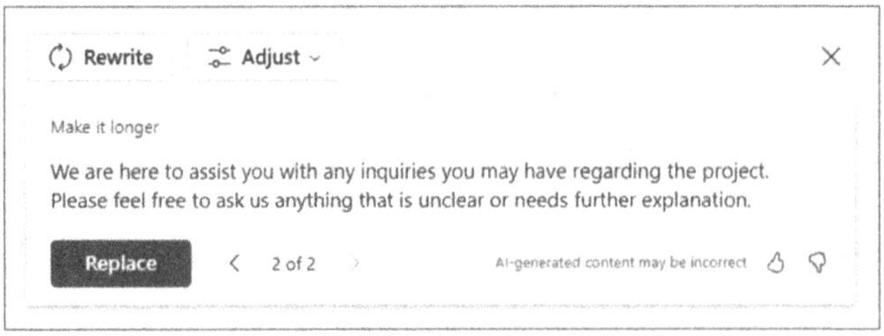

Rewrite Adjust

Make it longer

We are here to assist you with any inquiries you may have regarding the project. Please feel free to ask us anything that is unclear or needs further explanation.

Replace 2 of 2 AI-generated content may be incorrect

Figure 8.13: Example Copilot output after adjusting the prompt

Click Replace, and your initial prompt will be updated to the one shown in Figure 8.13. As with Copilot in any other desktop productivity applications, nothing is sent without your first being able to verify it and ensure that it doesn't contain incorrect or proprietary information you may not want to share on this channel.

Tone and Length

Tone and length are handled entirely within the context of the Adjust menu options. This is somewhat different from the Outlook Copilot input, which can take custom prompt refiners. This may change in the future, but it is currently how the Copilot Microsoft Teams interface functions.

NOTE **As of this writing, there are a number of things Copilot doesn't do. In Teams, Copilot won't generate documents based on tasks like "Recap the meeting" or "List action items." It also won't accept the forward slash (/) prompt like Copilot does in other applications to use a particular document as a basis for a template or to refine the prompt response. This shouldn't affect the productivity of the tool; rather, it is just something to note as a difference in how Copilot operates in Teams versus other applications.**

Copilot and Grammatical Issues

Finally, as is common in Microsoft desktop productivity tools, Copilot will also catch and correct common spelling errors in any prompts you provide. For example, it caught the misspelling of "documentaion" and corrected to "documentation" in the response.

Managing Project Meetings

Copilot in Microsoft Teams provides a great set of tools to manage meetings, especially those focused on projects. This can be especially useful if you missed the meeting, arrived late, want a summary of what was said, or want to review the action items from the meeting. For project managers, Copilot can provide a comprehensive starting point for meeting notes and to-dos coming out of the meeting.

To accomplish any of these tasks, the meeting *must* be recorded. If you're not the organizer, ask them to record it. This is covered in greater detail in Chapter 4, "Security/Purview Planning in Preparation for Copilot." Your company should have a policy in place regarding meeting recordings, and this should be taken into account when working with Copilot. The meeting also must be "owned" by someone in your organization. If you're joining a Teams meeting created and owned by a client or external partner, your organization's Copilot won't be able to access the meeting information to provide any of the aforementioned feedback.

Using Copilot During a Live Meeting

When recording a meeting with Copilot enabled, you'll receive an automatic prompt when there are only 10 minutes left, asking you if you would like Copilot's assistance and providing a good set of prompts. These prompts include:

- Recap meeting so far
- List action items
- Suggest follow-up questions
- What questions are unresolved?
- List different perspectives by topic
- List main ideas we discussed
- Generate meeting notes

When asked to generate meeting notes, Copilot will present a summary of key topics, as shown in Figure 8.14.

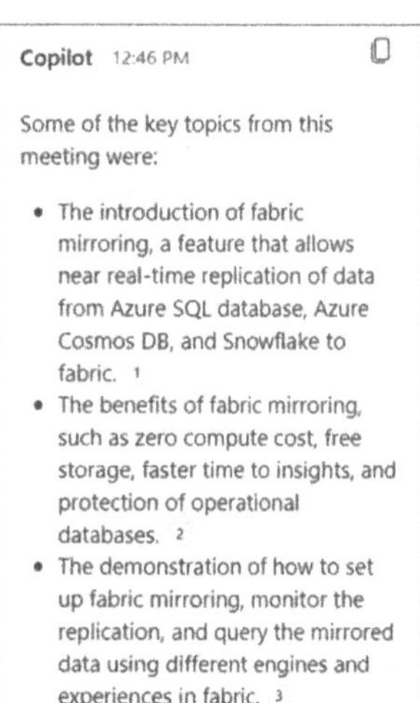

Figure 8.14: Example of Copilot's key topics generated from a meeting

As you can see in Figure 8.14, Copilot is aware of the key points covered in the meeting. It can also characterize the sentiment expressed during the meeting, which is something that a simple transcription of all words spoken during the meeting (a feature Microsoft Teams already has) can't provide.

You can also use Copilot to get a clear and concise listing of tasks and their assignees from throughout various parts of the meeting. If you're in project management or simply responsible for making sure things get done in your organization, you'll see the value here. Figure 8.15 shows the result of using the "List action items" prompt during one of the meetings.

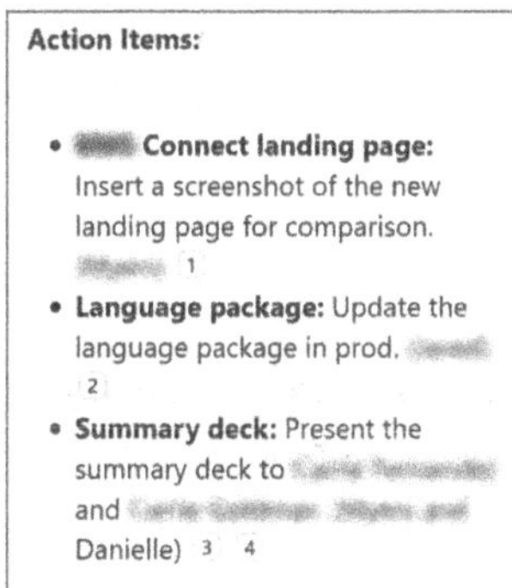

Figure 8.15: Example of Copilot-generated action items from a project meeting

TIP **Two great prompts to save in your toolkit are "What topic took the most time?" and "Write an agenda for our follow-up meeting based on open action items, next steps, and owners."**

Using Copilot with a Past Meeting

The previous section and examples are prompts for information on the meeting *while* you're in the meeting. Another very valuable use case is applying Copilot to meetings you were unable to attend. In that case, navigate to the past meeting in your Teams calendar view, open the meeting, and find the Recap option, as shown in Figure 8.16. Only after accessing the Recap section will you see the Copilot option.

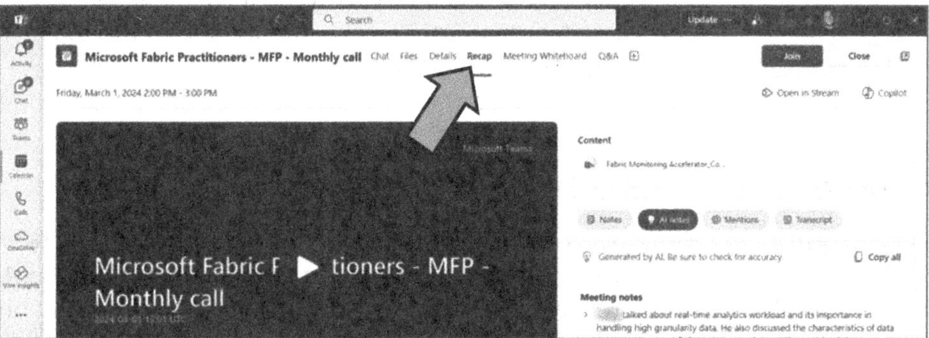

Figure 8.16: Accessing Copilot from a previous Microsoft Teams meeting

If the Recap option doesn't appear, you won't be able to take advantage of Copilot's functionality on the meeting's content. To rectify this problem going forward, you'll need to ensure that Recording and Transcription are on for future meetings,

Click the Recap option for the Teams meeting, then click the Copilot icon at the top. This opens the familiar Copilot pane on the right-hand side. It defaults to an open-ended prompt: "Ask me anything about this meeting," where you can ask the obvious such as "Give me meeting notes," "What were the action items?" or "What was the general sentiment of the meeting?"

You can also click the "More prompts" option at the very bottom to get a list of commonly used prompts.

TIP **These post-meeting options are available only as long as the meeting recording lasts. Depending on how long your organization retains recorded meetings, you may want to ensure that you use Copilot on past meetings before this period expires!**

Copilot in Microsoft Teams Phone

Another feature introduced in the Copilot ecosystem related to Microsoft Teams is Copilot in Microsoft Teams Phone. It's very similar to how Copilot appears in the Microsoft Teams desktop app, but it's good to know that it's there, in what has become the most quickly and broadly adopted phone productivity app in the Microsoft ecosystem.

To access Copilot within Microsoft Teams on your iPhone or Android phone, click into any chat or Teams channel post (with more than two replies), and find the Copilot icon on the upper right, just as you would in the desktop application, as shown in Figure 8.17.

Once there, click the Highlights option, as shown in Figure 8.18, or ask any specific question as you would in the desktop application.

NOTE **You might be wondering why Copilot chat, which is featured prominently in Microsoft Teams, is not covered in this chapter. That's because it's such a comprehensive topic on its own, both in Teams and in the browser, that it's covered in its own chapter, Chapter 6, "Microsoft Copilot Business Chat."**

Data Privacy and Security

As with any new technology, concerns about data and security with the new Copilot toolset may arise. These concerns are covered in greater detail in Chapter 4, but for now, keep in mind that Microsoft doesn't share any of your information with others via Copilot. It also doesn't share any data with third parties or use any personally identifiable information from one chat in the response for

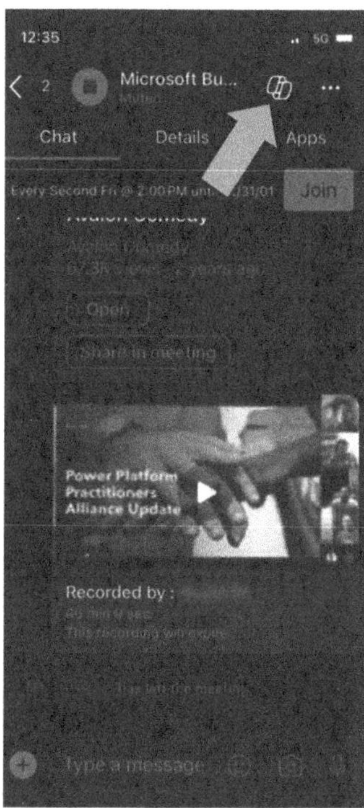

Figure 8.17: Accessing Copilot from the Microsoft Teams mobile app

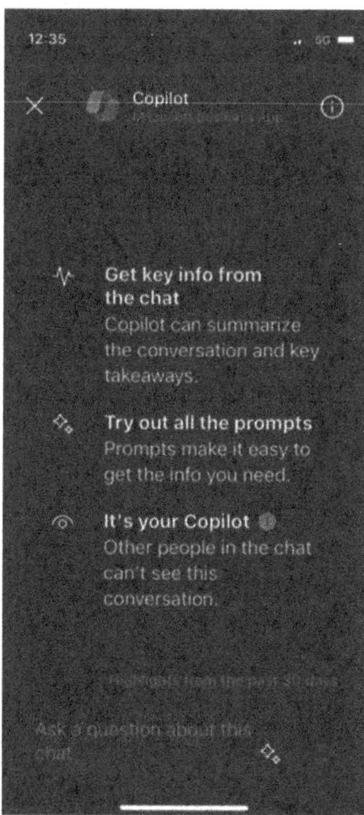

Figure 8.18: Copilot from within a Microsoft Teams chat on the mobile app

another. Furthermore, Copilot doesn't have access to your private documents or information. It operates strictly within the confines of the current meeting, focusing on real-time collaboration and summarization.

Conclusion

Copilot for Teams empowers you to stay informed, collaborate effectively, and focus on what matters most—achieving your goals together. Whether it's providing chat and channel summaries, assisting with meeting wrap-ups, or helping write messages, Copilot enhances your Teams experience and boosts productivity. (Remember to turn on recording!)

CHAPTER

9

Copilot in Microsoft Excel

Microsoft Excel can be one of the more daunting products within the Office suite, as it demands a high level of precision and care with the various formulas, numbers, etc. If you make a mistake, you can significantly affect the data being shown, which could have even more serious downstream consequences. This, along with the fact that many people get nervous when working with math, is what makes it a good candidate for an AI assistant.

In this chapter, you will learn how Copilot works within Excel. You will learn about some of the requirements for working with data and how you can use Copilot to complete complicated tasks, all with natural language.

Getting Started with Copilot in Excel

As just mentioned, Copilot will help you work with Excel. In this section, you will first learn how to set up your data to be Copilot-ready. Then, you'll be introduced to basic data manipulation capabilities, including how to create columns based on formulas that Copilot will create for you. Next, we will dive into creating charts with Copilot and how to ask questions about your data. Finally, we will walk through a couple of ways you can use Copilot to format your data to meet your business needs.

Identifying a Dataset

Your first step to working with Copilot in Excel is to obtain a dataset—ideally, an Excel file with relevant data. However, if you do not have a dataset, an amazing website called Mockaroo (`www.mockaroo.com`) allows you to generate your own fake dataset. They have a paid version of their service, or you can create a dataset with up to 1,000 records at no cost.

For this chapter, I created a mock dataset of employee survey feedback to help demonstrate the power of Copilot. You can choose to either create your own dataset or leverage the Excel workbook called *c09-Copilot-EmployeeData.xlsx*, which is available in the downloadable files for this book.

NOTE **You can find the *c09-Copilot-EmployeeData.xlsx* file at `www.wiley.com/go/copilotatwork`. This chapter also uses the *c09-Copilot-SalesData.xlsx* file, which is also included in the zip file.**

If you are unable to access Mockaroo or would feel more comfortable creating your dataset manually, then you'll need to create the following columns to follow along with the first set of exercises:

- **employee_id:** A number to signify a unique record
- **department:** Text containing either Finance, HR, IT, Marketing, or Operations
- **trust_in_leadership:** A number between 1 and 10 signifying a score
- **happiness_in_work:** A number between 1 and 10 signifying a score
- **work_life_balance:** A number between 1 and 10 signifying a score
- **job_satisfaction:** A number between 1 and 10 signifying a score
- **career_growth_opportunities:** A number between 1 and 10 signifying a score
- **overall_employee_engagement:** Blank for now

Preparing Your Workbook

There are a couple of requirements for you to be able to use Copilot with your Excel workbook:

- The Excel workbook must be saved as an .xlsx file.
- The file must be saved to a storage location in M365, such as a Microsoft Teams team, a SharePoint site, or your OneDrive.
- The data in the Excel workbook must be formatted as a table.

After saving your Excel workbook in M365, open it with the Excel client application. First, format the records into a table. To do this, select all the data in the open workbook. You can do this either with your mouse or by Command

+ A on a Mac or Ctrl + A on a Windows machine. From the Insert menu, click the Table button, ensuring that the "My table has headers" option is selected, and then enter Return, as shown in Figure 9.1.

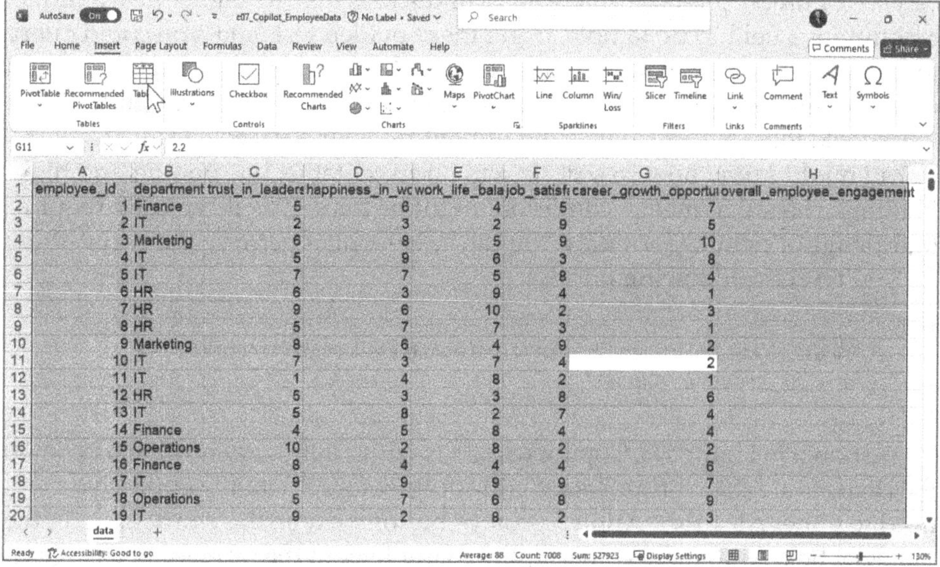

employee_id	department	trust_in_leaders	happiness_in_wc	work_life_bala	job_satisfa	career_growth_opportu	overall_employee_engagement
1	Finance	5	6	4	5	7	
2	IT	2	3	2	9	5	
3	Marketing	6	8	5	9	10	
4	IT	5	9	6	3	8	
5	IT	7	7	5	8	4	
6	HR	6	3	9	4	1	
7	HR	9	6	10	2	3	
8	HR	5	7	7	3	1	
9	Marketing	8	6	4	9	2	
10	IT	7	3	7	4	2	
11	IT	1	4	8	2	1	
12	HR	5	3	3	8	6	
13	IT	5	8	2	7	4	
14	Finance	4	5	8	4	4	
15	Operations	10	2	8	2	2	
16	Finance	8	4	4	4	6	
17	IT	9	9	9	9	7	
18	Operations	5	7	6	8	9	
19	IT	9	2	8	2	3	

Figure 9.1: Creating a table in Excel

You now have a dataset formatted as a table, which will allow you to interact with it using Copilot. For readability purposes, I am going to remove the color formatting, as shown in Figure 9.2, but feel free to perform whatever visual formatting you like for your own use case.

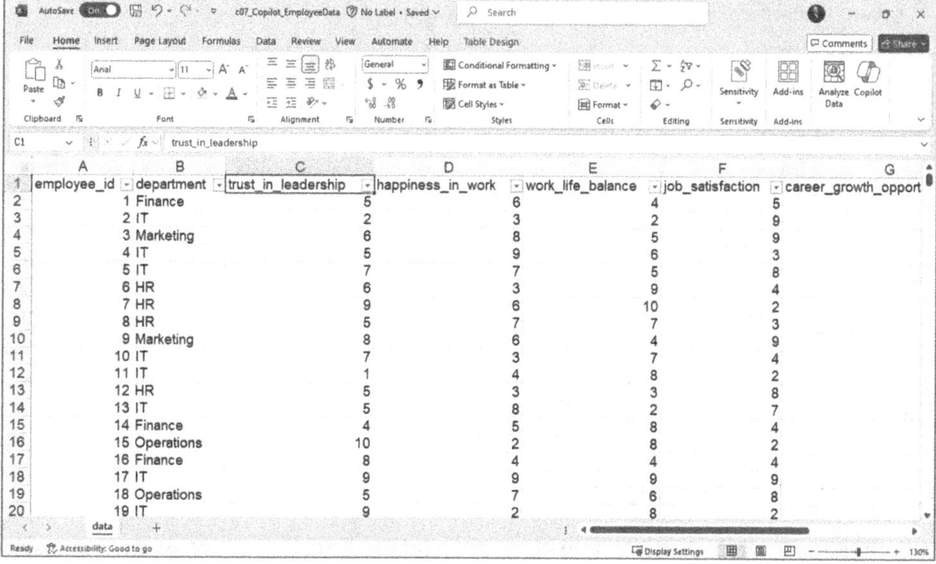

employee_id	department	trust_in_leadership	happiness_in_work	work_life_balance	job_satisfaction	career_growth_opport
1	Finance	5	6	4	5	
2	IT	2	3	2	9	
3	Marketing	6	8	5	9	
4	IT	5	9	6	3	
5	IT	7	7	5	8	
6	HR	6	3	9	4	
7	HR	9	6	10	2	
8	HR	5	7	7	3	
9	Marketing	8	6	4	9	
10	IT	7	3	7	4	
11	IT	1	4	8	2	
12	HR	5	3	3	8	
13	IT	5	8	2	7	
14	Finance	4	5	8	4	
15	Operations	10	2	8	2	
16	Finance	8	4	4	4	
17	IT	9	9	9	9	
18	Operations	5	7	6	8	
19	IT	9	2	8	2	

Figure 9.2: Formatted data in an Excel table

Manipulating Excel Data

One of the things you can do with Copilot in Excel is manipulate your data based on certain criteria. A common task in Excel is to find records that match a certain condition. Suppose you want to find scores that are higher than a certain amount for a field. For example, using the provided test data, you could query to find values higher than 8 for the "Trust in Leadership" question. You could then sort the table by the department. Then, as you're scrolling through the workbook, those records will stand out within your dataset.

You might know how to sort data in an Excel table, but finding and highlighting scores that meet a condition might be harder, as it typically requires knowledge of creating formulas. You can have Copilot perform the heavy lifting for you with the following prompt:

"Please sort by department ascending and bold the values greater than 8 in the 'trust_in_leadership' column."

As shown in Figure 9.3, Copilot responds with a summary of what it believes the changes are that you are looking to apply. Before it actually applies you will need to either click the "Apply" prompt button or type the word apply in the dialogue box. After requesting Copilot to implement the formatting changes it will confirm with "Done! I made the changes."

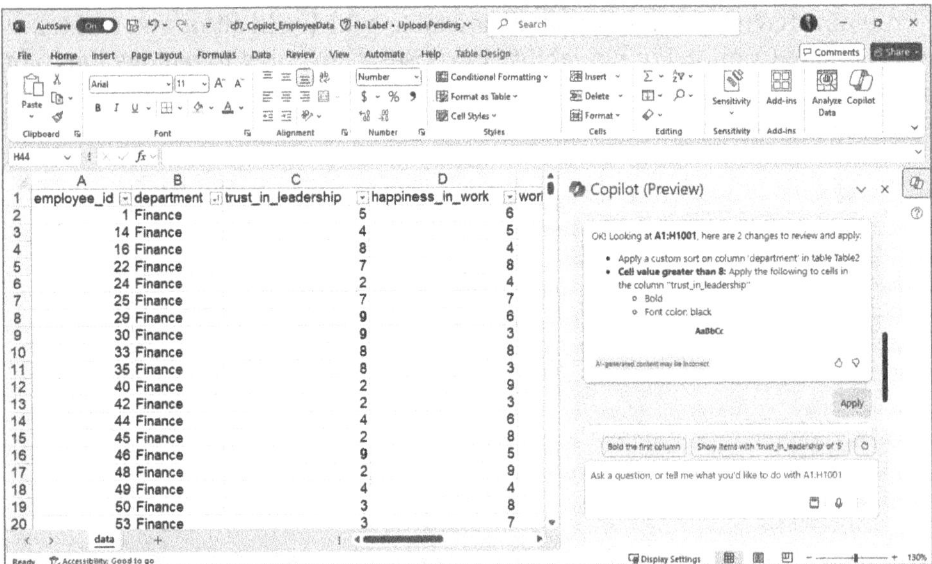

Figure 9.3: Sorting and highlighting data in Excel

Creating New Formulas

Another common task when working with data in Excel is to create new formulas based on your existing data. For some, creating formulas can be a series of trial and error to ensure that you have provided the appropriate syntax to perform the operation. With Copilot, however, you don't need to be a formula wizard; instead, you can describe the type of output you want to create. This might include adding two number columns together and storing the sum in a new column or performing a concatenation of two different text columns to generate a full name from a "first_name" column and a "last_name" column.

Building off the previous example, the last column in your file should be called "overall_employee_engagement," and at this point, the value should be blank. Let's use Copilot to help create a new value for the "overall_employee_engagement" column by getting the average value for all of the employee survey questions, which are in columns C through G in the same workbook.

From within your open workbook, open Copilot and enter the following prompt:

"Create a formula that populates column 'H' with the average of the values in columns C through G. Please format to include one decimal place."

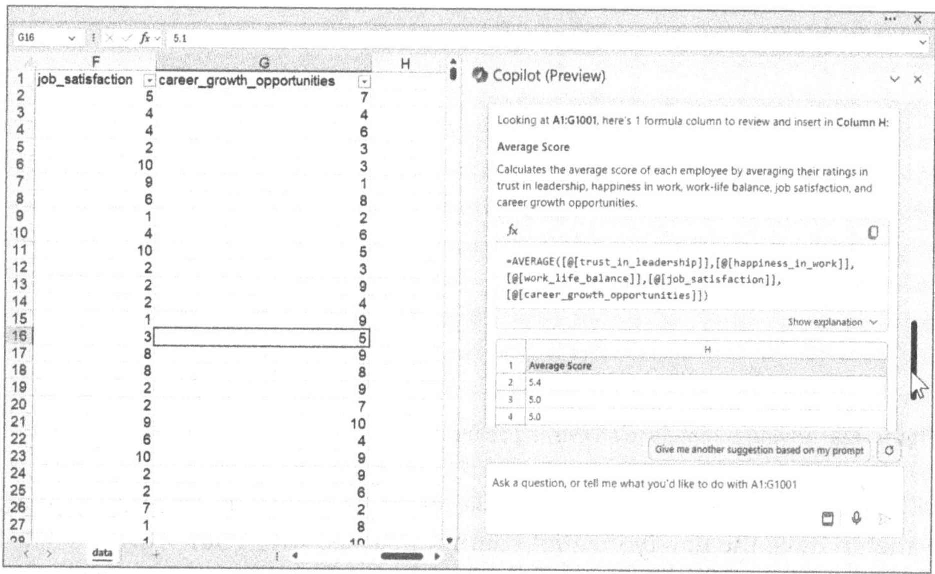

Figure 9.4: Creating a formula for overall employee engagement

Copilot returns the following (see also Figure 9.4):

"Here's 1 formula column to review and insert into A1:H1001:

> **Overall employee engagement** *Calculates the overall employee engagement by finding the average of the employee's trust in leadership, happiness in work, work-life balance, job satisfaction, and career growth opportunities."*

Copilot also provides the recommended formula for creating this new column:

```
=AVERAGE([@[trust_in_leadership]],[@[happiness_in_work]],[@[work_life_
balance]],[@[job_satisfaction]],[@[career_growth_opportunities]])
```

Now, your next step depends on what you want to do with Copilot's output. If you want to apply the formula to the existing Column H, then you can copy the formula from Copilot, select H2 in your open workbook, and then paste the formula into the formula entry drop-down, as shown in Figure 9.5.

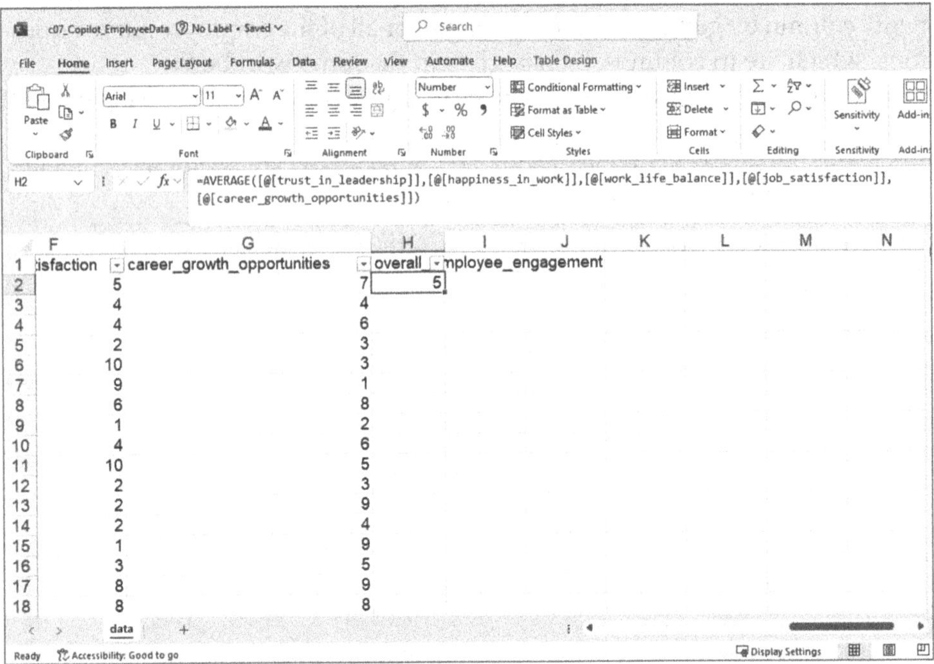

Figure 9.5: Adding a formula to an existing column

Alternatively, you can click the "Insert column" button in the Copilot panel to have the newly created column inserted into your worksheet, as shown in Figure 9.6. Then, to tighten things up a bit, you can delete the previous column I and either leave the new column as is or rename it to "overall_employee_engagement."

Creating Charts

While basic data manipulation is certainly a powerful capability, there are many use cases for creating visualizations to help interpret data and make decisions. Let's tap into the power of Copilot to create charts based on your data. You may be asking yourself what kind of charts Copilot can create. Rather than me providing an answer, why not ask Copilot?

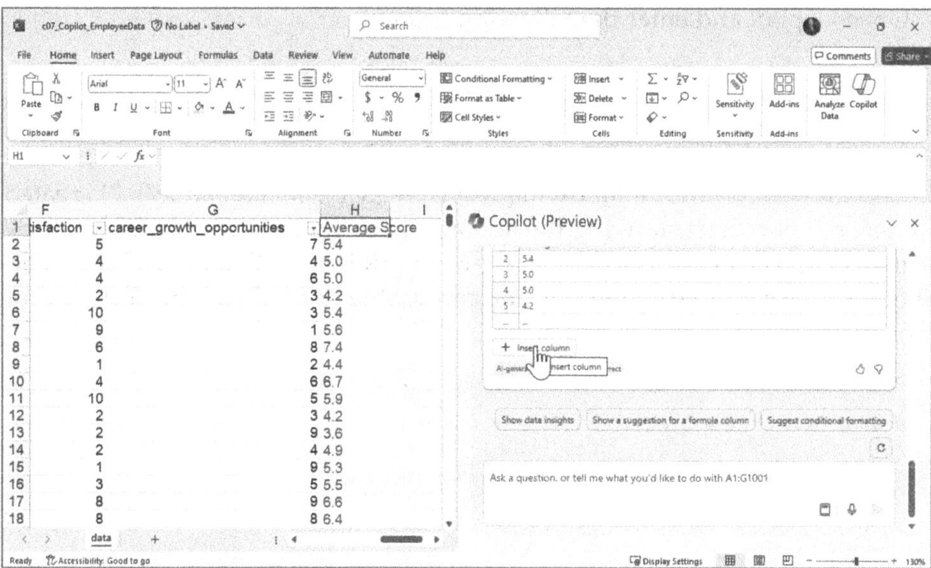

Figure 9.6: Inserting a new column

Open the Copilot panel in Excel and enter the following prompt:

"What kind of charts can you create?"

For me, Copilot responded with the following text: "I can create various types of charts, including line charts, pie charts, bar charts, column charts, area charts, scatter charts, and more. However, the specific chart type that is most appropriate depends on the data and your specific needs." At the time of writing, you are mostly limited to creating a chart without the ability to iterate much with it. Any changes to your dataset will generally require you to re-create the chart to reflect the latest data changes to your visualization.

Based on when you are following along, Microsoft may have released even more capabilities for Copilot; therefore, it would be helpful to keep an eye on the Microsoft 365 Roadmap for changes to available features.

NOTE **Microsoft maintains a roadmap of M365 Copilot features at** **`www.microsoft.com/en-us/microsoft-365/roadmap`.**

For now, we want to visualize the average score for the "Communication Effectiveness" question in the employee survey found in the *c09-Copilot-EmployeeData.xlsx* file to help better identify trends. As a business leader reviewing employee survey data, you might be interested to know if there are any trends related to specific questions, departments, or overall scores across the organization. For our first example, let's have Copilot create a chart to help visualize the scores for a specific question by department and allow it to select the chart that best supports the use case.

Open Copilot and enter the following prompt:

> *"Please create a chart showing the average score for 'trust_in_leadership' by department."*

Copilot will return the following response (see also Figure 9.7): "I created a clustered bar chart showing the average score for 'trust_in_leadership' by department. The average score for IT is 6, for HR is 6, for Finance is 5, for Operations is 5, and for Marketing is 5. You can see the chart above this message for more details."

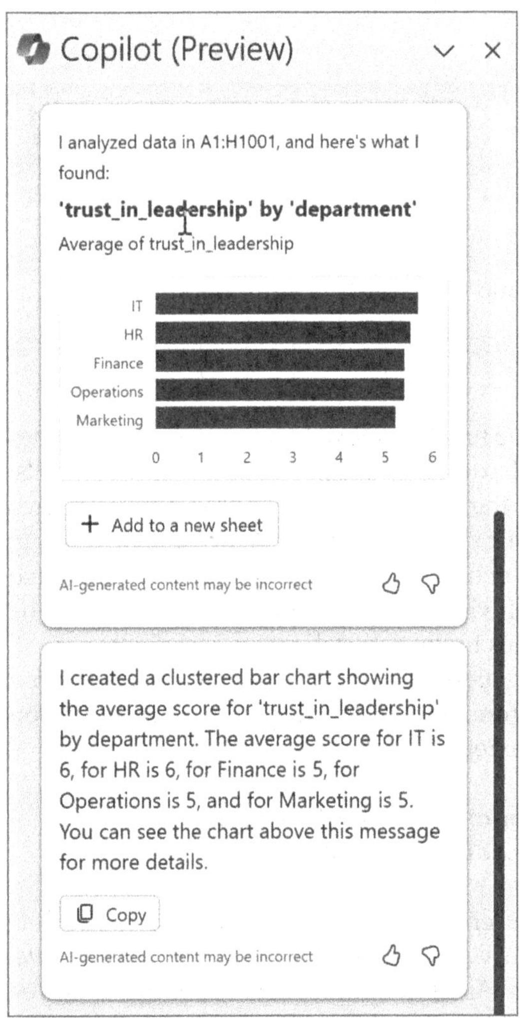

Figure 9.7: A clustered bar chart for trust in leadership

Next, if you like, you can click the "Add to a new sheet" button, and Copilot will create a new worksheet in your Excel workbook with the scattered bar chart, as shown in Figure 9.8.

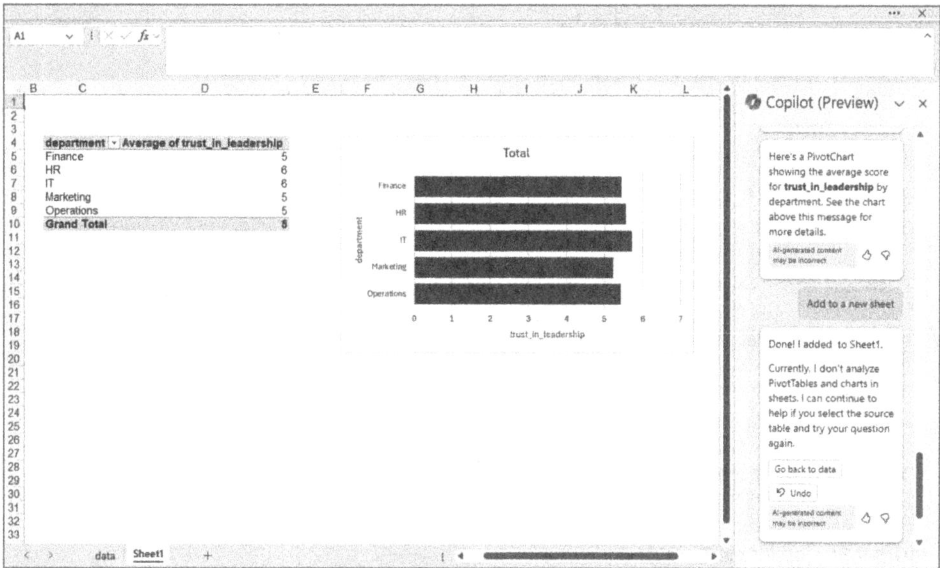

Figure 9.8: A clustered bar chart as new worksheet

Now, I would like to once again prove that despite best intentions, sometimes Copilot can be a bit misleading when it comes to providing answers—or what is commonly referred to as *hallucinating*. If you recall earlier, we asked what kind of charts Copilot can create and it listed off a variety of types, including pie charts. However, we can prove that this is not quite accurate by modifying the previous prompt to specify that the desired chart type should be a pie chart.

Go back to Copilot and enter the following prompt:

> *"Please create a pie chart showing the average score for 'trust_in_leadership' by department."*

At the time of writing, Copilot returns that it cannot create a pie chart, but it provides instructions as displayed in Figure 9.9. On the one hand, having Copilot provide you step-by-step instructions within your workflow is helpful in reducing the context switching between PowerPoint and performing an Internet search. On the other hand, it does make for a confusing user experience when it claims that it can perform an action that is later proven to be false. This again reinforces the need, as you onboard your users to Copilot, that you help set expectations that while it may appear to be an expert, Copilot can make mistakes.

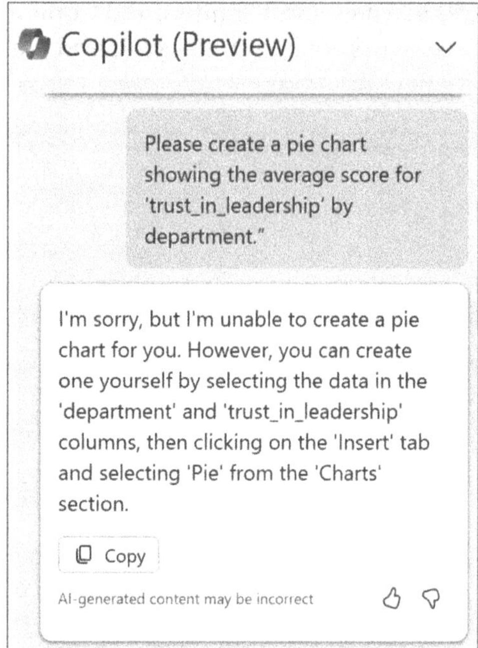

Figure 9.9: Copilot can't create a pie chart

Creating a PivotTable with Copilot

Charts are very helpful for visualizing datasets, allowing you to analyze and then make decisions based on them. However, an equally, if perhaps more, common way to analyze large amounts of data is with a PivotTable. In Excel, a PivotTable is a special table that summarizes data from a larger table by grouping individual values into categories. These summaries can include totals, averages, counts, or other statistics, making it easier to analyze and understand your data. Some use cases for PivotTables include:

- Querying large amounts of data
- Subtotaling and aggregating numeric data by categories
- Providing a hierarchical view of your data to allow you to further drill into specific sections of the data to gain key insights
- Enabling custom views of your data through filters and slicers
- Presenting a concise summary of your data or a subset of your data, for reporting purposes

While PivotTables are incredibly powerful features within Excel, they are not the easiest visualization to create if you are unfamiliar with them. However, Copilot can help you create a PivotTable without having to know all of the steps involved.

Go back to the Employee Survey data workbook, open the Copilot panel, and enter the following text:

"Please create a PivotTable with department and then a summary of the average scores."

Notice that you provided Copilot with a little bit of guidance in terms of what fields to consider for this action. You are empowering Copilot to interpret the data and make a recommendation for what it believes based on your dataset to be the desired outcome. Remember, at the end of the day, large language models are really good at predicting. While they're not like the Grays Sports Almanac from the popular *Back to the Future* movies, where they predict the future, they are trained on large amounts of data and can predict at a high level of probability the next sequence in the chain of text that you may be looking for.

For me, Copilot returns the following response: "I created a PivotTable that shows the average scores for trust in leadership, happiness in work, work-life balance, job satisfaction, career growth opportunities, and overall employee engagement, grouped by department. You can see the PivotTable above this message for more details."

In the Copilot pane, if you scroll up past that response, you can see the fields Copilot is selecting, as shown in Figure 9.10. Copilot provides you with the option to add that PivotTable to a new worksheet within your open Excel workbook.

Now, click the "Add to a new sheet" button in the Copilot panel to insert a new worksheet in your Excel workbook that includes this newly created PivotTable.

As shown in Figure 9.11, you should now have a second worksheet in your Excel workbook that contains the PivotTable Copilot created. As someone who has struggled with creating PivotTables for most of my professional career, this feels like absolute AI magic. It is very exciting to tell Copilot what I want, rather than having to visit numerous websites or follow tutorials on YouTube, which would interrupt my workflow and likely lead to other distractions.

Asking Questions About Your Data

While having AI create a PivotTable may be considered a neat parlor trick, the real power of Copilot can be witnessed by allowing it to analyze and provide insights on your dataset. What if you wanted to know which department had the lowest average score for a particular question? Depending on your Excel proficiency, you might start with creating a formula to average the scores, or maybe you would go back to creating a PivotTable to help quickly summarize them. These tasks may require Internet searches to help figure out what formula would work best, and there is a chance that you may not get it right the first or even second time. Rather than going through all of that hassle, however, let's go back to your first worksheet, which for me is called 'data,' and provide Copilot with the following prompt:

"Which department had the lowest score for work-life balance?"

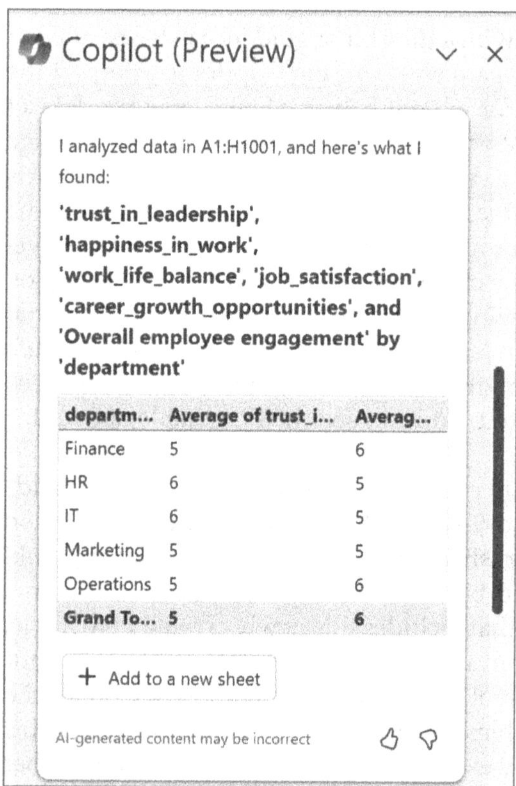

Figure 9.10: Adding a PivotTable to a new worksheet

Copilot provides a nice breakdown and explains how it arrives at the answer. For this example, it reasons through your prompt and concludes that you are looking for the "work_life_balance" column. It then reasons that to arrive at this answer, it must calculate the average score for the "work_life_balance" column. You can see the breakdown of Copilot's reasoning for your request in Figure 9.12. Extracting this information manually would typically require you to create a formula or two to replicate, but Copilot eliminates that need. It uses natural language to first understand your questions, does the appropriate analysis of your data, and then predicts what your desired output looks like and builds the appropriate formula behind the scenes to ultimately give you the answer to your question.

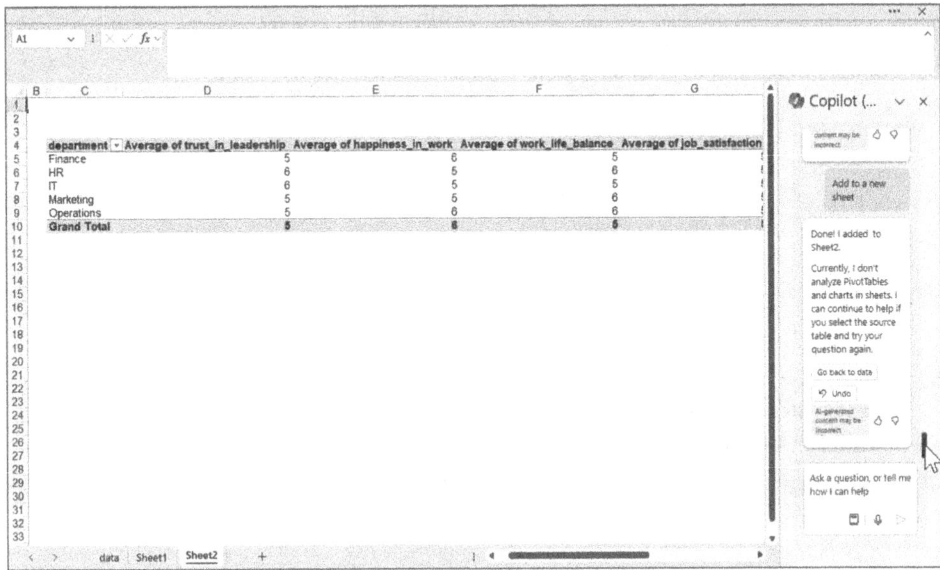

Figure 9.11: A PivotTable created by Copilot

Click the "Add to a new sheet" button to add that new PivotTable to your Excel workbook so that you can quickly check Copilot's math. Navigate to the newly created worksheet and notice that the PivotTable, as shown in Figure 9.13, has the average scores for the "work_life_balance" column.

At first glance, you may be slightly skeptical about how Copilot decided that the Finance team had the lowest scores, especially since the current PivotTable does not display decimal places. Unfortunately, as of this writing, you cannot have Copilot adjust the format of the values in a PivotTable for you. However, if you select the values shown in Figure 9.14, you'll see that the Finance department has an average score of 5.19 with trailing values, whereas when you highlight the IT department, the average score is 5.47 with trailing values. Therefore, Copilot is correct that, for this particular survey question, the Finance department has the lowest scores.

Copilot Suggested Prompts for Data Insights

You may have noticed while performing the previous actions that the Copilot panel suggested a number of prompts. In case you missed it, let's navigate back to the "data" worksheet in your Excel workbook and ask Copilot, *"Which 'employee_id' had the lowest 'overall employee engagement' scores?"* Notice that I wrapped the column names in single quotes to help Copilot understand that I am specifying columns. Copilot returns the following: "The employee with the lowest average overall employee engagement score is employee 787, with an average score of 2.2." If you scroll down, you will notice that Copilot also suggests some additional prompts you can use to further gain insights about your data (see Figure 9.15).

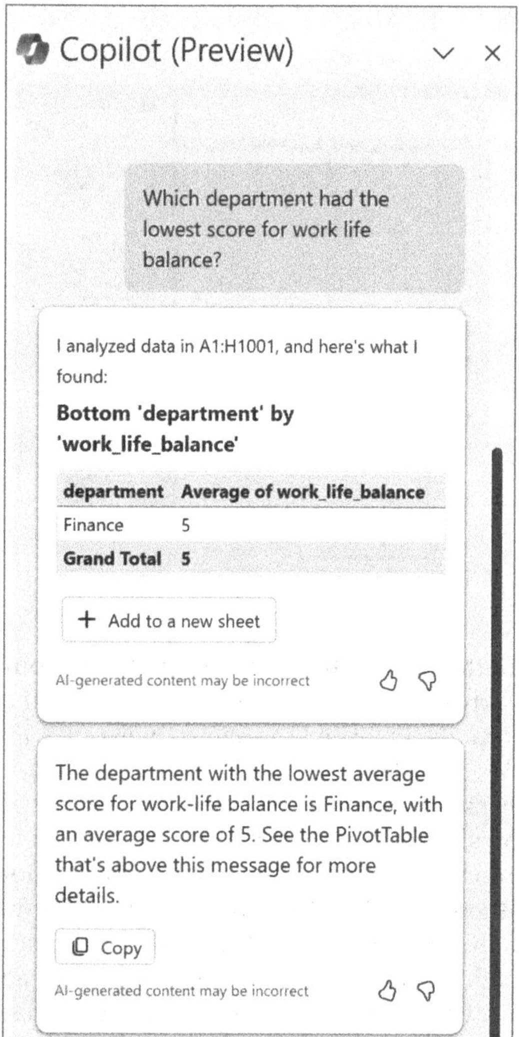

Figure 9.12: Lowest work-life balance score

department	Average of work_life_balance
Finance	5
IT	5
Operations	6
Marketing	6
HR	6
Grand Total	**5**

Figure 9.13: Average work-life balance score

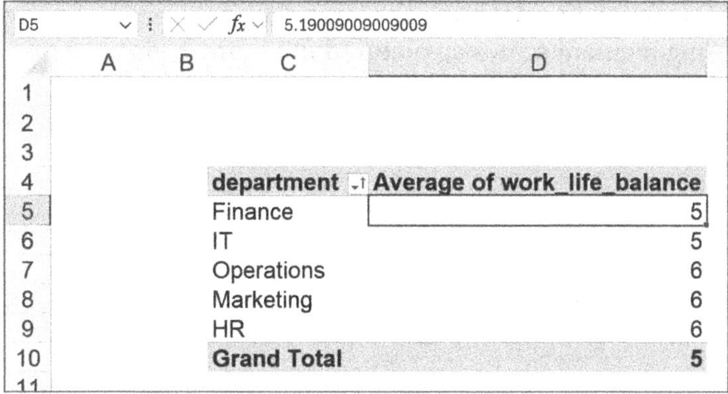

department	Average of work_life_balance
Finance	5
IT	5
Operations	6
Marketing	6
HR	6
Grand Total	**5**

Figure 9.14: Finance department scores

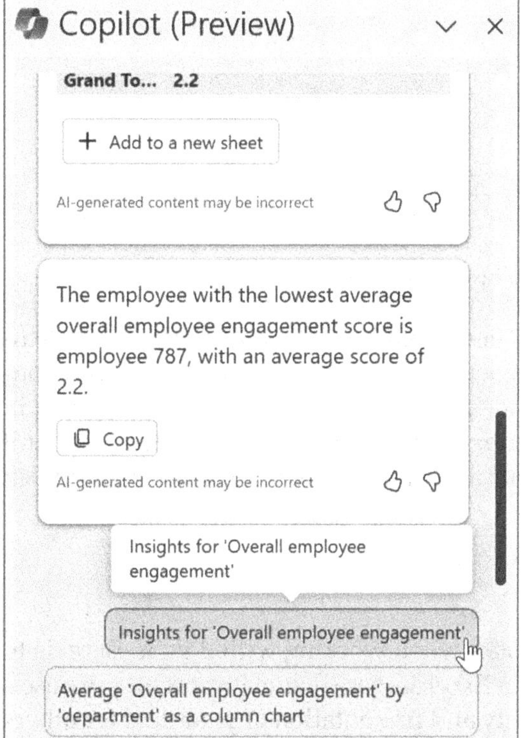

Figure 9.15: Insights for "Overall employee engagement"

Click the Insights for the 'Overall employee engagement' prompt, and Copilot will once again start to analyze your data. It will try to predict which charts might help you to better understand your dataset and then create an appropriate data visualization to help you understand that insight. In my case, Copilot returned a scatterplot with scores in the "job_satisfaction" column presented in the x-axis, and "Overall employee engagement" in the y-axis. Copilot suggests that you can gain important information by analyzing the impact job satisfaction has on the overall employee engagement scores as pictured in Figure 9.16.

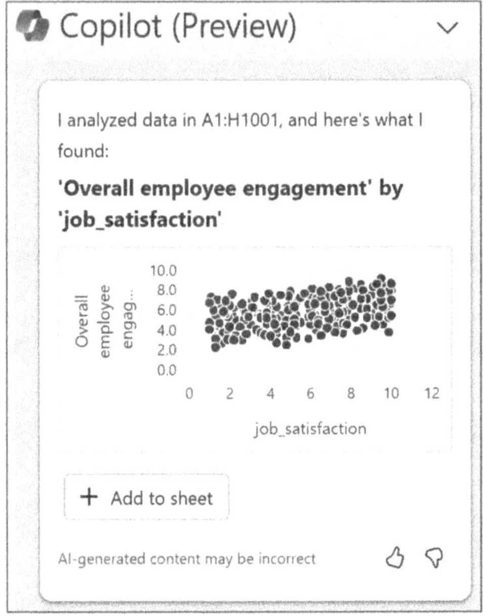

Figure 9.16: Overall employee engagement by job satisfaction

While the point of this exercise is not to pinpoint the root cause of this fictitious organization's employee satisfaction scores, it hopefully helps you consider how Copilot can serve as a data analyst assistant as you analyze data in your own Excel workbooks. Remember to keep an eye on the prompts that it suggests for potential helpful insights and data visualizations that may unlock new insights about your data.

Additional Formatting

Perhaps one of the most common tasks when working with data in Excel is to apply formatting. Formatting data in Excel serves several important purposes, including enhancing both the usability and presentation of your data for others to consume. Here are some examples of why you may be asked to format data in your Excel workbook:

- To improve the readability of your data
- To provide better organization
- To support data validation to catch outliers
- To highlight key information
- To provide consistency across multiple datasets
- To add visual appeal to make your data easier to work with

Prior to Copilot, you would need to know how to navigate Excel's many features to help achieve the goal of making your data more consumable for others. Continuing with the previous example of analyzing employee survey data, imagine that your leadership is so appreciative of how quickly you keep answering their questions that they continue to provide you with additional requests for your employee survey data spreadsheet. The next request is for you to identify all scores of less than 3 for the "Trust in Leadership" question and to filter the spreadsheet to those scores. This time, enter the following prompt in Copilot:

Please bold all values in the "trust_in_leadership" column that are less than 3, and then filter that column for values that are less than 3

Copilot should respond as follows: OK! Looking at **A1:H1001**, here are 2 changes to review and apply as pictured in Figure 9.17:

- Apply a filter on 'trust_in_leadership' to show only rows where the value is less than 3
- **Cell value less than 3:** Apply the following to cells in the column "trust_in_leadership"
  - Bold
  - Font color: black **AaBbCc**.

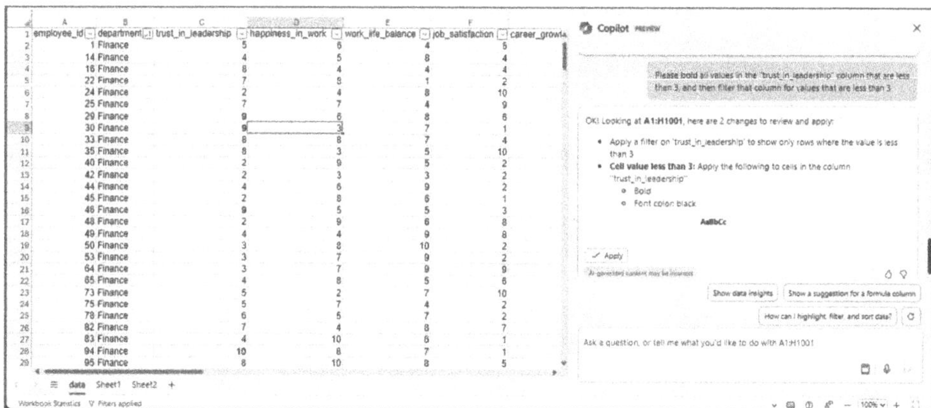

Figure 9.17: Formatting column data

Next, let's have Copilot help tell one more story about our dataset. Some information that might be helpful when trying to interpret data is to understand how many instances there are of a particular thing. For this example, it might be helpful to understand how many employees are in each department in order to better understand if there's any correlation between the size of the department and the overall employee satisfaction. Without data to back it up, you might assume that a smaller-sized department would have higher scores due to greater visibility to leadership or not feeling like they are lost in the mix of a large group of people. You can have Copilot analyze and provide a visualization to either prove or disprove this hypothesis.

Enter the following prompt:

"Can you please create a chart that helps show the correlation between number of people by 'department' and the 'overall employee engagement' scores?"

Copilot will create a new PivotTable, as shown in Figure 9.18, that you can add as a new sheet to your Excel workbook to further analyze. Notably, while perhaps not statistically significant, you can see from the data provided that the IT department has the lowest count of employees and the highest overall employee engagement scores. While department size alone may not dictate the reason behind the scores, it is one important insight that you could share with leadership.

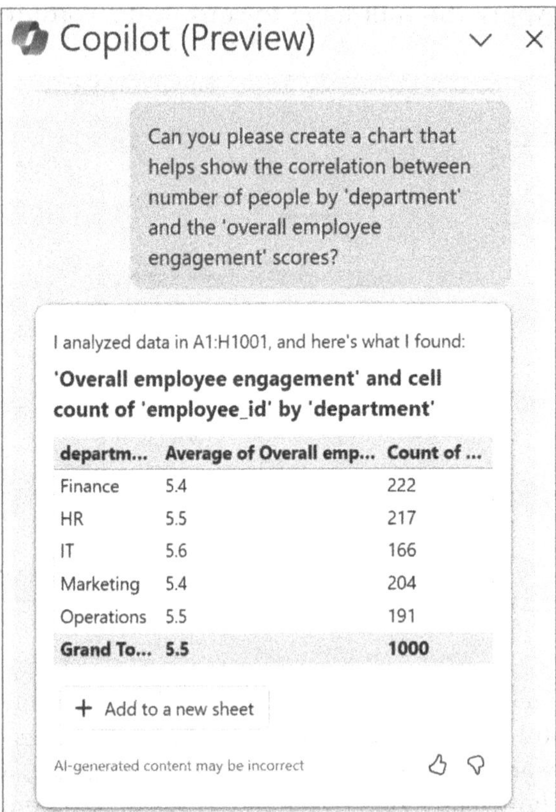

Figure 9.18: Overall employee engagement scores by department

Managing Sales Data with Copilot

So far, our examples have focused on employee survey data in Excel and used natural language to help filter, sort, and gain initial insights through lightweight questions and answers in addition to creating PivotTables and PivotCharts. Now, let's dive deeper into how Copilot can help create formulas to manipulate and format data. We'll do this by focusing on a sales dataset.

Once again, I recommend that you either create a dummy dataset using Mockaroo (`mockaroo.com`) or leverage the downloadable file *c09-Copilot-EmployeeData.xlsx* available for this chapter. Your starting point for this exercise is your data formatted in a table, as shown in Figure 9.19, and the Excel workbook hosted either on your OneDrive, SharePoint, or within Microsoft Teams.

If you are unable to access Mockaroo or would feel more comfortable creating your dataset manually, here are the columns that you'll need to create:

- customer_id: A number to signify a unique record
- customer_name: Text containing first name and last name
- purchase_date: A calendar date formatted as mm/dd/yy
- product_name: A random product with either A, B, or C as choices
- per_prod_amt: A number formatted with two decimal places reflecting the cost per product
- qty: A random number to reflect how many of a particular product was purchased

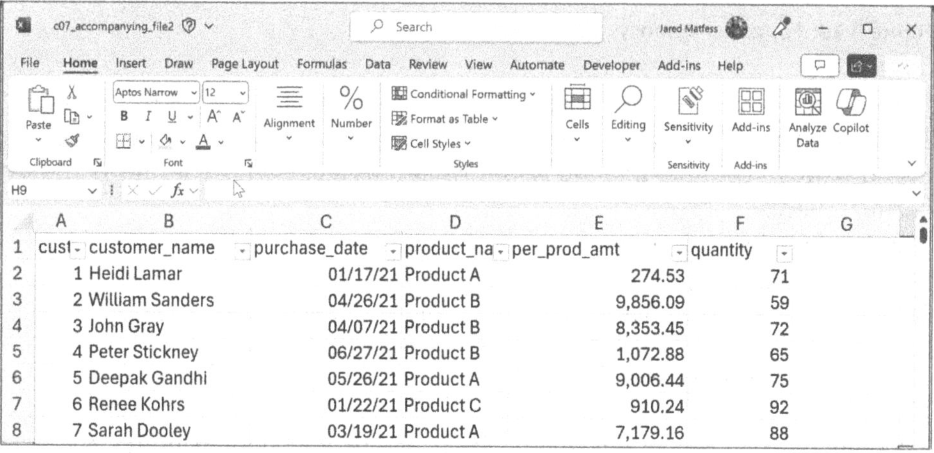

cust	customer_name	purchase_date	product_na	per_prod_amt	quantity
1	Heidi Lamar	01/17/21	Product A	274.53	71
2	William Sanders	04/26/21	Product B	9,856.09	59
3	John Gray	04/07/21	Product B	8,353.45	72
4	Peter Stickney	06/27/21	Product B	1,072.88	65
5	Deepak Gandhi	05/26/21	Product A	9,006.44	75
6	Renee Kohrs	01/22/21	Product C	910.24	92
7	Sarah Dooley	03/19/21	Product A	7,179.16	88

Figure 9.19: Sales data in table format

We are going to pretend that this sales data file was exported from another system and lost some of the formatting during the process. The first step is to format the "per_prod_amt" column to a currency. To begin, enter the following prompt within your Copilot panel:

"Please format the column 'per_prod_amt' as a Currency with two decimal places."

Copilot should return the following response, as shown in Figure 9.20: "I have formatted the column 'per_prod_amt' as a currency with two decimal places. Is there anything else you need help with?"

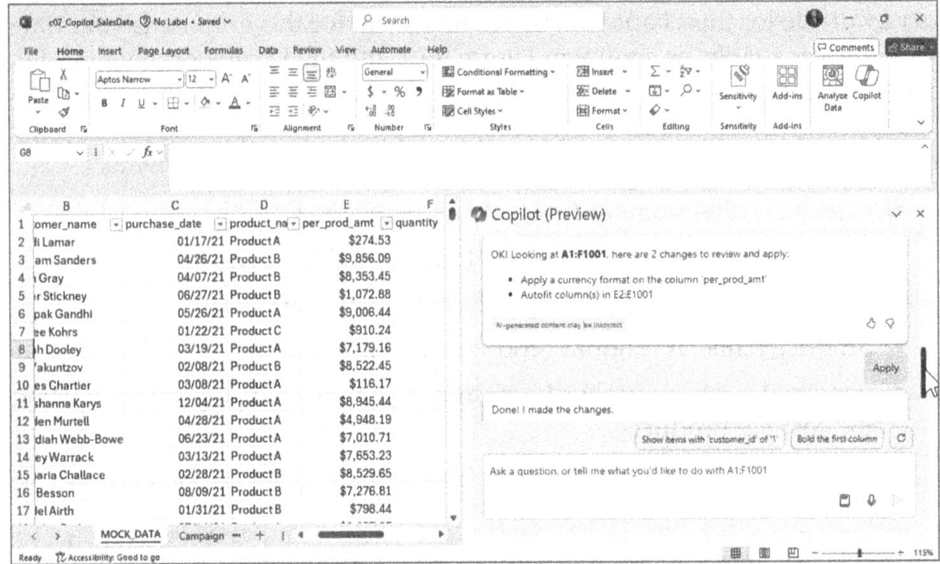

Figure 9.20: Format as currency

Now, let's have Copilot create a new column called "total_purchase_amt." This column will be a calculation of the column "per_prod_amt" multiplied by the "quantity" column, and we will format it as a currency column with two decimal places.

Enter the following prompt:

"Please create a new column called 'total_purchase_amt,' which is calculated by the column 'per_prod_amt' multiplied by the column 'quantity.' Format this as a currency and show two decimal places."

Copilot should return output similar to Figure 9.21, including the formula that it decided is required to create this new column, a rendering of the potential values for the first few records, and a button that allows you to add this new column with the formula to your workbook. Additionally, if you hover over the "Insert column" button within the Copilot panel, as shown in Figure 9.21, you can see that it also provides a real-time view as to how that new column will look alongside the rest of the data in your workbook. In this instance, it would be inserted as a new column to the right of all of your other columns.

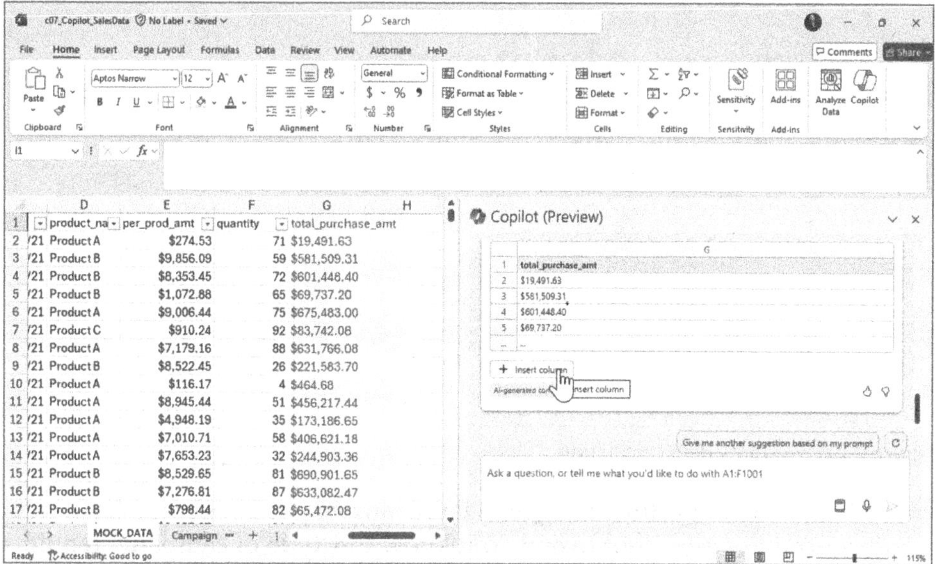

Figure 9.21: Creating the "total_purchase_amt" column

Next, let's create a new column called "Wty_Expiration," which will be a calculation based on the "Purchase_Date" column. For the purpose of this exercise, let's assume that Product A has a 3-year warranty; Product B has a 2-year warranty; and Product C has a 1-year warranty. Enter the following prompt into Copilot:

> *"Please create a new column called 'Wty_Expiration,' which should be calculated based on the 'Purchase_Date' column. If column 'Product_Name' is Product A, it should be 3 years, if Product B, 2 years, if Product C, 1 year from the column 'Purchase_Date.'"*

Again, Copilot quite impressively reasons over your request and creates the following formula, as shown in the Copilot panel in Figure 9.22:

```
=IF(EXACT([@[product_name]], "Product A"), EDATE([@[purchase_date]],
36), IF(EXACT([@[product_name]], "Product B"), EDATE([@[purchase_date]],
24), IF(EXACT([@[product_name]], "Product C"), EDATE([@[purchase_date]],
12), "")))
```

Click the "Insert column" button to add this new column to your spreadsheet.

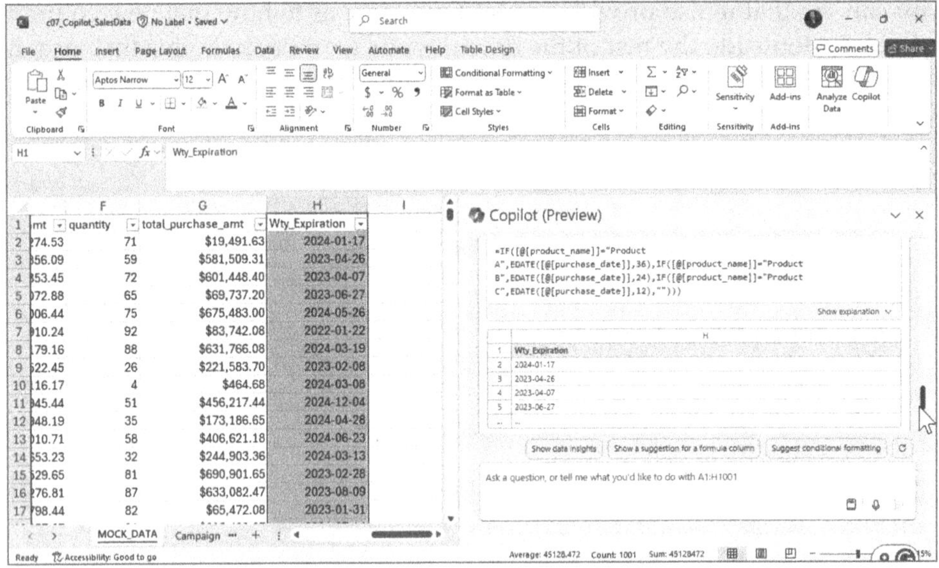

Figure 9.22: Warranty date calculation

Your warranty department suggests launching a special offer for customers whose warranties are about to end. You know this type of campaign requires some days to prepare and additional time for customers to respond. To provide a little bit of a buffer, you decide that you would like to have about 2 months between today's date and the warranty expiration date as your target pool. Let's begin by figuring out how many potential customers could be contacted to ensure that this campaign would be beneficial.

You can arrive at this count of potential customers with the following prompt:

> *"Please count how many records have the condition of 'warranty_expiration' being over 2 months later than today's date."*

Depending on when you perform this exercise, your results may vary, but at the time of writing, Copilot provides the following response: "There are 155 rows where the Warranty_Expiration is after July 27, 2024." When you share that with the head of the Warranty department, their eyes light up and request that you get started. As part of their campaign, they would like to include the warranty renewal amount as part of the email.

With the warranty manager all excited about the potential work this campaign could be bringing to her department, the next question they ask you is how much revenue this campaign could potentially generate. You respond by asking them what the pricing structure would be for these renewals. They provide the following breakdown of pricing based on the total purchase price of the customer's order:

- Total Purchase Price < $100,000: 3%

- Total Purchase Price $100,000–$500,000: 2%
- Total Purchase Price > $500,000: 1%

Your first step is to create a new column in your spreadsheet that will be calculated based on the breakdown provided by the warranty manager. As you can see, this is a much more complex formula that, without Copilot, would likely require a bit of trial and error, especially for those of us who are Excel novices.

NOTE **When working with Copilot, it is important to be very explicit with the columns that will be used in creating your formula. It is a good practice to use the word "column" and then include the name of the column within single quotes to help guide Copilot into knowing you are referring to a column. Additionally, you need to be very clear when asking Copilot to perform multiple calculations so that it will generate the appropriate syntax based on your desired output.**

For this particular calculation, Copilot needs to understand that there are two conditions: the warranty eligibility date based on today's date and the cost based on the value of the total purchase price.

Enter the following prompt into Copilot:

---

*Please create a new column called 'wty_ext_promo.' Set the value to 0 if the column 'warranty_expiration' is less than 2 months from today's date. If it's greater, then calculate the value based on the column called total_price. If 'total_price' is less than $100,000, then 'wty_ext_promo' would be calculated by the column 'total_price' * .03. If the column 'total_price' is between $100,000 and $500,000, then column 'wty_ext_promo' would be calculated by column 'total_price' * .02. If the column 'total_price' is greater than $500,000 then column 'wty_ext_promo' would be calculated by column 'total_price' * .01"*

Copilot will create the following formula to help calculate the pricing for the warranty extension and allow you to insert it as a new worksheet, as shown in Figure 9.23:

```
"=IF(FLOOR.MATH([@[warranty_expiration]] - TODAY()) < 60, 0, IF
([@[total_price]] < 100000, [@[total_price]] * 0.03, IF(AND([@[total_
price]] >= 100000, [@[total_price]] < 500000), [@[total_price]] * 0.02,
[@[total_price]] * 0.01)))"
```

Now that you have the calculation for the potential warranty extension costs for those customers who meet the eligibility requirements, you can either highlight column "L" and have it provide you with the sum in the bottom right-hand corner of Excel, or you can ask Copilot: *"What's the SUM of column L?"* Copilot will return the following: "The sum of column L, which is the 'wty_ext_promo' column, is $894,761.48." With that newly calculated information, you can inform the warranty manager what the potential total revenue would be if all customers were to respond that they want to extend their warranty.

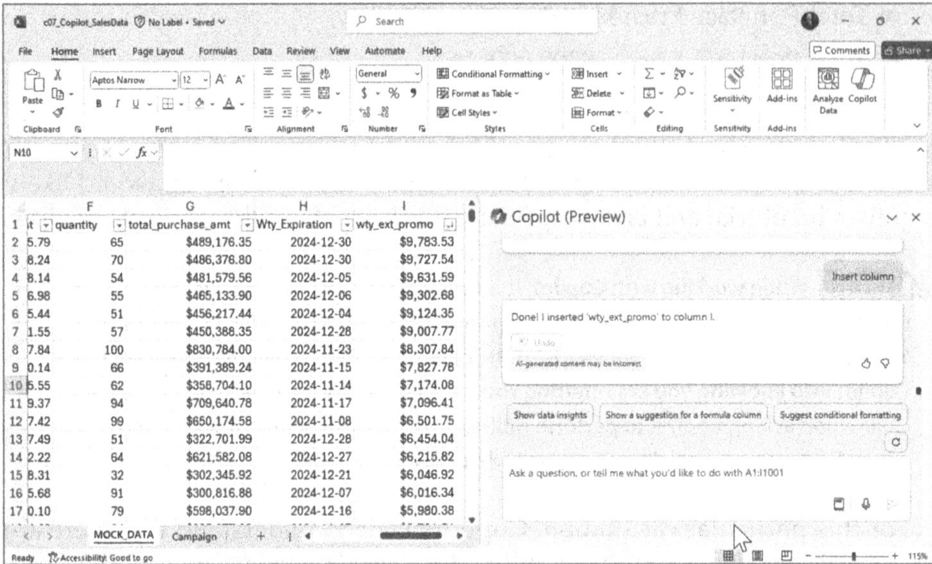

Figure 9.23: Warranty cost calculation

However, the more that the warranty manager thinks about, the more they realize this estimate is not very helpful for estimating potential revenue, because not every customer will respond to the campaign. Therefore, they ask you to perform one more calculation to be able to set the right expectations with the senior leadership team about how much revenue this campaign could potentially generate. The manager provides you with the following breakdown:

- Assume that 60% of the customers whose warranty renewals cost less than $1,000 will renew.
- Assume that 40% of the customers whose warranty renewals cost less than $5,000 will renew.
- Assume that 20% of the customers whose warranty renewals cost more than $5,000 will renew.

You create the following prompt:

"Calculate total for Column L less than 1000. Multiply that total by .4."

Copilot returns the following: "The total for Column L (wty_ext_promo) where the value is less than 1000 is $16,045.64. If you multiply that total by 0.4, the result is $6,418.26."

You can build off that prompt, so you craft the following new prompt:

"Calculate total for Column L less than 1000. Multiply that total by .4. Calculate total for Column L between 1000 and 5000. Multiply that total by .3. Calculate the total for Column L greater than 5000. Multiply that total by .2."

Copilot returns the following: "I'm sorry, but I'm not able to perform calculations on the data in the way you've requested. Could you please provide more information or clarify your request?"

You have just discovered one of the fun learning curves and decision points when working with Copilot. Sometimes it might be quicker to go with smaller targeted prompts to get what you're looking for. If you were to break that initial prompt into three separate prompts, Copilot would return the values you are looking for.

However, sometimes Copilot struggles with long-form prompts. Therefore, you must decide how much time you spend crafting the perfect long-form prompt versus using shorter prompts to get the answers you are looking for and then move on to the next task.

Conclusion

Copilot is a great feature for Microsoft Excel, which is one of the more complex applications in the Office suite. It can help you work with existing data, make charts and PivotTables, and conduct analysis on different datasets using natural language. Remember that the trick to getting the best output from Copilot is to be incredibly explicit with your desired output. This includes prefixing any references to columns with the word "column" and including the name within single quotes. It also means providing Copilot with the step-by-step instructions for how to create calculations, especially for some of the more advanced scenarios. It is also important to note that you can't take Copilot's responses as definitive. Large language models have been known to be inaccurate when dealing with numbers, so you should always check Copilot's work when possible. While the product still has some room for improvement, as evidenced in that last example, it can offer a lot of benefits. Chapter 10, "Copilot in Microsoft PowerPoint," explores how you can use prompts in Copilot to make PowerPoint presentations.

CHAPTER 10

Copilot in Microsoft PowerPoint

Microsoft PowerPoint is perhaps one of the most loved and hated applications within the Microsoft Office suite. Business professionals often lament the limitations of presenting information in PowerPoint slide format. However, despite these concerns, it is universally accepted as the default way to present information. If you are in the professional services field, you may be able to calculate the time spent agonizing over PowerPoint slides in years instead of hours. Perhaps one of the most time-consuming aspects of the PowerPoint creation and refinement process is focused on word choice and reformatting information to make it easier for the target audience to consume. Now, with the introduction of Copilot within PowerPoint, those long hours can hopefully be replaced with prompts that get you 80 percent of the way toward communicating key messages to your stakeholders.

In this chapter, you will learn how to leverage Copilot within PowerPoint to help you spend less time building slides and more time refining your messaging to ensure that it lands with the appropriate audiences. This chapter's use case focuses on how Copilot can help you build project management artifacts—in this case, PowerPoint files to support your own organizational rollout of Copilot. We will walk through the process of creating a Project Kickoff deck using the power of prompt engineering. You will also see how Copilot can analyze your content and serve as a second set of eyes to ensure your messaging is clear.

Preparing Your PowerPoint Template for Copilot

While Microsoft may live in the world of Contoso, many of us work for organizations that have made large investments in their brand and identity. Therefore, one of the first steps that you should take is to set up your organizational assets library to centrally store your PowerPoint templates. If you are unfamiliar with PowerPoint templates, unlike .pptx files, which are the modern file format, templates have the file extension .potx. This will not only make Copilot aware of your organization's PowerPoint templates and the various slide layouts but also make your desired template available as an option within the PowerPoint client when you create a new presentation. By establishing an organizational assets library and posting your company's PowerPoint template, you will also future-proof your Copilot implementation. According to Microsoft, future updates will leverage the organizational assets library for content creation, specifically PowerPoint files and images.

Initial Setup of an Organizational Assets Library

While this is not a mandatory step, I recommend considering it to stay aligned with the product roadmap for Copilot. Even the smallest organizations can benefit from having their PowerPoint templates centrally hosted. To complete these next steps, you will most likely need to engage with your Microsoft 365 Global Administrator or whoever has full control to make changes in your Microsoft 365 tenant. This would likely be someone in your IT group, but remember that each company is slightly different. The procedure entails creating a new SharePoint site collection, creating two document libraries, and then running a PowerShell command to establish your organizational assets library for Microsoft Office templates and images.

1. Create a new SharePoint site collection called "Branding."
2. Have your Microsoft 365 administrator set permissions on the site so that whoever is responsible for managing your company's PowerPoint template is a Member with Contribute access to the site collection. Additionally, you will want to grant everyone except external users Read access so that they can access the site.
3. Create two document libraries: one called "Templates" and another called "Images."
4. Upload your Company's PowerPoint template (.potx) file to the "Templates" SharePoint document library.
5. Upload your Company's Logo to the "Images" SharePoint document library.

6. Have your Microsoft 365 Global Administrator download the latest SharePoint Online Management Shell from `go.microsoft.com/fwlink/p/?LinkId=255251`.
7. Have your Microsoft 365 Global Administrator connect to SharePoint using the SharePoint Online Management Shell with the following command, replacing the **contoso** reference in the `Url` parameter, to match your SharePoint Online tenant name:

```
Connect-SPOService -Url https://contoso-admin.sharepoint.com
-Credential admin@contoso.com
```

8. The admin will then run the following PowerShell command, replacing `contoso` with the name of your SharePoint tenant, to set up your organizational assets office template library:

```
Add-SPOOrgAssetsLibrary -LibraryURL https://contoso.sharepoint.com/
sites/branding/Templates -ThumbnailURL https://contoso.sharepoint
.com/sites/branding/Images/contosologo.jpg
-OrgAssetType OfficeTemplateLibrary
```

9. Finally, run the following PowerShell command, replacing `contoso` with the name of your SharePoint tenant, to set up your organizational assets image document library:

```
Add-SPOOrgAssetsLibrary -LibraryURL https://contoso.sharepoint.com/
sites/branding/Images -ThumbnailURL https://contoso.sharepoint.com/
sites/branding/Images/contosologo.jpg
-OrgAssetType ImageDocumentLibrary
```

You are now all set for Copilot to recognize your company's PowerPoint template. Also, by establishing the organizational assets image document library as part of the previous setup, you have created a central location for company-approved stock photography images that can be inserted into Office documents such as Word, PowerPoint, etc. In the future we may see Copilot gain the ability to leverage this library when building content that contains imagery. However, at this current time, Copilot's source for images is the Microsoft Designer service, which uses a mix of Internet and AI-generated imagery.

PowerPoint Template Requirements

To improve Copilot's ability to produce well-formatted content, it's important to review your organization's PowerPoint template to ensure that it has a variety of different content layouts in the Slide Master. While this step is not mandatory, it will help provide Copilot with additional flexibility to generate engaging content. A good way to confirm that you have plenty of options is to open one of the default templates included with Microsoft PowerPoint (such as the template shown in Figure 10.1) and review the various content layouts within the Slide Master. From there, you can compare that to your organizational PowerPoint template to confirm whether any additional layouts are missing. The reason for doing so is to provide Copilot with multiple options for how it lays out content within your organizational PowerPoint template.

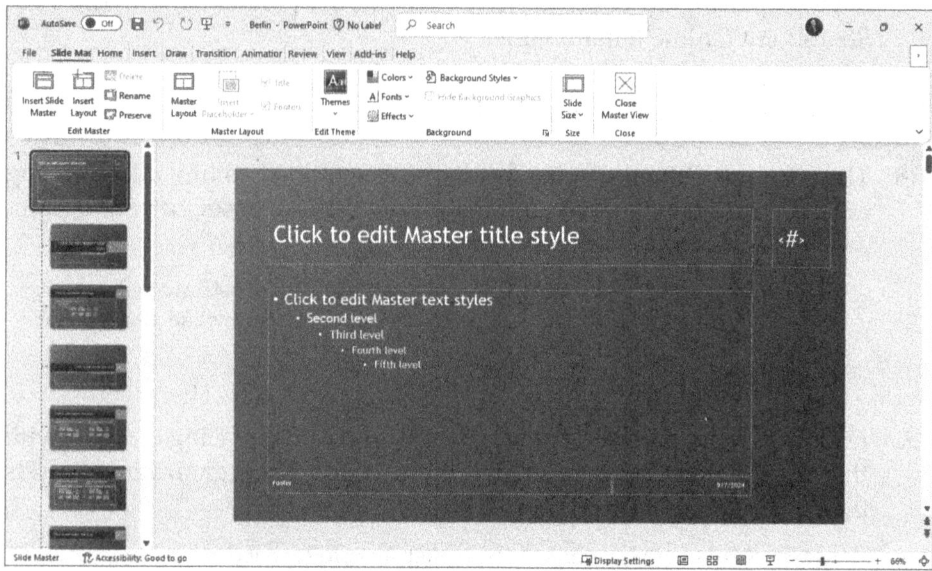

Figure 10.1: Example PowerPoint template

Creating Your First PowerPoint Presentation with Copilot

Now, let's use Copilot to help build your first PowerPoint presentation. This example walks you through creating a Project Kickoff deck for your Microsoft 365 Copilot rollout project. To help prove the point for how valuable prompt engineering is in providing Copilot with the appropriate level of detail to return something of value to you, enter the following prompt within a blank PowerPoint presentation file:

"Can you please create a Project Kickoff deck for a project where we will be implementing Microsoft 365 Copilot to 10,000 users across our enterprise."

Notice that this prompt provided Copilot with very limited information beyond the type of project and estimated number of users, which means we are giving Copilot some liberty to pull content from both its own knowledge base, the Internet, and other available information within Microsoft Graph. To set expectations, the presentation that Copilot creates is not going to be very useful for most real-world use cases, but it is meant to be illustrative for what your users may attempt when they are getting started.

The output you see may be similar to Figure 10.2 or vastly different, based on the information Copilot can access. As previously noted, one of the challenging aspects of Copilot is that it is highly dependent on user context in addition to data available within Microsoft Graph. The PowerPoint presentation that Copilot creates in this scenario is very generic and likely not very useful for any sort of real-world use cases. For a user who does not understand how Copilot works or how to interact with GenAI, this output might be considered a disappointing experience.

NOTE **At the time of writing, PowerPoint will not pull from your organizational assets library. Therefore, if you want to have it create a PowerPoint presentation in a defined template, you need to have a document with that template open and then enter your desired prompt.**

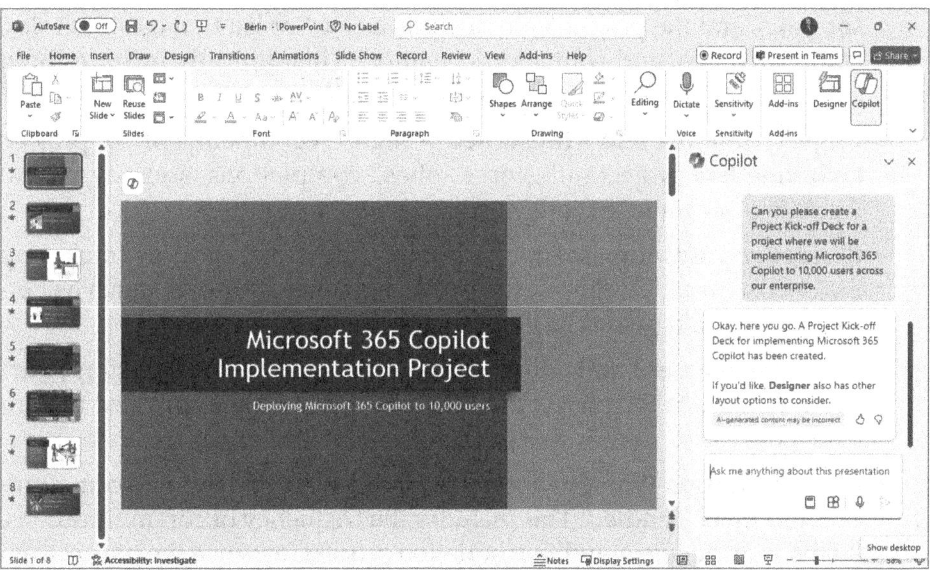

Figure 10.2: Project Kickoff deck version 1

Improving the Prompt

Let's try again, but this time we will first develop a prompt that better directs Copilot toward an output that might be more usable in a real-world scenario. For this example, we will provide additional information to the prompt to have Copilot hopefully create a more usable Project Kickoff deck. To help you get started, here is a list of common sections that are included in most large-scale IT projects:

- **Project Overview**: A summary of the project, including its name, purpose, and the value that it will be providing to the organization.

- **Background and Justification**: The origin story behind the project, including who requested the project, the problem or opportunity the project addresses, including any relevant history or context to help better align the project team with the project stakeholders.
- **Scope and Deliverables**: A clear definition of the project's scope, outlining what is included and what is excluded from the project. List the expected deliverables in terms of work products that will be delivered by the project team.
- **Objectives and Success Criteria**: An overview of what will be solved through this project. Typically, organizations define objectives using the SMART framework, meaning the objectives are specific, measurable, achievable, relevant, and time-bound. Additionally, stakeholders are informed about how success will be measured, with either quantitative measures, qualitative measures, or perhaps both.
- **Stakeholders and Roles**: An identification of key stakeholders, project sponsors, and the project team. Include a chart or list that outlines roles, responsibilities, and contact information. This typically includes both employees and contractors, where applicable.
- **Project Timeline and Milestones**: A high-level timeline of the project, including key project milestones, phase completions, and any critical deadlines or events that are worth noting.
- **Budget and Resources**: An overview of the project budget, including major cost areas, funding sources, and resource allocation (such as personnel, technology, and facilities).
- **Risk Management and Mitigation Strategies**: An identification of the potential risks to the project's success and the strategies planned to mitigate these risks.
- **Communication Plan**: An outline of how project updates and communications will be handled. This includes the frequency of communications, methods or channels, and the escalation process for when the project team encounters issues and needs to escalate them to key project stakeholders.
- **Change Management Plan**: A description of the procedures for managing changes to the project scope, timeline, or resources, including how stakeholder input will be incorporated.
- **Next Steps and Action Items**: The immediate next steps following the Kickoff meeting and the specific action items assigned to team members, including any upcoming deadlines.
- **Questions and Discussion**: An open section for stakeholders to ask questions, provide feedback, and discuss any immediate concerns or ideas they want the project team to consider.

You might be saying to yourself, if I have to list out each piece of content that I need Copilot to create, how is this going to make me more productive? And you are correct—if you had to spell out everything, you would probably spend more time building your prompt then copying a previous Project Kickoff deck and replacing it with the pertinent content. There is also content that I have outlined that will likely be ignored by Copilot if you were to include it within your prompt. However, my intent is for you to understand the delta between what Copilot can provide on its own and where you may need to either adjust your prompts or iterate further to get to your desired end state.

This time, let's start with your organization's PowerPoint template open so that the output will be branded. This example uses the "Berlin" PowerPoint theme, but you can choose to use your organization's PowerPoint template. At the time, Copilot will either use the theme of the existing PowerPoint file you have open or create its own custom theme. Here is your starting prompt:

> *"Create a presentation that will serve as a Project Kickoff deck. Use professional tone and imagery. Include the following sections: Project Overview, Background & Justification, Scope & Deliverables, Objectives & Success Criteria, Stakeholders & Roles, Project Timeline & Milestones, Budget & Resources, Risk Management & Mitigation Strategies, Communications Plan, Change Management Plan, and Next Steps & Actions. Please assume the project is for 6 months starting January 1st, 2025."*

The Copilot service will once again run and start to evaluate your prompt and assemble the content. Notice in Figure 10.3 that this time it adheres to the organizational PowerPoint template and creates a slide for each section you specified in the prompt. However, while some elements of what has been generated are helpful, other slides will require manual intervention. Copilot recommends leveraging Designer to help with formatting, providing you with different options for displaying text and images on your slides. You will also notice that it may ignore some elements of your prompt. For example, our prompt included information on the start date and project duration, which went mostly ignored by Copilot.

Improving the Content

Let's build out the Risk Management & Mitigation Strategies slide by including a couple of potential risks that might present themselves in an enterprise rollout of Microsoft 365 Copilot. Go to that slide in your current open PowerPoint presentation and replace the existing bulleted list with the following items as potential project risks so that your slide matches Figure 10.4 at a high level:

- Employees don't feel like they have time to learn how to use Copilot
- InfoSec concerns with M365 Copilot Service offering
- Managing multiple time zones and languages

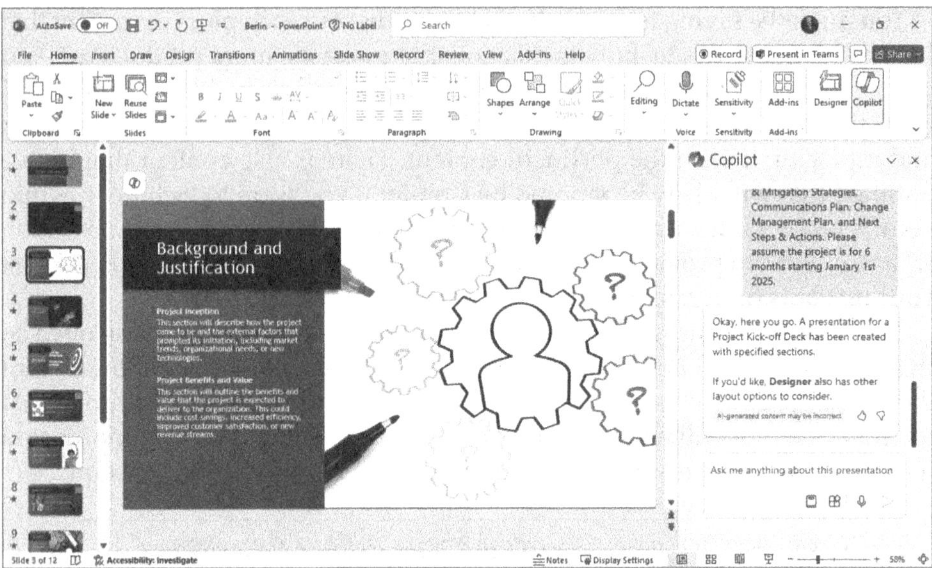

Figure 10.3: Project Kickoff deck version 2

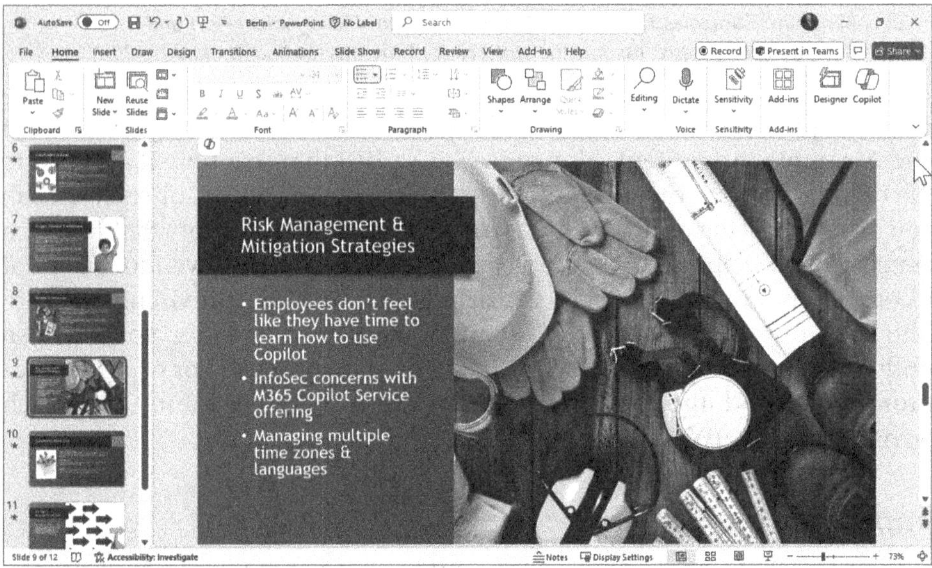

Figure 10.4: Project risks

At first glance, these risks all make sense as things that could potentially come up during an enterprise rollout of Copilot. However, for a Project Kickoff deck where there will be a mix of senior stakeholders and peers, the language of those bullets is kind of lacking and not very professional. This is where Copilot can really shine by performing an analysis of your content within your presentation and providing recommendations for how to better articulate your point.

With the Copilot panel open, enter the following prompt:

"What is a better way to articulate the 3 potential project risks?"

As shown in the Copilot panel in Figure 10.5, Copilot provides the following information and bullets, which you can use to update your slide:

Here are some ways to articulate the three potential project risks:

- **Lack of focus on selection or priority**: This risk can arise when there is a proliferation of use cases and a lack of focus on selection or priority. To mitigate this risk, you can create and fill in a risk log as a team in the early stages of your project, noting all possible risks that could arise during the project's life cycle. One example of this would be a RAID log, which is a project management tool used for tracking risks, actions, issues, and decisions. You can also set up recurring meetings with your team and the client to review and update your RAID log, in order to stay on top of any new risks that may appear later in the project.
- **Security and compliance issues**: Implementing solutions that are successful and robust involves merging security, technology, and compliance factors. Failure to take these into account and mitigate against security risks can lead to potential data breaches and the loss of confidential information and IP, leaving companies open to the threat of litigation.
- **Managing multiple time zones and languages**: This risk can arise when working with a global team or clients in different time zones and who speak different languages. To mitigate this risk, you can establish clear communication protocols and use tools to help manage time zone differences and facilitate communication in multiple languages.

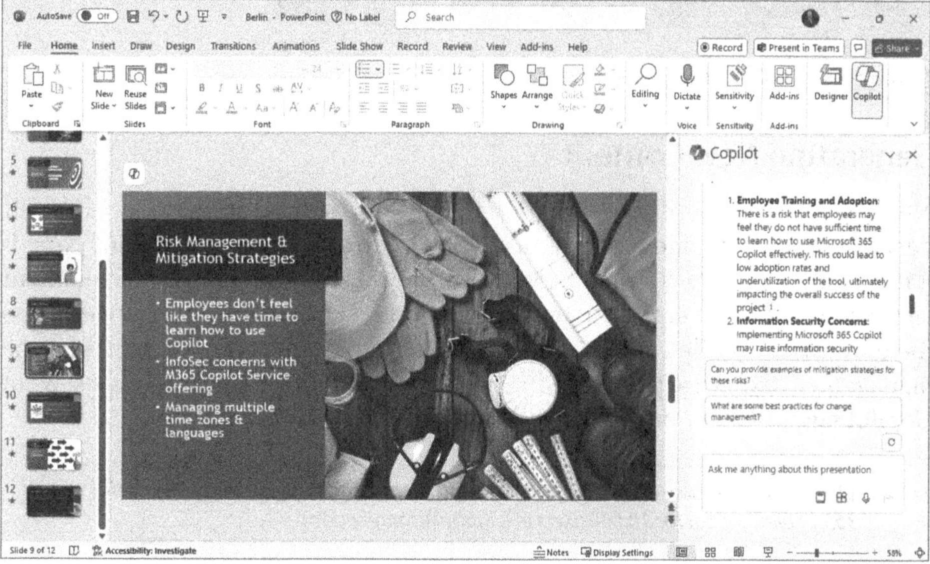

Figure 10.5: Copilot identifies risks

Currently, you will need to copy and paste the suggestions from the Copilot panel to the slide contents, but in the future I can envision Copilot being able to automatically update the slide content for you.

Your actual output will likely differ from Figure 10.5, but assuming it is somewhat similar, the text provided by Copilot is very long for the given space and probably not appropriate for an executive audience. However, you can have Copilot provide a more condensed output with the following prompt: "Can you please condense these bullets to no more than 18 words per bullet?" Note that Copilot is able to handle prompts with grammatical errors. As shown in Figure 10.6, Copilot is able to suggest a more condensed version of the bullets, which again you would need to copy and paste.

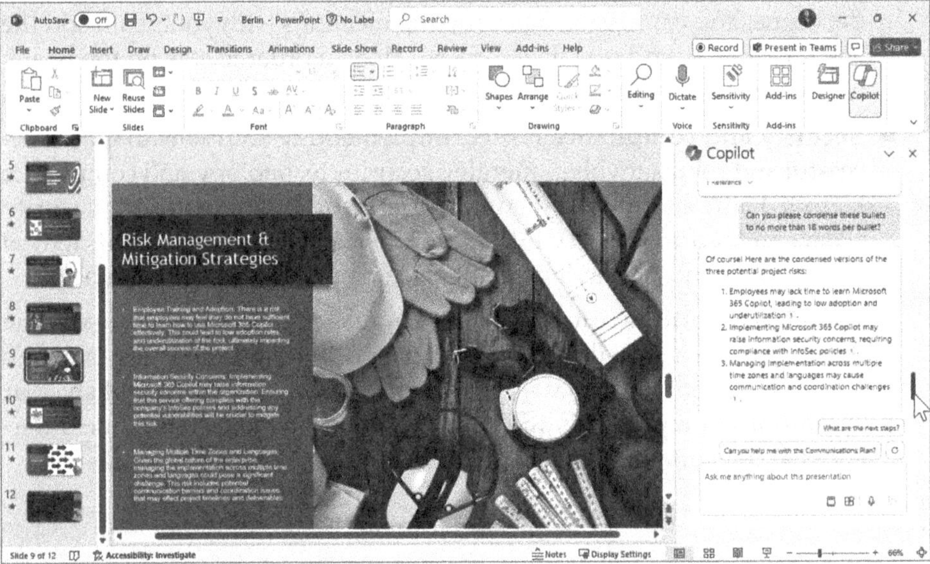

Figure 10.6: Copilot refines content

Generating New Content

Next, let's use Copilot to generate new content within your Project Kickoff deck. Go to the Change Management Plan slide and open the Copilot pane if it is not open already. We will prompt Copilot to suggest change management tactics that can be leveraged to help the project team manage this change across the enterprise. While certainly it is important to have someone with change management expertise provide a final review before presenting it, let's see what Copilot suggests. Try entering the following prompt:

"Please suggest three bullets for how to manage the change impact of a Microsoft 365 Copilot rollout for 10,000 users in a global organization."

While your actual output will likely differ, Copilot provided me with the following response:

"According to the presentation: Here are three suggestions for managing the change impact of a Microsoft 365 Copilot rollout for 10,000 users in a Global organization:

- **Develop a comprehensive change management plan that outlines the process for managing change throughout the project.**
- **Communicate regularly with stakeholders to keep them informed and engaged in the change process.**
- **Provide training and support to employees to help them adapt to the new technology and processes."**

Now, if you are not satisfied with the output or would like Copilot to provide an additional suggestion, try the following prompt, which includes context from the original request:

"Can you please suggest one more bullet for how to manage the change impact of a Microsoft 365 Copilot rollout for 10,000 users in a Global organization."

For me Copilot provided the following response:

"This response isn't based on the presentation: Here is one more suggestion for managing the change impact of a Microsoft 365 Copilot rollout for 10,000 users in a global organization:

- **Gather Feedback: Regularly gather feedback from employees and stakeholders to understand their concerns and challenges, and use this feedback to make necessary adjustments to the change management plan."**

Perhaps you have limited experience with change management and are unsure whether the suggestions Copilot provided are valid. While conferring with other project team members would certainly be an appropriate next step, you can also leverage Copilot to educate yourself on change management best practices. Type the following prompt into Copilot:

"What are key components of a change management plan not based on information in this document?"

Note that this prompt specifically requests Copilot *not* to provide information from this document, which means it will leverage either organizational data that it finds from Graph or Copilot's own knowledge.

Copilot provides the following response back to my prompt:

"This response isn't based on the presentation: Some key components of a change management plan that are not mentioned in the document include:

- **Training and Support: Providing training and support to employees to help them adapt to the changes and use new tools and processes effectively.**
- **Leadership Alignment: Ensuring that leaders at all levels are aligned with the change and are actively supporting and communicating it to their teams.**
- **Monitoring and Evaluation: Regularly monitoring the progress of the change and evaluating its impact to make necessary adjustments and ensure that the desired outcomes are achieved.**

This response helps demonstrate that Copilot itself has knowledge gathered from training the backend large language models. While it suggests that the response was not generated based on this document, I am quite curious where it found that information. I also subscribe to the philosophy of "trust but verify," so a helpful follow-up prompt to send to Copilot is:

"Was that last response from an Internet source, another document, or Copilot's own knowledge?"

Copilot responded as follows:

"The previous response was from my own knowledge and understanding of change management plans. The information provided was not based on the presentation or any other external source."

This helps to validate that Copilot itself has knowledge that it is able to provide. The process of creating content and iterating it with additional prompts to refine the output is one of the most powerful aspects of GenAI—and why Microsoft touts Copilot as an assistant versus an autonomous virtual being that does not require oversight.

Navigating Microsoft PowerPoint with Copilot

Similarly to how you can leverage Copilot within Microsoft Excel to create charts and PivotTables, you can also use it within the PowerPoint experience to help guide you through actions that you might not know how to perform. For example, accessibility is a very important topic when it comes to making your content available to people with diverse needs. Many people use screen readers or other assistive technologies to help navigate digital content. There are ways to make your presentations accessible for screen readers, including adding alt text to your images, charts, and other non-text elements. Alternative ("alt") text is essentially a brief description that explains the purpose and content of the element, which the screen reader software reads aloud for the viewer.

You may be saying to yourself that adding alt text to your images sounds easy, but you've never done it before. Normally, when faced with a task that you don't know how to perform, you might perform a Bing search or find a YouTube video for a visual how-to. However, this is a great example of how you can leverage Copilot within your workflow to learn how to perform an action without having to jump between PowerPoint and the Internet for instructions.

From within the Copilot pane, enter the following prompt:

"How do I add alt text to images?"

Copilot returned the following helpful step-by-step instructions for me:

"This response isn't based on the presentation: To add alt text to an image in PowerPoint on a Mac, follow these steps:

- **Click on the image to select it.**
- **Right-click on the image and select Format Picture from the context menu.**
- **In the Format Picture pane, select the Size & Properties tab.**
- **Expand the Alt Text section.**
- **Enter a title and description for the image in the Title and Description fields.**
- **Close the Format Picture pane."**

Another aspect of building inclusive content is color contrast. Color contrast is the difference in brightness and color between the text and the background of your slides. If the contrast is too low, some people may have difficulty reading the text, especially if they have low vision or color blindness. To make your presentation accessible for people with different visual abilities, you need to use high-contrast colors that are easy to distinguish. Microsoft PowerPoint has built-in capabilities to check the accessibility of your presentation, but you might not know where to find this setting.

To check the overall accessibility of your presentation, enter the following prompt from within the Copilot pane:

"How do I check this document for accessibility?"

Copilot returned the following to me:

"This response isn't based on the presentation: To check the document for accessibility in PowerPoint on a Mac, follow these steps:

- **Open the document in PowerPoint.**
- **Click on the Review tab in the ribbon.**
- **Click on the Check Accessibility button.**
- **The Accessibility Checker task pane will open, and any issues will be listed under the Inspection Results.**
- **Click on an issue to see additional information and suggestions for how to fix it."**

If you were to run that same prompt from a Microsoft Windows–based PC, you would likely see a very similar set of instructions:

"This response isn't based on the presentation: To check a PowerPoint presentation for accessibility, follow these steps:

- **Click on the File tab in the top left corner of the PowerPoint window.**
- **Select Info from the left-hand menu.**
- **Click on the Check for Issues button and select Check Accessibility from the drop-down menu.**
- **The Accessibility Checker pane will open on the right side of the window, displaying any accessibility issues found in the presentation.**
- **Review the issues and follow the provided suggestions to improve the accessibility of your presentation."**

It may seem obvious, but what is very exciting about this capability is that right now, Copilot is providing you with instructions on how to perform certain actions. In the long term, however, it is likely on Microsoft's roadmap[1] for Copilot to also execute those actions. For technical novices, the thought of using AI to navigate the complexity and make technology more accessible is very exciting.

Creating a PowerPoint Presentation from a Microsoft Word Document

Another very powerful capability of Copilot is its ability to create a PowerPoint presentation from an existing document. For this example, I will use an article published by Microsoft titled "Microsoft's Vision for AI in the Enterprise," which can be found at `info.microsoft.com/rs/157-GQE-382/images/Microsoft%20Enterprise%20AI%20white%20paper.pdf`. Feel free, of course, to use a document that is more relevant to your own particular use case.

---

1 `https://www.microsoft.com/en-us/microsoft-365/roadmap?filters=Microsoft%20Copilot%20(Microsoft%20365`

NOTE **Copilot uses Microsoft Graph to include documents as part of your prompt. Therefore, the file must be stored in your OneDrive, a SharePoint site, or a Microsoft Teams team that you have access to.**

I also want to preface that this example requires some time to work properly, so you may want to add this document to your OneDrive, make a few small edits, and then try to share it with others. Even then, you may have to wait a few hours for Copilot to become aware of this file. Behind the scenes, Microsoft Search is indexing your content and making it available via Microsoft Graph.

To get started, create a new PowerPoint presentation and select your preferred template. I am going to stick with the Berlin theme for this example. Next, open the Copilot panel and either select the "Create a presentation. . ." prompt suggestion or type it out yourself. Copilot will either start to suggest recent documents that you have been working on if you used the prompt suggestion, or you can enter a backslash (/) and start typing the name of the document you want Copilot to use. If Copilot cannot find the file you are referencing, it will display an error message, as shown in Figure 10.7, saying, "I can't find that file right now. Check the name of the file, or try again in a bit."

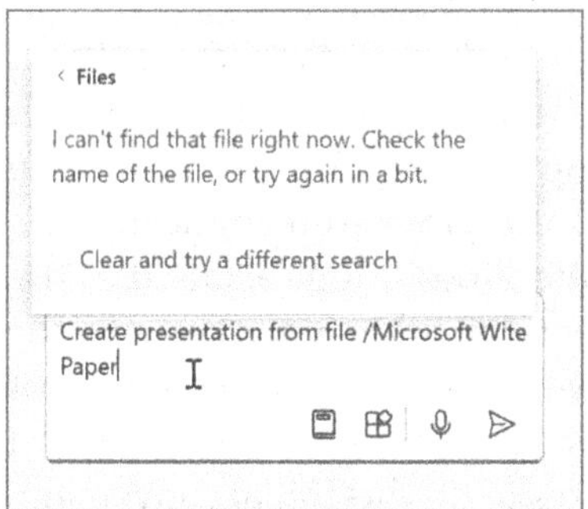

Figure 10.7: Copilot can't find the document

Once enough time has passed for the file to be indexed through Microsoft Graph, which for me was about 10 minutes after I had added the Word document to my OneDrive, Copilot can now find that document. My full prompt looks like this:

"Create presentation from file Microsoft-White-Paper.docx and please ensure that each industry has its own slide."

Notice that I added the last piece about including a slide per industry to guide Copilot on my preferred output for the presentation. Copilot will then analyze the Word document. It will then first create and display an outline and then start the process of creating the PowerPoint presentation. For me, Copilot created a presentation with 17 slides, as shown in Figure 10.8.

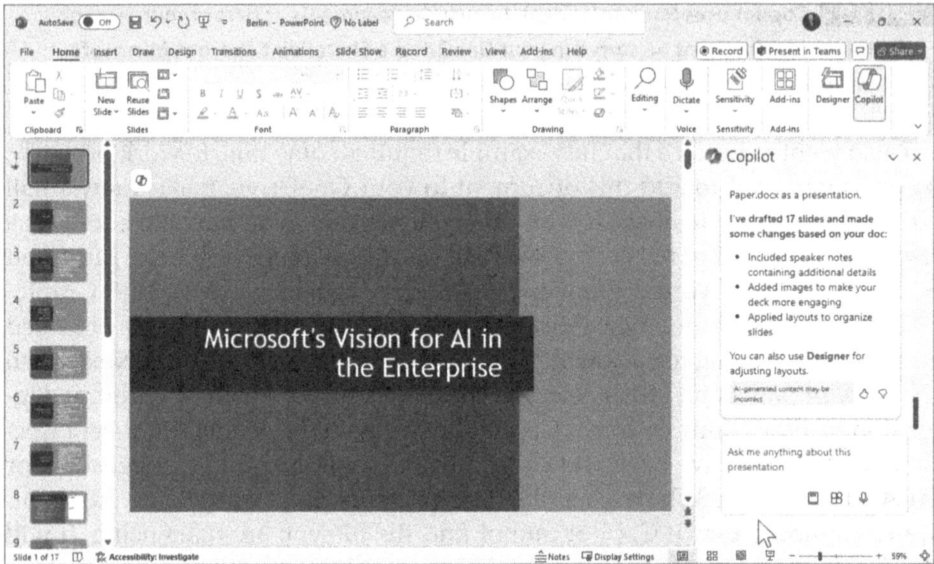

Figure 10.8: Creating a PowerPoint presentation from a Word Document

To set the appropriate level of expectations, the first draft that Copilot creates will likely not be something you can present within an executive setting. However, the process of converting files from one format to another is much more efficient and should give you a very strong starting point. An example of where I have seen this capability be very helpful is when responding to a request for proposal (RFP). The procurement guidelines often dictate that the submission for your response be a Word document, but when you present your proposal to the procurement and project teams, you tend to need a PowerPoint presentation. Copilot's ability to create a PowerPoint presentation from a Word document can certainly help reduce the time it takes to do this initial conversion, and then you can leverage Copilot to further refine your presentation to meet the needs of your intended audience.

Refining Your Presentation with Copilot

Once you've generated a presentation using Copilot, you'll likely want to refine it. The presentation might be too long or include things you didn't want to include. You can use Copilot to help with this as well.

With the presentation you just created from the Microsoft white paper, let's use Copilot to help refine the content. To start, 17 pages might be just a little bit too long for the intended audience. From the Copilot panel, enter the following prompt:

"Can you suggest any ways to consolidate this presentation into fewer slides?"

For me, Copilot provides the following response:

"This response is based on the presentation: Here are some ways to consolidate the presentation into fewer slides:

- **Combine related slides: Some slides contain related information and can be combined into one slide. For example, slides 26–29, which discuss the principles driving Microsoft AI innovation in the enterprise, can be combined into one slide.**
- **Use visual aids: Instead of using multiple slides to convey information, use visual aids such as charts, graphs, and infographics to present the information in a more concise and visually appealing manner.**
- **Remove redundant information: Some slides contain information that is repeated on other slides. Removing this redundant information can help reduce the number of slides.**
- **Summarize information: Instead of presenting all the information in detail, summarize the key points and present them in a more concise manner."**

Using Copilot to Get Feedback on a Presentation

Next, since this presentation is meant to help educate the consumer about Microsoft's vision for AI in the enterprise, it might be helpful to confirm if AI agrees that these topics are covered sufficiently. Again, from the Copilot panel, enter the following prompt:

"What are the key points of the presentation?"

Copilot then provides the following:

"Here's a summary of the deck:

Main ideas:

- **Microsoft's AI vision: Microsoft's vision for AI in the enterprise is to enable every company to transform by bringing AI to every application, business process, and employee**
- **AI transformation: The promise of AI is holistic transformation, with the potential to increase global GDP by 14% by 2030 and have a positive impact on growth, productivity, and job creation**
- **AI in applications: By 2021, 75% of commercial enterprise apps will use AI, with Microsoft providing a comprehensive set of offerings to developers in the enterprise**

- **AI in industries: AI has the potential to transform industries such as financial services, manufacturing, retail, public sector, healthcare, and education**
- **Microsoft's AI principles: Microsoft's AI investments for the enterprise are driven by three core principles: innovation, empowerment, and ethics**

Ask me to help with something else, or for more ideas see the prompt guide below."

Using Copilot to Clarify a Presentation

A benefit of using Copilot to analyze a presentation for key points is that it can help you gain a fresh perspective on your own content. I have found that when I am very close to the content, I may overlook some important details or make assumptions that could confuse or potentially alienate my audience. By using Copilot to extract the main points, you can see how potential readers may view your presentation and identify any gaps or inconsistencies that need to be addressed. This way, you can focus on improving the quality and clarity of the presentation and ensure that it conveys your intended message to your audience. To go one step further, enter the following follow-up prompt to Copilot:

"What parts of this presentation may be confusing for a reader?"

Copilot provides the following:

"This response is based on the presentation: Some parts of the presentation that might be confusing for a reader are:

- **The technical terms and jargon used throughout the presentation, such as 'Cognitive Services,' 'Azure AI platform,' 'Data Science VMs,' 'Knowledge Mining,' etc.**
- **The numerous statistics and data points presented, such as the increase in global GDP, the percentage of commercial enterprise apps that will use AI, the percentage of customers who believe their bank understands their current goals, etc.**
- **The various AI initiatives and programs mentioned, such as 'AI for Accessibility,' 'AI for Humanitarian Action,' 'AI for Earth,' etc.**
- **The numerous products and services mentioned, such as 'PowerApps for Dynamics 365,' 'Azure Bot Service,' 'Cognitive Services Language APIs,' etc."**

It's important to note that you can continue to use that same prompt as you further refine the content within your presentation. That is, as you address Copilot's feedback, you can continue to ask it to analyze your content, much like having your own personal editorial board to confirm that your content is consumable for your intended audience.

Using Copilot to Improve Engagement on a Presentation

Let's try one more prompt to gain additional feedback on your presentation. Enter the following prompt:

"What are some recommendations to make this presentation more engaging? Can you please specify recommendations per slide?"

Copilot will provide a slide-by-slide breakdown of recommendations to improve the presentation and make it more engaging, as shown in Figure 10.9. These suggestions include everything from how to improve graphics to how to better convey key concepts within the presentation. This is an incredibly powerful capability for both those who do not spend a lot of time building presentations and those who sometimes just need a second set of artificial intelligence eyes for coaching.

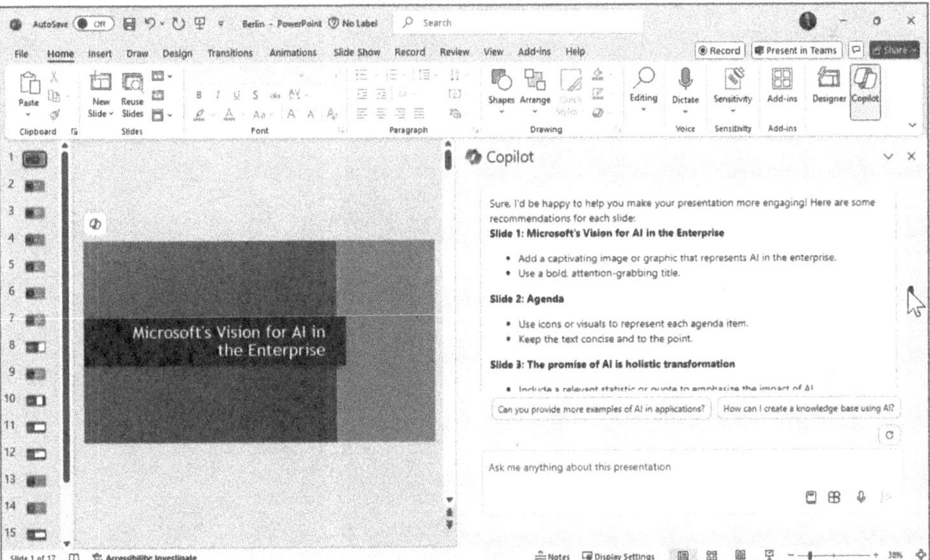

Figure 10.9: Copilot coaching to drive engagement

Conclusion

As you can see, Copilot has the potential to significantly disrupt the way people create and communicate presentations. It can assist you with everything from creating new presentations to serving as an editor, providing slide-by-slide feedback, and navigating PowerPoint's features and functions. Let's next look at how at Copilot works within one of Microsoft's latest collaboration offerings, Loop.

CHAPTER

11

Copilot in Microsoft Loop

Loop is yet another collaboration service that Microsoft has added to their ever-expanding catalog of capabilities delivered as part of their Microsoft 365 service. It was originally announced on November 2, 2021, and became generally available just a little over two years later, on November 15, 2023. This seems to be Microsoft's new strategy of releasing new services early as part of a public preview, allowing customers to test and provide feedback, and then releasing them as generally available once all the necessary enterprise controls and prioritized features have been included.

Let's first see what Loop is and what use cases it fits. We will then explore how Microsoft 365 Copilot can help accelerate your content creation capabilities using this powerful collaboration service.

Loop Overview

At a high level, Loop is a web-based collaboration platform within Microsoft 365, which is also a collaboration platform. What makes Loop appealing is how easy it is to use and the fact that multiple people can work together almost instantly.

Microsoft Loop removes some of the extra work that you might face when creating a Microsoft Teams or SharePoint site, such as setting up a channel strategy, creating metadata, designing workflows, etc. You know, those elements of governance that add a ton of long-term value but create some initial friction when you want to immediately begin working and not have to think about the long-term ramifications of your decision. This is not to say that Loop is collaboration without the governance, but rather that it is positioned as a tool meant for brainstorming, working through logistics for an event or activity, or lightweight management of ideas, tasks, and content in a modern web-based interface. The web interface is reminiscent of the SharePoint modern web experience, making it very easy for novice users to begin working without the need for extensive product training.

Microsoft has positioned Loop to let you directly access a space where you can focus on the business problem you are trying to solve. You can access Loop through `https://loop.cloud.microsoft` or from an iOS or Android app, both available in their respective app stores. Additionally, a very compelling aspect of Loop is that the data is synchronized across all of those various applications and experiences, allowing everyone to collaborate together no matter which channel they are using. Now let's jump in to the main pillars that make up the Loop application.

NOTE Other applications have similar functionality, but the one that feels closest to Loop is Notion (`www.notion.so`), which is also a lightweight collaboration service. Notion's first real commercial release was in March 2018 with their 2.0 version of their growing popular note-taking and task management application. So, one could perhaps infer that some of the inspiration for Loop may have been derived from Notion users within some of the Microsoft product teams.

What's in a Loop?

Microsoft Loop consists of the following three core components that shape the overall user experience:

Loop pages are akin to the modern SharePoint pages in that they are responsive, use a WYSIWYG editor that allows your changes to be seen in real time. They serve the purpose of providing a presentation layer for the various components, links, tasks, and data associated with what you are collaborating on. Loop pages can begin with a few elements and expand to accommodate your ideas. Loop pages can also be shared as a direct link or as an embedded Loop component across the Microsoft 365 apps.

Loop components are content pieces that are synced wherever they are used. Components help you work together in the context of your work—on a Loop page or in a chat, email, meeting, or document. They can be notes, tables, lists, and more; you always have the most updated information in your favorite app, like Microsoft Teams, Outlook, Word, Whiteboard, and the Loop app.

Loop workspaces are the main collaborative spaces that let you and your team view and organize everything relevant to your project. Workspaces make it simple for you to stay updated on what everyone is doing and monitor progress toward common objectives. You can think of a Loop workspace as a container, similar to a SharePoint site collection or a Microsoft Teams team.

Getting Started with Loop

Now that you have an initial grounding in Loop terminology, you might ask yourself where you should begin. Start experimenting with Loop from within the web application by logging in to `https://loop.cloud.microsoft`. As shown in Figure 11.1, the first time you log in to Loop, you will be presented with the "getting started" workspace created by the Microsoft Loop team. They have built a great starter workspace that provides an "art of the possible" view of pages with built-out content. They have also embedded a YouTube video that covers some of the basics of using and navigating Loop. The UI is very friendly and playful, mixing in emoticons while also showing some ways that you can style the Loop experience to help drive better engagement. Simple touches like including a banner image or changing the icon for the pages help make it feel less like a forced tool from IT and more like a consumer product.

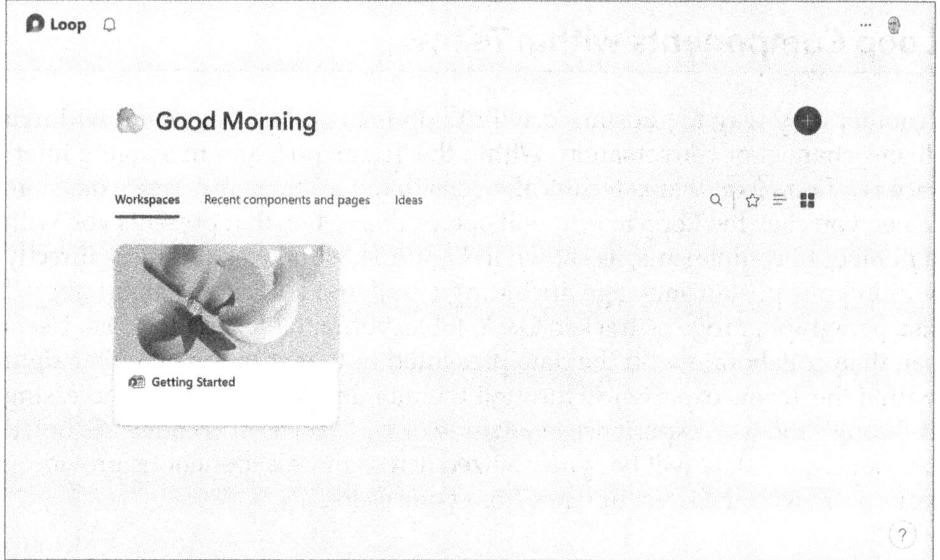

Figure 11.1: Microsoft Loop welcome workspace

Once you have established a few Loop workspaces, the welcome screen when you first log in to Loop will provide you with a lightweight user interface with navigation to the workspaces you are currently part of (see Figure 11.2). By default, it displays the name of the workspace, the banner image, and the last time you accessed it. If you are a member of many workspaces, you can search for the workspace by name.

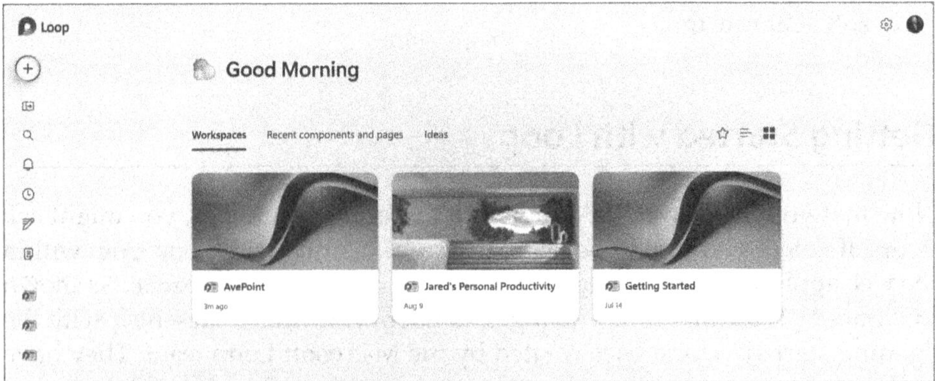

Figure 11.2: Microsoft Loop home workspace

NOTE **Users with only an Office 365 E3, E5, A3, or A5 plan cannot create workspaces. A Microsoft 365 E3, E5, A3, or A5 plan and a Microsoft 365 Extra Features plan is required.**

Loop Components within Teams

Another easy way to get started with Loop is to add a component within a Teams channel or conversation. Within the Teams post and messaging interface is a Loop icon that is technically considered a Teams message extension. When you click the Loop icon, it will open a dialog box that presents you with a number of components, as shown in Figure 11.3. You can add these directly within your post or message, including a bulleted list, checklist, numbered list, paragraph, progress tracker, Q&A, table, voting table, and task list. Users can then collaborate with the data presented in that component either right within the Teams experience, through the mobile apps, or even by accessing it through the web experience at `https://loop.cloud.microsoft`. As noted previously, the data will be synchronized across those experiences, providing your users with the latest updates from your users.

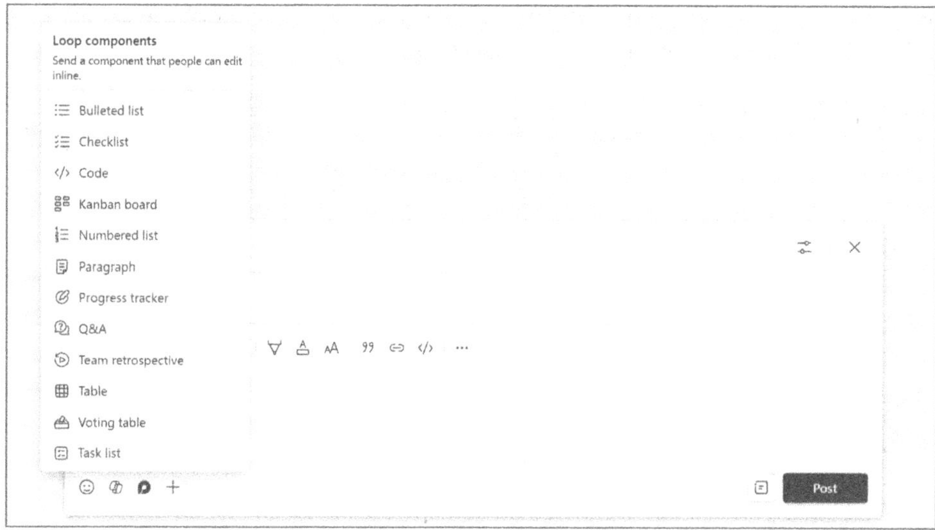

Figure 11.3: Adding a Loop component in Teams

NOTE **Loop components are available to anyone with access to Teams, Outlook, Word Online, Whiteboard, OneNote, SharePoint, OneDrive, the Loop app, and other supported Microsoft applications.**

Creating a Loop Workspace

Now that you've seen the Loop web experience, you are ready to create your first Loop workspace, which we will use to experiment with and to showcase how Microsoft 365 Copilot can further elevate your experience using GenAI. To get started, navigate to the Loop web experience (`https://loop.cloud.microsoft`). From the home screen, click the plus icon in the right-hand corner with the label "Create a new workspace." A dialog box will appear, enabling you to both name your newly created workspace and change its default icon. I titled my new workspace "Copilot Sandbox" and chose the hamburger emoticon to help it stand out. After clicking the Create workspace button, you will be routed to your newly created workspace with an Untitled page in edit mode.

There is a very helpful capability within Loop called "Templates," which includes a mix of components, pages, and content to help get you up and running quickly for lightweight collaboration scenarios. Loop presents a few of these templates at the bottom of the open page, as shown in Figure 11.4. You can also view all available templates by clicking the Template Gallery button located just below those examples. You can browse the interactive template gallery and then click the "Use template" button in the lower-right corner of the dialog box to insert that template within your workspace.

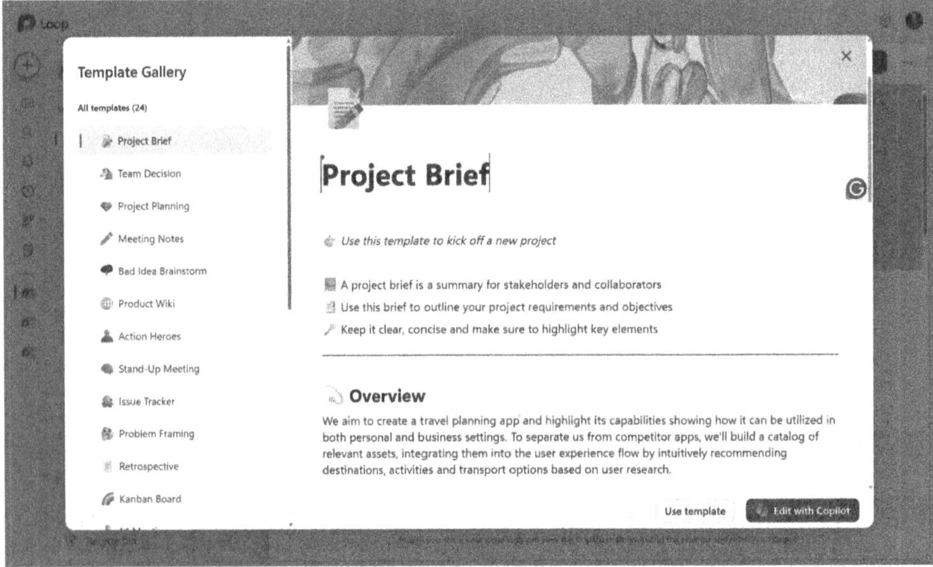

Figure 11.4: Template Gallery

NOTE **A Microsoft 365 E3, E5, A3, or A5 plan and a Microsoft 365 Extra Features plan is required to create a Loop workspace.**

Inviting Others to Collaborate

As mentioned previously, when you first create a Loop workspace, access is restricted to just the creator. However, you can easily grant others access through the Share button in the upper-right corner of your Loop workspace. The sharing options include:

- **workspace level:** You grant read and write access to all components and pages within the workspace, and also the ability to share with others.
- **page level:** You can grant access to individual pages within your workspace. You can use the traditional Microsoft 365 link sharing capability to enable read/write access or restrict it to just read-only for individuals or groups.
- **loop component level:** This behaves similarly to sharing at the page level, but it allows users to not only access but also surface Loop components in other Microsoft 365 experiences, including Teams, Outlook, Whiteboard, and Word.

From a permissions hierarchy perspective, granting access at the workspace level will cascade down to the pages and components within that workspace. A more restrictive way of sharing would be to grant access to only the page or component, which would prohibit the user from accessing any of the other pages or components within that workspace. You might consider going down this path of more restrictive sharing for users who need visibility to in-flight work versus enabling them to be active participants within the full workspace. While I can appreciate fine-grained controls, I believe that, in practice, users who adopt Loop will likely share at the workspace level or provide Edit access by default.

When to Use Loop

As Microsoft continues to invest in Microsoft 365 by creating new features for their existing services and announcing new services nearly every year, one of the biggest challenges organizations face is deciding when to use what. One of my most popular talks in the SharePoint Saturday community back in 2017 was "The Definitive Guide for When to Use What in Office 365." Back then, Skype for Business was still quite prevalent in most organizations, and Microsoft Teams had just entered the market. Microsoft's initial release of Office 365 Groups had also started to generate some additional confusion and governance challenges, as users were not clear about when to create a Group versus request a SharePoint site, and there was a lack of fine-grained access controls for content. Navigating the menu of choices between Office 365 Groups, OneDrive for Business, Planner, SharePoint, Teams, Yammer, etc. was many times more challenging than the technical work needed to enable those services.

While many folks, including me, tend to "geek out" over all the amazing bells and whistles included in the latest Microsoft 365 releases, average users are much more focused on how they can leverage the technology to get their jobs done more efficiently. Whether you are a consultant or working for an organization where you are responsible for managing or driving adoption of these collaboration capabilities, the trick is being able to help tie business use cases to product features. For example, when I was working with a corporate communications team that used to email copies of executive speeches and then reconciled all the feedback from the various editors, I introduced them to the document coauthoring feature in SharePoint Online. I showed them how they could just email a copy of a link and enable real-time collaboration from a central storage location. This helped them save a ton of time and eliminated a very unpleasant job while freeing them up to focus on other tasks of higher value or greater impact.

Positioning Loop in Your Organization

When it comes to positioning Microsoft Loop with all the other collaboration features in Microsoft 365, it is important to note that there will be scenarios where Loop is leveraged in addition to other collaboration capabilities such as Microsoft Teams. Additionally, there will be scenarios where it might make sense to use Loop instead of one of those services, due to the business use case or the overall outcome that you are trying to drive.

Use Cases for Loop

There are a number of use cases to consider as you think through positioning Loop within your own organization. Here are a few examples:

Personal Productivity Loop can be a real game changer from a personal productivity perspective. One of the biggest challenges many business professionals face is managing all the various random tasks that are either self-assigned or assigned by others. Microsoft's productivity offerings include multiple tools that perform similar functions, making it tricky to decide where to start. You may have attempted to become more diligent taking notes and capturing tasks in OneNote, but perhaps that falls off either due to lack of habit forming or to the fact that the user interface is a bit clunky, and trying to navigate various OneNote notebooks across multiple teams can be quite cumbersome. I am not sure exactly the root cause, but I believe OneNote does not play nicely with individuals who switch across multiple devices and accounts. The benefit of Loop over OneNote is that it brings together many features in a flexible canvas experience without carrying the legacy of OneNote, with multiple client application versions, all of which had different degrees of synchronization issues, usability issues, or even compatibility challenges.

Task Management Task management has been a staple of Microsoft's collaboration offerings, such as Outlook, SharePoint, To Do, Planner, etc. The biggest gap when using any of these services to manage tasks is that there is no single pane of glass to view everything you are working on across all of the various M365 services. I have seen individuals start with one or two of these services and then slowly abandon them when managing tasks becomes a full-time task in itself. They do their best to start creating tasks with due dates, but things shift, or they forget about the task altogether and revert to their previous methods of work management.

One could argue that it is not the technology that is failing but rather that the individuals have not committed to the new habits of maintaining information in this new digital resource. However, I believe that user experience also heavily influences adoption. It also helps when an application supports natural ways of working. Loop's lightweight nature makes it quite easy to create an action item tracking component to assign tasks. This creates transparency for where things stand, who has assigned tasks, and provides a simple UI to update the status of your assigned task across multiple experiences.

Comparing Loop to Planner and To Do Loop is not the first application Microsoft has introduced to help people manage their tasks. More recently, Microsoft has provided Planner or To Do. To Do is great for lightweight task management, but it is difficult to include all the necessary context that goes along with the request. For example, you could have a "Client Proposal" task with a due date, but then it is not connected to any of the assets that go along with that particular task. You may find yourself spending a lot of time flipping back between Teams, SharePoint, OneDrive, or other services, which could dissuade you from wanting to create tasks given how much setup work it takes.

I find that the sweet spot for To Do is the management of lightweight tasks, such as reminding myself to follow up with someone or anything that is recurring in nature. You should consider using To Do for tasks that might have previously been written on sticky notes scattered around your workstation or attached to your monitor, which are meant to keep you on task but are not intended for managing others' work.

Planner is similar to To Do but typically works much better when it is integrated within a Microsoft Teams team. When users have that one collaboration space using Loop that includes messages, documents, and Planner's Kanban board experience, it helps keep everyone organized and focused on driving initiatives forward. Again, the benefit of Loop is that you do not need all of the backend infrastructure that comes with provisioning a new team to get up and running.

Daily Work When it comes to daily work, Loop makes it simple to create your own personal workspace that is available across multiple devices, including Mac, Windows, and iOS. It is like having a personal scrapbook where you can add clippings to documents or generate tables to help further organize your data within a responsive format.

I recommend that you inventory the work you perform and then build a small workspace for productivity. Here is an example of how you might consider organizing your Loop workspace to accommodate various types of work and tasks to track:

- **Accomplishments page:** A running tab of highlights that have occurred throughout the year, including any feedback from customers or colleagues. This can be used to help with your annual performance review because you're capturing your accomplishments and can leverage Copilot to help summarize the page to generate the information to enter in to whatever system your organization uses for managing annual performance.

- **Brainstorming page:** A digital whiteboard where you keep new ideas. This is also a great page for you to experiment with Copilot and test your prompt engineering skills.
- **My Tasks page:** A place to manage the various work items that have been assigned to you. As noted, there may be some duplicative capabilities with Microsoft's other task management solutions such as Planner and To Do. However, using Loop for task management can provide a richer user experience by allowing you to easily include additional context, such as embedded media (images and video), links, tables, checklists, etc.

Managing Conversations Another great use case for Loop is managing conversations with your manager or direct reports. Loop has a premade 1:1 meeting template with preconfigured components such as Meeting Agenda, Meeting Minutes, and a Feedback component to track the effectiveness of your meeting.

If you have direct reports, consider creating a Loop page for each of them. The page can be used to drive your regularly scheduled check-ins. By sharing the page with your direct reports, you enable them to refer back to previous conversations, add items to the agenda, and come to a conversation prepared to be productive.

Microsoft 365 Copilot in Loop

Now that you have had a primer on Microsoft Loop, let's start to demonstrate how Copilot makes this lightweight collaboration solution even better. To get started, go to the Loop home screen from your web browser (`https://loop.cloud.microsoft`) and click on the + button in the upper-right corner, as shown in Figure 11.5, to open the "Create a new workspace" dialog box. Name your new workspace **Copilot Brainstorm**, and then press the Continue button to advance to the next screen.

Microsoft Graph, as discussed in Chapter 2, "Introduction to Microsoft 365 Copilot," makes Copilot an incredibly powerful tool due to its understanding of you and the context of your daily work, including meetings, chats, and files. The "Add files to your workspace" screen, shown in Figure 11.6, is an example of the type of personalization capabilities that can be delivered via the information that Copilot has available within Microsoft Graph. For example, assume you are preparing your organization for a Copilot implementation and have meetings and documents with the word "Copilot" in the filename or contents. Copilot will start to suggest including those documents that it finds to your Loop workspace. Select a few documents that you would like to include, and then click the "Create workspace" button.

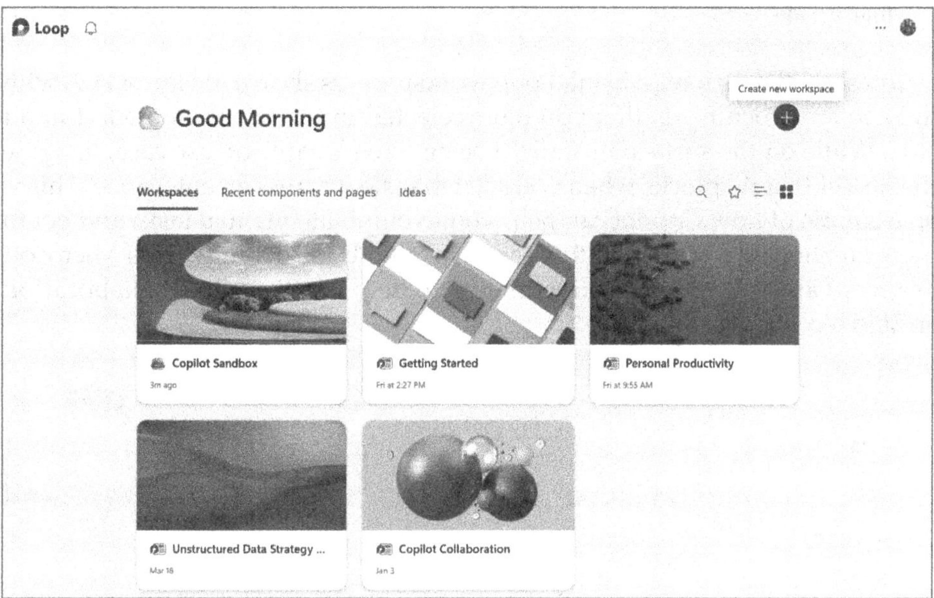

Figure 11.5: Creating a new Loop workspace

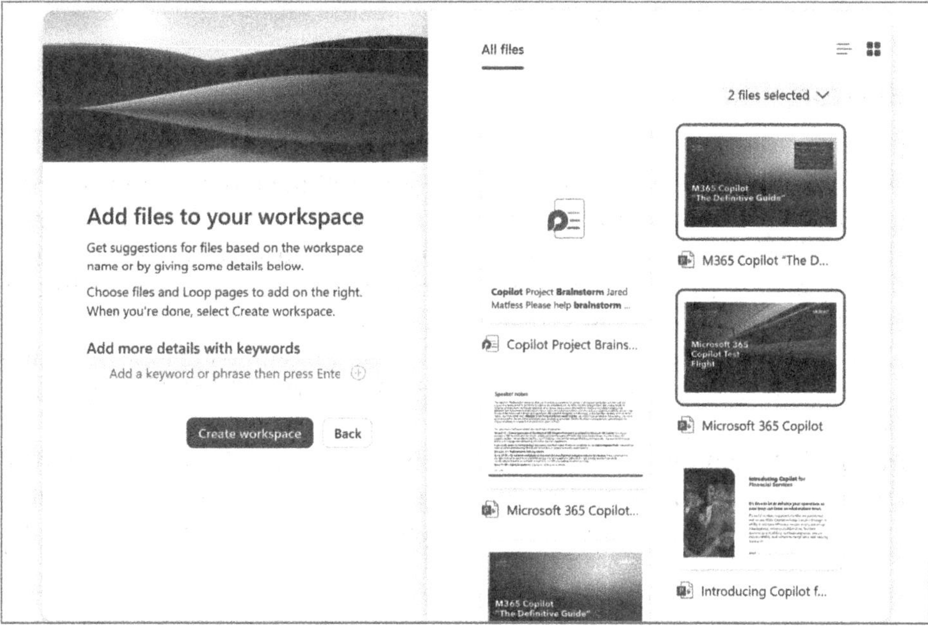

Figure 11.6: Adding files to your workspace

NOTE **Adding documents to a Loop workspace does not move them from their current location or change any existing permissions. They remain in their existing Microsoft Teams or SharePoint locations, with Loop providing a link or embedding it within a page.**

You should now have a blank Loop workspace, as shown in Figure 11.7, with links to any documents that you have selected in the panel on the left-hand side. While on the surface this might seem like a simplistic use case, imagine the power that it unlocks when you start to scale it across an enterprise. This is an example of how Copilot can help you to eliminate manual tasks and get to more creative work faster. In this case, it would be searching across Microsoft Teams to assemble relevant documents to help enable online collaboration around a particular topic.

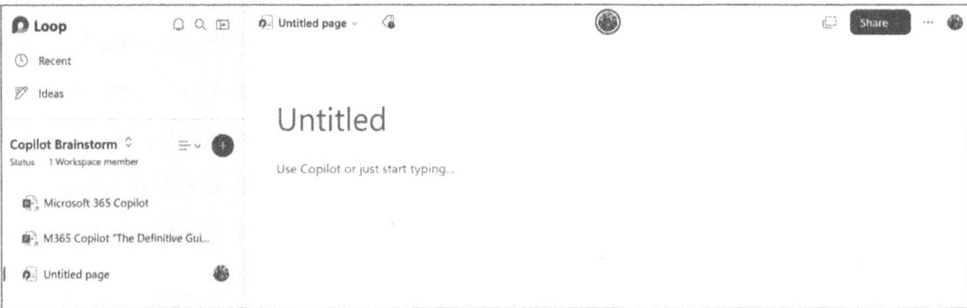

Figure 11.7: Initial Loop workspace

Brainstorming with Copilot

Let's continue to build this workspace for the use case of planning your Copilot implementation. First, name your Loop page something more descriptive than Untitled, such as **Copilot Project Brainstorm**, and then press Enter to return to the body of your Loop page. Optionally, you can add an icon and a cover photo to help set a more creative tone for your workspace. Feel free to get creative or stick with a "flight theme," as shown in Figure 11.8.

Next, type a backslash (/) to bring up the insert menu, which includes two Copilot actions, "Draft page content" and "Summarize page," as shown in Figure 11.9.

In this first example, we will have Copilot suggest activities, milestones, and deliverables for your own Copilot implementation project. The intent is to show how you can use Copilot to help with initial brainstorming around a particular topic, project, activity, etc. Select "Draft page content" and enter the following prompt:

"Please help brainstorm all the various workstreams that would be part of a large enterprise transformation for a Microsoft 365 Copilot rollout. Some examples include Project Management, Change Management, Governance, and Extensibility. Please include potential activities, milestones, and project deliverables as sub bullets under each workstream."

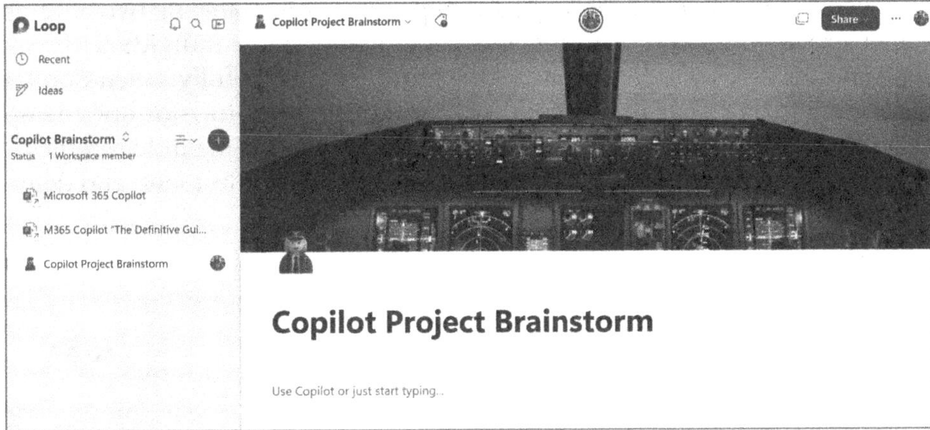

Figure 11.8: Copilot Project Brainstorm

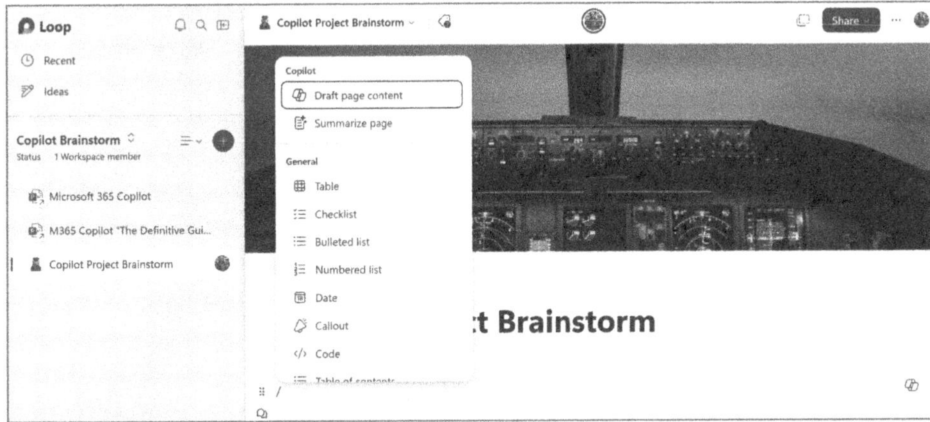

Figure 11.9: Copilot actions in Loop

After entering the prompt, click the paper arrow icon, shown in Figure 11.10, and wait for Copilot to finish evaluating your prompt, recent documents, etc. to begin creating a text summary within your Loop page.

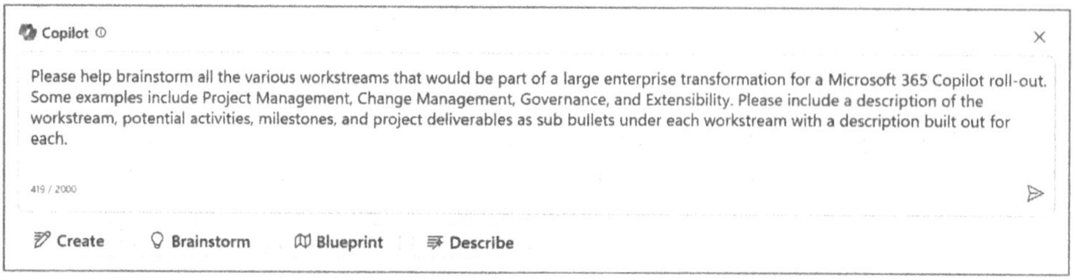

Copilot

Please help brainstorm all the various workstreams that would be part of a large enterprise transformation for a Microsoft 365 Copilot roll-out. Some examples include Project Management, Change Management, Governance, and Extensibility. Please include a description of the workstream, potential activities, milestones, and project deliverables as sub bullets under each workstream with a description built out for each.

419 / 2000

Create Brainstorm Blueprint Describe

Figure 11.10: Copilot Brainstorm prompt

Remember, the challenge and opportunity with GenAI is that no two outputs will be exactly the same, as inputs will differ based on the individual accessing it and the data included as part of the grounding. Hopefully, when Copilot is done analyzing your prompt and preparing its output to your open Loop page, it will somewhat resemble the output produced for me in Figure 11.11, highlighting each project phase and outlining activities, milestones, and deliverables in bullet points.

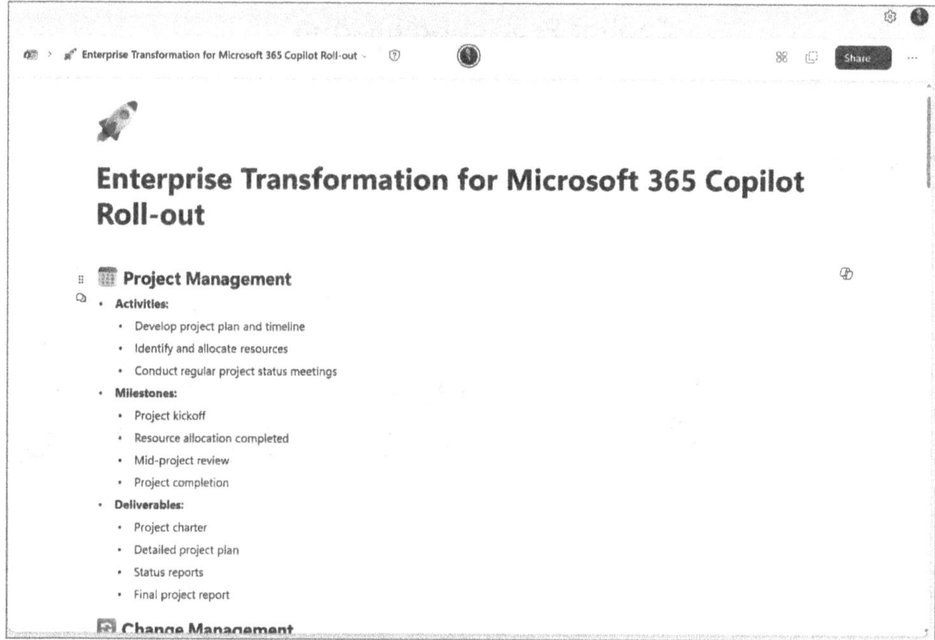

Figure 11.11: Copilot Brainstorm prompt output

The following is another example prompt:

"Please help brainstorm all the various workstreams that would be part of a large enterprise transformation for a Microsoft 365 Copilot rollout. Some examples include Project Management, Change Management, Governance, and Extensibility. Also propose workstreams that I have not included. For each workstream, include potential activities, milestones, and project deliverables for each."

That specific callout to provide workstreams that I have not included is what grants Copilot additional permission to get creative with its output. This is a great example of why it is important to think through the instructions you provide Copilot and to ensure that you are explicitly granting it permission to be creative with its output.

Remember that collaborating with Copilot does not have to be a "one and done" exercise. Since we know there will likely be more than four project workstreams for your Copilot implementation, let's have Copilot suggest some additional project workstreams. From the Loop page canvas, click on an open area of the canvas, ideally below the text content that was produced by Copilot, type a forward slash (/), and select the "Draft page content" action, and then enter the following prompt: *"Suggest up to four additional workstreams that I did not consider."* Notice that you did not need to restate the existing project workstreams, because Copilot already has access to the context of its previous output.

When Copilot finishes providing suggestions, it should show an output similar to Figure 11.12, including the addition of four new workstreams to the Loop page: Data Migration, Security, Infrastructure, and User Support, in my example. You could then further format the two outputs with a prompt such as: *"Please combine the two sets of output with workstreams numbered from 1 to 8."* Again, Copilot uses the conversation and page context to predict what you are looking to accomplish—combining the two text sections in to a single output.

This example of using Copilot to help brainstorm the different activities, milestones, and project deliverables is just the tip of the iceberg of what you can do. Below the last workstream, bring up the "Draft with Copilot" action again and this time enter the following prompt: *"Suggest some notable security risks that we should consider."* Again, it has the context that you are referring to a Copilot implementation project and that it also has called out Security as being a project workstream. Your output should look similar to Figure 11.13. Note that there are a few risks that probably are not applicable to Copilot specifically, such as the one referring to "weak passwords," which again reinforces the need for humans to review Copilot's output for accuracy and relevancy.

Based on the information provided in the page content, here are four additional workstreams that could be considered for a Microsoft 365 Copilot roll-out:

1. **Data Migration**: This workstream involves the migration of data from the enterprise's existing systems to the Microsoft 365 Copilot solution.
   - Activities: Identify data to be migrated; develop data migration plan; perform data migration; validate migrated data.
   - Milestones: Data migration plan approved, data migration completed, data validation completed.
   - Deliverables: Data migration plan, migrated data, data validation report.
2. **Security**: This workstream involves ensuring that the Microsoft 365 Copilot solution is secure and that enterprise data is protected.
   - Activities: Conduct security risk assessment; develop security plan; implement security measures; monitor security.
   - Milestones: Security risk assessment completed, security plan approved, security measures implemented.
   - Deliverables: Security risk assessment report, security plan, security measures.
3. **Infrastructure**: This workstream involves the setup and configuration of the infrastructure required to support the Microsoft 365 Copilot solution.
   - Activities: Identify infrastructure requirements; develop infrastructure plan; procure and set up infrastructure; test and validate infrastructure.
   - Milestones: Infrastructure requirements identified, infrastructure plan approved, infrastructure set up and validated.
   - Deliverables: Infrastructure requirements specification, infrastructure plan, infrastructure.
4. **User Support**: This workstream involves the provision of support to users of the Microsoft 365 Copilot solution, to ensure that they are able to use it effectively.
   - Activities: Develop user support plan; establish user support team; provide user support; monitor and improve user support.
   - Milestones: User support plan approved, user support team established, user support provided.
   - Deliverables: User support plan, user support team, user support reports.

Figure 11.12: Additional project workstreams

Some notable security risks to consider when implementing a large-scale enterprise transformation, such as a Microsoft 365 Copilot roll-out, are:

- The risk of unauthorized access to sensitive data and information
- The risk of data breaches or information leaks
- The risk of non-compliance with data protection regulations
- The risk of vulnerabilities in the software or infrastructure being exploited by cybercriminals
- The risk of insider threats from employees with access to sensitive data
- The risk of inadequate security measures being implemented, leading to vulnerabilities
- The risk of security breaches due to human error, such as weak passwords or falling for phishing scams.

To mitigate these risks, it is important to conduct a thorough security risk assessment, develop and implement a comprehensive security plan, and continuously monitor and improve security measures.

Figure 11.13: Notable security risks

Unlocking Insights with Copilot

While content creation tends to be the major selling point for Microsoft 365 Copilot, I am a very big fan of how it can be used to summarize and extract key points from within Loop pages. For this next example, create a new Loop page in your workspace and name it **Microsoft Earnings**. Next, navigate to the following URL, a press release for Microsoft's FY23 Q2 earnings: `www.microsoft.com/en-us/Investor/earnings/FY-2023-Q2/press-release-webcast`. Copy and paste the content of that website in to your "Microsoft Earnings" Loop page. Your Loop page should look similar to Figure 11.14, including the full text of the press release along with the accompanying tables and graphs.

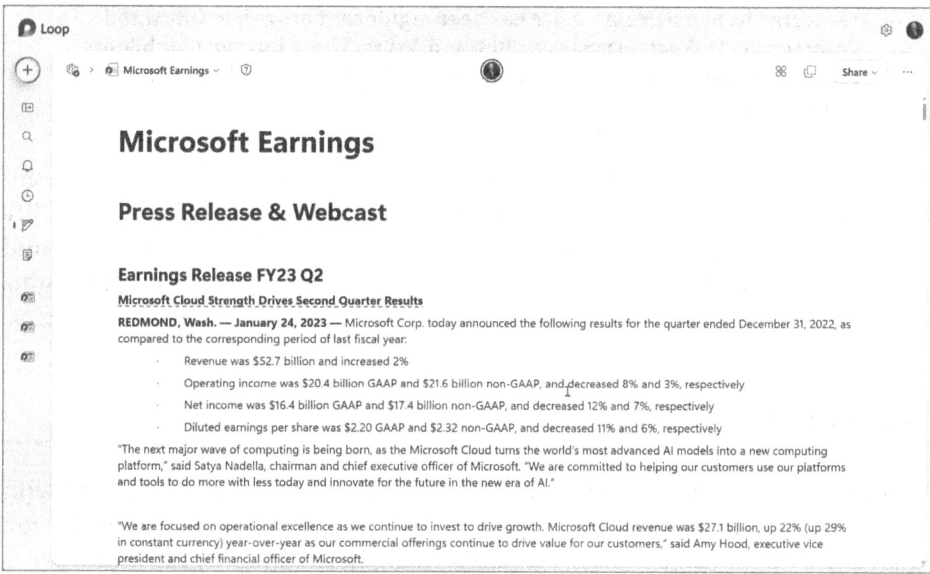

Figure 11.14: Microsoft earnings

Next, click within the body and enter a forward slash (/) to bring up a menu. This time, click the "Summarize page" button and enter the following prompt: *"Summarize Microsoft's earnings."* This should produce a much smaller bulleted list of specific callouts from that earnings report.

You can also ask additional questions, such as *"Which business area had the least amount of growth?"* Copilot produced the following response to my prompt:

"According to the given context, among Microsoft's main business areas, the area with the least amount of growth during Q2 FY23 was More Personal Computing, which had a revenue of $14.2 billion and decreased 19% compared to the corresponding period of the last fiscal year."

Next, let's start to push Copilot to perform additional analysis of the earnings report. Bring up the "Draft with Copilot" action again, and this time enter the following prompt: *"Why might someone invest in Microsoft?"* When Copilot finishes, it provides the following analysis of the earnings report on the Loop page:

"Based on the earnings report, someone might make an investment in Microsoft due to several reasons. One of these reasons is the growth of Microsoft Cloud, as stated by Satya Nadella, chairman and chief executive officer of Microsoft. Microsoft Cloud revenue was $27.1 billion, up 22% (up 29% in constant currency) year-over-year. This growth is driven by their commercial offerings and continues to create value for their customers. Another reason is the growth in the Productivity and Business Processes and Intelligent Cloud segments, which increased by 7% and 18%

respectively. In particular, there has been significant growth in Office 365 Commercial, LinkedIn, Dynamics 365, and Azure. These business highlights indicate that Microsoft is performing well in these areas, which may be attractive to investors."

This is a great example of how Copilot can help go through lengthy and complicated content and highlight key insights. You can use this same capability to analyze your content to ensure that it is readable and understandable, and to have a second set of "artificial eyes" provide recommendations and insights for how to ensure that your content is communicating your intended messages.

Conclusion

Microsoft Loop's simplified user experience makes it easy to get started with collaborating with others. By embedding the Copilot experience within it, you can tap in to the power of GenAI to help create new content, brainstorm ideas with teammates, or to summarize key points from within your Loop pages.

CHAPTER

12

Transforming Text with Copilot in Microsoft Word

Often considered the cornerstone of the Microsoft Office suite, Word has been a leading word processing application for decades. Its popularity stems from its versatility as an application that can seamlessly transition between business, personal, and academic domains. Microsoft Word is used for everything from drafting blog posts to capturing old family recipes, documenting essential research findings, formalizing business contracts, and telling stories. For many, it is one of the first applications they learn how to use and becomes a staple in their transition from student to business professional.

This chapter discusses how to integrate Copilot into your workflow in Microsoft Word. We will cover how to use Copilot to help ideate around a particular topic and then iterate on your draft until it's ready to move forward. We will walk through using Copilot to help create new content from existing content by incorporating reference documents as part of your prompt. Next, we'll explore how Copilot can act as your own personal editor, leveraging its grasp on language to suggest edits, rewrites, or recommendations for tone, clarity, and readability. Finally, we will look at using Copilot to quickly build an understanding of a document through natural language.

Getting Started with Copilot in Word

The Copilot experience in Microsoft Word is perhaps one of the most intuitive when it comes to partnering with an AI assistant. It all starts when you open Microsoft Word to create a new document. You are presented with a blank sheet of digital paper, as shown in Figure 12.1, and the Copilot dialog box is ready to assist you with creating your document. Helping users go from a blank sheet of digital paper to an initial draft of content is a key selling point of Copilot, but it requires a shift in mindset—from being the sole author of your content to becoming an editor of what AI produces.

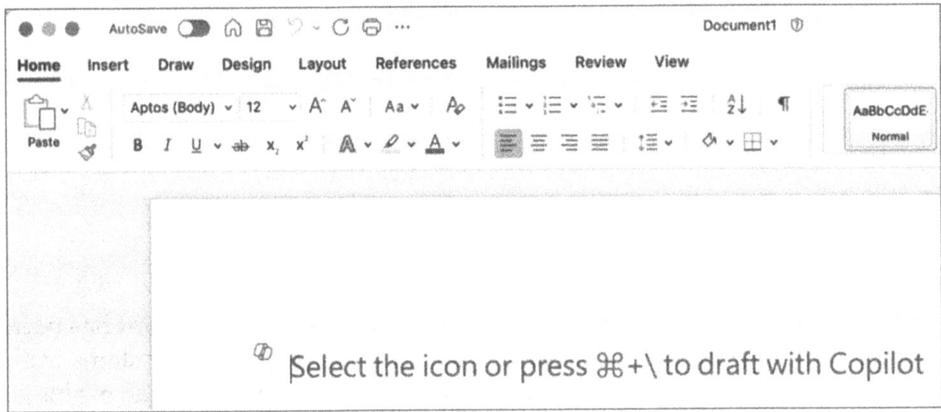

Figure 12.1: A blank Word document

Let's put theory into practice and use Copilot to help generate some content to serve as a starting point for a research paper on AI and its impacts on the manufacturing industry. Press Command + \ on a Mac or Ctrl + \ on a Windows computer to bring up the draft with the Copilot dialog box, as shown in Figure 12.2, and then enter the following prompt:

"As an industry advisor, please draft a white paper explaining the impact of AI on the manufacturing industry. Provide both quantitative and qualitative impacts and highlight a couple of use cases. Cite all sources you use at the end using APA style. Please do not exceed 1,000 words."

Notice for this prompt, we followed the R-T-F pattern, as outlined in Chapter 3,"An Introduction to Prompt Engineering," by setting the persona as an industry advisor, providing the context of AI's impact on the manufacturing industry, and being prescriptive about the required format by setting an expectation of output limited to 1,000 words and requiring APA-style citations for sources. Copilot will begin drafting your white paper with these specific instructions. As shown in Figure 12.3, it creates an initial draft with an opening paragraph and then begins to develop the content. In this example, Copilot's initial draft came in at 962 words, perfectly situated under the 1,000 word limit I had provided.

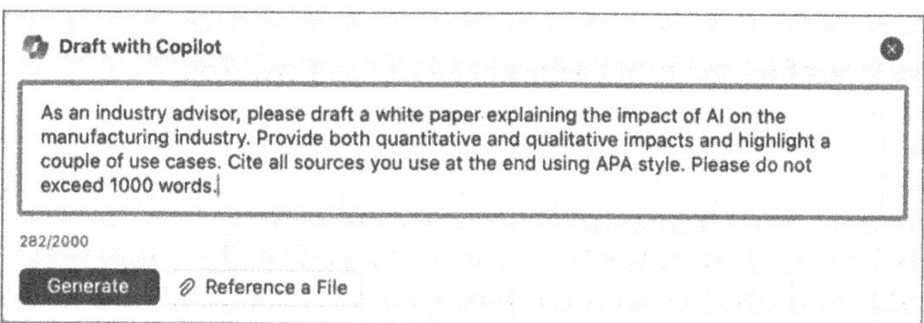

Figure 12.2: The Draft with Copilot dialog box

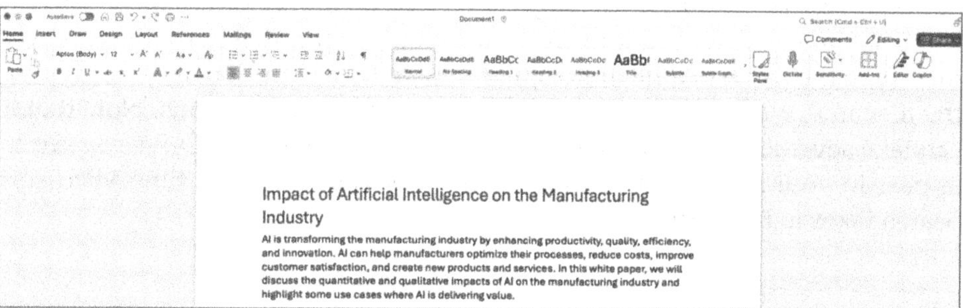

Figure 12.3: Creating your draft with Copilot

Once Copilot has created the initial draft of the content you requested, you can begin reviewing it to decide how to proceed. Sometimes, you might only make minor edits to what has been produced. Other times, you may find glaring holes or perhaps sections that are not relevant or not what you intend to include in your draft. You may choose to start this process over with a modified prompt that includes additional specificity or perhaps a different prompting technique, as outlined in Chapter 3.

Using Reference Documents to Enhance Copilot Results

As we discussed previously, the more information you provide AI services like Copilot, the better they will predict your desired output. An additional approach to using Copilot in Microsoft Word to get closer to your desired output is to include within your prompt a specific file that can be used as an example. This reference file can contain content you want Copilot to consider as part of its response or, alternatively, reflect a specific writing tone, style, or format required for your draft.

TIP Copilot can only locate files stored in Teams, SharePoint, or OneDrive. Additionally, these reference files must be in Word, PowerPoint, or PDF format.

Using the same prompt as before, let's try selecting the "Reference a file" option and adding up to three reference files to the prompt. This approach will source the AI-generated draft from the referenced documents, rather than sourcing additional material from your organizational graph or the Internet.

You will be presented with a list of recently accessed documents. Figure 12.4 shows the documents we were presented with, but keep in mind that this is a personalized list—Copilot will suggest files based on your individual activity. If the document you need appears here, simply select it. Alternatively, select the "Type the name of a file for Copilot to work from" option and start typing the filename, which will refresh the suggested list of documents. Note that it can take several minutes for newly added SharePoint or OneDrive content to appear in your suggested documents list, depending on the time Microsoft Search takes to index the new content.

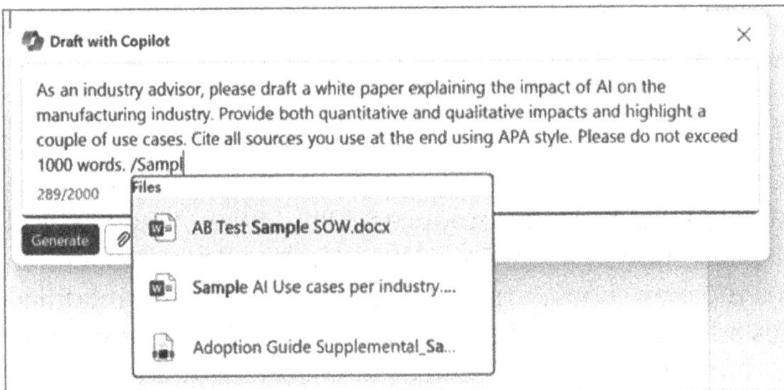

Figure 12.4: Including reference files in your prompt

This feature is beneficial when you already have the fundamental points captured in another file but need Copilot to flesh out the argument and generate the content in the desired format and tone. Also, using this feature, documents with one purpose and format can be transformed into very different content targeted for an entirely different audience. For example, system release notes from a SaaS vendor can be transformed into standard operating procedures, FAQs, staff blog posts, or user acceptance tests.

Rewriting with Copilot

If the Copilot output does not meet your needs, there are a couple of options to address this. The first is to discard both the prompt and the output and rewrite the text to better suit the intended audience or idea you are trying to convey. Refer to Chapter 3 to consider whether there are additional elements you can add to your prompt to get a more relevant or accurate output.

Another option is to have Copilot refine your text until it better meets your needs or until you decide to take over and manually finalize the edits. Using the chat window, as shown in Figure 12.5, you can insert additional prompts to refine that first draft. For example, you might want the draft to include a certain relevant point, or you may want to change the tone or the style of the generated output. Copilot will rework the draft in response to your prompt suggestions. You can continue to refine the text until you have a solid first draft that you are happy to finalize manually, remembering to keep the "human in the loop" on any AI-generated output.

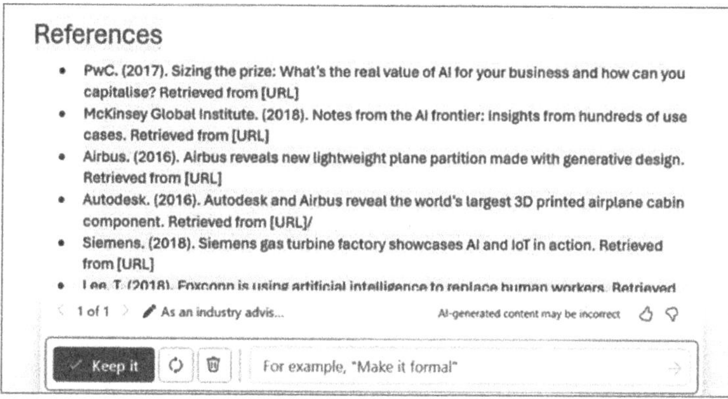

Figure 12.5: Refining your draft

An alternative approach is to use Copilot to do more targeted text edits. In this case, you can identify a paragraph that you want to rework or reword rather than the entire text. Highlight the paragraph, as shown in Figure 12.6, and select the Copilot icon to the right to be presented with editing options. You can decide whether to enter a new prompt for that specific highlighted text, to prompt Copilot to generate an alternative paragraph, or to convert the text to a table.

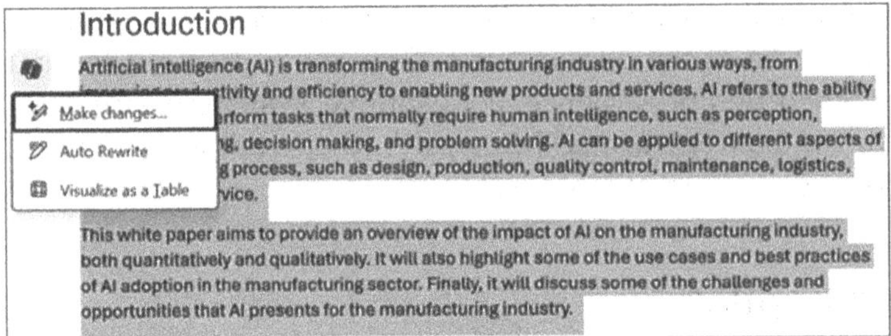

Figure 12.6: Refining a section of your draft

To refine the text via a new prompt, select "Make changes" and enter your instructions. For example, you could add, *"Include a reference to the disruptive force that AI is having in the manufacturing industry."* Copilot will regenerate the selected text to incorporate your suggested prompt and again present you with the option to retain, refine, or discard the generated text. The text is presented alongside the original, enabling a quick comparison of the two versions as shown in Figure 12.7.

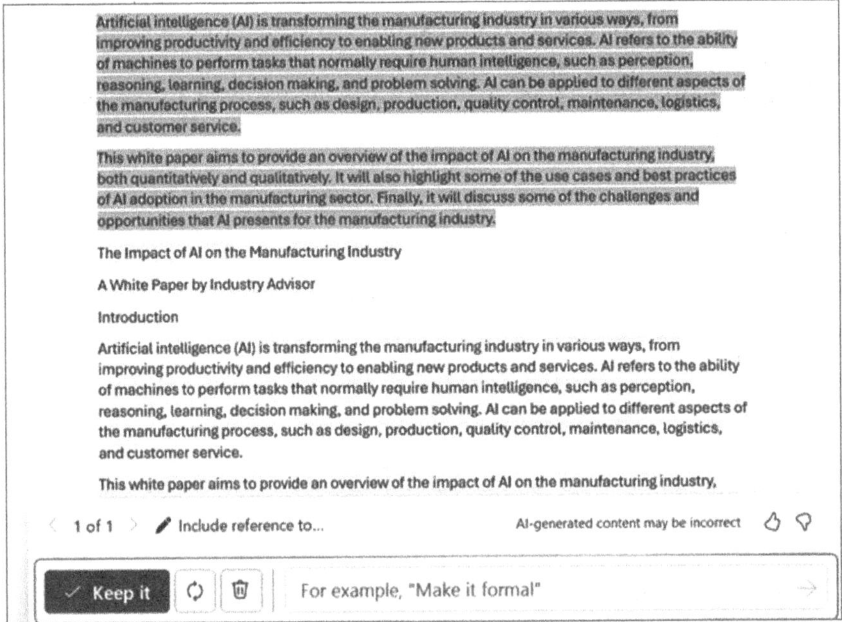

Figure 12.7: Comparing the two versions of a document

Another targeted refinement is to use the "Auto Rewrite" feature. Again, start by highlighting the text you want to change and select the "Auto Rewrite" option. This option works similarly to a thesaurus, suggesting alternative wording or phrasing without changing the essence of the text. It's a valuable tool to refine your writing, as it can elevate your written text or suggest alternative phrasing that adds variety and interest to your writing. The proposed rewrite does not overwrite your original text but appears below it, allowing you to choose whether to keep or discard it.

The third way to refine the text is to select the "Visualize as a Table" option, which quickly transforms a paragraph into a table format for more visual impact and clarity, as shown in Figure 12.8. Copilot analyzes the text, summarizes it, determines the appropriate column headers, and breaks out the content into its respective columns, resulting in a well-formatted table.

A target market can be defined by several characteristics, including:

- Demographics (age, gender, income, education, etc.)
- Psychographics (values, interests, lifestyle, etc.)
- Geographic location (urban, rural, country, zip code, etc.)
- Buying behavior (in-store, online, thrift, etc.)

Category	Examples
Demographics	age, gender, income, education
Psychographics	values, interests, lifestyle
Geographic location	urban, rural, country, zip code
Buying behavior	in-store, online, thrift

Visualize as a table 1 of 1 AI-generated content may be incorrect

Keep it Add more details for Copilot to generate

Figure 12.8: Visualizing text as a table

An alternative way to tap into Copilot's advanced editing capabilities is through the ribbon's Home tab, as shown in Figure 12.9. Select the Copilot icon and then select Ask from within the chat window. From here, you can ask Copilot to make suggestions to improve or rewrite your text, or you can chat with Copilot to refine the text according to your specific instructions, as described previously.

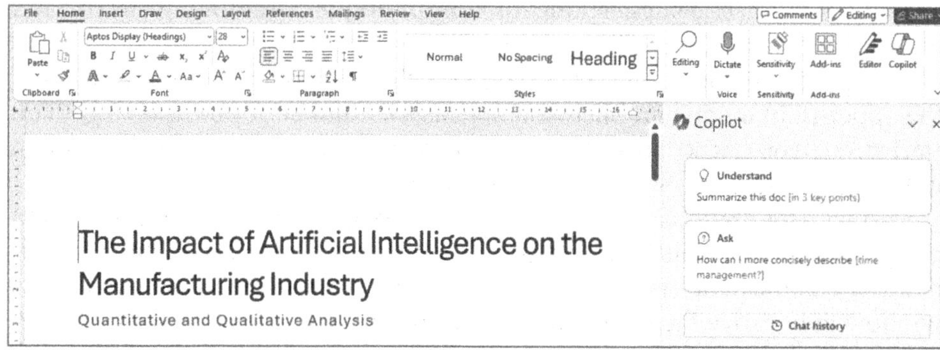

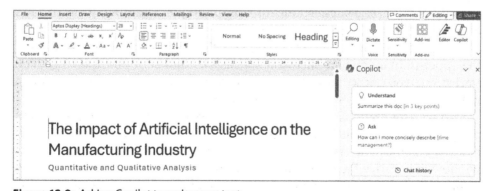

Figure 12.9: Asking Copilot to revise your text

You now have a draft you can work with, but perhaps you feel something is missing. Once you have text in your Word document, a new option, "Inspire me," appears, as shown in Figure 12.10. This is a great way to tap into the creative potential of Copilot. Based on the text you already composed, which can be as little as a heading, Copilot will generate additional related content, building upon your ideas and even suggesting new ones. This is handy if you hit the dreaded writer's block and are unsure what else to write. Again, the suggested text doesn't overwrite your original text but appears below it. You can choose to keep it, refine it, or discard it.

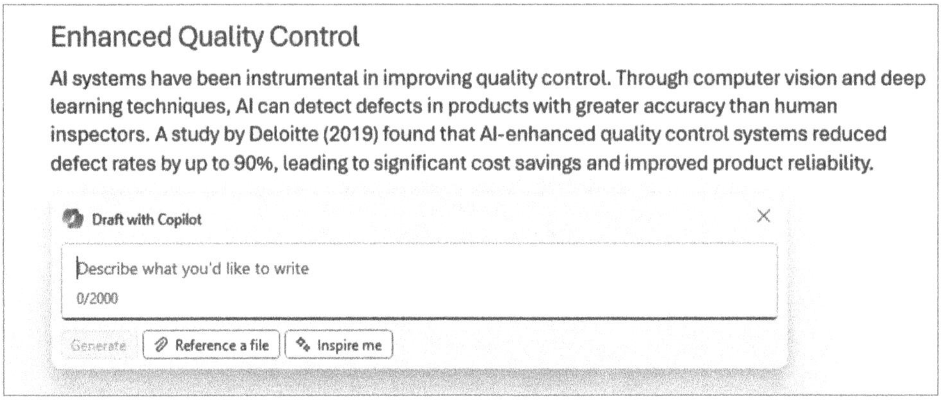

Enhanced Quality Control

AI systems have been instrumental in improving quality control. Through computer vision and deep learning techniques, AI can detect defects in products with greater accuracy than human inspectors. A study by Deloitte (2019) found that AI-enhanced quality control systems reduced defect rates by up to 90%, leading to significant cost savings and improved product reliability.

Draft with Copilot

Describe what you'd like to write

0/2000

Generate | Reference a file | Inspire me

Figure 12.10: Having Copilot inspire you

Copilot's Document Analysis Capability

In addition to creating content, Copilot can help you understand a document by answering natural language questions about its content. This document analysis feature offers considerable time savings for individuals who need to review and digest lengthy text. It can also help improve the quality of your documents by providing editor-like suggestions for simplifying text, removing jargon, and improving overall readability.

Using the document created earlier, launch the Copilot chat window from the upper-right menu bar. Microsoft suggests a number of prompts to get you started, and you can access additional prompts using the "View prompts" option in the chat window, as shown in Figure 12.11.

Start with the "Summarize the document" prompt. Copilot will return a summary of the main points in the document within the chat window on the right-hand side of the pane, as shown in Figure 12.12. Note that you can extend this window to improve the readability of the output. In response to your prompt, Copilot also links the information it returns to sources within the text, allowing you to cross-check it for accuracy. This is a great way to quickly scan a lengthy document and assess its relevance to your role or task.

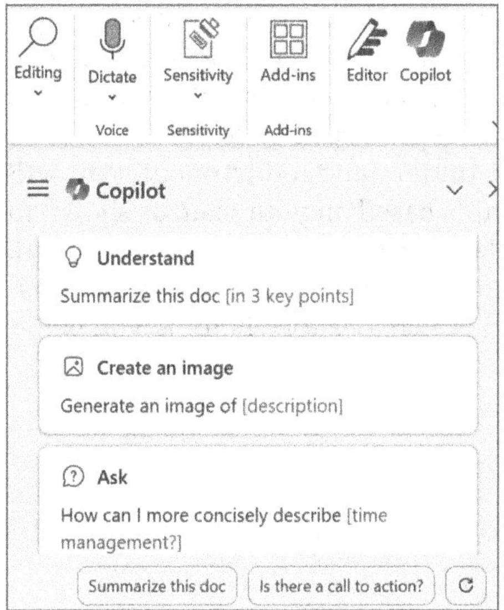

Figure 12.11: Using Copilot to improve document comprehension

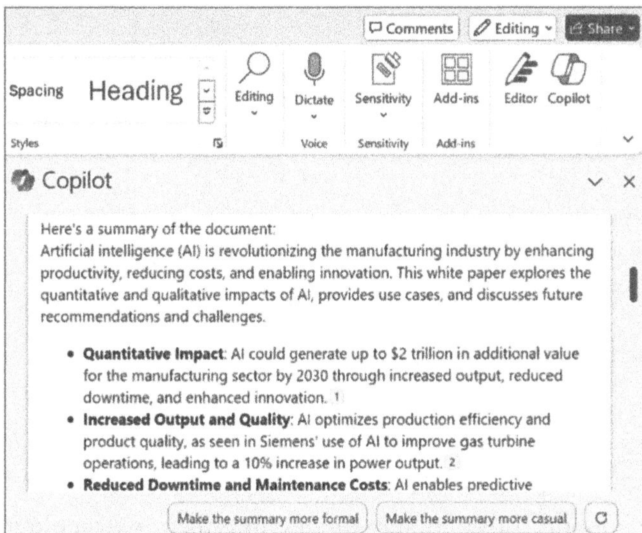

Figure 12.12: Summarizing your document

Copilot can currently handle texts of up to 20,000 words for a single query or prompt when using features like document summary and chatting with Copilot. If the document being summarized is particularly long, Copilot will break the task into parts and return results one part at a time. The user will be reminded to "continue" to complete the summarization.

When the summarization flags a topic of interest, you can use Copilot to explore that topic further and extract key insights. Try a natural language prompt such as *"Tell me more about the quantitative impacts"* or *"What does the paper say about AI's environmental impact"* to get more focused responses from Copilot.

Refer to the prompting examples in Chapter 3 to prepare document summaries that are on point and relevant for your target audience. You can alter the tone of the summary to be more formal or casual, generate an executive summary, or specify the output in a table format to meet your specific needs.

As you interact with Copilot to better understand a document, you will notice that it suggests other relevant prompts based on your chat, as shown in Figure 12.13. These prompts lead you to related topics covered in the document. This is a great example of contextual prompting within Copilot, as it dynamically suggests relevant prompts based on your chat history, helping you better understand the document.

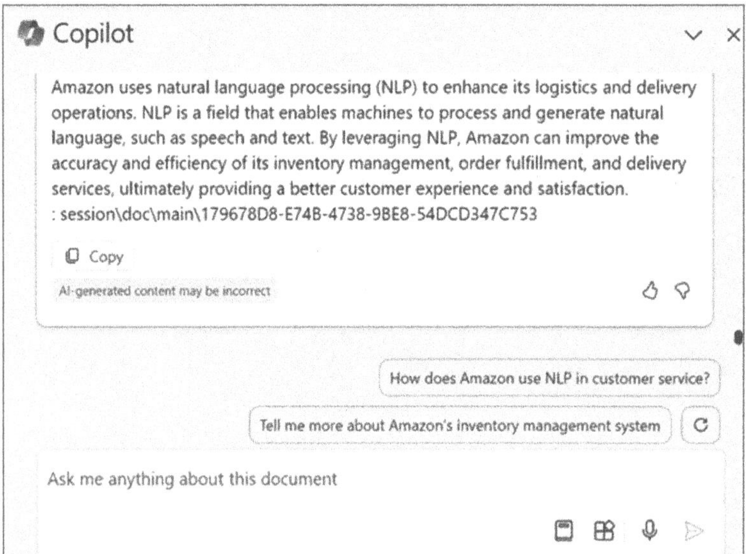

Figure 12.13: Copilot contextual prompting

Conclusion

Copilot can significantly enhance how you create documents or extract key information from existing documents. When you are faced with a new task, consider how it could be achieved with the aid of Copilot—and prepare to be amazed. At your fingertips, you have an intelligent assistant that can help you save time, improve your writing, and quickly uncover new insights from existing documents.

Part

II

Extending Copilot

In This Part

CHAPTER

13

Unlocking Real Value with Copilot

As discussed in Chapter 5, "Planning Your Microsoft 365 Copilot Rollout," defining your success measures and ensuring that you realize business value in your investment is critical to the success of your project. In this chapter, we will discuss building the business case for Copilot for Microsoft 365 and how to position this with your leadership team. Then, we will talk about measuring business value using both quantitative and qualitative measures. After that, we will cover how to map out business processes to help identify tasks that can be augmented with AI. Then, we will discuss using a third-party application called Prompt Buddy to help centralize your enterprise prompts and drive engagement. Finally, we will pull this together so you have an approach for communicating to your organizational leadership the business value you are realizing with your Copilot for Microsoft 365 implementation.

The Business Case for Copilot

While the technology industry has been abuzz with the potential transformational benefits that GenAI can potentially bring, the reality is that most businesses are measured on tangible things such as sales, revenue, market share, and profit. Therefore, your blueprint for Copilot should follow the same path as any other technology investment, where you carefully prepare a business case focused on demonstrating how this technology will yield positive business outcomes. Let's walk through the initial planning for preparing a business case for investing in Copilot for Microsoft 365.

As part of your initial business case planning activities, your first step is understanding how your organization evaluates investing in technology. Every organization operates differently; therefore, you want to understand the typical evaluation process, including the path to approval. For example, some organizations may require that you have an active sponsor for a functional business area, such as Communications, Human Resources, or Marketing, in addition to an Information Technology owner. Other organizations may have a more consolidated organizational structure, and decision-making may sit solely in the Information Technology department. Once you understand your path to approval, you need to understand the evaluation criteria for the approving body. Some examples that you may encounter within your organization include the following:

- **Return on investment (ROI):** A standard financial metric used to evaluate the profitability or efficiency of an investment. For example, what might be the productivity gains of Copilot by reducing the administrative burden for certain tasks? This could theoretically be calculated as hours saved by a full-time equivalent (FTE) rate subtracted by the investment cost. This should also factor in the total cost of ownership to provide a multi-year ROI.
- **Total cost of ownership (TCO):** A summary of a business's costs when implementing Copilot for Microsoft 365. This should include the internal costs, such as aligning a team to help support the rollout, licensing costs, and any additional costs, such as contractors or consultants, to help support the rollout.
- **Strategic alignment:** A narrative that helps connect how an investment would align with your organization's goals. For example, if your company has a strategic goal to attract top talent by providing access to cutting-edge technology, you could help connect that goal to your Copilot investment supporting that goal.
- **Business process improvement:** Examples of how this technology may drive efficiencies with existing processes or unlock new capabilities that your company does not have today. You should include a few examples depending on your business, such as "streamline social media content production, decrease turnaround time for proposals, improve quality of responses to customer inquiries, etc."
- **Employee engagement:** People are the lifeline behind every organization; therefore, you should highlight what impact this may have on your workforce.

Some examples may include "improve job satisfaction by reducing time spent on highly administrative tasks, reduce the number of meetings that employees need to attend, etc."

Once you have some insight into how your business case will be evaluated by the approving board, the next step is to start to pull together the necessary documentation to gain approval to proceed. Let's walk through some of the typical sections in business cases focused on implementing technology to help build your case for investing in Copilot for Microsoft 365.

Executive Summary

Your executive summary is the first thing that your stakeholders will read; therefore, it is important that you capture their attention immediately and concisely explain the key points of your business case. I would recommend you consider including an acknowledgment of the disruption that AI is having within your industry. You can build upon the fact that many businesses are challenged to deliver more value to their customers with less resources, and that strategic investments are needed to help not only compete but also to win in this current business climate.

Most executive summaries also provide a high-level snapshot of the forecasted investment amount, both in external costs—i.e., software licenses and third-party system integrators' support—in addition to the investment in internal resources to help deliver on the promises. You can drill down and provide greater detail for these costs in the investment section of your business case, but it is helpful to provide them that information up front so that they are not anxiously waiting for what the anticipated ask might be from an investment perspective.

The executive summary is also where you may want to paint the picture of how this investment aligns with your company's strategic business pillars. For example, if one of the pillars focuses on attracting and growing the best talent, you should include a statement about how investing in Copilot aligns with that goal. You could begin by explaining that Copilot is meant to help reduce the administrative tasks that employees prefer not to do, allowing them to focus on higher-value and more creative work. By having the balance of their time spent on work they enjoy, your workforce will be more engaged with their work, and focusing on higher-value work will contribute to their individual growth. Additionally, by investing in this cutting-edge technology, you are providing your recruiting team with an additional value proposition to present to prospective candidates about your organization's culture.

As a reminder, the intent of the executive summary is to provide a high-level snapshot of the "why" behind your request, including how much the investment might cost and a high-level overview of the direct benefits your company should expect to see through this investment. When crafting this, keep in mind that most executive audiences have a limited attention span and typically are most interested in knowing the potential cost and benefits of the investment.

Background and Introduction

Next is the background and introduction section of your business case. In this section, you should help establish the compelling event or events that are leading to the business need for this investment. For Copilot, you should acknowledge the impact that GenAI is having on your industry as one of the critical events accelerating the need. If any public case studies are available, you should be sure to reference them to help set the stage that this technology is something your peers are already investing in. There are not many executives who strive to be the first in their peer group or to take risks. However, they do like to follow leaders in their industry who have hopefully already encountered some of the learning pains of a new technology or initiative. Your tone should be professional but also create a small sense of urgency or that you may be lagging behind your peers and thus losing competitive ground.

Next, introduce your audience to what Copilot is. You can build on the disruption of GenAI to introduce Copilot as Microsoft's "GenAI-as-a-service" offering, an add-on to the core Microsoft 365 offering. Depending on your audience's familiarity with GenAI, you might describe Copilot as making ChatGPT available in all the Office applications and core Microsoft 365 services. It would also be helpful to provide a few examples of what it can do to better frame it for your audience, such as "draft emails, summarize Teams meetings, create PowerPoint slides, or tap into enterprise knowledge." Since this is an executive audience, you should also be transparent about the fact that Copilot still needs human oversight to ensure the quality and accuracy of the information provided. By doing so, you are getting ahead of the inevitable ask that some executives will inquire about in terms of how many jobs could potentially be displaced by investing in Copilot.

Next, you should explain the need that Copilot will be serving. Copilot's sweet spot is focused on end-user productivity. However, that alone will probably not spark any excitement from leaders who have heard that pitch before. If your organization is like others that were greatly disrupted by the COVID-19 pandemic, then you may have also witnessed a large uptick in Microsoft Teams meetings and a decrease in in-person collaboration. I suspect that years from now, there will be studies highlighting the mental and social tolls that this large swing from in-person to virtual connection has had. With this new Teams meeting culture, have you also witnessed a shift to more 30-minute calls to help be more "efficient" with meetings? Do those meetings seem to go back-to-back throughout your whole day? Do you feel more accomplished at the end of the day, or do you feel less accomplished as you have had to endure more context switching throughout your day?

If you are unfamiliar with the term, "context switching" is basically shifting one's attention from one task to another, often in response to interruptions or competing demands. Context switching reduces productivity by increasing the time and mental effort required to resume a task after switching from another one. For example, if you are in the middle of writing an email and then must jump to a meeting, the time and effort it takes to complete that email will be much greater later than when you are already in the process of writing. When you are in the middle of a task, your focus is already set, and you have the context needed to complete it. However, when you are forced to abandon that task and then pick it up later, you have lost all context of what you hoped to achieve through the completion of that task. Therefore, the switching between tasks is imposing both a mental and productivity burden on you as the individual to complete the work.

Copilot has a couple of different capabilities that address this context-switching problem, which should be highlighted in your business case. The Teams meeting experience, as we reviewed earlier, is highly compelling in addressing some of the downsides of our new normal of context switching. Copilot can provide a nudge 10 minutes before a meeting is set to end. This nudge is valuable in that you can quickly recap key decisions, action items, and next steps while directly in the context of the meeting. This allows you to ensure that you not only captured the events correctly but it also can serve as a forcing function to end the meeting on time or early to allow others a moment to reflect and start to build context for the next activity on your schedule. The intelligent recap can also be quite helpful in switching back to the context of that meeting later by having it provide a summarization or answer questions you may have as your brain attempts to recall the context of events.

Finally, you want to communicate the purpose of this project. Each organization will differ slightly given the project scope and investment; however, at a high level, what you will be documenting is the breadth of your Copilot project. This could be a small evaluation of Copilot within a particular group or department or a larger rollout to a business unit or perhaps multiple departments. It all depends on your organization's culture for embracing new technology and your own hypotheses about the impact Copilot will have on the users you have identified. To keep it simple, you are helping your executive stakeholders understand the level of commitment they are signing up for as part of this investment. Despite Microsoft licensing requirements, evaluations come with an assumption of a much smaller commitment, whereas implementation will likely require some level of data showing that you've already completed an evaluation, which resulted in a recommendation to proceed with a larger investment.

Business Objectives

When documenting your business objectives, describing how this project aligns with your organization's strategic priorities is important. Depending on the makeup of your business, you may want to focus on the following objectives as part of your business case:

- **Increasing employee productivity:** Leveraging AI as an assistant to automate routine tasks or provide an initial draft document, allowing the author to become the editor.
- **Improving data-driven decision-making:** Helping empower employees within your organization to make decisions more quickly and accurately based on AI-driven insights.
- **Foster innovation and creativity:** Using AI as a partner in brainstorming new ideas, ideating on potential new products or service offerings, or helping provide opposing views for an idea or hypothesis.
- **Increasing employee engagement:** As previously mentioned, helping employees better appreciate how their work rolls up to higher-level organizational objectives, and shifting the focus from administrative to creative tasks. Also, demonstrating that the organization is focused on investing in their employees to help improve their overall work experience.
- **Enhance customer experience:** Organizations exist to help serve their customers, and Copilot is positioned to help you respond more quickly and with higher-quality output. You can cite using Copilot to help respond to customer inquiries while ensuring that you are maintaining the tone and brand in the response. Or you can talk about being able to use Copilot to help with your response to compelling events, allowing you to better serve your customers.
- **Drive competitive advantage:** Gaining an advantage by leveraging these new capabilities to help differentiate you from your competitors.

NOTE There is a compelling article put out by the *Harvard Business Review* that highlights how humans with AI will replace humans without AI. You can find it at `hbr.org/2023/08/ai-wont-replace-humans-but-humans-with-ai-will-replace-humans-without-ai`.

The business objectives you choose to highlight in your business case will depend highly on your organization. Remember that the most compelling business cases are elaborate stories rather than documents that only focus on profits and cost. Next, you will want to provide an overview of the current situation analysis to help your stakeholders understand how Copilot fits within your organization's journey to becoming AI-enabled.

Current Situation Analysis

The current situation analysis of your business case should be focused both externally on the greater industry you are aligned with and then on the internal initiatives and investments you are making. For example, if you are in higher education, you may help begin the narrative of how ChatGPT has impacted faculty as students begin to use it to help draft essays, or how GenAI is being introduced to contact centers to help agents resolve issues, ultimately reducing call time and increasing customer satisfaction.

You should also highlight where your organization is with evaluating GenAI and any active in-flight experiments or use cases. Some organizations may still be in the planning stages of trying to establish a governing body to oversee experimentation or bring new capabilities with GenAI to market. Regardless of where you are on your AI journey, it is important to set the current context as part of your business case narrative, which will help expand upon how Copilot fits in.

Copilot might be the first practical application of AI to many employees. Copilot has an advantage because Microsoft has used its "responsible AI" framework for the service. As mentioned in Chapter 1, "Introduction to Artificial Intelligence," one of the issues with AI is that it responds based on the data it learned from. If that data contains hidden biases, the outcome could also be biased information, which could affect some people, customers, or assumptions. Therefore, if Copilot is in fact your first widespread use case of AI, you should highlight that to your executive stakeholders. You should also highlight the fact that Microsoft has integrated responsible AI into the service in addition to educating them about the value of doing so.

NOTE **You can find details about Microsoft's responsible AI framework at** `microsoft.com/en-us/ai/responsible-ai`.

Alternatively, if your organization has already invested in building its own GenAI applications, there may be an opportunity to replace those early experiments with a more production-ready service. For example, suppose your organization was one of the many that built its own "secure ChatGPT" chatbot using Azure OpenAI. In that case, it might make sense to position this as replacing some of that capability while providing additional functionality with its integration into the various Microsoft 365 applications. No matter where your company is in AI, this section of your business case is meant to help ground everyone on the current state.

Solution Description

The solution description will give your stakeholders a high-level overview of the Copilot for Microsoft 365 service offering. Some of the key elements that you should highlight include:

- **SaaS-based product:** Microsoft 365 is a software-as-a-service (SaaS) product offering that does not require any on-premises or cloud-based infrastructure to support.
- **Subscription-based model:** Copilot for Microsoft 365 is an add-on to your existing Microsoft 365 licensing agreement, with a monthly cost per user licensed.
- **User experience:** You should provide examples of how Copilot will be accessed, including web, mobile, and client applications. You should also mention that users will interact with the Copilot service using prompts, with the ability to leverage Copilot Lab as a source of inspiration.
- **Model training:** Microsoft doesn't train the models based on your data, which is one of the concerns of many legal and compliance groups. You will want to highlight Microsoft's Data Protection Addendum, highlighting how your data is managed as part of the Copilot service.

NOTE The Data Protection Addendum, which is included as part of your enterprise agreement with Microsoft, can be found at `microsoft.com/licensing/docs/view/Microsoft-Products-and-Services-Data-Protection-Addendum-DPA`.

- **Data access:** You should provide a high-level overview of how Copilot maintains the same level of access within Microsoft 365 as the user leveraging it. You should highlight the advantages of this to ensure that users do not have additional access rights using this service, as well as call out the potential need to evaluate your current Microsoft 365 for potential examples of oversharing.
- **Solution extensibility:** You can talk about how Copilot can be extended to access other line-of-business applications, such as ServiceNow, Salesforce, SAP, etc., to increase its overall knowledge. Additionally, it can be further extended to transact in those backend systems by creating actions in Copilot Studio or Microsoft Teams message extensions.

The granularity level and technical details you need to provide about the Copilot service will likely vary by organization. Some very technical stakeholders may request to see architecture diagrams to understand how the service works. Others may request representatives from your Microsoft account team provide reassurances that the Copilot service is not trained on your organization's data.

However, hopefully, what has been provided will be helpful as a starting point for describing the Copilot service to your executive stakeholders. Next, we will focus on providing a high-level cost-benefit analysis.

Implementation Plan

Whether you call it a project plan or an implementation plan, you will want to provide your stakeholders with a timeline of activities that makes up the total effort for your deployment. As discussed in Chapter 5, this implementation plan will likely include an initial onboarding of the core project team to Copilot to help ensure that those overseeing the deployment are also evangelists.

Cost-Benefit Analysis

This next section of your business case will likely be the most important since it outlines the required investment you are asking for and the justification for why this would make business sense. As with most other business case sections, we have covered multiple variables for you to consider for your specific project. However, the following are likely to be considered universal across most Copilot deployments:

- **Licensing costs:** These will be based on the number of users included in your deployment. You will likely want to show the annual costs for your subscription. For companies with a Microsoft Enterprise Agreement or those purchasing through a third-party licensing provider, there may be opportunities to negotiate a discount based on the number of licenses purchased and the duration of the agreement. Those numbers are highly dependent on any existing agreements and negotiations. Therefore, your mileage may vary depending on how much of a discount you can negotiate.
- **Professional services fees:** Many organizations may decide to solicit the assistance of qualified Microsoft partners to implement new products or services. These fees would be one-time costs based on the duration and type of services they provide. Some examples of professional services that you may consider include adoption and change management, training, technical advisory, and project management. Additionally, if you decide to extend Copilot to additional line-of-business applications, you may consider professional services expertise to build out those integrations.
- **Additional third-party licensing:** As discussed throughout this book, some organizations may be in a situation where their current Microsoft 365 environment is lacking any content governance policies or controls. There may be a need to provide visibility to instances of content oversharing and technical controls to remediate and then enforce ongoing issues.

Some Microsoft ISV partners, such as AvePoint and Orchestry, offer solutions designed for organizations that want to manage their data assets in Microsoft 365. If your company requires these services, you should consider including their costs in your total cost of ownership.

- **Internal resources:** Some organizations may have a model where employee costs are tied to projects. Therefore, when planning your implementation, you may need to consider the cost of the internal project team, including their time and appropriate cost structure, in your business case.
- **Materials for go-live:** Depending on your company culture, you may treat the rollout of Copilot as a key event. This could include the production of posters and signage as part of your communications campaign, establishing a "Copilot and Coffee" series of educational sessions to help demonstrate use cases, or any other potential swag or giveaways to either raise awareness or reinforce the adoption of Copilot.

Then, from a benefits perspective, you will likely be challenged to estimate how Copilot will positively impact your organization. This is perhaps one of the more challenging aspects of your business case for several reasons. First, the target audience is knowledge workers who tend to have tasks that vary widely based on the day, week, and month, depending on their role. Second, the variability of their role in those tasks can also fluctuate widely. For example, a proposal targeted at a large enterprise customer would likely be more detail-oriented and require more effort than perhaps a proposal targeted at a nonprofit account or one where you have friendly buyers. Therefore, when you are trying to calculate potential time savings, there are so many nuances that impact both the usual effort without AI versus the potential time savings with it. Finally, from a pure ROI perspective, the salaries of knowledge workers vary greatly based on role, experience, title, etc., which makes performing any sort of true mathematical calculation challenging.

So, when it comes to providing a cost-benefit analysis as part of a business case for Copilot, you may want to start with the following:

- Microsoft, which currently is the largest Copilot user base, has found through surveying both their employees and participants in the Early Access program that, on average, users report a time savings of approximately 14 minutes a day, or 1.2 hours a week.
- Repeatable productivity use cases for Copilot include meeting recap and summarization, drafting of emails, finding enterprise knowledge, and performing research. You can perform A/B tests to simulate the gains and will likely observe a 40–60% time savings, depending on the complexity of the task.

- User productivity will become greater as employees become more familiar with Copilot.
- Additional business benefits can be gained by extending Copilot into other line-of-business applications to help reduce context switching between applications and to deliver new data-driven insights that were previously unavailable.

NOTE You can find Microsoft's Work Trend Index special report about early Copilot user experience at `microsoft.com/en-us/worklab/work-trend-index/copilots-earliest-users-teach-us-about-generative-ai-at-work`.

You should not underestimate the complexity of articulating the value of Copilot. As we will discuss in the next section, both qualitative and quantitative measures are used to help paint a full picture of how people are using Copilot within your organization.

Evaluation and Measurement

To support the previous section of your business case, you will describe your approach for measuring and communicating business value in the evaluation and measure section. As noted, this can be quite challenging given the nature of knowledge workers' daily tasks. However, from a quantitative perspective, Microsoft has a Copilot Adoption Dashboard, available through the Viva Insights application, that measures how many people are using Copilot, which applications they are using it in, and whether they are using it to create or summarize content. This dashboard would be considered a quantitative measure, as it provides numbers associated with the usage of Copilot.

Next, you will want to understand not just how often people use Copilot or which applications they use, but also whether it's helpful. Surveying your user base is considered a qualitative measurement of Copilot's effectiveness. There are no right or wrong ways to solicit this feedback, whether it be through 1:1 interviews, small focus groups, self-reporting, or even surveying your users. The goal is to capture the reported value, time savings, and how Copilot makes them feel about their work to help qualify the impact to your stakeholders.

When you present your business case to stakeholders, you should communicate that you will use both quantitative and qualitative measures to evaluate the effectiveness of Copilot. You should also help them understand that measuring knowledge worker productivity is not only based on data but also on narrative to show the impact. Additionally, you should mention that improving productivity is one goal, but another goal is to leverage that higher engagement for pursuing new initiatives.

Presenting Your Business Case

Prior to presenting your business case to executives, it is very helpful to practice your pitch in front of others. This will help you prepare for questions they may ask you during your presentation. Additionally, when preparing your presentation, you may try to incorporate Copilot into part of your presentation. You can either obtain a few licenses to provide a real-time demonstration of the capability, or you can download content from Microsoft's adoption site (`adoption.microsoft.com`), including prerecorded Copilot videos. By incorporating Copilot into your business case review, you will have the ability to tell a story about how this technology can help drive productivity in your organization and make it real for them, which is important from a storytelling perspective.

Measuring Business Value

Hopefully, with your stakeholders signed off on moving forward with your Copilot implementation, it's time to get organized for measuring usage and adoption. The first step is to ensure that you and others tasked with driving adoption have access to the Copilot Adoption in Viva Insights. Viva Insights, formerly Workplace Analytics, focuses on improving employee productivity and well-being through data-driven insights and recommendations. While Viva Insights typically requires a paid license to access the reporting features, Microsoft has made the Copilot Adoption Dashboard available to all Microsoft 365 users without needing additional Viva Insights.

Copilot Adoption Dashboard Setup

If you are not an organizational leader, you may need to ask your Microsoft 365 Global Admin to first help grant you access to the Copilot Adoption Dashboard. First, log in to the Microsoft 365 admin center at `admin.microsoft.com` and then follow these steps:

1. Go to the Settings tab and select Microsoft Viva, then Viva Insights.
2. Under Viva Insights in Microsoft 365, select "Manage settings for viewing Copilot."
3. Click the Assigned tab.
4. From here, you can add users for which you want to grant access to the Copilot Adoption Dashboard.

Accessing the Copilot Adoption Dashboard

Now that you have access to the Copilot Adoption Dashboard, open your Microsoft Teams client and click the Viva Insights application from your Teams application list. If you do not have Viva Insights, click the Apps button in your Microsoft Teams client, and then enter **Viva Insights** into the search menu. Then, you can install Viva Insights so that it will appear within your list of Microsoft Teams applications.

When you click Viva Insights from Microsoft Teams, you should see the Microsoft Copilot Dashboard, as shown in Figure 13.1, which defaults to a tab called Readiness that provides a high-level overview of the number of users in your Microsoft 365 tenant and active Copilot users. Active Copilot users are defined as people with a license who have used it over the defined period, which is 4 weeks by default. This screen is most helpful in gauging from a macro level if, overall, your Copilot users are engaged with the product. For example, if the number of active Copilot users is low, you may have some work to do to help promote Copilot usage across your user base, including sending more communications, hosting office hours, or surveying individuals to better understand why they are not using Copilot.

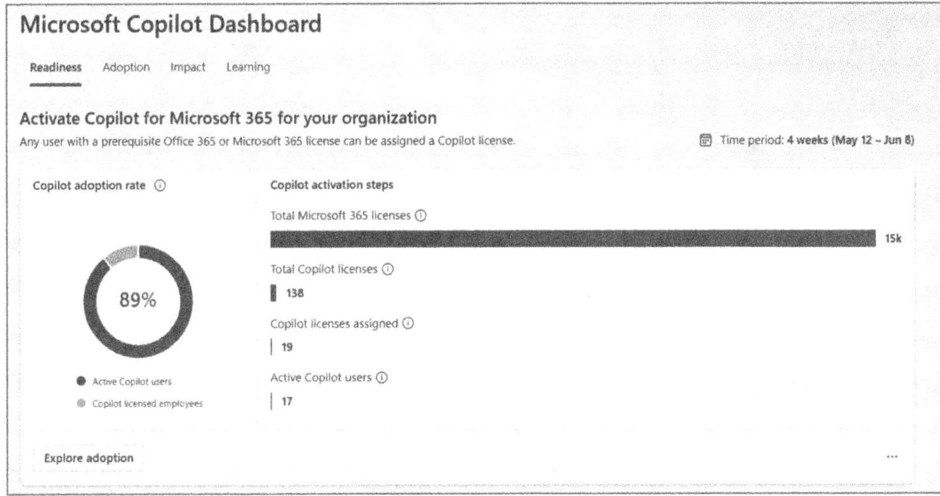

Figure 13.1: The Microsoft Copilot Dashboard

If you scroll down on the Readiness view of the Copilot Dashboard, you will find additional statistics about your tenant, aligned to potential Copilot benefits. Microsoft is very invested in ensuring that Copilot is adopted, given their significant financial investment in OpenAI, in addition to all the internal engineering effort that has been aligned to Copilot. Therefore, in addition to their investments in engineering effort, they have been very transparent with the research around the impact of AI on people's work, as published on their Work Trend Index site `microsoft.com/en-us/worklab/work-trend-index`.

Part of that research has been geared toward helping to quantify the impact Copilot can have on knowledge workers by studying their own Copilot deployment. Based on their research, they have developed assumptions of time savings that can be realized by actions such as summarizing meetings, synthesizing Teams chats, creating content, and processing email, as shown in Figure 13.2. For each of these activities, they have documented their own observed productivity gains and then correlated them with the number of Teams meeting users, Teams chat users, Office application users, and Outlook email users to help you understand how Copilot could potentially impact your user base.

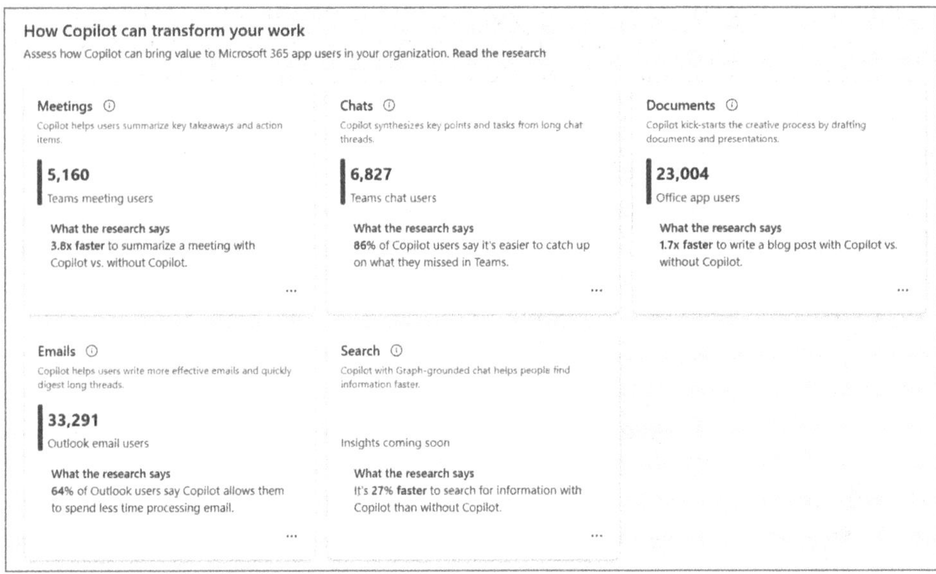

Figure 13.2: The Copilot activity report

Next, let's look at Copilot adoption within your tenant. Assuming you have already assigned licenses to users, and they have been using it for a week or two, you should be able to click the Adoption tab on the Copilot Adoption Dashboard. Based on the number of users, you should see an overview as shown in Figure 13.3, which provides a breakdown of Copilot usage within your tenant. The two views of this adoption data are as follows:

- **Active user count:** This captures the number of users who have interacted with Copilot, with a breakdown per application, including Microsoft Teams, Word, PowerPoint, Excel, etc. They would minimally have to use

Copilot within one of those applications once during the defined time period of the report to influence that metric. However, it does not tell you how many times they acted in one of those applications.

- **Actions per user:** This captures the average number of times a user performed an activity using Copilot per application. Some example activities include drafting documents in Word, summarizing email threads, generating email threads, and summarizing meetings.

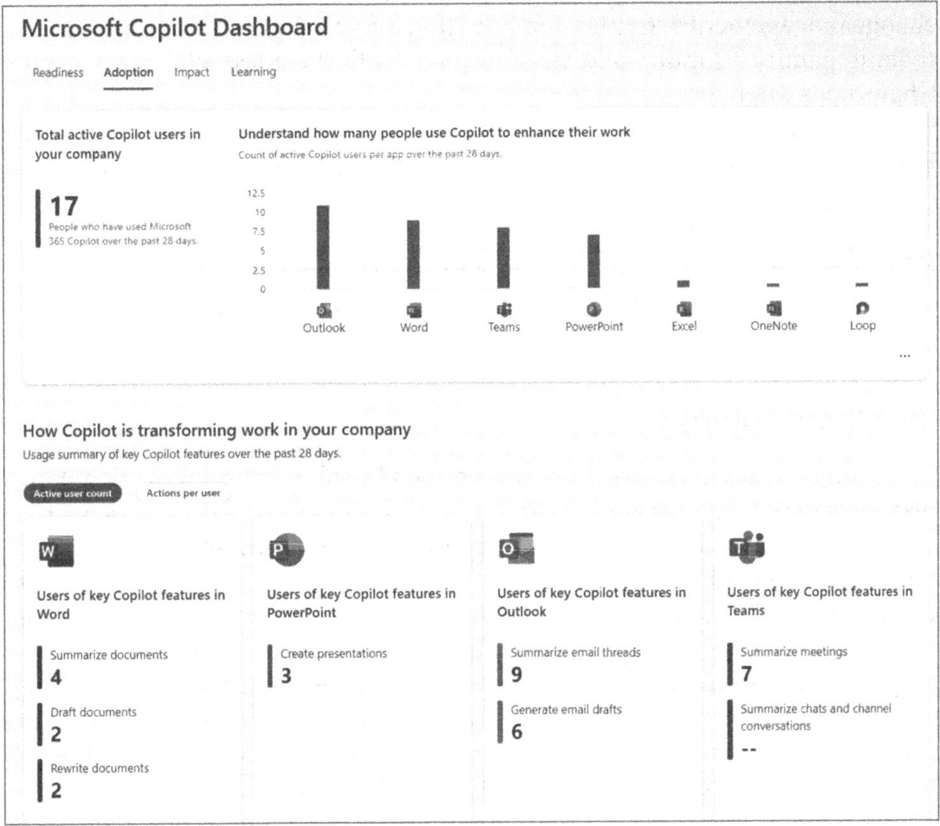

Figure 13.3: Copilot adoption metrics

This view of which applications are seeing the most Copilot usage is helpful as you start to craft your narrative around your ROI. While this reporting does not specify the types of work content that people are using Copilot for, it does provide some insights into where your users are realizing the most value. It can also inform where you might want to target from a change management perspective, to help promote use cases for the applications that are not being used as frequently. You can then measure usage over time and adjust your approach depending on how your users respond.

Copilot Adoption Dashboard "Advanced Features"

If you have Viva Insights as part of your licensing agreement with Microsoft, you are also entitled access to Advanced Features, which is essentially greater insight into your Copilot adoption metrics. The dashboard shows the same metrics as the dashboard without a subscription, but the adoption, impact, and sentiment types offer more metrics and filters. For example, you can create Copilot "cohorts" of users and then track their progress. This might be helpful if you are coordinating internal activities to help measure the impact of change management activities and how they drive adoption, or you could use them to gamify adoption and track users by cohorts to see who your Copilot Champions might be.

You can learn more about the advanced features of the Copilot Adoption Dashboard at `learn.microsoft.com/en-us/viva/insights/org-team-insights/copilot-dashboard-advanced-features`.

NOTE **Users will need both Copilot for Microsoft 365 and Viva Insights licenses to have their activity captured in the Copilot Adoption Dashboard.**

Viva Pulse Surveys

As mentioned previously, the Copilot Adoption Dashboard provides quantitative measures of how many users are leveraging Copilot. However, it does not provide much insight into the end work products or types of documents or data that users are creating with Copilot. It also does not gauge user sentiment as to whether or not Copilot is providing value. Therefore, the way for you to capture those additional metrics as part of your qualitative measures will include surveys and user interviews. One of the ways to quickly capture this data from users is through Microsoft's Viva Pulse survey tool. From a licensing perspective, Viva Pulse is an add-on service that can be purchased separately or as part of one of the various Viva licensing bundles offered by Microsoft.

NOTE **It is important to note that only users creating Viva Pulse surveys and viewing the responses require a license; survey takers do not require a license to complete a survey.**

Once you have been assigned a Viva Pulse license by your administrator or have obtained a trial license, navigate to `pulse.cloud.microsoft` to access the Viva Pulse home screen, as shown in Figure 13.4. Alternatively, from within Microsoft Teams, you can access Viva Pulse by clicking the Apps button on the side rail and then searching for **Viva Pulse** in the Microsoft Teams App Store. Once added, a chatbot will message you that Viva Pulse is now available.

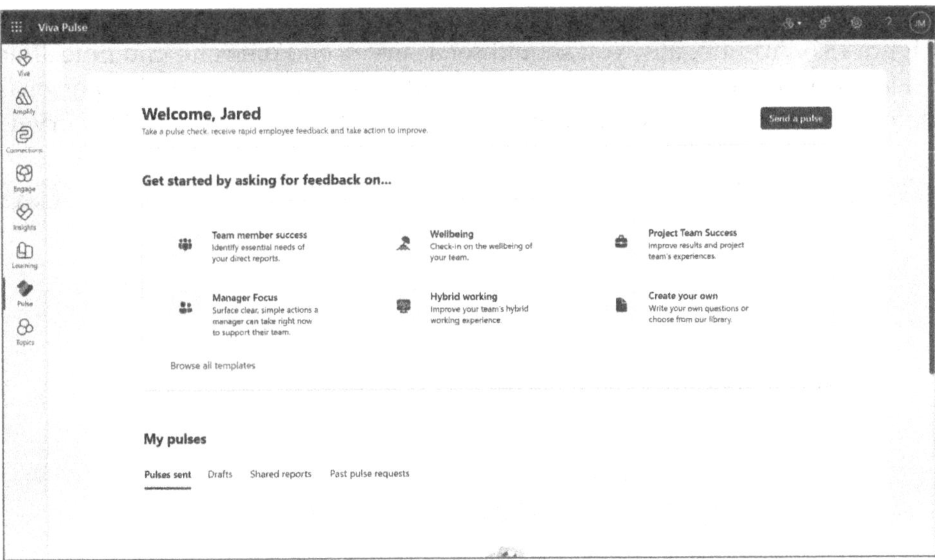

Figure 13.4: The Viva Pulse home page

From here, click the "Browse all templates" link to access the preloaded survey templates that Microsoft provides out-of-the-box, as shown in Figure 13.5.

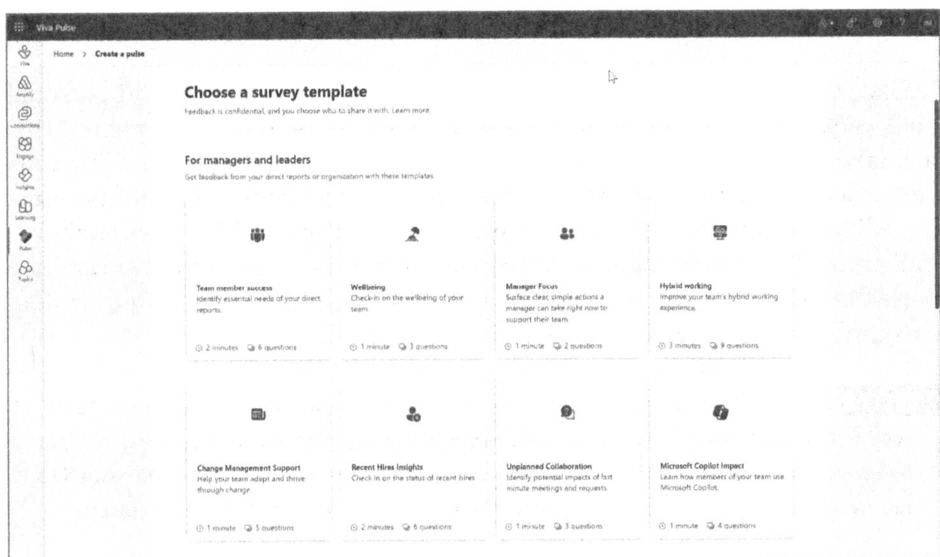

Figure 13.5: The Viva Pulse survey templates

Select the Microsoft Copilot Impact template, which includes four initial questions that you can choose to either keep or delete. Once you have finalized your list of questions, click Next. Here, you can pick the recipients of your survey by selecting individual users, a group, or a Microsoft Teams channel, as shown in Figure 13.6. Additionally, you should set a survey end date and end time after which no additional responses can be submitted. You can also include a personal note that will be displayed to users to encourage them to complete the survey.

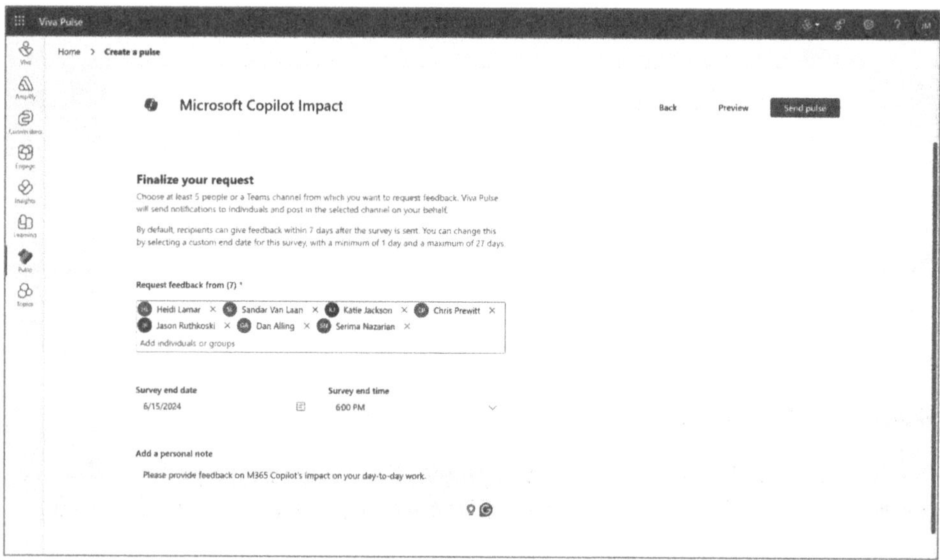

Figure 13.6: The Viva Pulse recipients list

Once you have entered the survey end date, survey end time, and personal note, click the "Send pulse" button to send the survey to your recipients. This will take you to a confirmation page, as shown in Figure 13.7. Your recipients will be alerted by Viva Pulse to complete the survey by the end date and time. In addition to being alerted, you can also click the "Copy link" button, as shown in Figure 13.7, to copy the URL to the survey to your clipboard. You can then paste the copied link into an email, Teams channel, Teams message, etc. to help encourage completion of your survey prior to its closure.

NOTE **Viva Pulse requires a minimum of five survey responses for you to be able to see the results. Therefore, you should ensure that not only are you surveying more than five people to account for those who may not take the survey, but you may also need to follow up with those who perhaps procrastinate in responding to feedback requests.**

You can check in on the progress of your survey from the Viva Pulse home screen, as shown in Figure 13.8. However, you will not be able to see the results until the confidentiality threshold has been met, which by default is 25% of the users you sent the survey to.

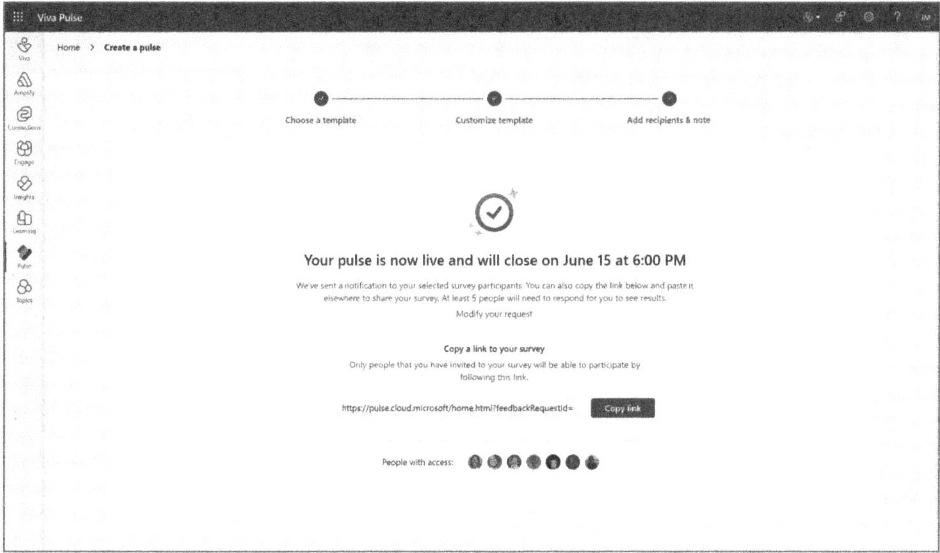

Figure 13.7: The Viva Pulse survey confirmation screen

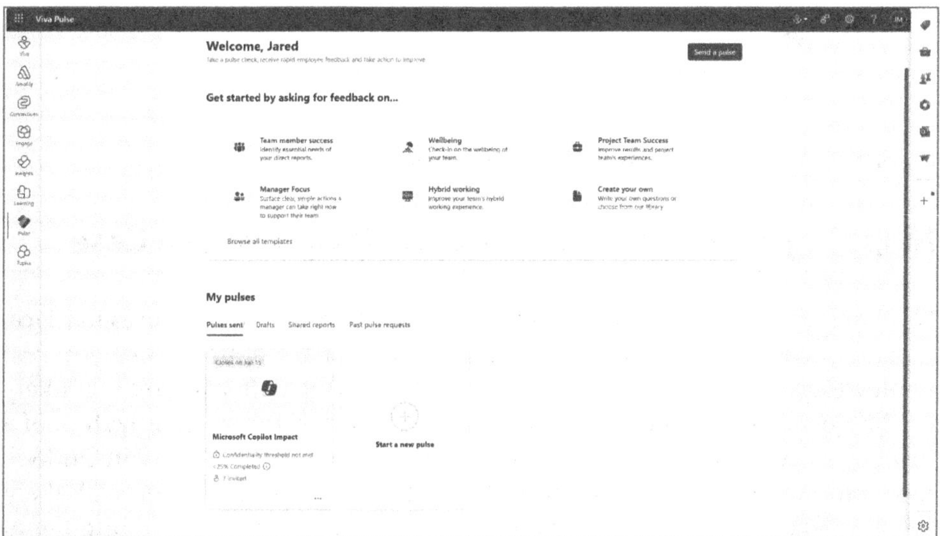

Figure 13.8: The Viva Pulse survey response tracking confirmation screen

After either the completion date of your Viva Pulse survey or once everyone has completed your survey, you can view the results, as shown in Figure 13.9. In addition to reviewing the results, you can click the "Share report" button for others to view the results.

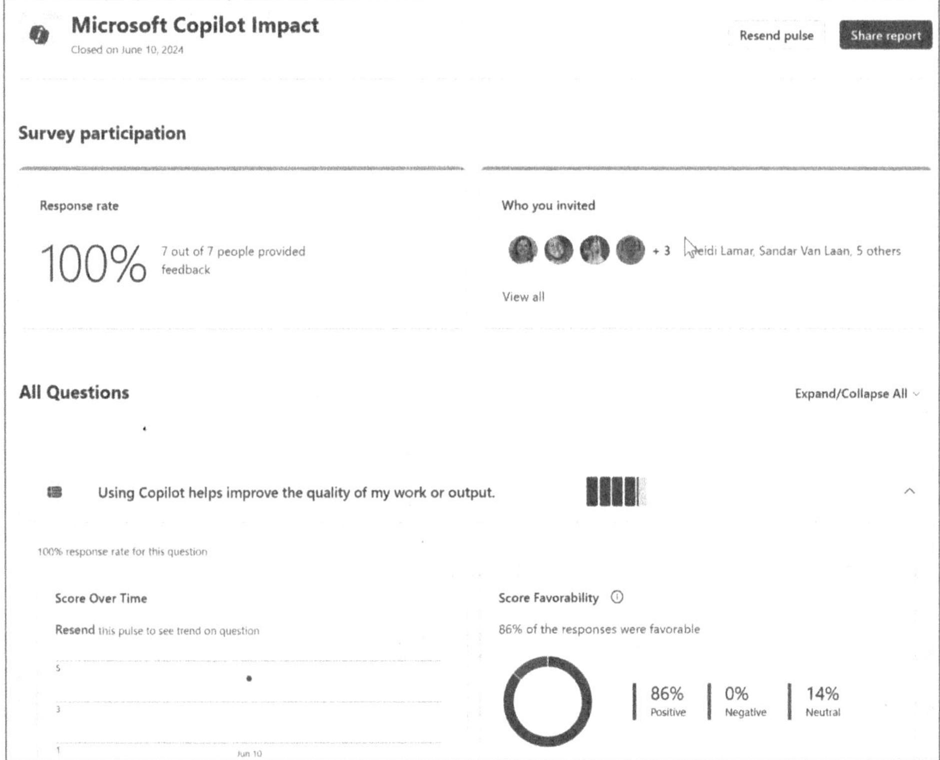

Figure 13.9: The Viva Pulse survey results confirmation screen

Mapping Business Processes: The Proposal Use Case

Now that you have both your qualitative and quantitative measures in place, you can focus on how to drive additional value out of Copilot. When you first deploy Copilot to your users and observe their usage patterns, you will likely see Microsoft Teams as the most used application and the summarization of a meeting as the most popular use case. Following that may be Copilot in Outlook to summarize an email thread or to draft an email, and then usage will likely vary depending on the organization. These popular use cases of intelligent meeting recap and drafting emails are universal regardless of role. However, to unlock the true power of Copilot, you need to help transform the power of complicated business processes. It takes a bit more effort to help people understand and eventually adopt an AI-assisted workflow, but the benefits, if realized, could be game-changing for individuals.

To help illustrate what I mean, let's break down the process of creating a proposal for a customer. Imagine working for a software company, and a major Fortune 500 manufacturer releases a request for proposal (RFP) for a new GenAI application that will automate claims processing. You are one of the sales leads responsible for responding to this RFP and have decided to leverage Copilot to help with the response. Your initial instinct may be to try and create the perfect prompt to begin pulling together a proposal deck to respond to the RFP. Maybe in a year or two, as Copilot continues to mature, that may be possible, but the technology isn't there just yet in this first year of being generally available. As previously mentioned, Copilot's sweet spot is automating individual tasks rather than handling true end-to-end processes, which means you could try to craft the perfect prompt, but there's another way to approach this. You can break the request down into smaller tasks and use Copilot for each individual task.

Mapping Your RFP Response Process

The simplest way to map out a nonlinear process, like responding to an RPF, is to start listing the tasks. While not exhaustive, here are some tasks that typically align with responding to an RFP:

- Reviewing the RFP document to extract key information such as the due date, scoring criteria, and initiative objectives
- Finding other similar proposals that you have previously submitted
- Developing "win themes" based on the RFP document
- Researching information about the company and industry trends to help inform anything that might better personalize the response
- Finding customer stories or references in your various SharePoint sites and Microsoft Teams
- Drafting a cover letter for your response outlining your commitment to ensuring the success of the overall project
- Reviewing the proposal before sending it to ensure that it is logical and communicates your differentiators to the buyer

Aligning Tasks to Copilot Capabilities

Now review those tasks and begin mapping out how you might use Copilot to help pull together your response. For example:

- You can open the RFP document in Word and ask Copilot specific questions such as "When is our response due?", "How will our response be scored?", and "What are they hoping to accomplish with this initiative?"
- You could create similar proposals by prompting Copilot in Teams. You can ask, "Find me proposals for our GenAI claims processing solution that we submitted in the past 4 months," and it will perform a search against resources that you have access to.

- From within either the Teams, Loop, or even Word applications, you can direct Copilot with a prompt such as, "I would like you to brainstorm win themes for a proposal that we are going to submit for a GenAI claims processing solution that we have developed. The target audience is a procurement manager who's worked at that company for 30 years. We have built a software package that can satisfy their needs. What could we propose that would help differentiate us from our competition? Please be very specific and outline no more than four themes, in bullet format, that we should articulate in our proposal. An example win theme may be that we have been doing business with this company for over a decade, so we understand how they work."
- From within Microsoft Teams, you can ask Copilot, "What are the top four biggest challenges for manufacturers these days according to the Web?"
- Again, from within Microsoft Teams, you can ask Copilot, "Please find me customer stories for our claims processing solution."
- From within Word, you can ask Copilot, "Please draft a cover letter to include in our proposal thanking Company X for considering our bid. Highlight our long-standing partnership and commitment to ensure they are successful."
- Finally, before sending the proposal, within PowerPoint, you can ask Copilot questions about your proposal, such as, "Are there any portions of this proposal that might be considered confusing? Where in this proposal do we highlight that our understanding of Company X is our differentiator?"

These examples are not intended to be an exhaustive list of everything that Copilot can do. However, they should help illuminate that the value of Copilot is not just in creating a document but in assisting the pulling together the final work product. You are tapping into it to locate, create, and analyze your existing content. When you tap into those three capabilities, you will start unlocking Copilot's true potential as your AI assistant. This is also why adopting Copilot is not a straight line from an end-user perspective. Everyone has their own personal workflow, and it is not about trying to conform to how Copilot works but rather how you can start to incorporate Copilot into how you work.

Building an Enterprise Prompt Library

Some users may struggle to break down their work into tasks and figure out how Copilot can help them. The challenge may be that they have been approaching tasks in the same way for a long period of time, and the thought of breaking that rhythm may be hard for them to imagine. It may be helpful to provide these individuals with suggestions of potentially helpful prompts they can use. We discussed Copilot Lab earlier and how Microsoft provides a curated list of prompts that you can use across the core Microsoft 365 applications. However, at the time of writing, this list is not customizable; therefore, you are reliant on Microsoft to publish updates for your users to take advantage of.

As with any product gap, someone always looks to fill that gap with a creative solution. In this case, an open-source solution called Prompt Buddy was developed by two Microsoft employees, Stuart Ridout and Erik Olsson. Prompt Buddy is an enterprise prompt library, which basically means an application that is meant to store examples of prompts and outputs from GenAI that can be reused by others. This solution is a Teams application developed using the Power Platform. Therefore, you do not need to purchase any additional licenses to take advantage of it. See Figure 13.10 for the end-user view of Prompt Buddy once loaded into Microsoft Teams.

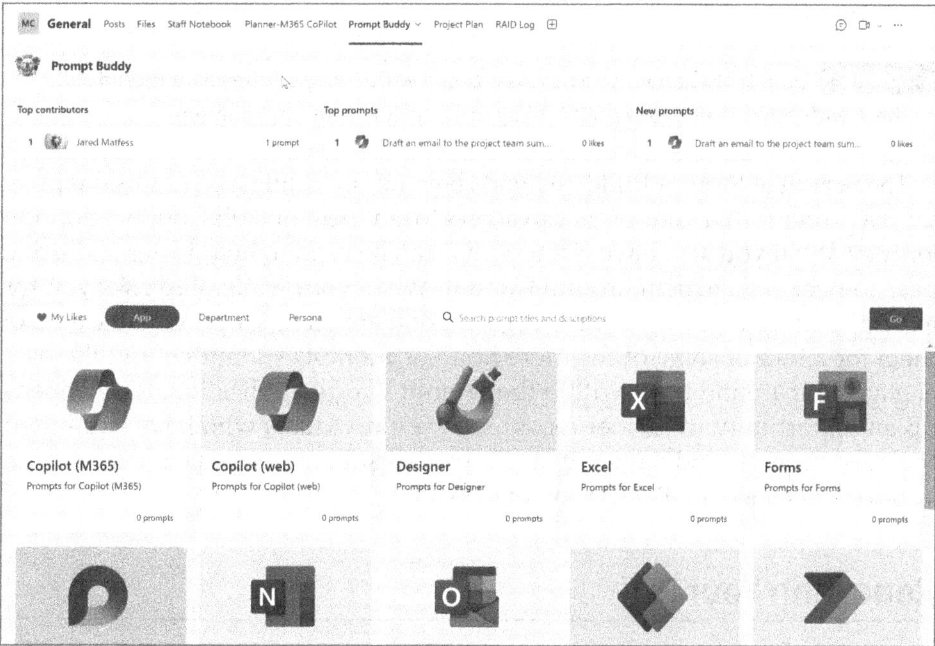

Figure 13.10: The Prompt Buddy home screen

The core functionality for Prompt Buddy includes the following:

- A centralized prompt repository that can be used for Copilot or any other GenAI application
- The ability to create categories for your prompts so that you can organize based on persona, application, or other custom categories

- The ability for users to submit prompts and assign categories based on department, use case, or custom categories that you create
- The ability for users to upvote prompts they find useful
- Leaderboard functionality to help showcase the top contributors to Prompt Buddy and the most popular prompts
- Analytics to track engagement with Prompt Buddy, including upvotes and comments
- Integration with Microsoft Teams
- Extensibility available via Power Platform

The Prompt Buddy project is maintained at the GitHub repository found at `github.com/stuartridout/promptbuddy`. There is a great set of instructions that walk you through the installation process. The final steps of installation include identifying a Teams channel where users can access the Prompt Buddy administrator functionality and then a Teams channel where users can access the main functionality.

NOTE **Despite there being no cost associated with Prompt Buddy, you should still check with your IT team to see if it is okay to install it in your environment.**

The benefit of Prompt Buddy extends beyond providing a centralized repository of prompts that your users can access to aid them in their Copilot adoption journey. What you also have is a tool that can be used to help foster and drive peer-to-peer engagement around Copilot. When your leadership asks you for examples of how people in your organization are using Copilot, you can take them for a tour of some of the more popular prompts submitted and the user engagement around them within the Prompt Buddy application. It also opens up an opportunity to further recognize the individuals who have submitted the most prompts and have the most upvoted submissions as ambassadors to your company's overall adoption of GenAI.

Reporting Your ROI

Now that you have your Copilot Adoption Dashboard in place, a Viva Pulse survey template prepared, and an example of breaking down a business process into tasks to incorporate Copilot and Prompt Buddy to help provide inspiration and proof of Copilot usage, it is time to talk about how you report progress to your senior stakeholders. As previously mentioned, this will be a bit of art mixed with science to help tell the story of Copilot's impact on your organization.

You will want to create a PowerPoint deck to help drive the conversation, and your slides should include the following:

- A high-level overview of your Copilot deployment that recaps the number of users, the departments and locations involved, and the duration of time that you are reporting out on
- A screenshot of the Copilot Adoption Dashboard so that your stakeholders can see quantitatively how many people are using Copilot, which applications, and the number of transactions
- Self-reporting through the Viva Pulse survey tool, including:
  - Copilot's impact on work quality
  - Copilot's reduction in mundane or lower-value tasks
  - Perceived productivity gains using Copilot
  - Any notable quotes captured during any 1:1 user interviews or through surveys
  - A screenshot of Prompt Buddy highlighting both user engagement and showcasing some of the most impactful use cases submitted

Now comes the tricky part, as your stakeholders may ask you to help quantify the return on your investment. If your organizational culture is one that is highly focused on data, then you may want to create a high-level roll-up similar to Figure 13.11, which helps provide an illustrative overview of what you are seeing from a Copilot ROI. One of the key inputs that you will need to establish is what might be considered full-time equivalent (FTE) rates for the personas to which you have deployed Copilot. The FTE rate would be the hourly rate inclusive of benefits used to help calculate what the value of time savings using Copilot might equate to. However, even with those savings, the true benefit is when you can take advantage of that additional capacity to help drive additional value to the business.

Quantitative				Qualitative		
PERSONA	FTE RATE	TIME SAVINGS	PRODUCTIVITY IMPACT	QUALITY IMPROVEMENT	NET PROMOTER SCORE INCREASE	RISE IN JOB SATISFACTION
Project Manager	$60/hr	16 hrs/mo	**$960/mo**	15%	10%	**20%**
Finance Analyst	$65/hr	12 hrs/mo	**$780/mo**	20%	15%	**25%**
Recruiter	$50/hr	8 hrs/mo	**$400/mo**	25%	20%	**30%**
Operations Manager	$70/hr	16 hrs/mo	**$1,120/mo**	20%	15%	**20%**
Contact Center Agent	$38/hr	12 hrs/mo	**$456/mo**	25%	30%	**30%**

Figure 13.11: Copilot ROI roll-up

Conclusion

This chapter walked through creating a business case for investing in Copilot for Microsoft 365, using the Copilot Adoption Dashboard to monitor usage, building surveys using Viva Pulse to capture qualitative data, leveraging Prompt Buddy to show real-world use cases of Copilot, and, finally, reporting the collective findings to your stakeholders. The next chapter will discuss how to extend Copilot for Microsoft 365 to access additional line-of-business applications to further drive even more value out of your investment.

CHAPTER

14

Introduction to Microsoft Copilot Studio

Satya Nadella has been quoted as saying that "Microsoft is the copilot company" and described "a future where there will be a copilot for everyone and everything you do." Copilot Studio represents Microsoft's commitment to this vision by empowering people to extend existing first-party products, such as Microsoft 365 Copilot, or build stand-alone Copilots to fit unique business needs. Copilot Studio, built on top of the Power Virtual Agents (PVA) platform and Power Platform, is the next evolution in low-code application development. Microsoft has also integrated a copilot specifically to help you build out these customizations. We have officially reached the era of copilots helping you build new copilots. Hopefully, they won't become self-aware and decide to take over the world.

In this chapter, we will discuss when you might need to extend an existing copilot or consider building a stand-alone solution. We will then explore the Copilot Studio platform and how to start building your first copilot, taking you through the development and publishing processes. Finally, we will briefly examine how you might want to plan for this influx of AI assistants in your enterprise.

Who Should Use Copilot Studio?

One of the initial questions that you may have is, "Who should use Copilot Studio?" The answer will differ from one organization to the next, but Microsoft has positioned Copilot Studio for individuals who might consider themselves to be "citizen developers." If you are unfamiliar with that term, the most straightforward definition is someone who is not part of the IT organization but is performing IT tasks, such as creating or enhancing existing applications using low-code platforms. Often, these individuals do not have any formal training in software development or IT, but they are masters of their business domain.

When I refer to low-code application platforms, I'm speaking specifically about applications or platforms that allow you to build software solutions without leveraging a programming language such as C#, JavaScript, Python, etc. These systems have a configuration-based approach to building out the experience, leveraging a vast menu of options to help guide you through the steps to create a fully functioning solution. Other examples of low-code platforms within the Microsoft ecosystem include Power Apps and Power Automate, which also leverage a configuration-based approach to building out business solutions. The key benefit of these platforms is they empower people who are closest to the business domain to stand up a compelling technical solution.

While I call out citizen developers specifically, the reality is that there are also many IT professionals and IT consultants who will leverage low-code application platforms for their business solutions. Another benefit of going with low-code is that you can sometimes transition ownership of the solution to non-IT personnel for long-term support. For example, an IT consultant may develop a copilot for Human Resources, but rather than transferring the solution to IT, they could help transition responsibility to business owners. This would enable these business owners to perform lightweight maintenance of applications without having to engage with IT to make changes. By enabling self-management, this approach helps business users to rapidly respond to changes in processes without the overhead of having to track down an IT developer to make the change.

Customizing Existing Copilot vs. Creating a Stand-alone Copilot

One of the first decisions you will need to make is whether you are extending the capabilities of an existing Copilot product, such as M365 Copilot, Copilot for Sales, Copilot for Service, etc., or if you intend to create a stand-alone solution. From a project perspective, this first requires understanding the business problem you are attempting to solve, confirming the audience who will be using this solution, and then starting to plan for the user experience—how people will interact with your solution. If your target users will have M365 Copilot licenses, then you might want to consider extending that product and deploying a Copilot Agent. However, if your users are, for example, frontline workers who have a Microsoft 365 F1 or F3 license, which provides a limited set of capabilities within Microsoft 365, these users most likely will not have a Copilot license. Therefore, you might want to consider building a stand-alone copilot for performing inventory lookup or whatever their particular use case might be.

A second factor to consider is the licensing costs for Copilot Studio. While Microsoft pricing is always subject to change, at the time of this writing, Copilot Studio is included as part of your M365 Copilot license when you extend M365 Copilot and deploy your solution as an action. However, if you publish it as a stand-alone copilot, there is a cost associated with that channel. We will talk about channels later in this chapter, but for now, just keep in mind that if you are deploying a custom copilot and not extending M365 Copilot, there is a cost associated with that solution.

At a high level, Microsoft has implemented a usage-based cost model associated with the number of queries and responses your solution processes. Prior to any volume-based discounts, the starting point is $200 USD per month, which provides you with a tenant license for Copilot Studio and access to 25,000 messages per month. The concept of "messages" refers to the queries you send to Copilot and its responses. To further complicate the matter, there is a tiered level of messages that you will need to take into account.

Microsoft considers standard actions and responses—meaning you are fully controlling the inputs and outputs of your copilot—to be a single message. However, if your copilot provides a generative AI answer, meaning an LLM is evaluating your data and using its reasoning to provide an answer, that will count as two messages against your quota. Therefore, when building solutions with Copilot Studio, time may need to be spent up front to forecast how much your solution may cost based on an estimated usage.

An approach that can be helpful is to plan for a couple of different customer scenarios, map them out in terms of the user first invoking your copilot and then carrying on the conversation, and then extrapolate how many messages this may entail. From there, you can start to estimate the potential number of customer interactions you may service, and finally, that should hopefully help you arrive at a high-level estimate. However, the reality is you may not have a firm handle on how much your solution will cost until you move it into production and start to service actual users. From there, you can look at ways to either reduce the cost by limiting the generative AI answers or perhaps look for ways to make the content people are using your copilot for more easily available. If you are unsure what I mean by generative AI answers, no problem, we will dig into that later in this chapter.

NOTE Additional licensing information can be found in Microsoft's Power Platform licensing guide, maintained at `go.microsoft.com/fwlink/?linkid=2085130`.

Getting Started with Microsoft Copilot Studio

Microsoft has made getting started with Copilot Studio incredibly easy by making trial licenses available. To get started, navigate to the Copilot Studio website at `copilotstudio.microsoft.com` and authenticate with your Microsoft Entra ID. Note that to use Copilot Studio, you must authenticate using a work account and have either a Microsoft 365 E3 or E5, Office 365 E3 or E5, or Microsoft 365 Business Standard or Business Premium license. When it comes time to move your solution to production, you will need to work with your Microsoft account team to acquire a Copilot Studio tenant license. However, as noted earlier, you can obtain a 30-day trial license to begin developing your solution. Then, you can extend that trial for another 30 days while you work with the necessary parties to obtain the proper long-term licenses needed for your solution.

Navigating the Copilot Studio User Interface

Once you have authenticated with your Microsoft Entra ID on the Copilot Studio website, you should see a screen similar to Figure 14.1, welcoming you to Copilot Studio and providing a brief click-through overview of the platform provided by Microsoft. You can choose to either skip reviewing this overview or walk through it by clicking the Next button. This welcome screen only appears the first time you access Copilot Studio with your Microsoft Entra ID.

Once you have chosen to view or skip the walk-through, you should arrive at the Copilot Studio home page, as shown in Figure 14.2. As you can see, right at the top of the user interface is a Copilot chat window, which you can use to describe the type of Copilot you want to create. As mentioned earlier, Microsoft enables you to leverage generative AI to help create a custom copilot solution.

Below the chat window are example templates that help provide a starting point for building out your copilot, including:

- **Safe Travels:** A policies and procedures solution to help support employees planning their business travel
- **Store Operations:** A policies and procedures lookup targeted at frontline workers in a retail organization
- **Sustainability Insights:** Helping users quickly look up how a company is progressing against their sustainability goals

- **Team Navigator:** To navigate an organization's hierarchy to find the right person based on a need
- **Weather:** To look up weather information
- **Website Q&A:** To ask questions and leverage a website as the knowledge base for answers

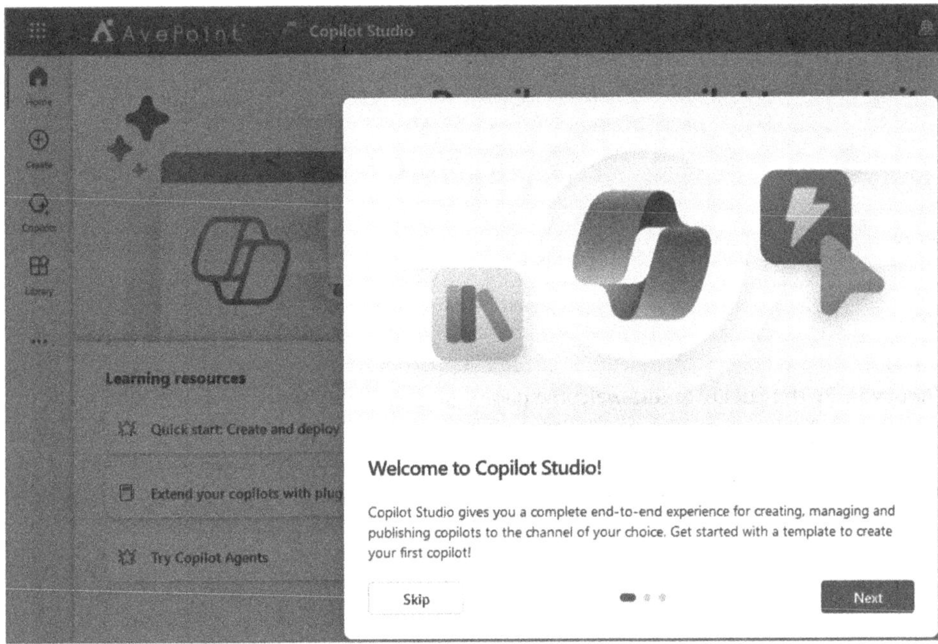

Figure 14.1: The Copilot Studio welcome screen

Below the templates is a section dedicated to learning resources, including Quick Start guides, full solution documentation, and links to a support community and Microsoft Responsible AI resources. Microsoft did a good job centralizing many of the key resources needed when building out a new copilot or developing customizations.

On the left navigation rail, you will notice a few additional buttons to help navigate the Copilot Studio user interface. The first button, Create, takes you through the process to begin developing a new custom copilot or to begin creating a customization to be leveraged by an existing copilot. Below that, the Copilots button enables you to see copilots in your Power Platform environment that you have access to. Next, the Library button lists the Power Platform connectors in your environment and the Copilots to which they are currently connected. Finally, there's a button with an ellipses, which will bring up a launcher window to navigate to other integrated Power Platform services, as shown in Figure 14.3.

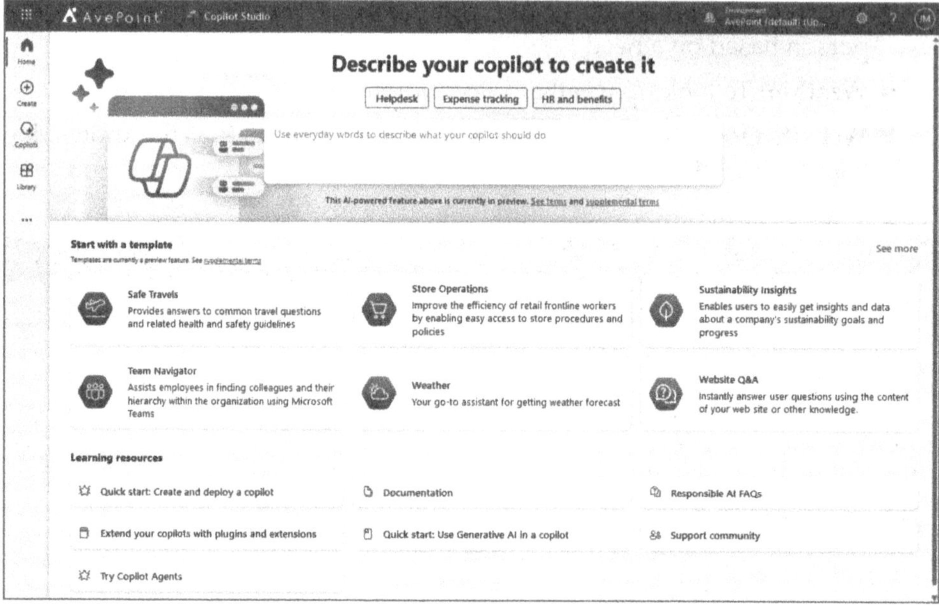

Figure 14.2: The Copilot Studio welcome page

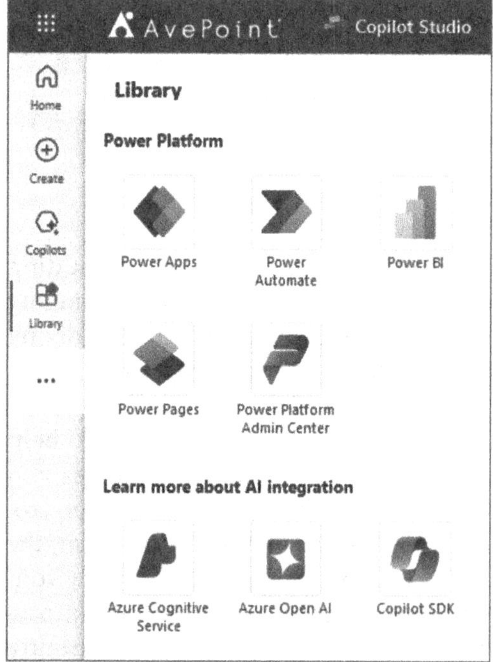

Figure 14.3: Power Platform and AI integration resources

Building Your First Copilot

Now that you've been oriented to the Copilot Studio user interface, let's go ahead and create our first custom copilot. One of the common scenarios that I have seen is building a copilot for a customer-facing website. For this example, we are going to use one of the starter templates to help create our custom copilot.

To start, click the Create button on the left rail to begin the Copilot creation process. This should bring up a new dialog, as shown in Figure 14.4, that allows you to choose between creating a new copilot from a blank template or using one of the prebuilt templates, as mentioned earlier. For this example, select the Website Q&A template to get started.

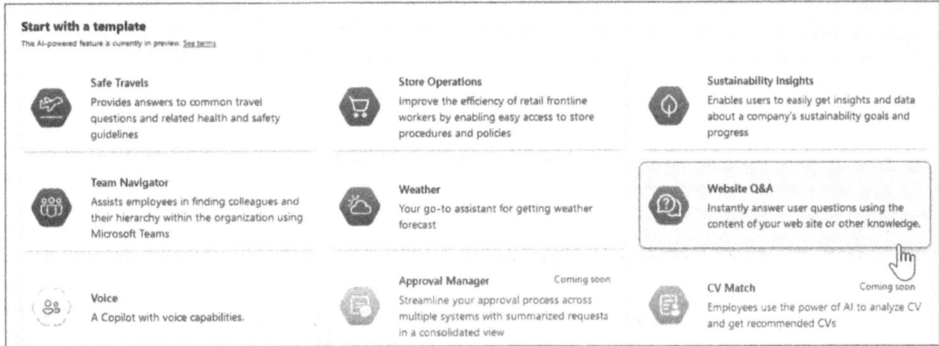

Figure 14.4: The Website Q&A template

This will open up a new dialog box that allows you to start to customize this new copilot. You can choose to follow along exactly as I configure my solution, as shown in Figure 14.5, or you can use the following instructions as a guide to build your own copilot. You can set the following parameters:

- **Language:** You can choose the default language for your copilot, though note that you cannot change this after it has been set.
- **Name:** You can name your copilot so that when you return to Copilot Studio, you can easily find it within the list of what may be dozens of copilots in some organizations.
- **Icon:** You can choose an icon, which must be a PNG file and less than 30 KB in size.
- **Description:** This should be a high-level description written so that others in your organization will know what function this copilot serves.
- **Instructions:** This is perhaps one of the most critical components of your copilot, as it will provide the LLM with clear instructions around behaviors and which topics are appropriate for it to respond to.

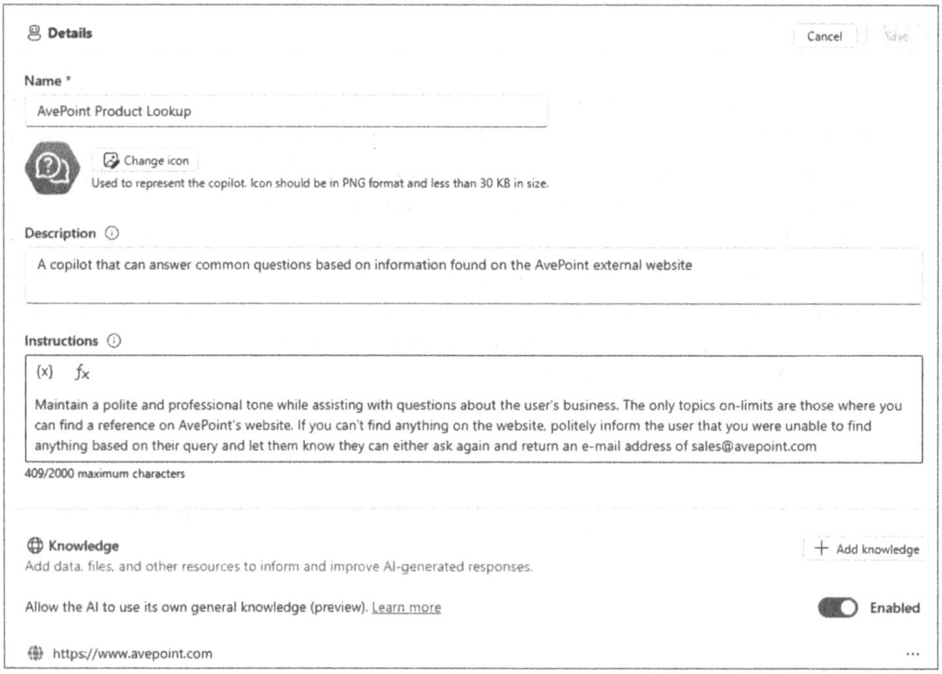

Figure 14.5: The AvePoint Product Lookup copilot

The final configuration that you will set is the knowledge base for your copilot. When you click the "+ Add knowledge" button, a new window will appear, as shown in Figure 14.6, that allows you to configure the data sources your new copilot should use. Notice that it says that these sources are powered by "Copilot Connectors." Connectors are used to help integrate with systems such as Salesforce, Zendesk, Mailchimp, etc. They follow a very similar pattern as Power Platform connectors. A number of Microsoft-certified connectors are available. Additionally, you can have custom connectors created within an organization or tenant. Custom connectors let your copilot retrieve and update data from external sources accessed through APIs.

For this use case, click the "Public websites" button to configure your external website. A new dialog box will open, as displayed in Figure 14.7, that allows you to enter the URL for the website that you want to connect to. You can add one or multiple websites to leverage as your copilot knowledge base.

When adding a website, you should provide the public website link, which is the URL for the website. Then, you can provide a name, which might be the URL again, or you can give it a distinct name that will be distinguishable for others who may be reviewing your copilot configuration as they develop copilots. Finally, you can provide a short description of that website in case anyone needs to refer back to your copilot's configuration. You may want to consider developing a naming standard within your organization for URLs to help distinguish between internal and external websites. This may be as simple as prepending all names with "[Internal]" or "[External]" as appropriate.

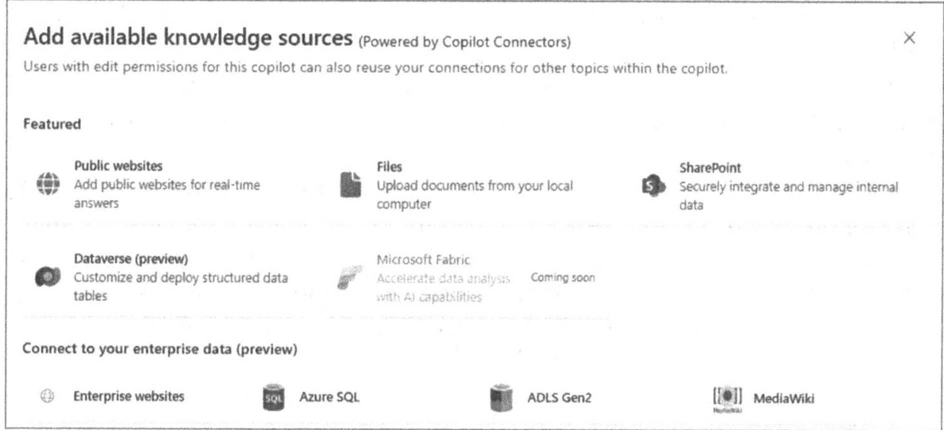

Figure 14.6: Adding available knowledge sources

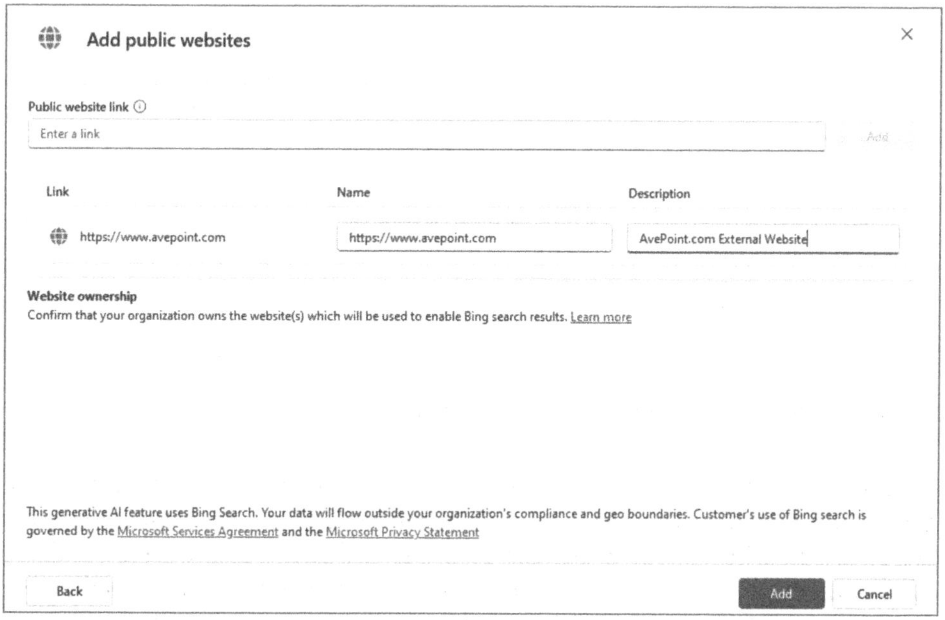

Figure 14.7: Adding public websites

Additionally, you can provide your copilot with multiple data sources, including SharePoint sites, Files, Microsoft Dataverse, Microsoft Fabric, etc. Microsoft is continuing to make new data sources available.

NOTE Some data sources may not be available at the initial creation of your copilot, but you can go back and add them afterwards.

Once you've filled out all the information, as shown in Figure 14.7, click the Add button in the open dialog box. Finally, click the Create button in the upper-right window. Copilot Studio will begin creating your new custom copilot and display a "Setting up your copilot" status message until the initial provisioning is finished.

Once it finishes provisioning, you should see a screen similar to Figure 14.8, which allows you to customize your copilot further or go back and make changes if there were initial mistakes. Also, if you click the "+ Add knowledge" button within the Knowledge panel, you'll notice that additional data sources are available for you to add to your copilot now that it has been provisioned.

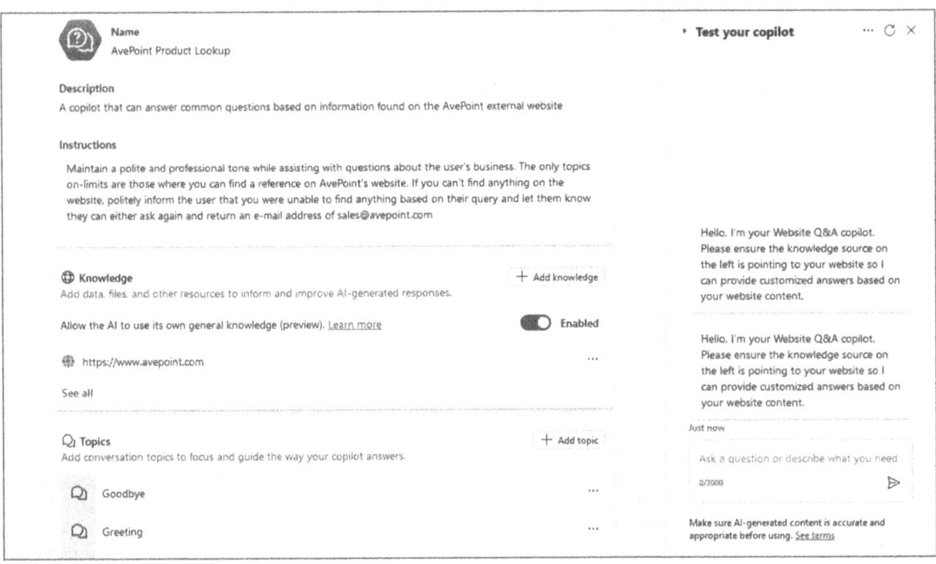

Figure 14.8: The custom copilot configuration screen

You should also notice a "Test your copilot" dialog box with a chat interface on the right-hand side of the Copilot Studio UI. As you might assume, this chat window allows you to start interacting with your copilot in a sandbox environment to ensure that it is working as expected and to iterate on the user experience. Note that at this point, you have not published your copilot to any channels, so it is only available through Copilot Studio.

Below the Knowledge section is a panel called Topics, which we will expand on further in a few pages. For now, understand that this is how you can start to design your conversation flow within Copilot Studio. Of course, there will be the option to leverage generative AI to further build out Topics. Finally, below Topics is the current "Published copilot status" which, as of now, is "Not published" since you have just provisioned it. Let's start to test your new copilot, and then we will work through the process to publish it so that others can interact with it and provide feedback.

Testing Your Copilot

So, you have provided Copilot Studio with the bare minimum needed to create a custom copilot that will return information from a website you defined. For this example, I have pointed my copilot at `avepoint.com`; therefore, I expect that when I engage with this custom copilot, it will not only return answers from that website but also cite the page on the website where it found the information included in its response.

Rather than exchanging pleasantries with this copilot, let's hop right in and see what it can do. Try the following prompt, and then either click Return or press the paper airplane message icon to send the following prompt to your custom copilot:

"Does AvePoint offer any products that can back up Microsoft 365?"

Just like magic, it comes back with a positive response that AvePoint offers Cloud Backup solutions and cites where it found that information, as shown in Figure 14.9.

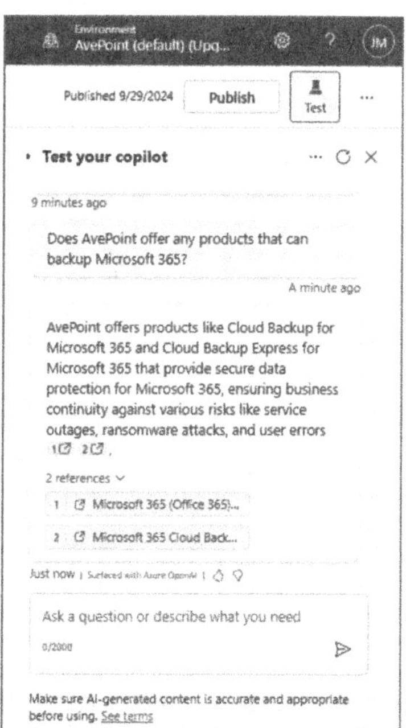

Figure 14.9: Testing your custom copilot

If you have ever attempted to build a professional code chatbot from scratch, you will know there are many steps to achieve what we just accomplished in minutes. There's all the infrastructure provisioning, building of web applications, writing the code, testing the code, building the pipelines to deploy the code, conducting all the security reviews, etc. What we have configured in just a matter of minutes could serve as a chatbot you can deploy to your website to help answer standard queries about your company's products and services. Now, before releasing something like this, you'll want to go through a few more rounds of testing to ensure there aren't ways to "jailbreak" or otherwise bypass the inherent security controls provided by Microsoft. However, this is definitely a great jumpstart at quickly scaffolding up an impactful solution.

Publishing Your Copilot

Once you are at a point where you feel that your copilot is ready to be used, you will want to publish it for others to consume. First, click the Publish button in the upper-right corner of the Copilot Studio interface, and then click the Publish button in the dialog box, as shown in Figure 14.10.

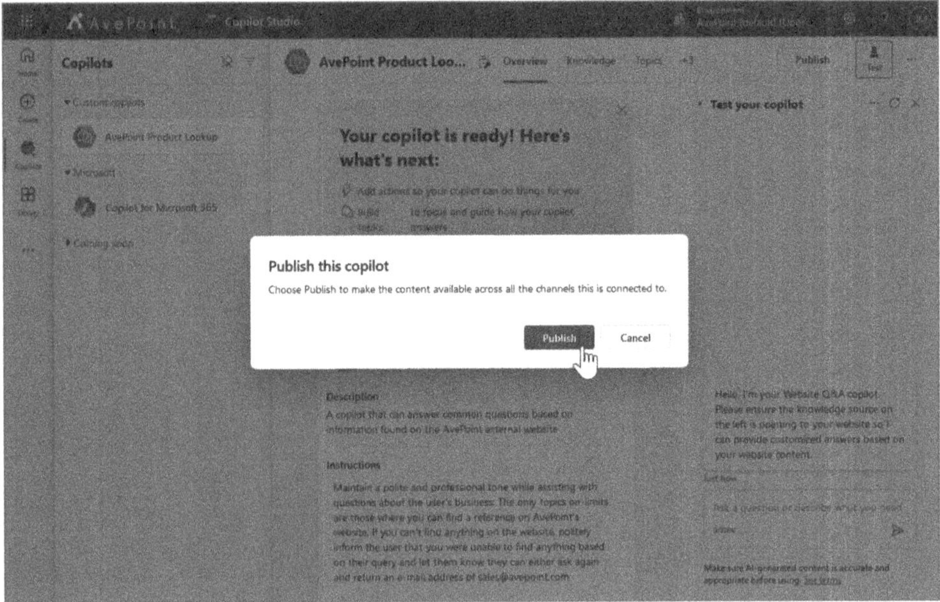

Figure 14.10: Publishing your custom copilot

You will see a confirmation dialog box that lets you know your copilot is being published. Feel free to close this window. Your copilot will publish in the background. In the background, Copilot Studio is making your copilot available through the channels you have associated with it. Copilot Studio is configured for you to publish to Telephony and Microsoft Teams as the default channels. If you click the Channels button in the navigation in Copilot Studio, you will arrive at the Channels screen, as shown in Figure 14.11.

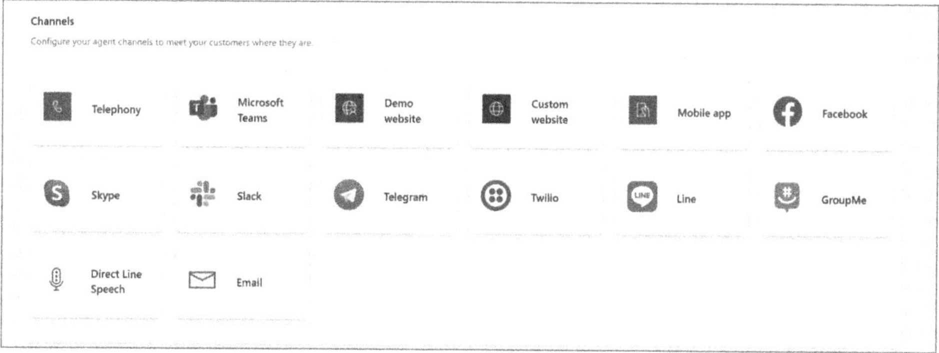

Figure 14.11: Copilot Studio channels

You will notice that there are many channels through which you can publish your copilot, including a website, mobile app, Facebook, Slack, etc., along with the ability to hand off a chat session from copilot to an enterprise solution such as Genesys, LivePerson, Salesforce, etc. This is where Microsoft differentiates itself from the competition by enabling seamless interoperability across many of the most popular communication channels. This makes your Copilot Studio solutions very portable and easy to integrate into your existing enterprise workflows.

Let's finish configuring your copilot by clicking the Microsoft Teams button within the list of channels. This will open a new dialog window, as shown in Figure 14.12, where you will then click the Turn on Teams button to finalize the setup configuration.

After a few minutes, Copilot Studio will finish publishing your copilot to Microsoft Teams, making it available for you to add to your client as a virtual assistant. When Copilot Studio finishes its configuration setup, it redirects you to a window that suggests you open the link in the Microsoft Teams application. It also provides a link to download Microsoft Teams if it is not installed on your computer.

You can continue this setup through the web browser, or you can open Microsoft Teams. If you decide to open the Microsoft Teams client, you will be presented with a dialog box similar to Figure 14.13 that prompts you to add your new copilot to your Microsoft Teams client.

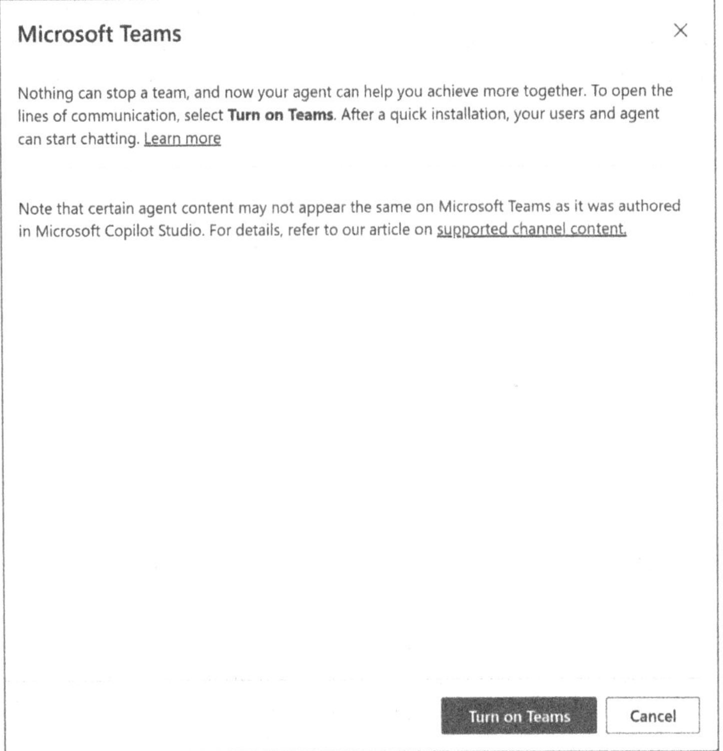

Figure 14.12: Microsoft Teams channel configuration

For me, Microsoft still references Power Virtual Agents as part of the copilot manifest, as shown in Figure 14.13, but rest assured that being powered by Power Virtual Agents is synonymous with being powered by Copilot Studio. It also provides a rundown of the features and permissions that this new copilot will have, such as the ability to complete tasks, find information, and chat, while having permission to send and receive notifications. This new copilot has capabilities like a colleague you are interacting with through standard Microsoft Teams messaging.

To bring this experience full circle, you can now chat with your new copilot as though it were another chatbot or person. For this example, I sent it a similar prompt to what you sent earlier:

"Does AvePoint provide solutions to back up Microsoft 365?"

As you can see in Figure 14.14, the AvePoint Product Lookup copilot responds with, "AvePoint provides solutions for Microsoft 365 backup, ensuring secure data protection and efficient recovery processes." It also provides three sources that helped inform its response, including the following URL from the AvePoint website, which we defined as a knowledge source as part of our original copilot configuration:

```
avepoint.com/products/cloud-backup/microsoft-365-backup
```

The channel was added.

Microsoft Teams

Excited to make your agent available for others to use in Microsoft Teams? Review how your agent will appear. Select **Edit details** to modify. Once you are ready, select **Availability options** to continue.
Learn more

Agent preview

AvePoint Product Lookup
AvePoint Product Lookup

Edit details Open agent Settings (coming soon)

Disconnect from Teams

Availability options

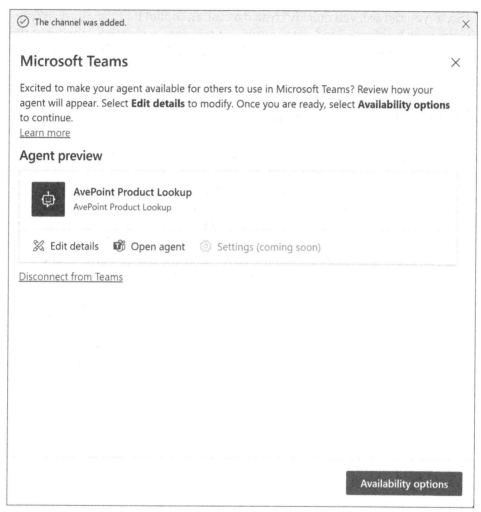

Figure 14.13: Adding your custom copilot to Teams

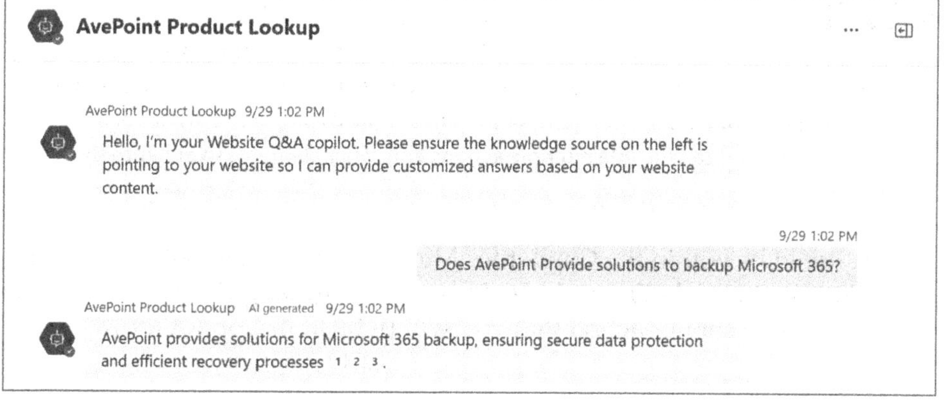

Figure 14.14: Teams Chat with your custom copilot

So, as you can see, you quickly created a custom copilot that seamlessly returns information from a defined data source—in this case, a website—as part of the Microsoft Teams chat experience. Next, let's extend Copilot for Microsoft 365 to provide a similar capability.

Creating a Copilot Plugin

Copilot actions are customizations that you develop to extend the out-of-the-box capabilities of Copilot for Microsoft 365. Similar to our custom copilot example, we are going to extend Copilot for Microsoft 365 to perform a lookup from the AvePoint external website to provide product information within the Copilot experience. To get started, navigate back to the Copilot Studio home page or go directly to `copilotstudio.microsoft.com` and authenticate with your Microsoft Entra ID. Click the Copilots button on the left-hand rail navigation, and then click the Copilot for Microsoft 365 option, as shown in Figure 14.15.

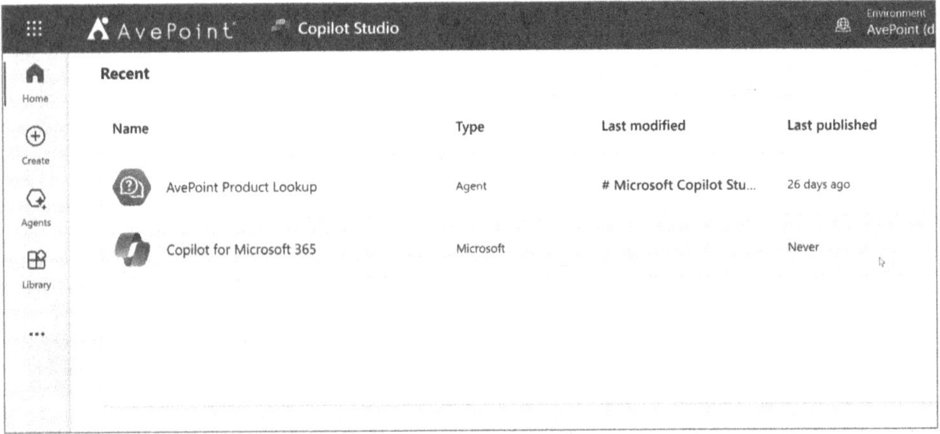

Figure 14.15: The Copilot for Microsoft 365 option

NOTE **The terms "Copilot agents" and "Copilot plugins" are often used interchangeably as Microsoft marketing continues to change the name of products and features. For the sake of clarity, we will refer to them as plugins to reflect the current user interface for Copilot Studio. Copilot agents or plugins are the deployable instance of the customization, and can include multiple actions and other elements to enhance the copilot's skills.**

You should be within the Copilot for Microsoft 365 screen within the Copilots menu, as shown in Figure 14.16. Now, click the "+ Add action" button to begin creating a copilot action that you will publish to Copilot for Microsoft

365. Actions are specific tasks or operations that a copilot can perform. They enable the copilot to interact with external systems, apply business logic, or access data sources.

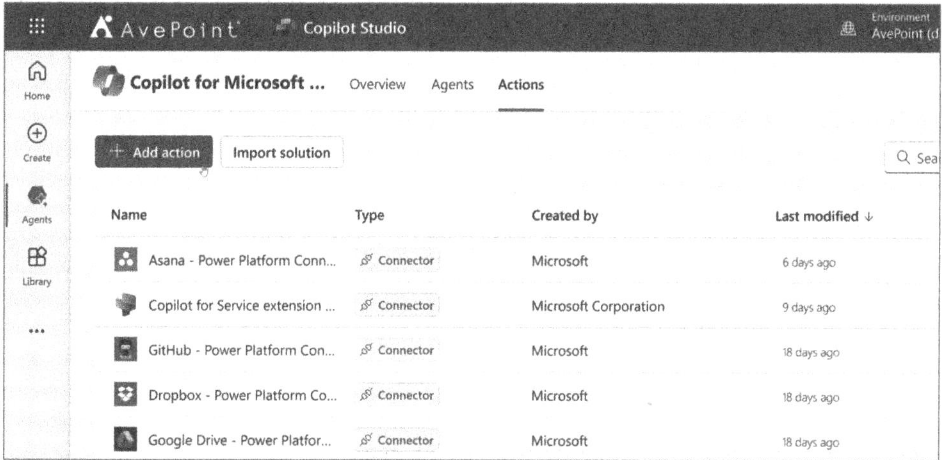

Figure 14.16: Adding an action to Copilot for Microsoft 365

You can create several types of actions, as shown in Figure 14.17, but for this instance, you are going to create a conversational action to mimic the user experience from the custom copilot you just created.

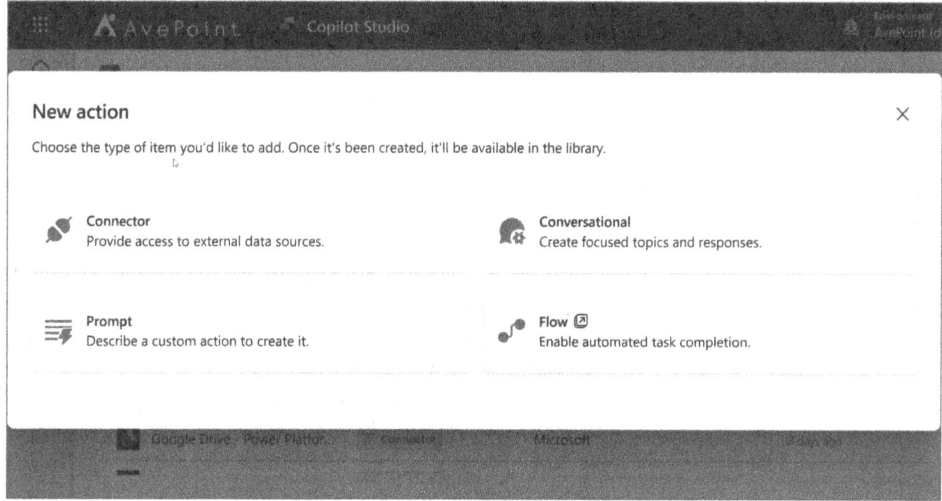

Figure 14.17: Adding a conversational action

If you try to name this new action the same as the copilot you created earlier, you will receive an error message similar to the one shown in Figure 14.18, indicating that the "Copilot name already exists." Currently, there is no way to publish a custom copilot as a plugin for Copilot for Microsoft 365. To bypass this error message, provide a unique name for your action, and then click the Create button.

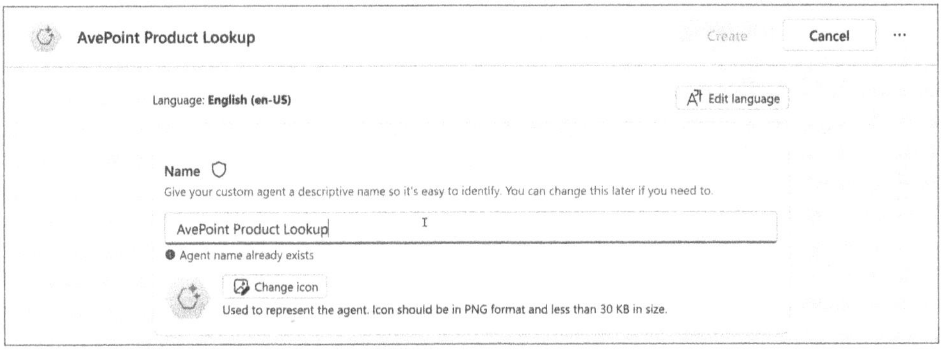

Figure 14.18: The "Copilot name already exists" error message

If you have ever worked with Power Virtual Agents, the page you will be brought to, shown in Figure 14.19, should look fairly familiar. You are in the Topic builder interface of the old Power Virtual Agents user experience. Each topic starts with a trigger as the initial node for the conversation workflow. For the sake of simplicity, in this example, you are not designing a complete conversation workflow with multiple topics to guide the user. This scenario is leveraging a single topic where the copilot does not know the intent of the user.

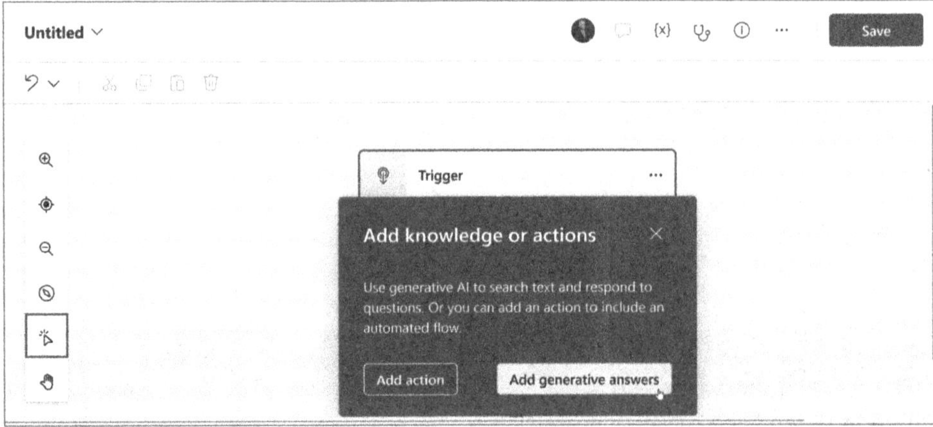

Figure 14.19: The "Add knowledge or actions" dialog box

Sometimes this is referred to as the "fallback topic," meaning if all else fails, invoke this set of logic.

NOTE Microsoft provides an in-depth overview of Topics on Microsoft Learn at `learn.microsoft.com/en-us/microsoft-copilot-studio/guidance/topics-overview`.

You can either click the "Add generative answers" button from within the blue dialog box or click the "+" button underneath the box labeled Trigger to bring up a menu. Then, under Advanced, there is an option called "Generative answers." In both scenarios, this will add a new node to your conversation flow, beneath the initial box labeled Trigger.

Generative answers, at a high level, mean you will leverage Azure OpenAI to understand the intent of what your users are looking for, ground that prompt with data from the `AvePoint.com` website, and then return it to the user.

A dialog box should appear on the right side of the screen, helping you configure the generative answers properties for this node, as shown in Figure 14.20.

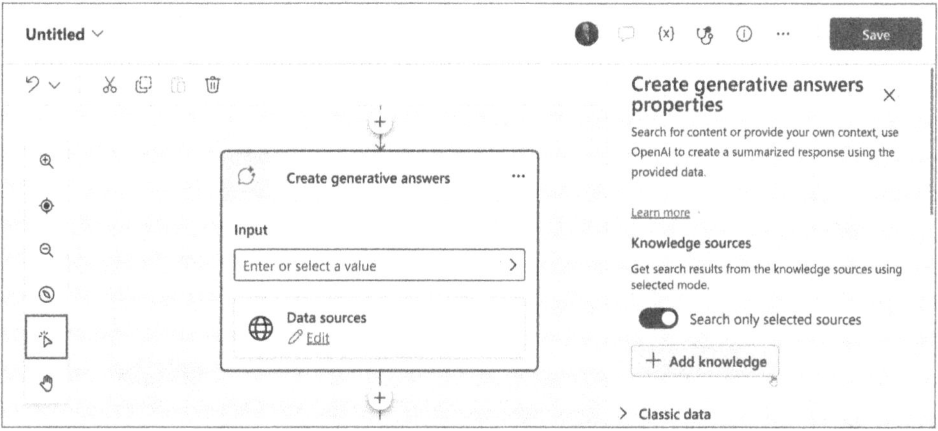

Figure 14.20: Configuring generative answers

Click the "Search only selected sources" toggle to ensure that only responses from the `AvePoint.com` website are returned as part of the response. This ensures that the large language model that is passed this prompt will not try and respond based on its knowledge but instead will follow the retrieval augmented generation (RAG) pattern of basing its responses on retrieved data as specified by the user.

Next, click the "+ Add knowledge" button to open the "Add available knowledge sources" dialog box, as shown in Figure 14.21.

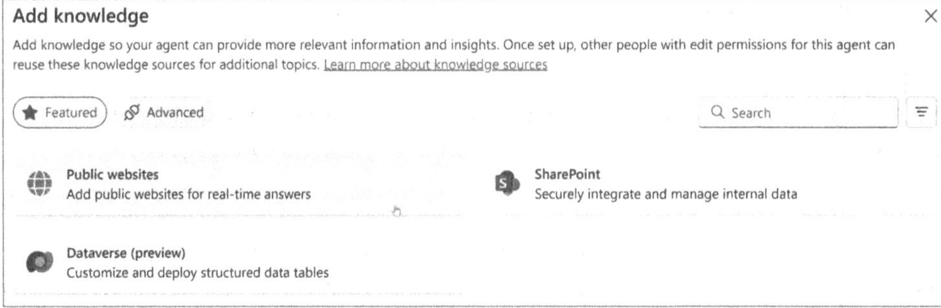

Figure 14.21: Adding available knowledge sources

You will then enter the URL for the website that you intend to have this action refer to. For my example, I entered `avepoint.com` and provided a description of AvePoint External Website, as shown in Figure 14.22. Click the Add button to close this dialog box and return to the Copilot Studio topic authoring canvas.

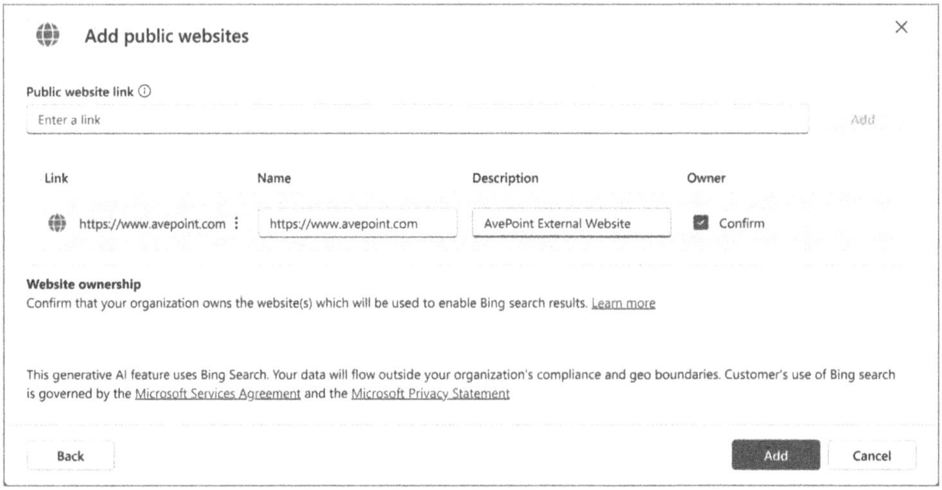

Figure 14.22: Adding public websites

Next, you must configure the Input property for this "Create generative answers" node. You can do so by clicking the Input box of the "Create generative answers" node. The input is the text that the user sends to this copilot. For this instance, select the system variable *Activity.Text*, as shown in Figure 14.23, as a string, which is the text sent from Copilot for Microsoft 365 to this Copilot Studio topic.

NOTE **Microsoft Learn has excellent resources for further understanding how to build conversational plugins. You can find them at `learn.microsoft.com/en-us/microsoft-copilot-studio/copilot-conversational-plugins`.**

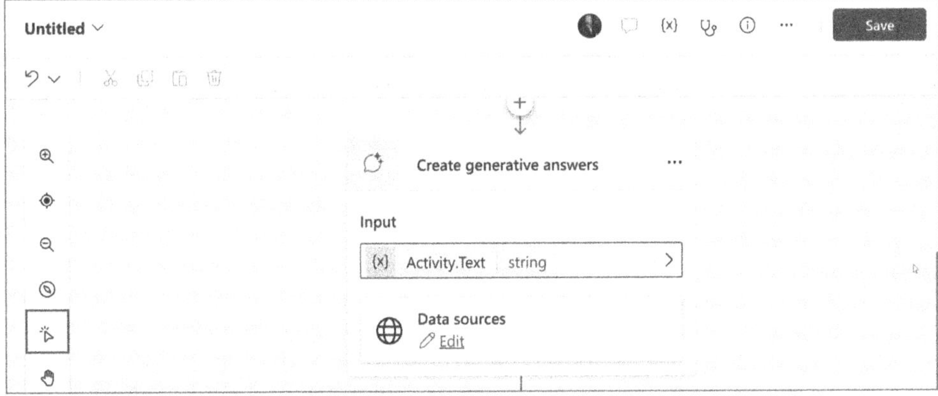

Figure 14.23: The "Create generative answers" dialog box

Before publishing, you need to provide a name for the topic. Double-click Untitled in the upper-left corner, and then rename the topic to "**Product Lookup**" or something unique, as shown in Figure 14.24.

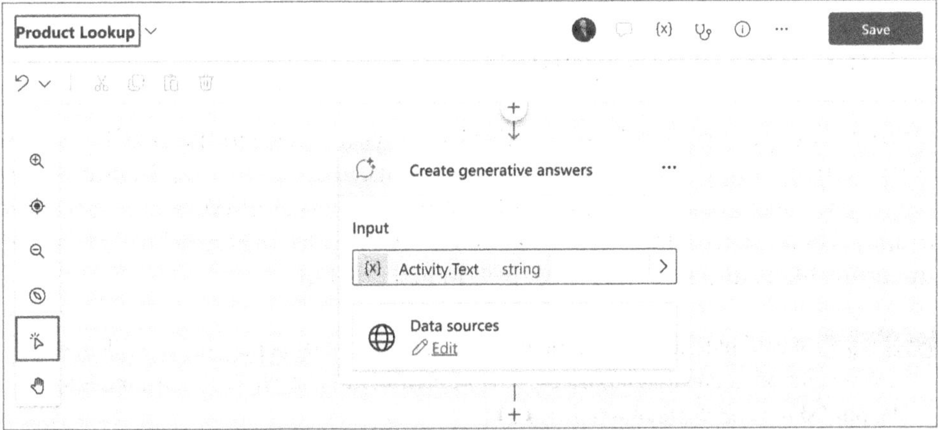

Figure 14.24: Naming the topic

Finally, click the Publish button in the upper-right corner and confirm that you want to publish this plugin, as shown in Figure 14.25. You will need to wait a few minutes for Copilot Studio to package your solution and make it available.

NOTE You can find administrator resources for managing and deploying copilot plugins at `learn.microsoft.com/en-us/microsoft-copilot-studio/copilot-plugins-enable-admin`.

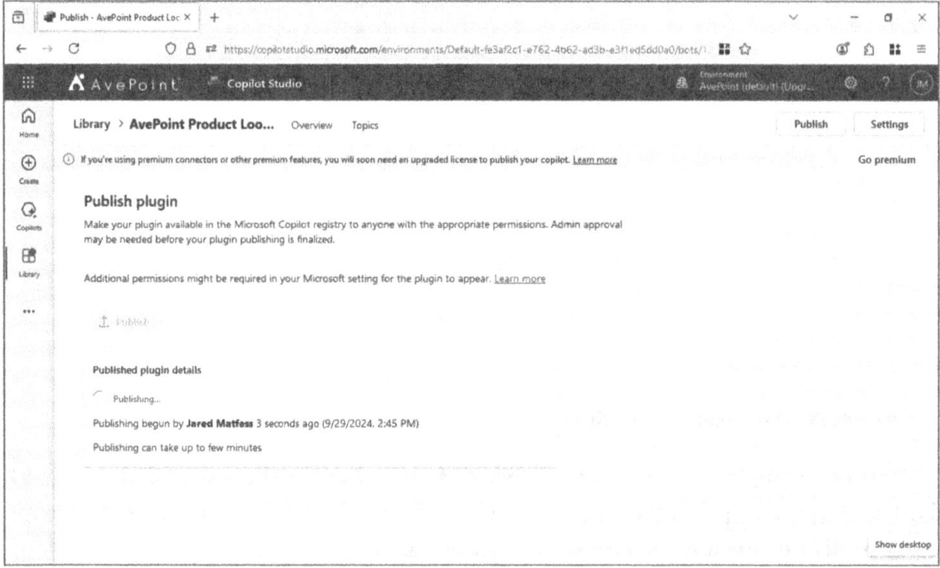

Figure 14.25: Publishing the plugin

Testing Your Copilot Plugin

Once your copilot plugin has been deployed, you can go to the BizChat experience either in Microsoft Teams or at `copilot.microsoft.com`. In either scenario, you must ensure that the Work/Web toggle is set to Work to select your plugin. Then, click on the right-hand side of the copilot message box, as shown in Figure 14.26, and select the plugin you just created.

NOTE **If your plugin does not show up in the list of available plugins, you will need to work with someone that has access to the Microsoft 365 Admin Portal to complete the publishing and deployment process.**

Finally, try to re-enter the prompt you used previously to validate that your plugin is working as expected. For this scenario, I am going to send the same prompt:

"Does AvePoint provide solutions to back up Microsoft 365?"

As you can see in Figure 14.27, the plugin is returning data from the `AvePoint.com` website that we previously configured. To recap, users can now toggle the custom plugin that you developed to provide additional specificity to the content they are looking for from M365 Copilot. From a user experience perspective, this starts to set the foundation that M365 Copilot is the single entry point for the work that they perform.

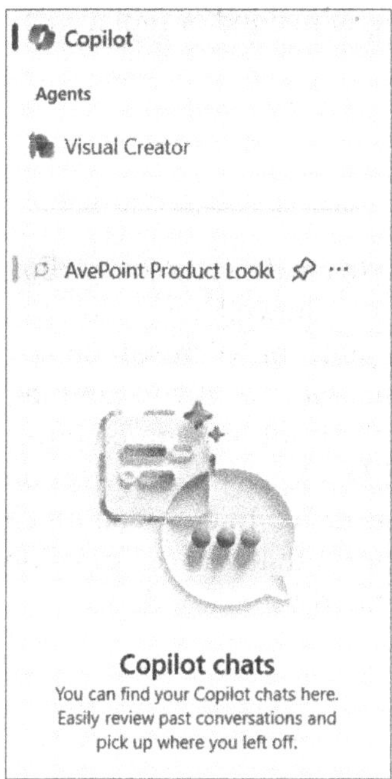

Figure 14.26: Enabling an M365 Copilot plugin

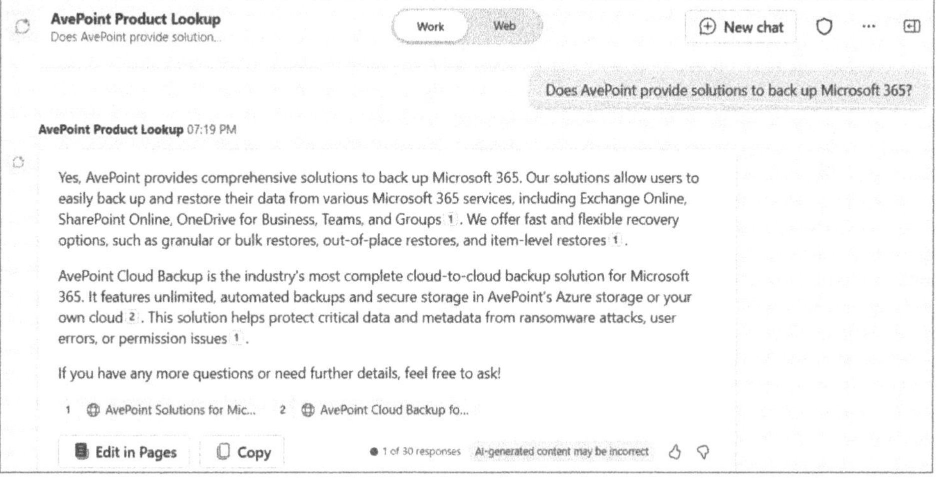

Figure 14.27: Copilot plugin success

As organizations begin to mature their M365 Copilot implementations, you can expect the list of plugins to grow as business use cases are identified and solved. It is also important to have up-front conversations around governance to ensure that, just like any other application within an IT environment, plugins are maintained, supported, and pruned when no longer needed or replaced by more advanced capabilities.

Conclusion

In this chapter, we covered how to use Copilot Studio to create a custom copilot. We published this custom copilot in Microsoft Teams and showed how to interact with it just like a colleague. Then, we extended Copilot for Microsoft 365 by creating a custom plugin mimicking that same external search. These examples, while simple, are pretty impressive when you think about how much effort they would take if you were to develop them outside a low-code application environment. The extensibility of Copilot for Microsoft 365 makes it so much more than just a singular product; rather, it is a platform that you can develop and deploy customizations on to provide a more refined user experience.

CHAPTER

15

Creating a Custom Teams Copilot

There will be instances when Copilot Studio may not satisfy the business use case you want to solve. Some reasons for this might be that the application logic is far too complex for what you can develop using a low-code application platform, or you may have unique performance or logging requirements based on your organization's governance requirements. For these types of scenarios, you will need to develop these customizations using familiar programming languages such as JavaScript, TypeScript, C#, etc. There are a few benefits to this, including the ability to utilize developers who are already familiar with these programming languages. The learning curve will be relatively manageable, and you will have full control over the customization and its functionality.

Much like any other software development project, the key is to set up your development environment for optimal productivity. Doing so ensures that developers like us have the right tools, such as computing, data manipulation, and debugging options, all in one place. Additionally, for building custom Copilots or extending existing ones, writing full code means you can tap into Azure AI Studio, which will help unlock additional functionality for your use case. In this chapter, we will walk through setting up your environment to take advantage of all these capabilities and more. This makes it easy to add exactly what your project needs. You start by defining the plugin's purpose, setting up the environment with Azure SDKs, and writing some custom code. Testing is simple with Microsoft's tools, and once it's all good, you can deploy the plugin for others to use. It's a great way to share your work and give your network access to custom solutions you've built!

Extensibility Options

With the Copilot Wave 2 announcement, Microsoft introduced even more changes to the extensibility options for Copilot. These new extensibility patterns or options include the following:

- **Declarative agents:** These can be used to extend the Copilot chat-based experience within Microsoft Teams or the Web to focus on a particular set of data sources or domain knowledge areas.
- **Connectors:** Connectors can be used to extend the Microsoft Graph within your tenant to additional data sources to increase Copilot's knowledge base. Some examples include ServiceNow, Salesforce, and SAP.
- **Power Platform connectors:** You can develop custom connectors that can be leveraged by both Copilot and Power Platform applications.
- **Plugins:** These are applications that allow you to interact with resources both inside and outside of the boundaries of Microsoft 365. These can be deployed to Microsoft Teams as message extensions, work stand-alone, or be leveraged by Copilot Studio, enabling you to mix the benefits of low-code and full-code solutions.

Knowledge and Software Prerequisites

There are a number of prerequisites for you to be able to use Azure AI Studio and build AI projects. You should make sure you know or have the following before you install and configure Azure AI Studio:

- An understanding of the general architecture of plugins for Microsoft applications
- A coding background
- A Microsoft Developer account
- Node.js and npm
- A .NET environnent on your machine
- A configured integrated development environment (IDE)

Let's take a look at each of these areas.

In this chapter, we will focus on Copilot extensibility via plugins and getting your development environment prepared to help create the customizations. For additional information on the other extensibility options, you can reference the information at Microsoft Learn at `learn.microsoft.com/en-us/microsoft-365-copilot/extensibility`.

An Understanding of the General Architecture of Plugins

Microsoft plugins expand software functionality by adding new features or integrating with other tools. It usually breaks down into three parts: the host application (like Office or Teams), the plugin (which adds specific features), and the APIs/SDKs (tools that help the plugin communicate with the host). For Office add-ins, you can use web tech like HTML, CSS, and JavaScript, connecting to Office via the JavaScript or Copilot API. If you're diving into plugin development, check out the Office Add-ins documentation, as shown in Figure 15.1, or the Teams platform:

- Office Add-Ins: `https://learn.microsoft.com/en-us/office/dev/add-ins`
- Teams platform: `https://learn.microsoft.com/en-us/microsoftteams/platform`

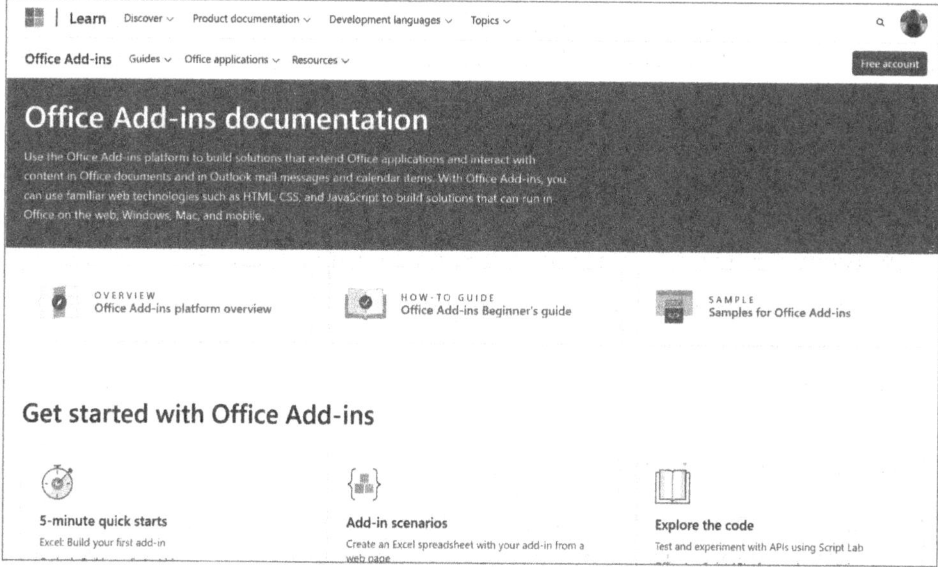

Figure 15.1: The Microsoft Office add-in home page

A Code Background

JavaScript is one of the most popular programming languages for building applications. Since it's so versatile, you can use it for pretty much anything, from small tasks like form validation to full-scale applications. On the other hand, TypeScript builds on JavaScript by adding static types. It's great for larger projects where catching errors early and having a more structured codebase are important. With TypeScript, you get better tooling, like autocompletion and type checking, which can make development smoother. However, the setup for a TypeScript environment can be more complicated.

When it comes to Microsoft plugins, both JavaScript and TypeScript are often used, depending on the complexity of the project. For simpler plugins, JavaScript is quick to set up and get running. But for more intricate builds, such as a plugin that needs to interact with Excel or Word, TypeScript can help keep the codebase clean and maintainable. For example, a basic Office add-in could consist of a manifest file, a web page, and a script written in either JavaScript or TypeScript. If you're using TypeScript, you'll get the added benefit of type definitions, which makes working with Office objects easier and more reliable.

If you're just getting started or want to level up your skills, plenty of resources are available. Mozilla's JavaScript Guide is a great starting point, offering tutorials for both beginners and advanced developers. If TypeScript is more your speed, the official TypeScript docs are full of useful tips and examples. And if you're curious about how this works in the real world, some awesome sample projects are available on GitHub, such as the Office Add-in Samples and TypeScript Samples. These repos are packed with examples showing how to build plugins and solve common challenges using these languages.

Whether you're new to coding or looking to dive deeper into Microsoft plugin development, the following tools and resources will set you up for success. The combination of JavaScript's flexibility and TypeScript's structure is powerful, especially when building something as customizable as Microsoft plugins.

- JavaScript Guide: `https://developer.mozilla.org/en-US/docs/Web/JavaScript/Guide`
- Typescript Documentation: `https://www.typescriptlang.org/docs`
- Office Add-in Samples: `https://github.com/OfficeDev/office-js-docs-pr`
- TypeScript Samples: `https://github.com/microsoft/TypeScriptSamples`

A Microsoft Developer Account

You will need a Microsoft Developer account to use Azure AI Studio. This section guides you through the process of creating your own Microsoft Developer account if you don't already have one. This includes navigating to the registration page, signing up for an account, understanding the requirements and verification process, and exploring the benefits and responsibilities associated with having a Microsoft Developer account.

To begin the process of creating a Microsoft Developer account, open your web browser and visit the Microsoft Developer registration page at `https://developer.microsoft.com/en-us/microsoft-365/dev-program`. You can then sign up for an account by clicking the Sign Up button.

The following steps walk you through the requirements for signing up and verification process:

1. Sign in with a Microsoft Account. If you do not have a Microsoft account, you can create one during the sign-up process. You should use an email address that is not associated with a school or company domain to avoid verification issues.
2. Fill out basic information about your location, company name, and preferred language.
3. Choose your focus as a developer. For this example, choose "Personal Projects."
4. Choose which areas of Microsoft 365 you are interested in. For this example, choose Copilot for Microsoft 365, Office Add-ins, Microsoft Teams, and SharePoint Framework.
5. Input a valid phone number; Microsoft will text you a code.

Congratulations, you are now part of the Microsoft 365 Developer program!

NOTE For detailed instructions, refer to the Microsoft Developer Program Sign-Up Guide found at `https://learn.microsoft.com/en-us/office/developer-program/microsoft-365-developer-program`.

Node.js and npm

Another prerequisite is having Node.js and npm. In this section, we'll cover how to install Node.js. This will be followed by information on how to configure npm.

Introduction to Node.js

Node.js is a JavaScript runtime built on Chrome's V8 engine, created in 2009 by Ryan Dahl. It uses an event-driven, non-blocking I/O model, making it perfect for data-heavy real-time apps. Since its launch in 2009 and the introduction of npm in 2010, Node.js has rapidly grown. Key milestones include performance upgrades, modern JavaScript support, and the establishment of the OpenJS Foundation.

Using JavaScript on both front- and backends streamlines development, reducing context switching. Node's non-blocking I/O can handle multiple connections at once, which is ideal for high-performance apps like gaming platforms or chat services. Its huge npm library also speeds up the development process.

Installing Node.js

Node.js can be installed on Windows, macOS, and Linux, and the process is straightforward for each platform. This section provides the installation instructions for each operating system.

Windows Installation

Use the following steps to install Node.js onto a Windows system:

1. Download the Windows Installer:
   - Visit the official Node.js website at `nodejs.org` and download the Windows Installer. Choose either the LTS (Long Term Support) version for stability or the Current version for the latest features.
2. Run the Installer:
   - Execute the downloaded .msi file. Follow the prompts in the setup wizard. Accept the license agreement, select the installation folder, and choose the components to install, including npm.
3. Verify the installation:
   - Open Command Prompt and type **node -v** to verify that Node.js was installed correctly. Then type **npm -v** at the Command Prompt to confirm that npm was also installed correctly. The system should display the installed versions of Node.js and npm.

macOS Installation

Use the following steps to install Node.js onto a macOS system:

1. Using Homebrew:
   - Install Homebrew if it's not already installed. Open Terminal and run:

     ```
     /bin/bash -c "$(curl -fsSL https://raw.githubusercontent.com/
     Homebrew/install/HEAD/install.sh)"
     ```
   - Once Homebrew is installed, you can install Node.js by running:

     ```
     brew install node
     ```
   - This command installs the latest version of Node.js and npm, setting them up for immediate use.

2. Verify the Installation:
   - To check if Node.js and npm were installed correctly, type the following commands in Terminal:

     ```
     node -v
     npm -v
     ```

   - This will display the installed versions of Node.js and npm, confirming a successful installation.

Linux Installation

Use the following steps to install Node.js onto a Linux system:

1. Use a package manager to perform the installation:
   - For Debian and Ubuntu-based distributions, enter:

     ```
     sudo apt update
     sudo apt install nodejs npm
     ```

   - For Red Hat and Fedora-based distributions, enter:

     ```
     sudo dnf install nodejs npm
     ```

   - These commands install both Node.js and npm from the package repository.
2. Verify the installation:
   - Confirm the installation by checking the versions of Node.js and npm:

     ```
     node -v
     npm -v
     ```

   - The successful output of version numbers indicates that Node.js and npm have been installed correctly.

Selecting the Correct Version of Node.js

When installing Node.js, you should confirm that you are installing the correct version to work with Copilot. You will want to evaluate the needs of your project and team. If stability and long-term support are priorities, opt for the latest LTS version. If accessing the latest features is critical, consider the Current version, but be prepared for more frequent updates and potential changes.

Understanding LTS vs. Current Versions

The LTS (Long Term Support) version is recommended for most users, as it receives all the critical bug fixes, security updates, and performance improvements.

LTS versions are ideal for production environments due to their stability and extended support period.

The Current version contains the latest features and updates. It is suitable for developers who want to experiment with new capabilities or need features that are only available in the latest version. However, this version may not be as stable as the LTS and has a shorter support life cycle.

Using Version Managers

Tools like nvm (Node Version Manager) for macOS and Linux, or nvm-windows (`https://github.com/coreybutler/nvm-windows`) for Windows, allow developers to easily install and switch between different Node.js versions. This is particularly useful for testing applications across multiple versions.

To install nvm on macOS or Linux, enter the following:

```
curl -o- https://raw.githubusercontent.com/nvm-sh/nvm/v0.39.1/install
.sh | bash
```

To install a specific Node.js version using nvm, enter the following:

```
nvm install 14.17.0  # Replace with the desired version number
nvm use 14.17.0
```

Deciding Which Version to Use

To decide which version to use, you should evaluate the needs of your project and team. If stability and long-term support are priorities, opt for the latest LTS version. If accessing the latest features is critical, consider the Current version, but be prepared for more frequent updates and potential changes.

npm Configuration Tips

The following are essential npm configuration tips:

- **Manage Node.js versions with nvm, as explained earlier in this chapter.** Using nvm (Node Version Manager) allows you to easily switch between different versions of Node.js, ensuring compatibility and testing across versions without requiring reinstallation. Figure 15.2 shows an example nvm command to list the available versions of node on your system.
- **Set up npm for a project.**
  When setting up npm for a project, it's crucial to configure it correctly to avoid common pitfalls like package version mismatches.
  - Use a local npm registry: This can speed up the installation and ensure availability of all packages.

```
PS C:\Users\thomas.flock\TeamsApps\CopilotBook> nvm list

  * 18.20.4 (Currently using 64-bit executable)
PS C:\Users\thomas.flock\TeamsApps\CopilotBook>
```

Figure 15.2: An example nvm command to list the available versions of NodeJS on your system

- Configure npm scripts: Standardize scripts like start, test, and build in your package.json to ensure consistency.

  ```
  "scripts": {
    "start": "node app.js",
    "test": "jest",
    "build": "webpack"
  }
  ```

- **Use .npmrc for configuration.**
  The .npmrc file allows you to set configuration parameters at the project or user level. Common configurations include setting a custom registry, configuring proxy settings, and more.

  ```
  registry=https://registry.npmjs.org/
  strict-ssl=true
  save-exact=true
  ```

- **Use dependency management.**
  - Locking dependencies: Use package-lock.json or npm shrinkwrap to lock the versions of your project's dependencies. This ensures that installations are repeatable, and dependencies do not update unexpectedly.
  - Audit for vulnerabilities: Regularly run `npm audit` to check for vulnerabilities in installed packages:

    ```
    npm install --save lodash
    npm audit fix
    ```

- **Optimize npm performance.**
  - Use npm ci for CI/CD pipelines: npm ci is faster than npm install, as it skips certain user-oriented features and focuses on reproducibility.
  - Configure npm caching: npm caches packages locally. Configuring these caches can speed up installation times and reduce network overhead.

    ```
    npm config set cache /path/to/cache -global
    ```

- **Secure npm projects.**
  - Enable 2FA for npm accounts: Protect your npm account by enabling two-factor authentication, reducing the risk of unauthorized access.
  - Use scoped packages for private code: Scoped packages (@your username/projectname) can be used to manage private projects and share them within a team or organization.
- **Use environment variables.**
  - To avoid hard-coding sensitive information in your package.json, use environment variables. This is crucial for keeping API keys and other secrets out of your codebase.

```
"scripts": {
  "start": "API_KEY=${API_KEY} node app.js"
}
```

- **Document npm scripts.**
  - Document npm scripts for better collaboration: Ensure that all npm scripts used in the project are well documented in your package.json file or a separate documentation file. This helps new developers understand what each script does and how to use them effectively. For example:

```
"scripts": {
  "start": "node app.js",
  "test": "jest",
  "build": "webpack",
  "deploy": "npm run build && npm run publish"
}
```

- In your documentation, explain each script:
  - start: Launches the application
  - test: Runs the test suite using Jest
  - build: Bundles the application into static files for production with Webpack
  - deploy: Builds the application and publishes it to a server

Installing .NET

.NET, or `dotnet` in the command line, is a free, open-source, cross-platform code for building various types of applications. Created by Microsoft, .NET is one of the most widely used frameworks for developing applications. Many of the SDKs provided by Azure AI Studio rely on .NET in the background to function properly. To install .NET on your local machine, follow these steps:

1. Visit the official .NET download page at `https://dotnet.microsoft.com/en-us/download`.

On this page, you'll see options for different .NET versions. For the latest long-term support version, look for .NET 8.0 or the highest non-preview version available.

2. Click the Download .NET SDK button for your operating system (Windows, macOS, or Linux).
3. Once downloaded, run the installer:
   - On Windows: Double-click the downloaded .exe file and follow the installation wizard.
   - On macOS: Open the .pkg file and follow the installation steps.
   - On Linux: Follow the distribution-specific instructions provided on the download page.
4. After installation, open a new terminal or Command Prompt window, and then verify the installation by typing:

```
dotnet -version
```

If .NET was installed correctly, you should see the version that is installed in the terminal.

A Configured Integrated Development Environment

Picking the right IDE for your JavaScript or TypeScript development can really make a difference in how smoothly your project runs. Here's a quick rundown of some popular options:

Visual Studio Code (VSCode) VSCode is a favorite among developers for its lightweight feel and huge plugin library. It's easy to use, has cross-platform support, and integrates well with Git. It supports tons of extensions, but adding too many can slow it down. VSCode works especially well with TypeScript since they're both Microsoft products.

WebStorm WebStorm is a commercial IDE made for JavaScript and TypeScript. It comes with a lot of built-in features, great debugging tools, and deep code assistance. It's more resource-intensive and has a steeper learning curve, but it's a powerhouse for big projects.

Atom Atom is an open-source text editor from GitHub, fully customizable with a range of plugins. It's free and flexible but can slow down if you add too many packages. Atom is best for smaller projects or personal use since it's no longer officially maintained.

Visual Studio Microsoft Visual Studio is a full-featured IDE mainly for .NET, but it supports TypeScript. It's powerful with tons of tools, but it can be overkill for smaller projects. Visual Studio is great if you're working in a mixed tech environment with both .NET and JavaScript/TypeScript.

Cursor: The AI-First IDE Cursor takes code editing to the next level by embedding AI directly into its fork of Visual Studio Code. It's packed with features like AI-integrated code chat, code generation, refactoring, and natural language editing, making it very intuitive to use. You get all the benefits of VSCode, plus the added AI perks. It also has a "Privacy Mode" to keep your code secure, and it's SOC 2 certified. There's a free tier, but you can also use your own OpenAI API key to save on costs.

Installing and Setting Up VSCode IDE

We have chosen to use the VSCode IDE. This section walks you through downloading and installing VSCode and introduces some essential extensions you might want to use.

Downloading VSCode

VSCode works on Linux, macOS, and Windows. Head to the official website at `https://code.visualstudio.com/download` and choose the version for your operating system. Download the installer file (.exe for Windows, .dmg for macOS, or .deb/.rpm for Linux), and then follow the corresponding instructions:

- Installing on Windows:
  1. Double-click the downloaded .exe file.
  2. Follow the setup wizard.
  3. Launch VSCode from the Start menu or desktop shortcut.
- Installing on macOS:
  1. Open the downloaded .dmg file.
  2. Drag the VSCode icon to the Applications folder.
  3. Double-click VSCode in Applications.
- Installing on Linux (Ubuntu/Debian):
  1. Open a terminal in the directory where you downloaded the .deb file.
  2. Run **sudo dpkg -i <filename>.deb**.
  3. Launch VSCode by typing **code** in the terminal or by using the application launcher.
- Installing on Linux (Red Hat/Fedora):
  1. Open a terminal in the directory where you downloaded the .rpm file.
  2. Run **sudo rpm -i <filename>.rpm**.
  3. Launch VSCode by typing **code** in the terminal or by using the application launcher.

Essential Extensions for VSCode

Adding the right extensions to your IDE can really improve your productivity! Here are some must-haves:

- **Azure Tools:** A must-have for developing with anything Microsoft
- **GitHub Copilot:** AI-powered code suggestions to speed up coding
- **Prettier:** Keeps your code formatted and clean
- **ESLint:** Helps catch errors and maintain code quality
- **Bracket Pair Colorizer:** Makes nested code easier to read
- **Path Intellisense:** Auto-completes file paths for quick access
- **Code Spell Checker:** Catches typos in your code
- **REST Client:** Tests APIs directly in the IDE
- **Live Share:** Enables you to collaborate and code with others in real time

These extensions help maximize VSCode's AI capabilities while keeping your workflow smooth. Check them out on the VSCode marketplace (as shown in Figure 5.3) or through VSCode's extension manager!

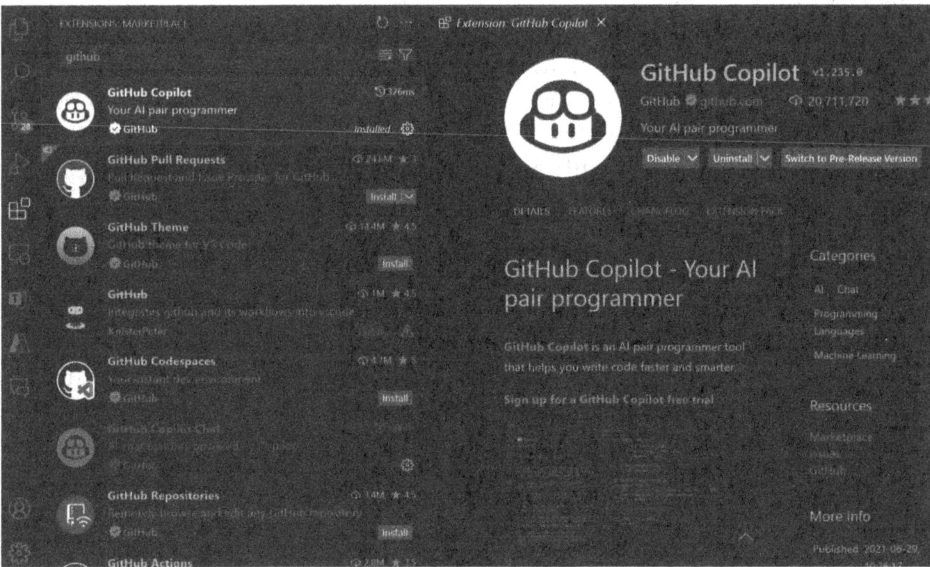

Figure 15.3: Example IDE extensions

Customizing the IDE for Productivity

Customizing your IDE is key to boosting productivity. Whether it's changing the color theme, adding extensions, or tweaking settings, these adjustments can make coding smoother and more enjoyable. The following are suggestions you should consider for customizing your IDE:

- **Pick a theme:** Choose a theme that's easy on your eyes, like Material Theme Icons or Peacock.
- **Improve navigation:** Use extensions like Bookmarks and Project Manager to jump between lines of code or projects quickly.
- **Streamline writing:** Use Prettier for formatting and GitHub Copilot for AI suggestions.
- **Enhance code quality:** ESLint and Error Lens help spot bugs fast.
- **Add collaboration:** Live Share allows for real-time coding with teammates.
- **Personalize shortcuts:** Modify keyboard shortcuts to speed up common actions that you find repetitive!

Customizing your IDE isn't just about looks; it's about making tools work for you, saving time and improving code quality.

Installing Azure AI Studio SDKs and Necessary Libraries

When building plugins for Azure AI Studio, setting up your development environment is the first step. In addition to installing the IDE, this also means installing the necessary SDKs and libraries to interact with Azure services efficiently. To get started with these, you'll need to install the Azure AI Studio SDKs and any other required tools. This guide will walk you through the setup to ensure that you have everything you need for smooth plugin development.

Setting Up TypeScript for Azure AI Development

TypeScript is well suited for AI development, particularly due to its strong typing system on a non-strongly typed code (JavaScript). This feature is especially valuable when working with complex AI algorithms and large datasets. With that being said, let's get into TypeScript configuration! You can first install TypeScript globally with the following:

```
npm install -g typescript
```

After installing typescript globally, you can begin using TypeScript in your projects by initializing a tsconfig.json file. This file should include compiler options suitable for Azure AI development:

```
{
  "compilerOptions": {
    "target": "ES6",
```

```
    "module": "commonjs",
    "strict": true,
    "esModuleInterop": true
  }
}
```

You will also need to install the TypeScript libraries. You can install the necessary TypeScript libraries and type definitions in your project by using the following command in your project's root folder:

```
npm install typescript @types/node
```

Git

Git is a distributed version control system, perfect for both small and large projects. Created by Linus Torvalds in 2005, it lets multiple developers work on a project without overwriting each other's changes. Key features of Git include:

- **Distributed system:** Each clone has a full history and version-tracking, not needing a central server.
- **Branching and merging:** You can experiment with new features without affecting the main project.
- **Data assurance:** Git uses checksums to maintain data integrity.
- **Staging area:** Git allows you to control which changes are committed.

Installing Git

If you don't already have Git installed, you will need to install it. The steps required vary depending on the platform you are using:

On Windows:

1. Go to `git-scm.com` and download the installer.
2. Run the .exe file and follow the setup wizard. (The default options work fine.)
3. Open Command Prompt and type **git --version** to check if it's installed.

On macOS:

1. Install Homebrew if you don't have it:

   ```
   /bin/bash -c "$(curl -fsSL https://raw.githubusercontent.com/
   Homebrew/install/HEAD/install.sh)"
   ```

2. Run **brew install git**.
3. Type **git --version** in Terminal to verify.

On Linux:

- On Debian/Ubuntu, run the following:

  ```
  sudo apt update
  sudo apt install git
  ```

- On Red Hat/Fedora, run the following:

  ```
  sudo dnf install git
  ```

- Check the installation by typing **git --version** in Terminal.

Initial Git Setup

Peform the following steps to initialize your Git setup:

1. Set your username:

   ```
   git config --global user.name "Your Name"
   ```

2. Set your email:

   ```
   git config --global user.email you@example.com
   ```

Once you've set up Git, there are a number of basic Git commands you can use:

- **Initialize the repo**: `git init`
- **Clone the repo:** `git clone https://github.com/user/repository.git`
- **Check the status:** `git status`
- **Add to staging:** `git add <file> (can use "git add ." to add all files to staging`
- **Commit changes:** `git commit -m "Your commit message"`
- **Push to cloned remote repo:** `git push origin main`
- **Pull from remote repo:** `git pull origin main`

For more details, visit `https://git-scm.com/doc`.

Building a Custom Teams Copilot

Now that your development environment is configured, you need to set up a SharePoint Online environment to be used to build and test a custom copilot. First, you need to create a SharePoint site to build the copilot off of. Navigate to a SharePoint site that you have permission to add sites to and create a new site by selecting the "+ Create site" option in the upper-left of the web page (see Figure 15.4).

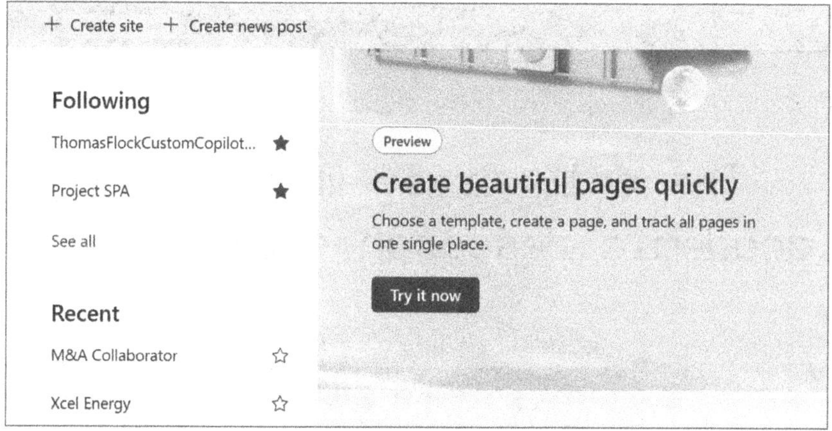

Figure 15.4: The SharePoint "Create site" landing page

Next, select Team Site, as this is the one we will be using in this demonstration. Enter the site's name, description, and configure privacy settings. You can choose to use a template if you wish. When selecting the language, you must select English, as this is the only language supported for custom copilots at the time of writing. For this example, once the site is created, you are going to upload documents into the documents area on the left, as shown in Figure 15.5.

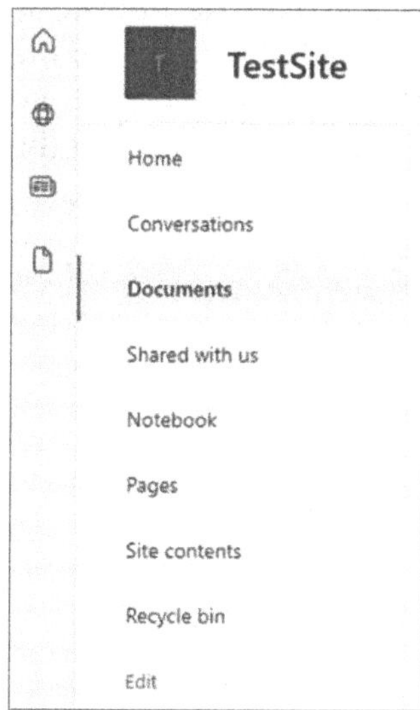

Figure 15.5: The SharePoint new site landing page

In this example, I chose to go to `https://oa.mg`. This is a free service that lets you search for free academic papers in PDF format. As shown in Figure 15.6, I searched for "tides," and I am going to upload three to four documents into the SharePoint library to test on.

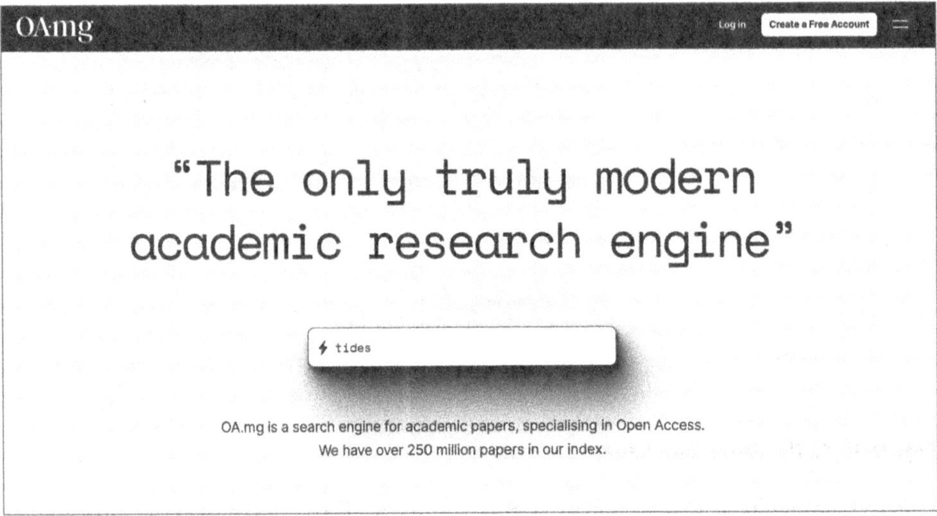

Figure 15.6: The OA.mg research landing page

After uploading these PDFs, you need to create two pages: Privacy Policy and Terms of Use. (These PDFs will be used later).

You need to have access to an Azure Subscription where you are the Administrator because you need to create an app service and an app registration. So, go to `https://portal.azure.com`. On the top left, click Create Resources, as shown in Figure 15.7, and then search for "Web App." Click the Web App tile with the small circle icon and then Create. Provide the required information. You should pick Node for the runtime environment. For Pricing Plan, select the free version, as shown in Figure 15.8.

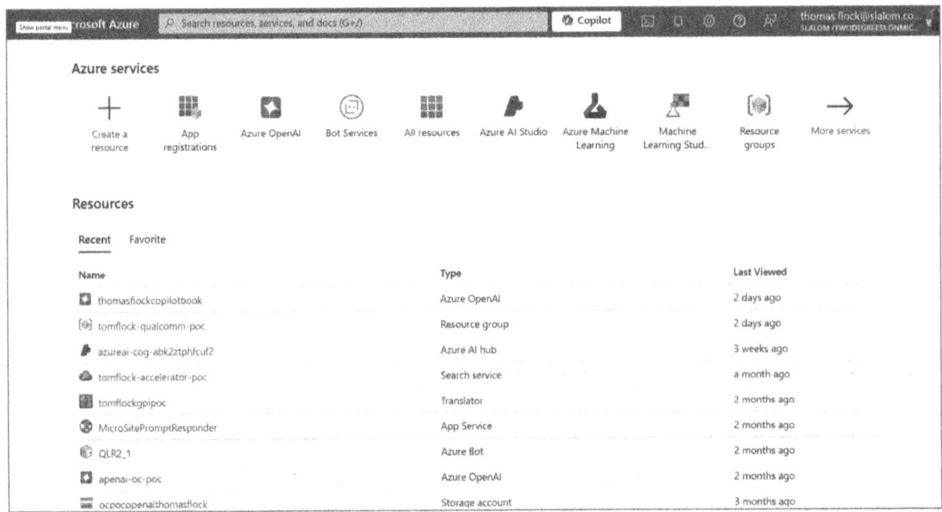

Figure 15.7: The Azure portal

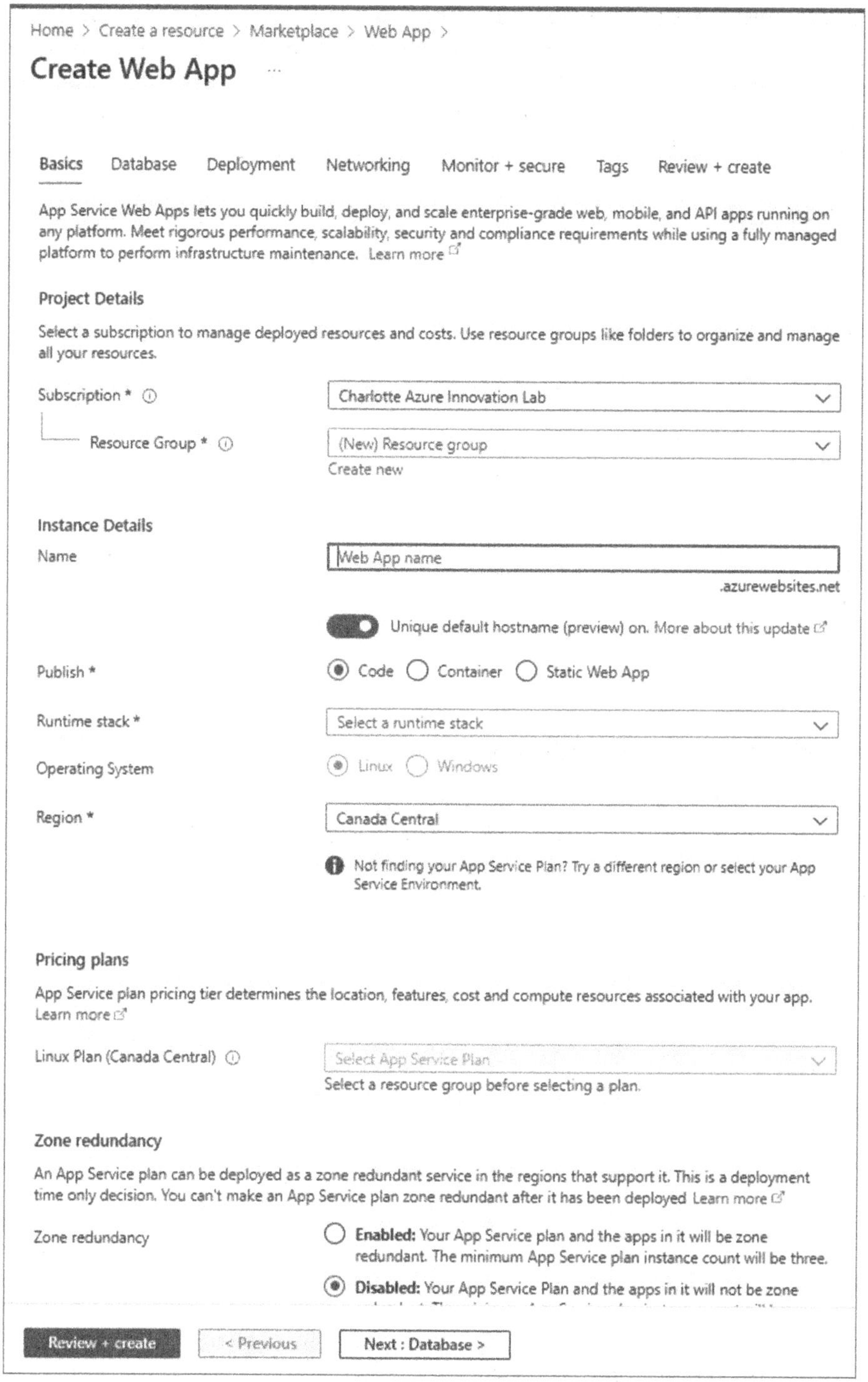

Home > Create a resource > Marketplace > Web App >

Create Web App ...

Basics Database Deployment Networking Monitor + secure Tags Review + create

App Service Web Apps lets you quickly build, deploy, and scale enterprise-grade web, mobile, and API apps running on any platform. Meet rigorous performance, scalability, security and compliance requirements while using a fully managed platform to perform infrastructure maintenance. Learn more

Project Details

Select a subscription to manage deployed resources and costs. Use resource groups like folders to organize and manage all your resources.

Subscription * — Charlotte Azure Innovation Lab

Resource Group * — (New) Resource group
Create new

Instance Details

Name — Web App name
.azurewebsites.net

Unique default hostname (preview) on. More about this update

Publish * — Code / Container / Static Web App

Runtime stack * — Select a runtime stack

Operating System — Linux / Windows

Region * — Canada Central

Not finding your App Service Plan? Try a different region or select your App Service Environment.

Pricing plans

App Service plan pricing tier determines the location, features, cost and compute resources associated with your app. Learn more

Linux Plan (Canada Central) — Select App Service Plan
Select a resource group before selecting a plan.

Zone redundancy

An App Service plan can be deployed as a zone redundant service in the regions that support it. This is a deployment time only decision. You can't make an App Service plan zone redundant after it has been deployed Learn more

Zone redundancy — **Enabled:** Your App Service plan and the apps in it will be zone redundant. The minimum App Service plan instance count will be three.
Disabled: Your App Service Plan and the apps in it will not be zone

Review + create < Previous Next : Database >

Figure 15.8: Creating the web app

After creating the web app, you need to create an app registration for it. From the portal dashboard, search for "app registration" in the top search bar (see Figure 15.9) and click "+ New Registration" in the upper-left corner. Enter the name, choose the first option on the radio buttons for Single Tenant, and then select Register at the bottom of the screen (see Figure 15.10).

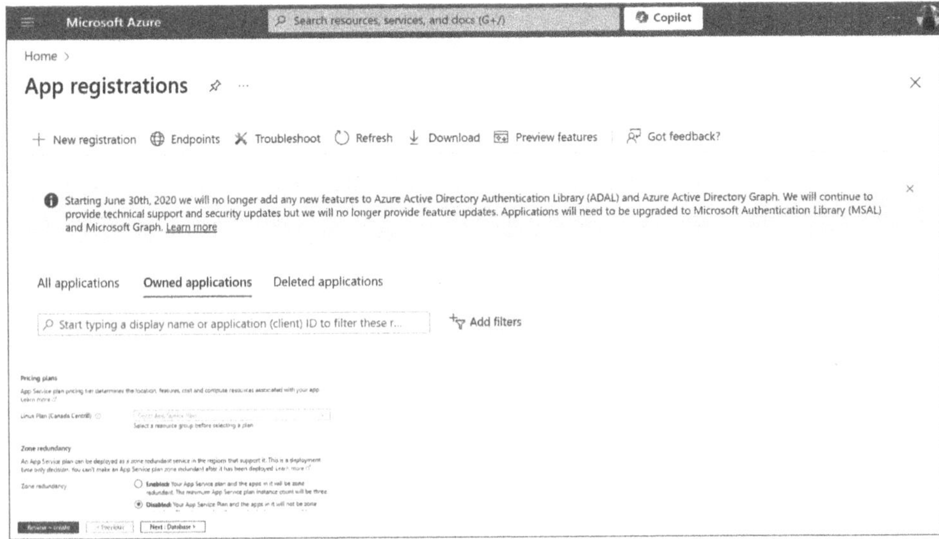

Figure 15.9: Searching for an app registration

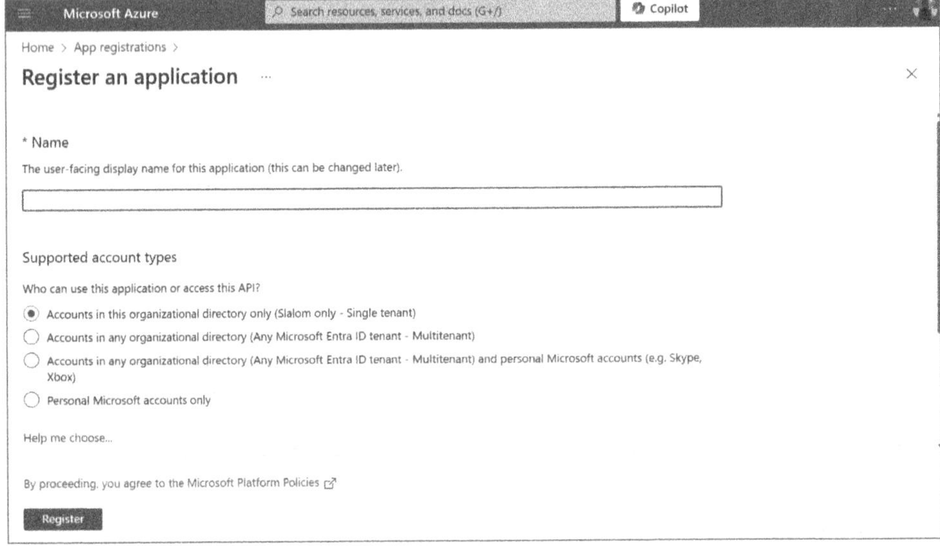

Figure 15.10: Creating a new app registration

Now that you've created the app and the app registration, head to `dev.teams.microsoft.com`, click Apps on the left side of the page, and then select "+ New App." This will present a form with a lot of information.

Under App Names, you must enter a name and an optional full name. Under Descriptions, enter descriptions for both the web app and the app registration. Then, under Developer Information, enter the name of the company you are representing or, if you have a personal website, you can use that. App URLs are next. Enter the URLs of the SharePoint pages you made earlier (Terms of Use, and Privacy Policy). Finally, for Application (client) ID, you need to enter the app registration ID you created earlier in the Azure portal (see Figure 15.11).

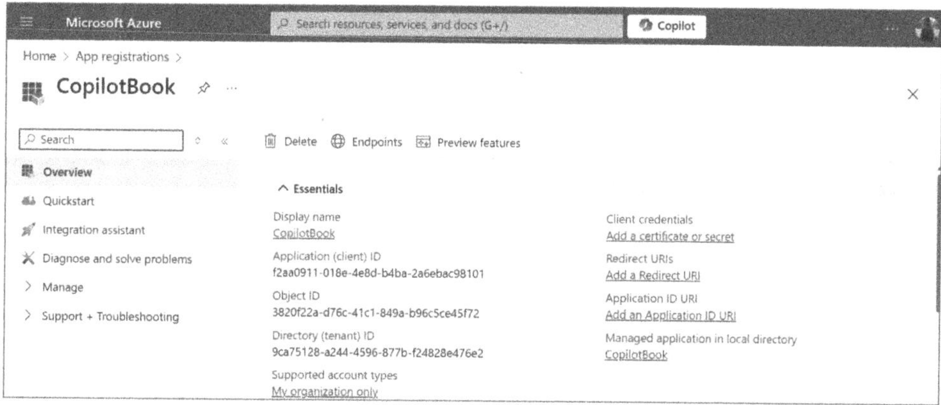

Figure 15.11: Where to find the app ID

The final piece you need to create is an Azure OpenAI service. In your Azure portal home, search for "Azure OpenAI," select the open AI service, and then enter the required information. There is only one pricing tier you can select.

After the resource is provisioned, select Go to Resource. On the left side of the portal, you will see Keys and Endpoint under Resource Management. Copy KEY 1 and the endpoint, as shown in Figure 15.12.

After the OpenAI service is created, you need to deploy a model for the Teams Copilot to chat on. On the Azure OpenAI service (as shown in Figure 15.12) on the left under Resource Management is a tab called Model Deployment that you can select. This will cause a pane to come up that says, "Model deployments have been moved to Azure AI Studio." When you click this, the browser will navigate to the Azure AI Studio portal, as shown in Figure 15.13. Once there, select "+ Deploy Model" on the upper left of the screen. You are going to use gpt-4o as the model, so in the next prompt, select gpt-4 and name the deployment. Save this name because you will need it later. You can leave the rest as is, although you can add more tokens on the slider as necessary.

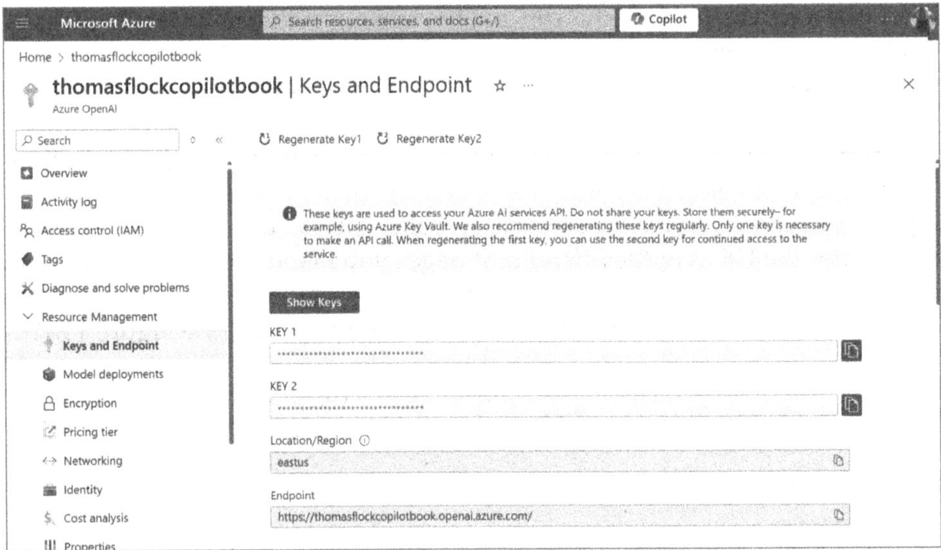

Figure 15.12: Copying the Azure OpenAI access Key

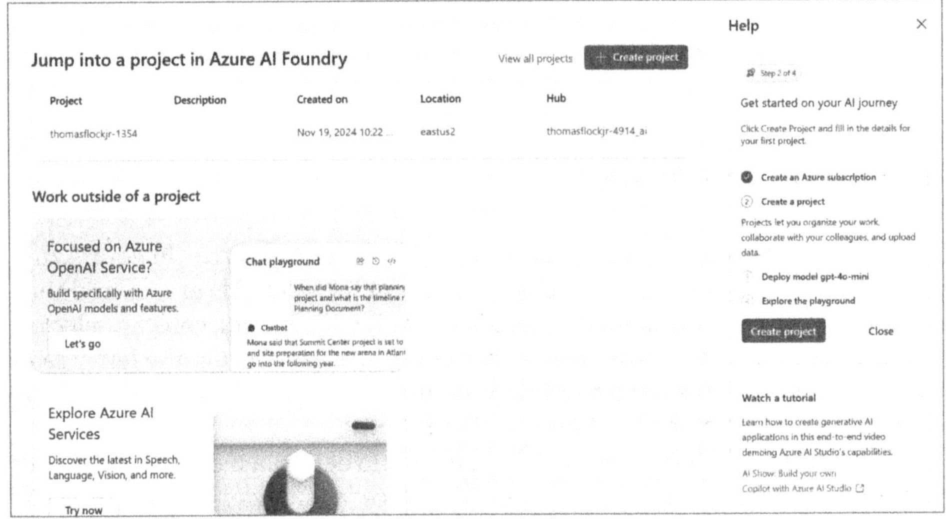

Figure 15.13: The Azure AI Studio landing page

Now that you have all the backbone set up to create the Teams Copilot, it's time to start coding! First, create a folder named CustomCopilot on your C drive, and then open that folder with Visual Studio Code. You are going to have to install the Teams Toolkit for Visual Studio Code found at https://learn.microsoft.com/en-us/microsoftteams/platform/toolkit/install-teams-toolkit?tabs=vscode#install-teams-toolkit-for-visual-studio-code, or you can just search for "Teams Toolkit" in the extension manager. Once the Teams Toolkit is installed, you can go back to the app you just created in the Teams Dev Center. As shown in Figure 15.14, select Develop and then Open in Teams Toolkit. You should then be able to select Open in Visual Studio Code (JS/TS).

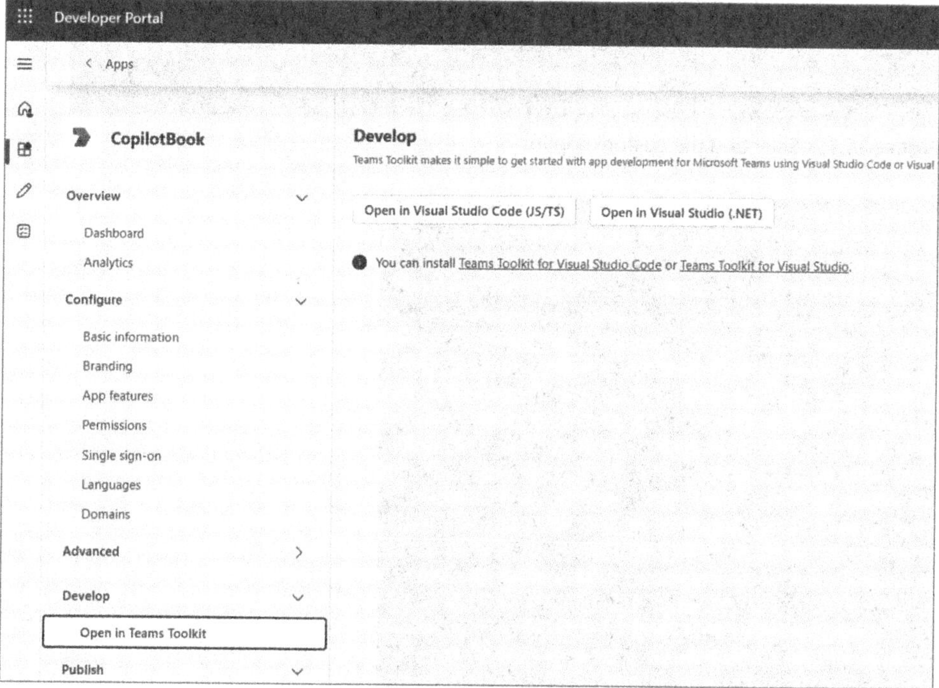

Figure 15.14: The Teams Toolkit Dev Center landing page

If the Teams Toolkit VSCode extension was installed correctly, with the selection you just made, the app will open in VSCode and ask you to create a new project. Select Create a Custom Copilot, which should be the first option, as shown in Figure 15.15. Then, select Basic AI Chatbot. On the next prompt, select JavaScript as the code to be written. The next prompt will ask whether you are using Azure OpenAI or regular OpenAI. For this example, you will use the Azure OpenAI that you created earlier. The next three prompts will ask you for the key, endpoint, and name that you copied earlier.

After you select these items, VSCode will create a folder scaffolding to start customizing your new custom Copilot, as shown in Figure 15.16. This might be done in a new window or the current one.

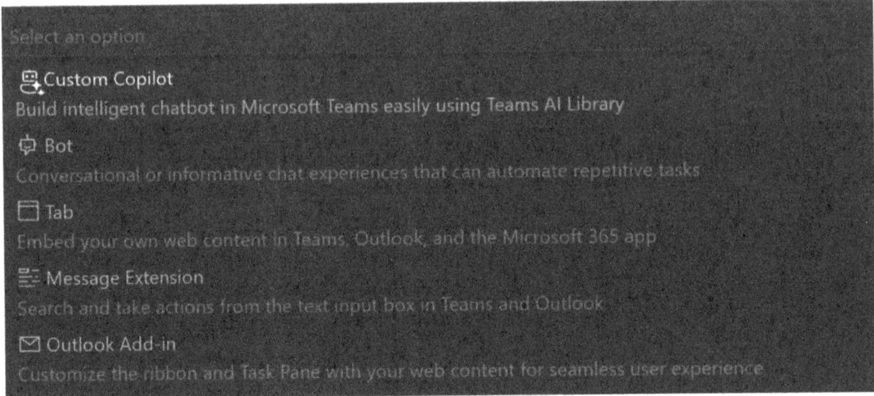

Figure 15.15: Selecting the custom copilot

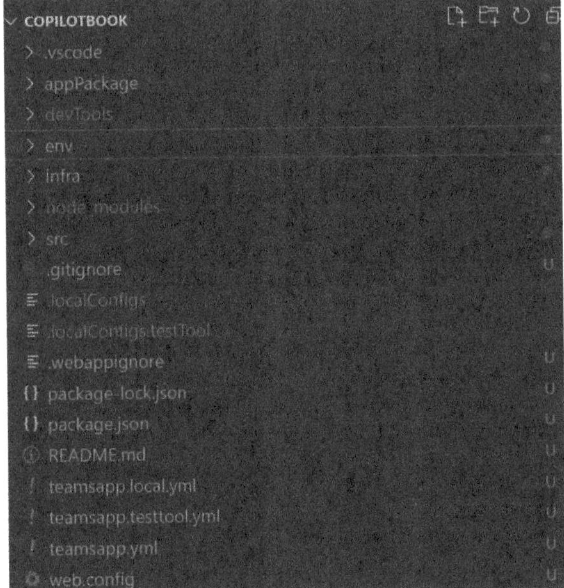

Figure 15.16: The custom copilot folder structure

The following is a high-level overview of the folder structure:

- **vscode/:** Contains VSCode-specific configuration files:
  - extensions.json: Recommends extensions for the project
  - launch.json: Configures debugging settings
  - settings.json: Includes project-specific VSCode settings
  - tasks.json: Defines custom tasks for the project

- **appPackage/:** Contains files related to the Teams app package:
  - color.png: The color icon for the Teams app
  - manifest.json: The manifest file that defines the Teams app properties
  - outline.png: The outline icon for the Teams app
- **.env/:** Contains environment-specific configuration files:
  - .env.dev: Development environment variables
  - .env.dev.user: User-specific development environment variables
  - .env.local: Local environnent variables
  - .env.local.user: User-specific local environment variables
- **infra/:** Contains infrastructure-as-code files for Azure deployment:
  - botRegistration/: Likely contains files for bot registration
  - azure.bicep: Azure Bicep template for resource deployment
  - azure.parameters.json: Parameters file for the Azure Bicep template
- **src/:** The source code directory for the application:
  - app/: Contains core application logic:
    - app.js: The main application file
    - graphDataSource.js: Handles Microsoft Graph data source
  - data/: Contains data files used by the application:
    - Contoso_Electronics_PerkPlus_Program.txt
    - Contoso_Electronics_Company_Overview.txt
    - Contoso_Electronics_Plan_Benefits.txt
  - prompts/chat/: Contains files related to chat prompts:
    - config.json: Configuration for the chat prompt
    - skprompt.txt: The actual prompt template. This is using Semantic Kernel (covered later in this chapter).
  - public/: Contains public-facing files:
    - auth-end.html: Authentication end page
    - auth-start.html: Authentication start page
  - adapter.js: Sets up the bot adapter
  - config.js: Contains configuration settings
  - index.js: The entry point of the application

- **.gitignore:** Specifies files and directories to be ignored by Git
- **.localConfigs:** The local configuration file
- **.webappignore:** Specifies files to ignore when deploying to Azure Web App
- **aad.manifest.json:** The Azure Active Directory app manifest
- **package.json:** Defines project dependencies and scripts
- **README.md:** Project documentation and instructions
- **teamsapp.local.yml:** Teams Toolkit configuration for local development
- **teamsapp.yml:** The main Teams Toolkit configuration file
- **web.config:** The configuration file for IIS web server

You can now run the program! Hit F5 or press Debug to start the debugging process. A prompt will display asking you to sign in to the Microsoft 365 Developer account you created earlier. After you click Accept and Sign In, a browser window will appear and ask for your credentials.

NOTE **If you get an error with running debug that says "(x) Error: /bots/0/scopes/2 must be equal to one of the allowed values," check the manifest.json file under the appPackage folder. Inside the array "bots," there is a value "scopes." The groupchat scope should be camel case "groupChat," as shown in Figure 15.17.**

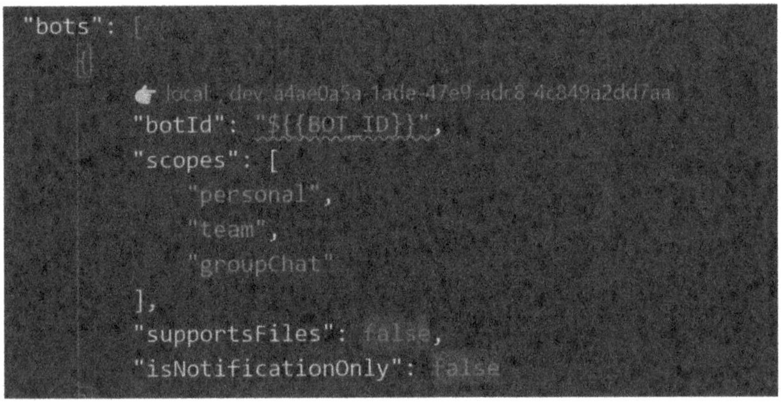

```
"bots": [
    {
        "botId": "${{BOT_ID}}",
        "scopes": [
            "personal",
            "team",
            "groupChat"
        ],
        "supportsFiles": false,
        "isNotificationOnly": false
```

Figure 15.17: The bots scope

A couple minutes after you start the debugging process, a new browser window will open to the Teams App, and a prompt will ask you to add the app that was just created to Teams. Click Add, as shown in Figure 15.18.

NOTE **VSCode Teams Toolkit has a new option, "Debug in Test Tool." If you have this option, you can debug locally without a Microsoft Developer account. The Test Tool debugger will also give you better error handling in the browser (see Figure 15.19).**

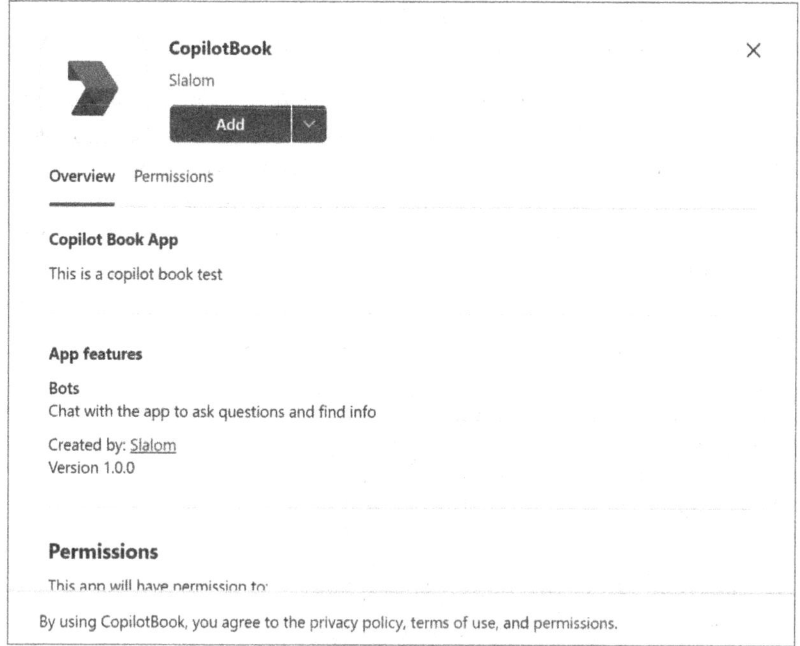

Figure 15.18: Adding the custom copilot

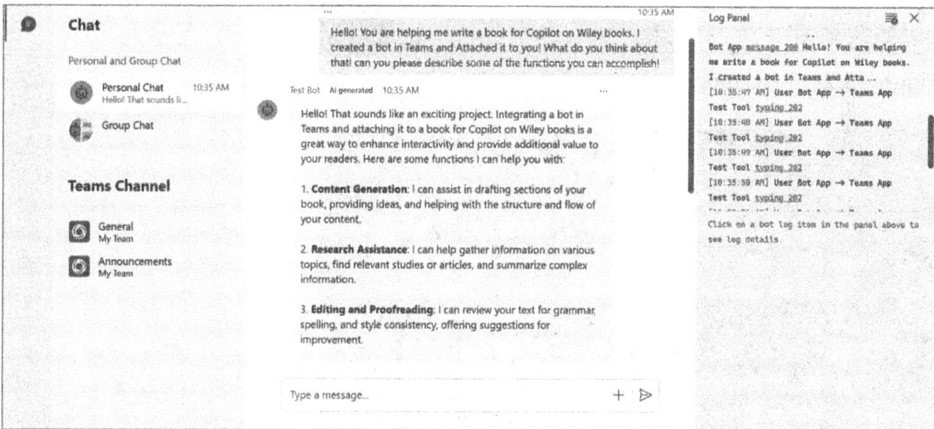

Figure 15.19: The new Test Tool debugger

You now have a custom copilot ready to be deployed to your company! To read more in depth about what you can modify your copilot to do, visit `https://learn.microsoft.com/en-us/microsoftteams/platform/overview`.

Deploying a Custom Teams Copilot

Before deploying your custom copilot, you should save a version of it to Git. On the top of your IDE, you should see an icon that looks like a Git repo symbol; this is your source control. When you click this icon, a new sidebar will appear and ask you to initialize a repository. Select Initialize Repository, as shown in Figure 15.20. A new prompt will appear with all the changes in your folder. Go ahead and add a message and select Commit. This will save a snapshot of your code to Git, and you can now modify your code and always have stepped "backups" of your code to go back to using Git (see Figure 15.21).

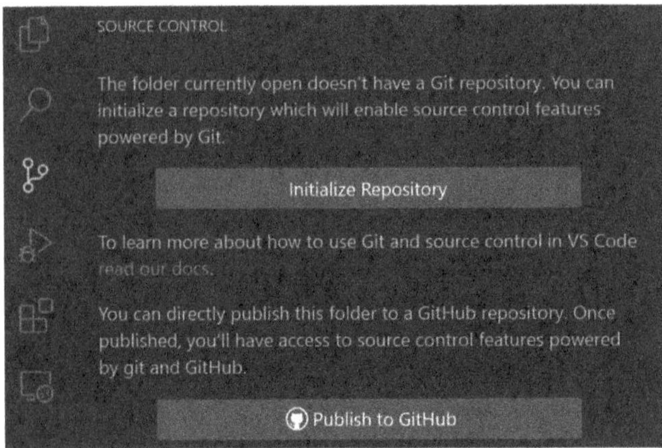

Figure 15.20: Initializing a repository in VSCode

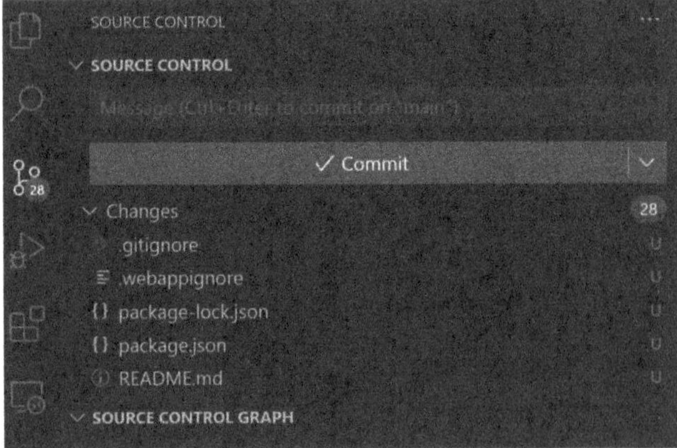

Figure 15.21: Checking in your code to local Git

After successfully creating and testing your custom copilot, you need to get it out to the world. Microsoft makes this easy with the Teams Development Admin Center we set up earlier in the chapter. As shown in Figure 15.22, you should have options on the side of your IDE under the Teams Toolkit Extension for deploying and publishing.

Figure 15.22: The Teams Toolkit Lifecycle menu

First, select Provision under the LIFECYCLE menu. You will be prompted to put in a subscription and a resource group. These are the same subscription and resource group of the web app you created earlier in the chapter. Azure will provision your application after some time. When provisioning ends, a prompt will pop up on the bottom right of your IDE, and you can select "View provisioned resources," as shown in Figure 15.23. A new browser window will open, bringing you to your resource group. You will see new "bot" resources provisioned. This is what your organization needs to deploy your Teams app.

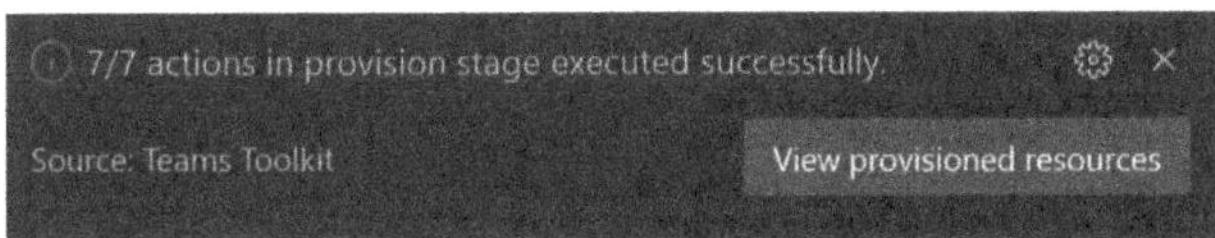

Figure 15.23: The new provisioned bot services

After you have successfully confirmed that the resources are provisioned, go back to the IDE and select Deploy under the same LIFECYCLE menu you used earlier. Then, you can go back to your app in the Teams Development Dashboard (`dev.teams.microsoft.com`). You should now see options at the top for Preview in Teams and Publish, as shown in Figure 15.24.

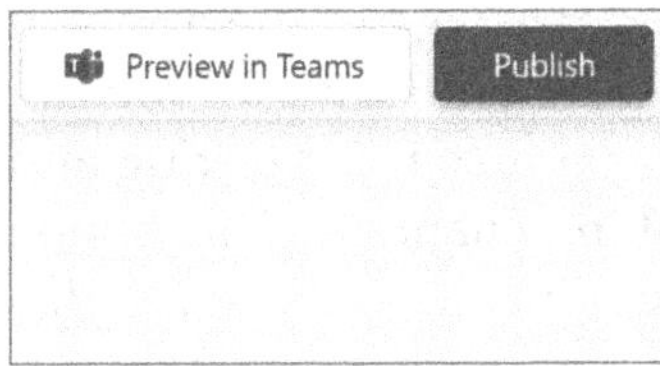

Figure 15.24: Deployment options in the Teams Development Dashboard

These two options are controlled by your organization. If you select Preview in Teams and the prompt for adding to Teams comes up and there is no Add button, you will need to contact your administrator to be able to publish to Teams. A high-level overview of how to do this is provided later in the chapter. If you have the necessary permissions, you can select Add, and the Teams Custom Copilot app you just created will be available to you inside your organization's Teams. Your application is not published yet, so let's take care of that.

If you select Publish on the top right, you will be prompted with three options: "Download the App Package," "Publish to your org," and "Publish to the Teams Store," as shown in Figure 15.25. I will briefly touch on each of these options. These options are also available on the left side of the Teams Dev Center menu. If you click each one of these options, a new dashboard will come up showing you more in detail the options available.

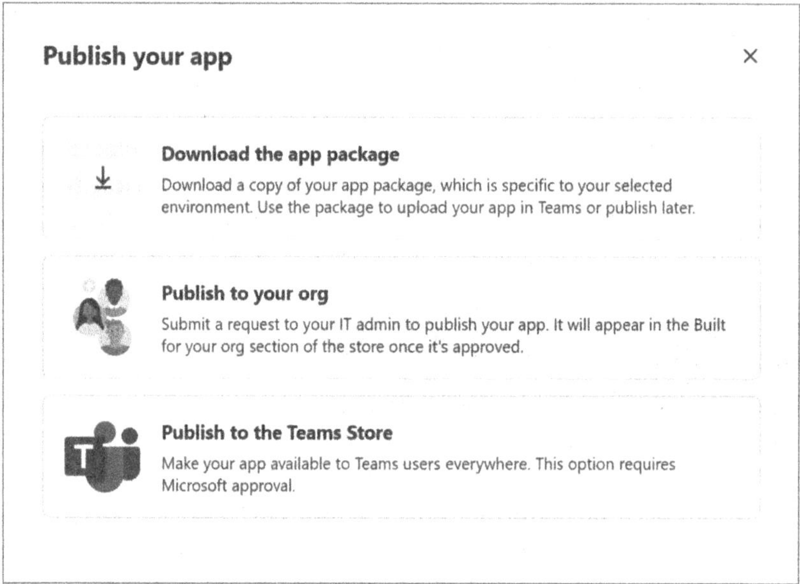

Figure 15.25: Publishing your custom Teams app

The first option, "Download the app package," allows you to obtain a copy of your app package. This will create a streamlined package of the app you just created for deployment to any Azure service. By downloading it, you can manually upload and install the app in Teams later or use it for testing and distribution purposes outside of the official publishing channels. This option is useful if you want full control over the deployment process or need to distribute the app through alternative means.

The second and third options involve publishing your app to make it available to users. "Publish to your org" submits a request to your IT administrator to approve and publish the app within your organization. Once approved, the app will appear in the "Built for your org" section of the Teams app store, making it accessible to users within your company. Selecting "Publish to your org" will create a ticket and send it automatically, so make sure that your IT department knows your intentions ahead of time. As shown in Figure 15.26, you can hit "Cancel app publish" in the top left to stop this transaction. This option is ideal for internal apps or when you want to limit the app's availability to your organization. For more information about deploying to your organization, go to `https://learn.microsoft.com/en-us/microsoftteams/teams-custom-app-policies-and-settings`.

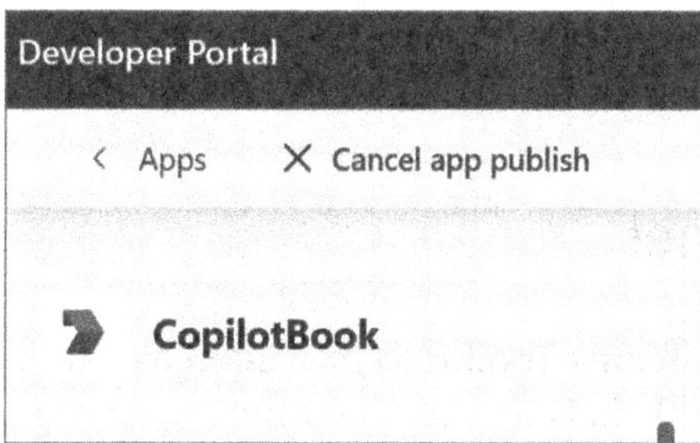

Figure 15.26: Canceling your Teams app

The "Publish to the Teams Store" option, as shown in Figure 15.27, makes your app available to Teams users everywhere. This requires Microsoft approval and is suitable for apps intended for a wider audience. It allows your app to be discoverable and usable by Teams users anywhere. You can find detailed instructions for distributing to the Teams Store at `https://learn.microsoft.com/en-us/microsoftteams/platform/concepts/deploy-and-publish/appsource/publish`.

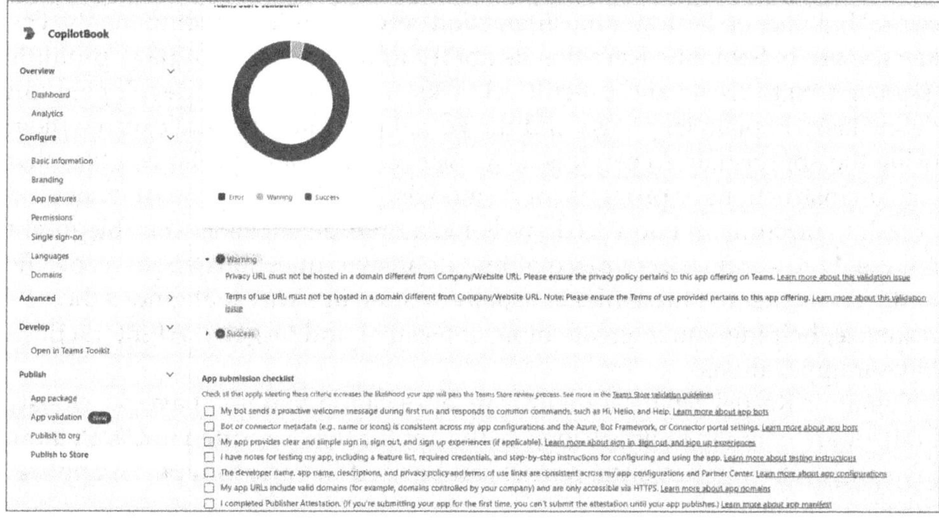

Figure 15.27: Publishing to the Teams Store

To complete these publishing processes, you'll need different requirements for each option. For downloading the app package, you simply need to have your app fully developed and configured. For publishing to your organization, you'll need appropriate permissions within your organization and may need to provide documentation or justification for the app to your IT administrator. Publishing to the Teams Store requires meeting Microsoft's app submission guidelines, which typically include providing detailed app information, privacy policies, terms of service, and passing a review process to ensure the app meets Microsoft's standards.

Introduction to Semantic Kernel

Earlier in the chapter when you used the Teams Toolkit to provision a custom copilot, you saw a file called *skprompt.txt*. This is less of a text file and more a "function" for Semantic Kernel. Semantic Kernel is at the heart of all Microsoft-based AI services.

What is Semantic Kernel? Microsoft Semantic Kernel is an AI software development kit (SDK) designed to integrate large language models (LLMs) such as OpenAI, Azure OpenAI, and Hugging Face with conventional programming languages like C#, Python, and Java. At its core, Semantic Kernel provides a programming model that allows developers to add advanced natural language processing (NLP) capabilities to their applications.

The primary purpose of Semantic Kernel is to simplify the integration of AI into software applications. It achieves this by offering a framework that manages working with various AI services and plugins. Semantic Kernel acts as a central hub that orchestrates the interaction between different components. The key feature of Semantic Kernel is its ability to use natural language prompts (*skprompt.tx*) to create and execute AI tasks. This means that developers can define tasks in plain language, and the kernel will interpret and execute them using the appropriate AI services. `skprompt.txt` files are special text files that contain instructions or prompts for AI models. These files tell the AI what kind of task to perform and how to do it. For example, an `skprompt.txt` file might tell the AI to summarize a piece of text or answer questions about a specific topic. The content of these files is usually written in a way that guides the AI's response, helping you to create more consistent and targeted AI interactions in your applications.

Semantic Kernel can be added to any application that you have previously built, or are going to build, as long as the application is written in C#, Python, Java, or JavaScript. Semantic Kernel can be used in various types of applications, including:

- Web apps
- Desktop apps

- Mobile apps (through backend services)
- Command-line tools
- Microservices
- Serverless functions

It also provides abstractions for various AI services, making it easier to switch between different providers (like OpenAI, Azure OpenAI, or Hugging Face) without major code changes. You can also create modular, reusable AI components. These plugins can easily be shared between different applications or parts of your application.

Conclusion

Setting up a development environment is crucial for building and deploying custom AI solutions with Azure AI Studio and related Microsoft technologies. This chapter covered the components needed to create a productive workspace, from installing core tools like Node.js, npm, and .NET to configuring integrated development environments like Visual Studio Code and Cursor. We also explored the importance of version control with Git and the process of setting up Azure resources necessary for AI development. The knowledge of preparing your development environment extends beyond just installing software. It involves understanding the intricacies of TypeScript for type-safe coding, leveraging the power of Azure AI Studio SDKs, and grasping the concept of Semantic Kernel for advanced natural language processing capabilities. These tools and frameworks form the base foundation on which you can build AI applications, chatbots, and custom copilots that integrate with Microsoft Teams and other platforms.

We walked through the practical steps of creating and deploying a custom Teams copilot, demonstrating how the various components of your development environment come together, from setting up SharePoint sites and Azure services to coding and debugging your application—each step builds upon the last. The deployment and publishing options discussed highlight the flexibility you have in distributing your AI solutions, whether internally within your organization or to a larger audience through the Teams Store. As you move forward in AI development, remember that the environment you've set up is not static. It will evolve with advancements in AI technologies. Regularly updating your tools, exploring new features in Azure AI Studio, and staying informed about best practices in AI development will ensure that your development environment remains optimal. With this solid foundation in place, you are well equipped to tackle complex AI projects.

CHAPTER 16

Copilot Wave 2 Features

One of the challenges with new technology like Copilot for Microsoft 365 is trying to keep pace with the speed at which Microsoft releases new product features. As we were in the final stages of publishing the book, Microsoft made another wave of announcements during their September 16th Copilot "Wave 2 Event." These announcements were significant enough to warrant this chapter, which helps address some of the most impactful changes to the product, while also covering what Microsoft sees as the future of humans collaborating with AI.

In this chapter, we will cover the relaunch of Copilot Chat as "BizChat," which is the first step in Microsoft's investment toward more agentic AI collaboration. Next, we'll go through some of the changes to using Copilot for Microsoft 365 with Outlook, Teams, PowerPoint, and Excel, which, as part of the event, were made generally available. Finally, we'll end with a look to the future with Copilot agents and Microsoft's vision of semi-autonomous AI within your workflow.

BizChat, aka Copilot Chat

Chapter 6, "Microsoft Copilot Business Chat," introduced Microsoft's GenAI-powered chat product, which supports a ChatGPT experience over your organizational data or web searches. With the Wave 2 rollout, this chat experience has been rebranded as Business Chat (BizChat), as shown in Figure 16.1. The vision for BizChat is that it will serve as a central hub where business data, web data, and other non-Microsoft 365 data sources all come together. Consolidating the data you need right where you do your work minimizes both context switching and the resulting loss of focus when you toggle between applications to complete a work task.

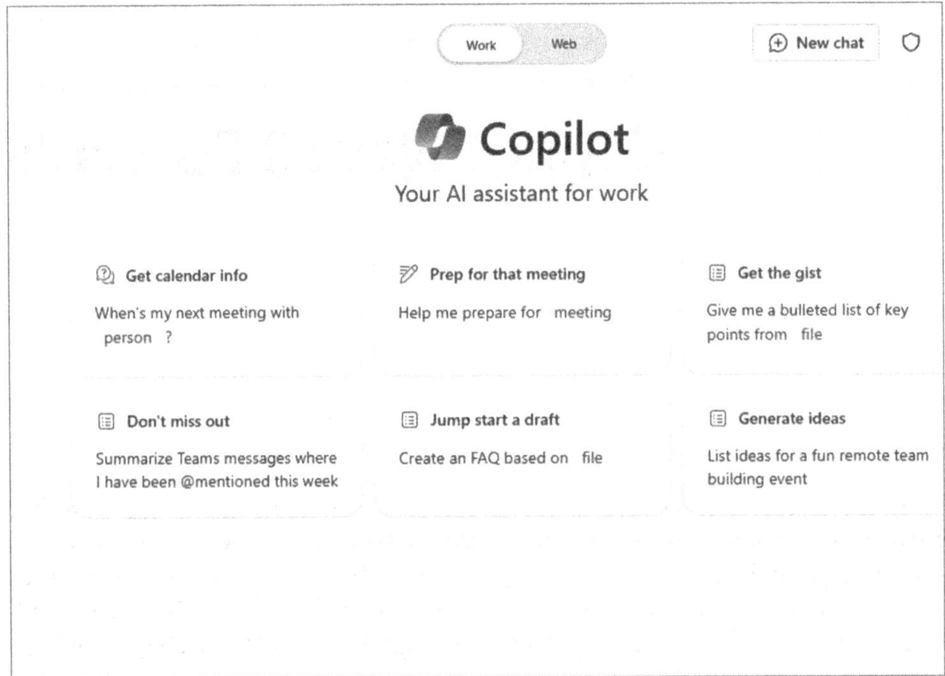

Figure 16.1: Microsoft 365 Copilot Business Chat (BizChat) interface

With the new Wave 2 release, we can really see this vision taking shape. Microsoft has now incorporated the ability to create Copilot agents directly within BizChat, supported by a user-friendly conversational interface. By removing any coding or technical requirements, this new feature puts the power of agents in the hands of your business teams, with more complex use cases addressed in Copilot Studio.

Integrating agents within BizChat, directly in the flow of your work, aims to streamline workflow and processes, delivering increased efficiency and productivity. This not only optimizes current processes but also sets the stage for what is to come. As we anticipate processes becoming increasingly "agentized" in the near future, BizChat will serve as the control tower from which processes are orchestrated. More discussion on the agents feature follows in this chapter.

Copilot Updates in Outlook

As we discussed in Chapter 7, "Microsoft Outlook," email remains perhaps one of the most pervasive forms of communication, and the promise of technology to help manage the mountains of unread messages is quite appealing to many. The initial launch features of Copilot for Microsoft 365 included the ability to summarize email threads within Outlook, leveraging GenAI to extract what it believes to be the most important points to provide a quick inbox scanning capability. New to Copilot Wave 2 Outlook functionality is "Priority by Copilot," as shown in Figure 16.2, implemented as a new filter for your inbox. This new capability prioritizes emails based on your role, the chain of command in your organizational structure, or other contexts from your inbox.

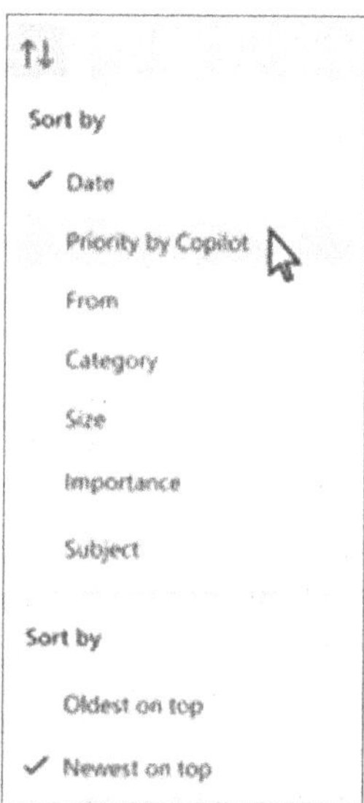

Figure 16.2: Priority by Copilot

This release adds an AI dimension to Outlook's existing Focused Inbox feature. Bringing its existing knowledge of your organizational structure from Microsoft Entra ID to bear, Copilot will prioritize and summarize emails from your supervisor, from those email contacts where you have been most active and responsive, or based on specific keywords. It will also explain why this email has been prioritized and recommend actions to take in response to the email.

You can specify an email's prioritization, as shown in Figure 16.3, or correct the prioritization suggested by Copilot if you disagree. Additionally, you can configure Copilot so it knows which topics, keywords, and people are critical for you and flags any communication that matches these criteria as a high priority.

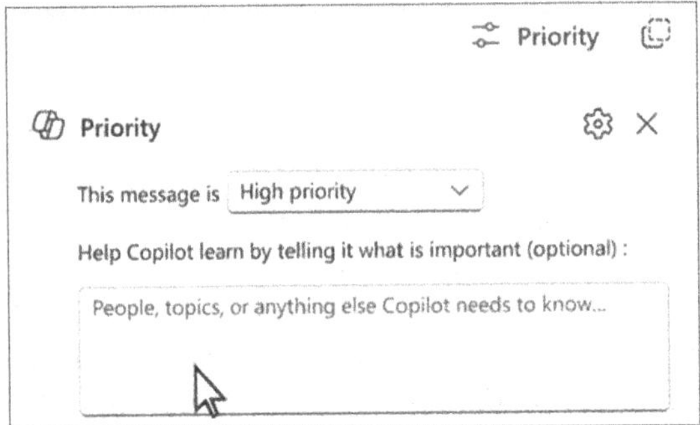

Figure 16.3: Setting email prioritization

If you are frequently overwhelmed by an overflowing inbox, the capabilities that Copilot offers for inbox management will, no doubt, be most welcome. Building on the initial Copilot release features for Outlook covered in Chapter 7, your AI-powered personal assistant can quickly get you back in control of your mailbox and help you craft a tailored response in your desired tone.

Copilot Updates in PowerPoint

As we covered in Chapter 10, "Copilot in Microsoft PowerPoint," Copilot in PowerPoint shows great promise, but there is a learning curve to help you realize real productivity gains. The challenge is that PowerPoint presentations are complex documents subject to personal preferences, organizational norms, customized templates, and maintaining a balance between telling a story while also helping to guide the audience toward an outcome. On top of that, you have the challenge of trying to craft a context-rich prompt to help ground Copilot with your intent while also getting through Microsoft's multiple AI safety checks. At the end of the creation process, you may find the results to be mixed depending on the use case.

To help improve the Copilot experience in PowerPoint, Microsoft released a new "Narrative Builder" capability in Wave 2. This is a bit of a paradigm shift from the initial approach to creating presentations in PowerPoint. Instead of trying to craft a master prompt to generate a perfect presentation, you first collaborate with Copilot to develop an outline, and then Copilot uses that full context to create your presentation.

To start, open PowerPoint and select your preferred template, which should align with your organization's branding. Click the Copilot icon, as shown in Figure 16.4, and then click the "Replace with presentation about..." option from the dialog window.

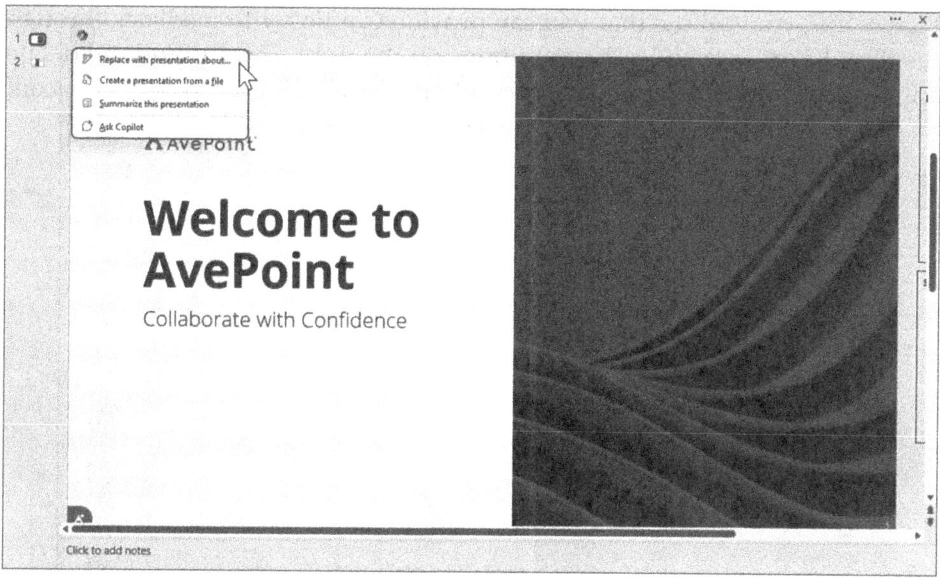

Figure 16.4: The "Replace with presentation about. . ." option

This will open the Copilot Narrative Builder experience, which is essentially a chat interface. Here, you create your first prompt to begin working with Copilot to build an outline for your presentation. As you can see in Figure 16.5, it will prepend the "Create a presentation about" prompt to whatever you enter in the Copilot chat window. For my prompt, I entered the following:

"Create a presentation about the value of investing in Generative AI technologies such as M365 Copilot. Include topics such as talent acquisition, workforce planning, increasing productivity, and improving our work quality. Also, touch on how we might measure ROI and propose a high-level approach that will maximize adoption while managing cost."

After pressing Enter, you will see that rather than generating slides, as we saw with the initial release, Copilot will start to create an outline for the presentation with slide headers and key bullet points, as shown in Figure 16.6.

Next, you can continue to collaborate with Copilot by refining each of the individual sections. You can edit the outline by using follow-up prompts or provide additional grounding for the presentation topics by pulling in content from other files or emails. If you hover your mouse over the ellipses to the left of each section, you will notice that you have the ability to change the section order by clicking and then moving your mouse either up or down. Also, as shown in

Figure 16.7, you can see that you can provide Copilot with feedback through the thumbs up or thumbs down buttons on the right. Finally, you can delete any sections not relevant to your presentation by clicking the recycle bin icon.

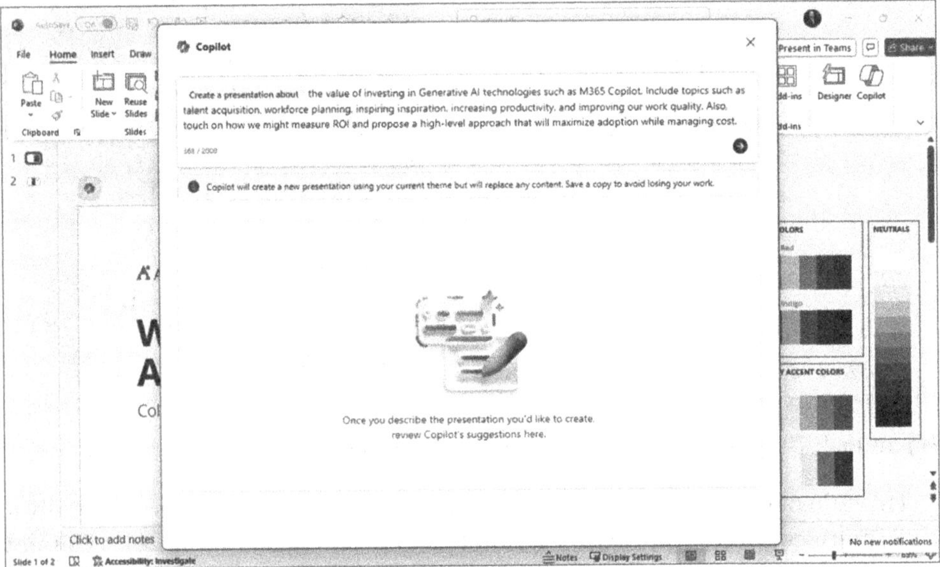

Figure 16.5: Copilot Narrative Builder

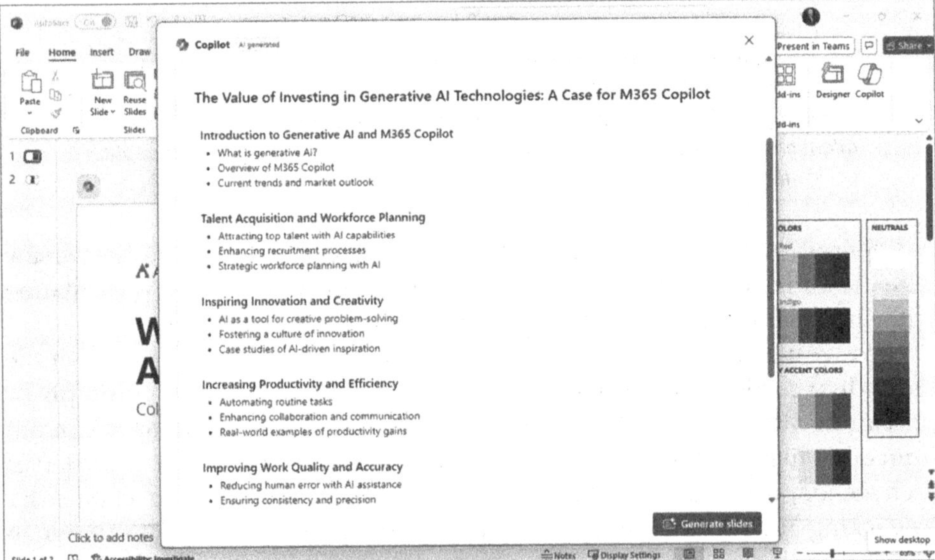

Figure 16.6: Creating a PowerPoint outline

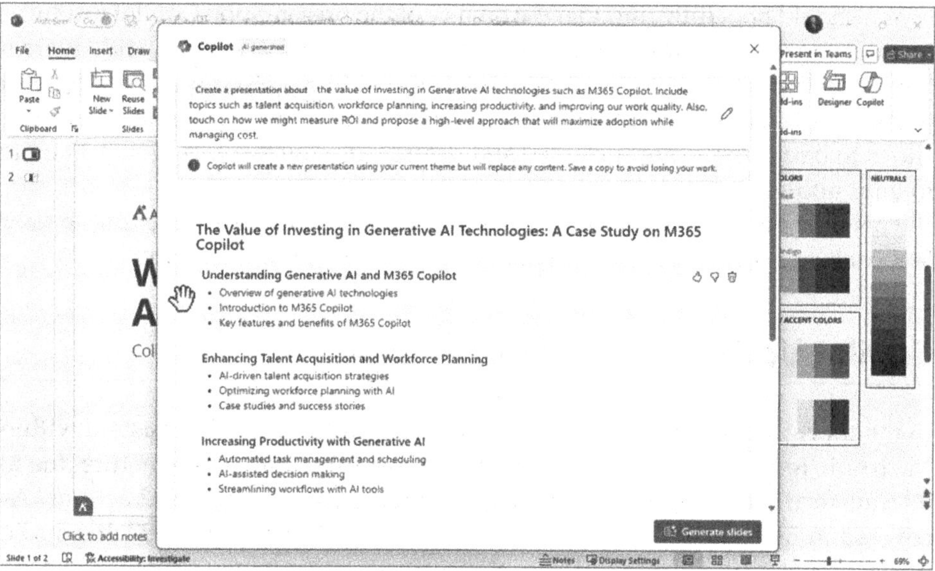

Figure 16.7: Iterating with Copilot Narrative Builder

After finalizing your presentation outline, you can click the "Generate slides" button in the lower-right corner of the Narrative Builder user interface. Copilot will leverage the outline that you co-created to build out your presentation. It will provide updates such as "Creating narrative, adding titles to slides," and then "Putting slides together," until finally it finishes and drops you into the PowerPoint slide sorter view, as shown in Figure 16.8.

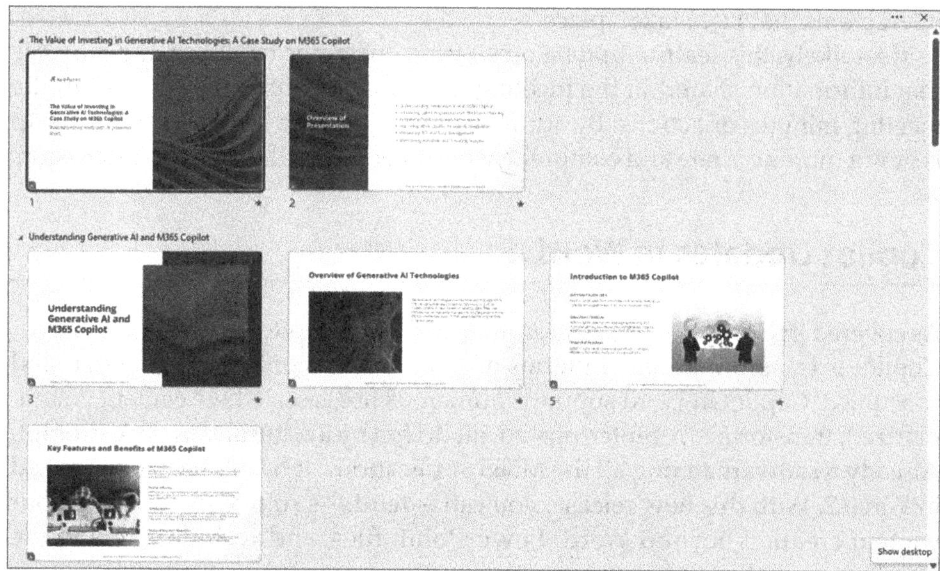

Figure 16.8: Copilot-generated slides

You should hopefully find that the quality of the presentation Copilot produces is much closer to your desired end state than if you were to try and create a "mega prompt" to help build out the full presentation. I also find it very helpful that Copilot creates PowerPoint sections, enabling you to easily rearrange your slides to better represent the story and messaging you are trying to articulate to your audience.

This new narrative experience is an example of Microsoft listening to user feedback and incorporating it to help improve the Copilot experience.

Copilot Updates in Microsoft Teams

In the short time since its launch, the use of Copilot as your AI assistant within Microsoft Teams meetings has become the most frequently cited feature due to its transformational impact on managing meetings, minutes, and actions. As covered in more depth in Chapter 8, "Copilot in Microsoft Teams," the audio voices of meeting participants are transcribed, and a file is generated based on that transcription, which Copilot can interrogate to generate meeting summaries, the sentiments of those involved, or things like action items or to-dos.

Prior to the recent Wave 2 rollout, the meeting recap only captured what was said in the meeting; it did not include anything that was asked, answered, or commented on in the chat associated with that Teams meeting. With Copilot Wave 2, all the content of the meeting chat is now integrated into and available to Copilot, giving a more complete picture of the discussion and interaction in the meeting. If a team member joins a meeting late and prompts Copilot for what they may have missed, the response generated will also include any chat interactions that have taken place.

Most likely, this feature update arose from customer feedback and surprise that information shared in the meeting chat was not subsequently part of the meeting minutes or actions. By addressing this gap, the Teams' meeting recap is now a more accurate and comprehensive reflection of the meeting discussion.

Copilot Updates in Word

As covered in Chapter 12, "Transforming Text with Copilot in Microsoft Word," Copilot is transformational in terms of how written content is generated and consumed. Copilot in Word supports numerous use cases where content is summarized, transformed, or interrogated, all driven by a natural language prompt. Already a stalwart among all the M365 applications, it hasn't been overlooked in Wave 2. With this new release, you can extend the source material for your content creation beyond Word, PowerPoint, files, and web data to include emails and meetings.

This streamlines the flow for business users who want to integrate conversations and emails from Teams and Outlook within their documents. Before this release, you would have needed to perform this action in the BizChat experience, copy and paste the response into Microsoft Word, and then deal with the additional formatting steps required to have it fit within your final work product. It's a good example of Microsoft using this release to iron out a few wrinkles, creating more streamlined and intuitive user experiences within Copilot.

Copilot Updates in Excel

As noted in Chapter 9, "Copilot in Microsoft Excel," there remained room for improvement with the initial release of Copilot in Excel. It struggled with complex data evaluations, was unable to work with anything but the most basic table format, and produced limited data visualizations. As part of the Wave 2 announcements, Microsoft signaled that Copilot in Excel will soon include integration with one of the best programming languages for data analysis, Python. This feature, now in public preview, represents a significant advancement of capability for Copilot within Excel. Python's rich visualization capabilities can now be applied to the data in your worksheet via Copilot. Excel users can conduct advanced data analysis such as forecasting, risk analysis, and visualization of complex data without needing to be proficient in Python. Using natural language prompts to explain the analysis you want to perform, Copilot will automatically generate, explain, and insert the required Python code within your Excel spreadsheet.

Let's take a look at how this works. First, select the new "Advanced analysis" prompt within your Copilot panel in Excel, as shown in Figure 16.9. Then, click "Start advanced analysis," as shown in Figure 16.10, to prompt Python to reason over your data sheet, conduct analysis, and return data insights.

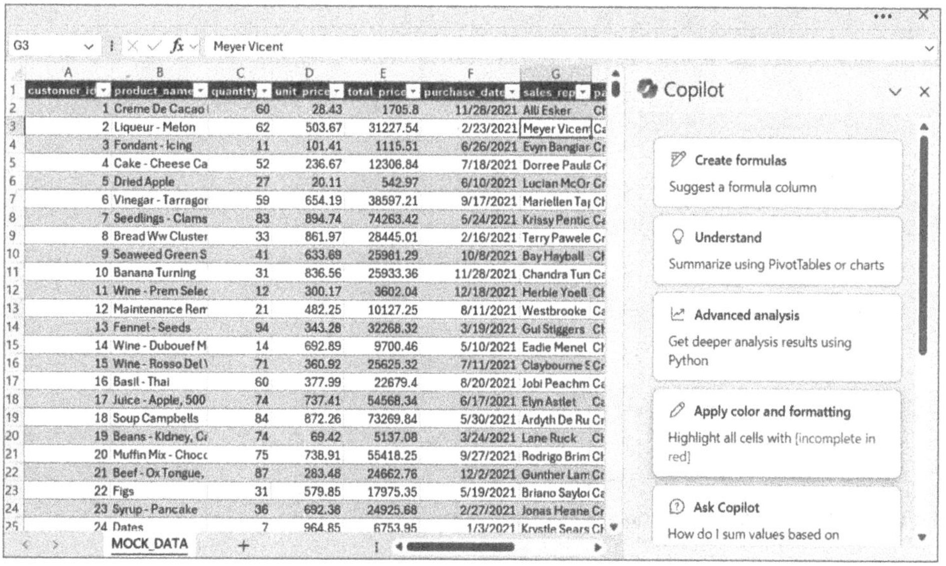

Figure 16.9: The Advanced analysis prompt

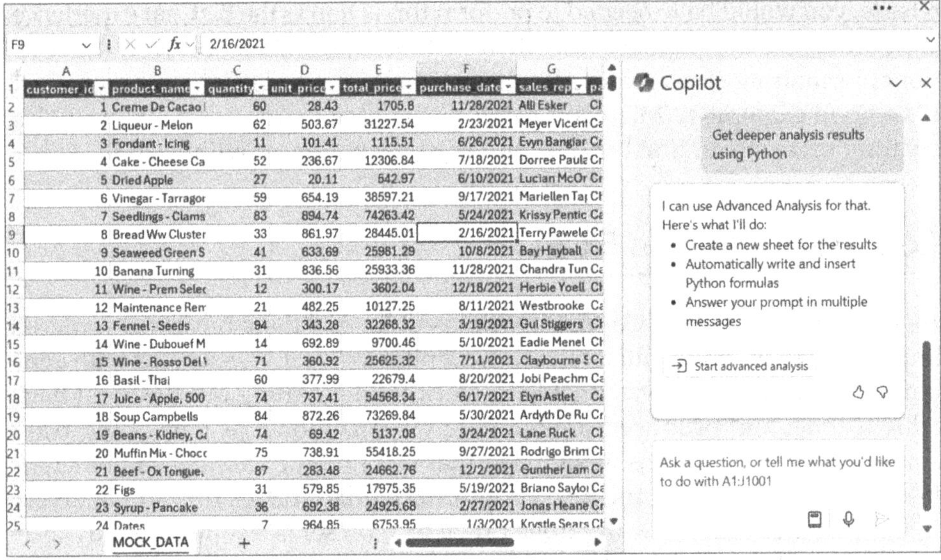

Figure 16.10: The Start advanced analysis option

The data insights are output to a new sheet, called Analysis, from where you can also see the Python code that has been used to generate these insights and suggested prompts for more in-depth analysis.

In the Copilot panel in your new Analysis tab, as shown in Figure 16.11, Copilot will present a preview of the data that it is analyzing, outline its plan for the advanced analysis requested, and execute this plan by writing and running Python code, returning a quick visualization of your data.

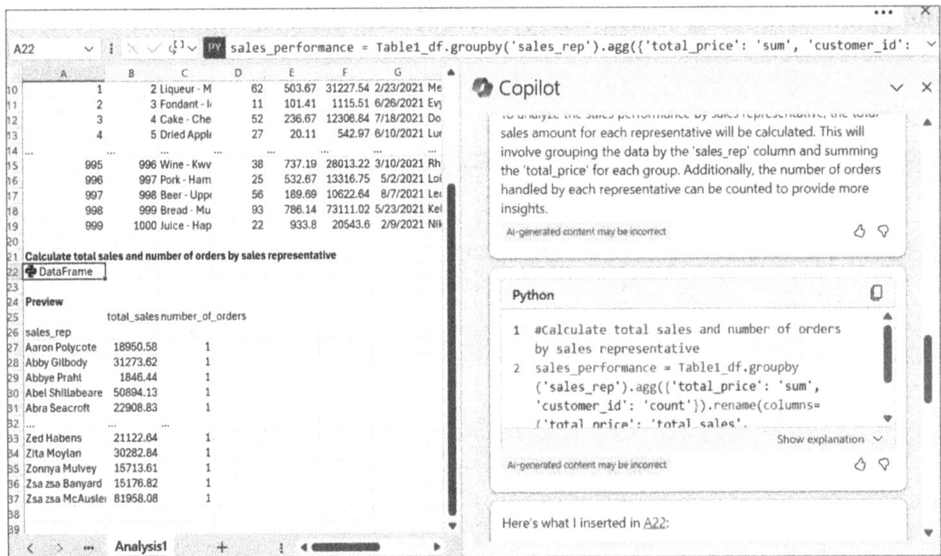

Figure 16.11: Analysis sheet showing Python code

You can then prompt Copilot for other insights from your data by selecting the suggested prompts or by entering your own prompt in the Copilot panel, giving you the tools to refine and adjust the suggested charts and visualizations to best suit your needs.

As shown in Figure 16.12, you can also edit the Python code directly within your workbook.

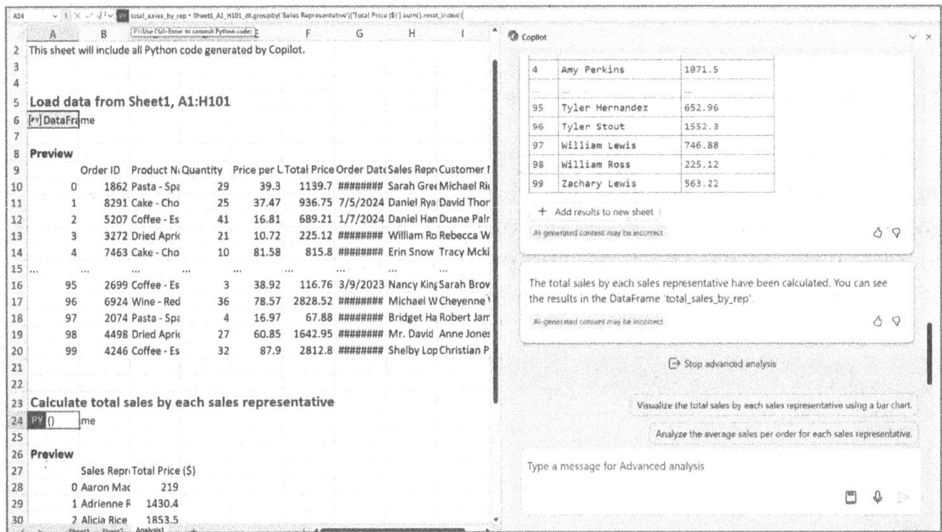

Figure 16.12: Editing Python code

Another change to highlight is that your workbook data is no longer required to be formatted as a table, and Copilot can also reason over text as well as numeric data. Lastly, the simplification of complex formulas within Excel is one of the key benefits of Copilot. Wave 2 extends support for additional formulas such as XLOOKUP, SUMIF, as well as conditional formatting rules.

These new features propel Excel from a laggard position to the forefront of the Copilot applications and unlock a range of additional use cases for your business teams.

Copilot Updates in OneDrive

Copilot could already summarize files in your OneDrive. Now, with Wave 2, a document summary can be generated directly from the file list view without opening the file, as shown in Figure 16.13. You can also generate a FAQ from the selected file to share across your teams or to update your corporate knowledge base, for example.

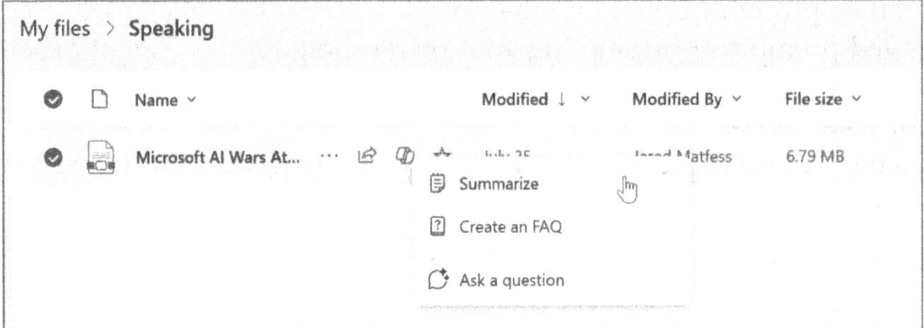

Figure 16.13: Summarizing files in OneDrive

Furthermore, as part of Wave 2, you can compare and highlight differences across up to five files stored in your OneDrive. The files can be in a range of formats, such as Word docs, PDFs, or PowerPoint slides. As shown in Figure 16.14, Copilot will compare each file and present a detailed comparison to help you locate the file you need without having to open and scan each file.

2 files selected
Why Trustworthy AI is Essential.pptx, Conversation is the new UI.pptx

Here is a comparison of the two files. "Why Trustworthy AI is Essential.pptx" and "Conversation is the new UI.pptx":

Aspect	Why Trustworthy AI is Essential.pptx	Conversation is the new UI.pptx
Author	Jared Matfess	Jory Tan
Last Modified Time	August 13th	August 2nd
Main Theme	Trustworthy AI, including transparency, ethics, and safety	The evolution of user experience and conversational interfaces
Key Points	- Importance of Trustworthy AI - Benefits and risks of AI - Challenges and solutions for achieving Trustworthy AI	- Evolution from command prompt to conversational interfaces - Impact of AI on consumer behavior and enterprise services - Microsoft's GenAI offerings
Structure	- Definition and principles of Trustworthy AI - Benefits and risks - Challenges and solutions	- Evolution of user experience - Consumer expectations - Overview of Microsoft's GenAI offerings

1 : Why Trustworthy AI is Essential.pptx 2 : Conversation is the new UI.pptx
Let me know if you need more details or any other assistance!

AI-generated content may be incorrect

Copy
Ask a question
Show hidden icons

Figure 16.14: Comparing OneDrive files

An additional feature coming in Wave 2 is the ability to select and interrogate specified files to quickly get an answer to a question or locate key information, as shown in Figure 16.15. Within OneDrive, you first select the source file(s) that contain the information you need, and then, using the chat panel, you can enter the natural language prompt to return the information you need from those files.

Copilot continues to drive organizational efficiency. If you are someone who spends too much time trying to locate the correct documents, this feature is sure to resonate.

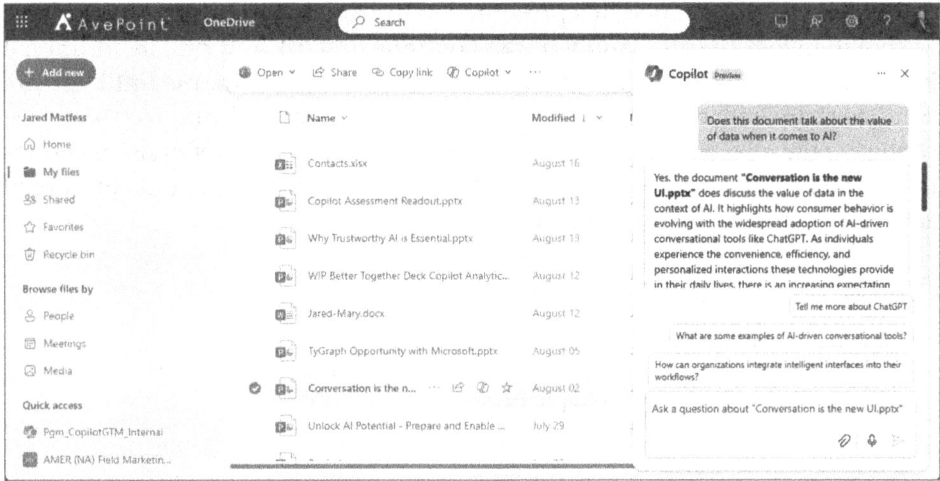

Figure 16.15: Querying OneDrive files

Copilot Pages

Copilot Pages is a new feature launched as part of the Wave 2 release. Billed by Microsoft as a "dynamic, persistent canvas for multiplayer AI collaboration," Copilot Pages is based on Microsoft Loop files and offers a new AI-enabled collaboration tool. Copilot Pages elevates AI from an individual to a team activity by bringing colleagues together to collaborate using Copilot. Using Copilot Pages, your generated responses from BizChat can form the basis of a permanent collaboration space where data can be shared, edited, and extended by other team members. As shown in Figure 16.16, the BizChat response can be converted to a page by selecting Edit in Pages.

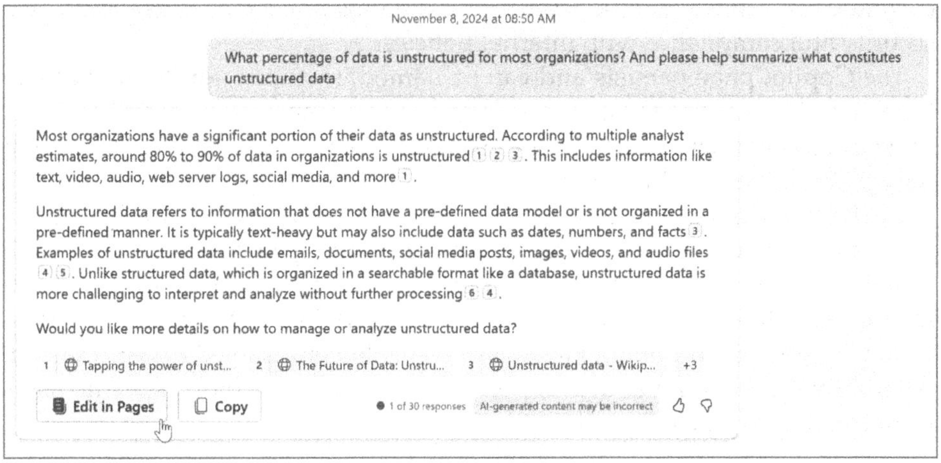

November 8, 2024 at 08:50 AM

What percentage of data is unstructured for most organizations? And please help summarize what constitutes unstructured data

Most organizations have a significant portion of their data as unstructured. According to multiple analyst estimates, around 80% to 90% of data in organizations is unstructured 1 2 3. This includes information like text, video, audio, web server logs, social media, and more 1.

Unstructured data refers to information that does not have a pre-defined data model or is not organized in a pre-defined manner. It is typically text-heavy but may also include data such as dates, numbers, and facts 3. Examples of unstructured data include emails, documents, social media posts, images, videos, and audio files 4 5. Unlike structured data, which is organized in a searchable format like a database, unstructured data is more challenging to interpret and analyze without further processing 6 4.

Would you like more details on how to manage or analyze unstructured data?

1 Tapping the power of unst... 2 The Future of Data: Unstru... 3 Unstructured data - Wikip... +3

Edit in Pages Copy 1 of 30 responses AI-generated content may be incorrect

Figure 16.16: Converting a BizChat response to a page

Once the page is created, it's presented to the right of your BizChat window, as shown in Figure 16.17, and you can continue to work and pull in additional information from files, emails, or additional web/work prompts until you are ready to share with colleagues. You can toggle between work and web searches, capturing the relevant responses on your page. You can even reference meetings that have been transcribed by Copilot and extract meeting details or agreed actions into your collaboration space.

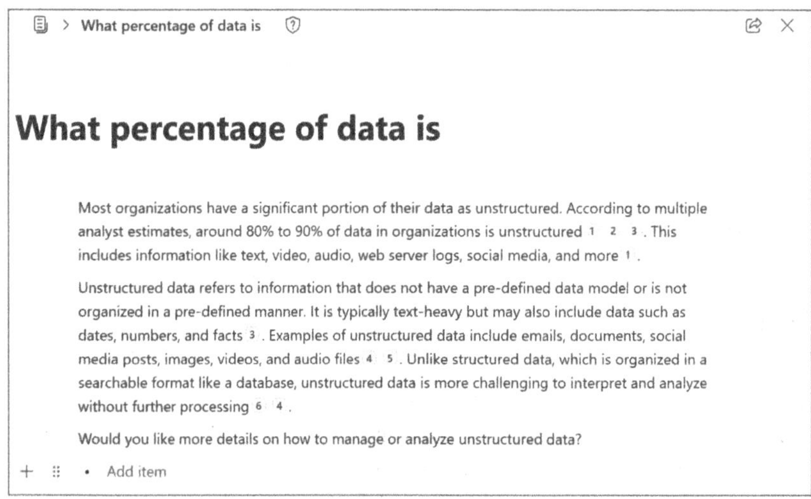

Figure 16.17: Working with Pages

Collaboration with your colleagues is simple. Simply select the Share button in the upper-right corner and tag your colleagues. Once shared, they too can also start to work on the collaboration space with dynamic team updates visible online so the page remains in sync and up-to-date. Sharing of Copilot Pages is currently restricted to people within your organization's tenant to ensure data security and compliance with internal policies.

The Copilot page persists and can be named, revisited, and edited at any time. Individual pages are stored as .loop files in a new user-owned SharePoint Embedded container and can be retrieved via a SharePoint search or via recent files in SharePoint or OneDrive.

By default, Copilot Pages are enabled in your tenant. Your IT admin team can manage the creation, use, and sharing of Copilot pages using Loop admin switches within the Microsoft 365 admin center. In Configure Settings, search for the "Create and view Loop files in Microsoft 365 Copilot Chat" setting, from where access to Copilot Pages can be enabled or disabled for your tenant. Alternatively, conditional access policies can be used to block specific users from creating pages, if more limited use is preferred.

Copilot Pages also adheres to your organization's Sensitivity Labels, which can be manually applied to individual pages. (Select the Sensitivity Label in the toolbar and assign the appropriate label from the drop-down menu. Note that this assumes that Sensitivity Labels are already configured within Purview.) If Copilot locates content with a higher Sensitivity Label than the Copilot page, it will automatically upgrade the Sensitivity Label of the page once this content is added. Your data loss prevention policies, as discussed in Chapter 4, "Security/Purview Planning in Preparation for Copilot," can detect and block the sharing of very sensitive information in any form, including Copilot pages.

Copilot Pages has the potential to transform team collaboration, especially for remote workers or dispersed teams. By enabling teams to consolidate their inputs in one shared space, Pages has a big role to play in eliminating silos, facilitating idea sharing, and streamlining communication.

Copilot Agents

Saving the best for last, perhaps the most impactful announcement made during the Wave 2 event was the introduction of Copilot agents. Copilot agents represent an evolution from the initial use cases of searching for content, summarizing data, and generating content. This next evolution of AI capability is focused on knowledge and actions, enabling Copilots to partner with humans to complete dynamic and complex business tasks, all within the guardrails of Microsoft's security boundaries.

A use case for this new capability would be to develop a Copilot agent that returns content from a finite set of resources. For example, an operations team could create an agent to help support questions about policies and procedures. The configuration of this agent could be constrained to a single SharePoint document library containing all the relevant policies and procedures. Then, you could publish this agent to Microsoft Teams and make it accessible just as if it were another person on your team. So instead of messaging your colleague in operations with a question about a given policy, you can message an agent in Teams at any hour and have it respond to your query, citing the source as a link to the policy in the defined SharePoint document library.

The thought of developing this new agent capability might seem overwhelming at first. However, Microsoft has simplified the setup with a user-friendly creation process available across multiple experiences. Supported by a conversational exchange via Copilot, you can quickly build out your agent.

Figure 16.18 shows an example of how you can create an agent directly from BizChat. You can click the Copilot button in the upper-right corner to expose a drop-down list.

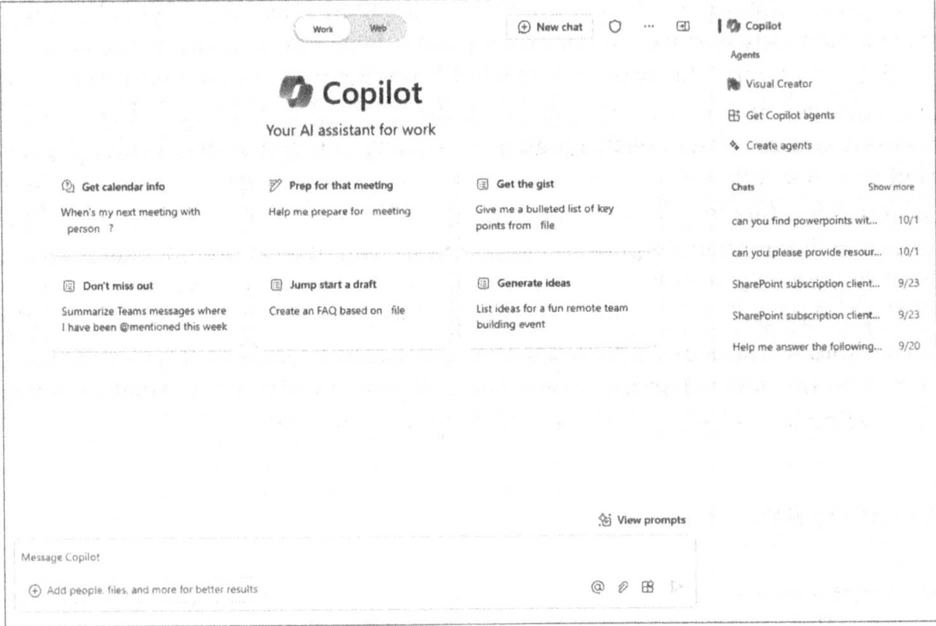

Figure 16.18: Creating a Copilot agent

Once you click the "Create agents" button, a dialog box will pop up, as shown in Figure 16.19, which uses Copilot to guide you using natural conversational language. You'll provide Copilot with the name for your new Copilot agent.

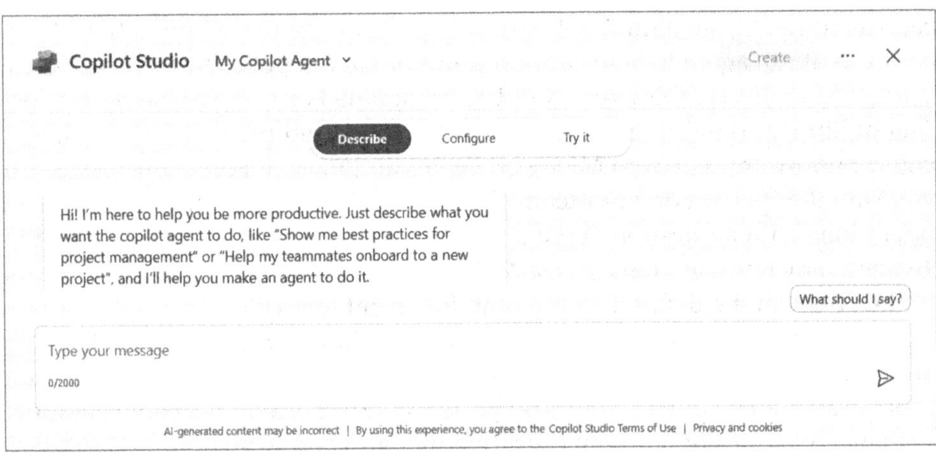

Figure 16.19: Describing your Copilot agent

From here, you essentially tell Copilot what you want the agent to do, what the data source should be (generally SharePoint or Teams at this point, but other

IT-approved data sources may be enabled), and then what you want it to be able to do with that information. Then, click Create, and the agent gets automatically built. Once created, it will be available in BizChat or in the Copilot mobile app for use by other users. Or you can make it available in Microsoft Teams, and anyone can @mention the agent to interact with it.

You may be wondering whether an agent respects your organizational data and security permissions once it is deployed. Microsoft has baked in privacy considerations by design into Copilot agents. Anyone with existing access to the SharePoint site referenced as the agents' data source can use the agent to access information. If a user does not have existing access to the SharePoint site, they will not be able to retrieve any information via the agent. Instead, they will see a message indicating that they do not have the required permissions to access the data.

This is just the tip of the iceberg for what you can do with Copilot agents, and you should expect Microsoft to continue to invest in this capability to further promote the adoption of M365 and Copilot for Microsoft 365. In Chapter 14, "Introduction to Microsoft Copilot Studio," we covered Copilot extensibility in greater detail to help you understand the various patterns for delivering even more value through Copilot for Microsoft 365.

Conclusion

The Wave 2 features covered in this chapter will be released throughout Q4 2024, solidifying Copilot for Microsoft 365 as the "UI for AI" across the Microsoft 365 applications. Based on the features described in this chapter, it is evident that Microsoft remains committed to infusing AI throughout our most frequently used Office applications to further drive adoption. Microsoft has also responded to customer experience and feedback with these features, particularly the PowerPoint and Excel changes, which represent significant improvements to the AI capabilities within these applications. With each new release, we can look forward to our AI experiences becoming increasingly intuitive and efficient.

As of this writing, we are just 18 months into the Copilot journey. There is much more to come as this technology moves at an unprecedented pace. With Copilot agents, we are at the cusp of another seismic change. Agents offer a range of capabilities, from basic prompts and responses to agents that process repetitive tasks to more advanced agents, ultimately becoming more autonomous and self-directed. Positioning agents at the forefront of our Office applications will make them more familiar and accessible to users. This will fuel demand for more sophisticated and advanced agents as we appreciate their full potential to transform work processes.

Index

D

E

Q

R

S

X–Y–Z